P9-DVJ-282

Coaching TENNIS

CHUCK KRIESE

MASTERS PRESS

A Division of Howard W. Sams & Company

Published by Masters Press
(A Division of Howard W. Sams & Company)
2647 Waterfront Pkwy E. Drive, Suite 100
Indianapolis, IN 46214

© 1997 Chuck Kriese
All rights reserved. Published 1997

Printed in the United States of America.

No part of this publication may be reproduced, stored in a retrieval system, or transmitted, in any form or by any means, electronic, mechanical, photocopying, recording, or otherwise, without the prior permission of Masters Press.

     97 98 99 00 01 02   10 9 8 7 6 5 4 3 2 1

Library of Congress Cataloging-in-Publication Data
Kriese, Chuck, 1950-
      Coaching tennis / Chuck Kriese.
           p.   cm.
      Rev. ed. of: Total tennis training. c1988.
      Includes bibliographical references.
      ISBN 1-57028-123-8
      1. Tennis -- Training. 2. Tennis -- Coaching. 3. Tennis -- Psychological aspects.
      I. Kriese, Chuck, 1950-   Total tennis training. II. Title.
GV1002.9.T7K74   1997   97-26803
796.342'07'7--dc21   CIP

TABLE OF CONTENTS

• •

DEDICATION

•••

You never know when you touch a life! I would like to thank those coaches who touched mine:

♦ Tennis: Rowland Leverenz, Paul Ditzenberger, Brother Rowland Driscoll, Larry Ware, Alan Cornelious, Harry Hopman, Bill Branch;

♦ Basketball: Vic Sahm, Mike McGinley, John McLeod, Bill Green, Tom O'brien, Ron Bargatze, Mr. Wilder, Tony Corsaro;

♦ Track & Cross Country: Mr. Edwards, Bill Green, Ron Volpatti, Bob Knoyce;

♦ Football: Art Phelan, Dutch Roembke, Tom Snyder;

♦ Baseball: Maurice "Pop" Kriese, Vic Sahm.

As I continue my coaching for as long as God allows, my prayer will be one of great gratitude for allowing me to teach:

"O God, thou hast taught me from boyhood, all my life I have proclaimed thy marvelous works and now that I am old and my hairs are gray, forsake me not O God...Songs of Joy shall be on my lips; I will sing thee psalms, because thou has redeemed me. All day long my tongue shall tell of thy righteousness.

Psalm 71:17, 18, 23, 24

Kent Kinnear celebrates an ATP Tour victory.

FOREWORD

• •

I first met Coach Kriese as a junior tennis player, a time that found me in search of a college program that would hopefully be my springboard into a professional career in tennis. I was a long way from that pro career at the age of 16, but sensed that if I was indeed serious about pursuing such an endeavor, Kriese's coaching philosophy and knowledge could give me the bounce I needed. Now, after spending nearly a decade on the professional tour, I look back at that decision and feel thankful, realizing how important acquiring a solid foundation was to the successes I have since experienced. Chuck Kriese has had a great influence on my life just as he has upon the thousands of others with whom he has come in contact; and not just in ways that help on the tennis court, but in disciplines that are beneficial throughout life. This, I know, is his ultimate goal.

In his book *Coaching Tennis*, Coach shares important insights and keys to success that he has compiled over his twenty-plus years of coaching. In all my years of competitive tennis, I have never come across anyone as dedicated to coaching and thirsty for knowledge of the game as this man. He has observed, charted and studied literally thousands of competitive matches, always looking for new ideas on how to better prepare and compete. If one man is qualified to write a book with this title, it's Chuck Kriese.

Coaching Tennis is a must read for anyone who wants to really get inside the sport of tennis.

Whether you're a player, coach or enthusiast — and regardless of age or level of play — this book is truly a tool by which to better understand the sport. Coach Kriese touches on many of those components of tennis that are too often overlooked yet remain important variables of this complex game. Study the sound principles and ideas presented, incorporate them into your game, and discover a more disciplined, more efficient approach to this great sport.

I have been playing tennis now for nine years on the ATP Tour since graduating from Clemson University in 1988. I am convinced that the four years I spent under Coach Kriese gave me the strong foundation that has enabled me to deal with the various adversities faced on the tour, both on and off the court. Professional tennis has been an incredible education for me, enabling me to travel an average of 40 weeks a year, compete in over 35 countries, and participate in over 30 Grand Slam Tournaments. Without hesitation, I can say that had it not been for Coach Kriese and the lessons I learned from him that are shared in this book, my career as a professional tennis player would have been minimal, if not non-existent. I am forever grateful to Coach for his incredible sacrifices of time and for his genuine care that has played such a big part of where I am today. Please enjoy the book, and apply the information...it works!

— Kent Kinnear, Professional Tennis Player

Models: Bernardo Martinez, Eduardo Martinez, David Mercado, Shelly Mercado, Raphael Bochent, Kris Huff, Richard Matuszewski, Joe Defoor

All photographs by Robert Waldrop except for the following:
pp. 5, 73, 76, 249, 257, 261, 265 and Chapter 3 (female model pictures) by Scott Harke;
pp. 34, 88, 131, 192, 196 (Fig. 17-2) and 214 by Kerry Capps;
pp. 154 by Rob Biggerstaff;
pp. viii, 201, 212 and 225 courtesy of Clemson University Sports Information Department.

Note: While not wishing to minimize the full participation of women in tennis or their contribution to the sport, to facilitate smooth reading and to avoid awkward phrasing, the editors of this book have chosen to use masculine pronouns when referring to both genders.

CREDITS:
Proofreader: Pat Brady
Diagrams: Terry Varvel, Kelli Ternet, Christina Smith, Jason Coates
Text layout: Chad Woolums
Cover design: Kelli Ternet
Cover photographs: Robert Waldrop, Kerry Capps
Edited by: Chad Woolums

Coaching Tennis

PREFACE

Every coach needs a philosophy to train and to work by. It gives purpose. It gives passion to continue when the task is hard. With it we gain direction; without it, we are at the fate of the prevailing wind. Your philosophy for training must be yours and yours alone. Your unique style will alone satisfy your inner needs and desires as a teacher. The following story explains my personal philosophy for coaching, for training, and for teaching. It also sets the tone for what is expressed in this book.

> Everybody wants to be tough, but no one ever wants tough times. Each must learn to earn their own way.

If you are an athlete, I hope this book will inspire you. If you are a coach, I hope that it will give you some guidance and insight into the awesome job we have as teachers and mentors of youth. If you are a parent, this book should give you a perspective into the depth that goes into the teaching and coaching of this fantastic sport of tennis. Most of all I hope that this book will be a guide that illustrates and describes completely the balance between the Physical, Mental and Emotional dimensions of the game.

Pain is often the Teacher

I was not looking for profound wisdom as I sat in a restaurant with my mother on a cold rainy evening in Charlotte, North Carolina.

We were both solemn and concerned over my brother-in-law, John, and the diagnosis of colon cancer that he had just been given. At 35, John had moved up the corporate ladder until it looked like only a matter of time before most of his goals in business would be realized. He was also, and had been, my best friend in life.

John would suffer through a terrible 18 months before dying. During that time, he would show me what courage really is and much about true friendship. In those last months, he helped me with coaching and personal problems, and he seemed to gain strength and enthusiasm from doing so.

That evening in Charlotte, when we first received the bad news about John, I had been moaning about some of my problems. I had shared my deep concerns, as I often still do, with my mother. Mostly, I complained of my inability to properly motivate the players on my team. "It seems that it means so much more to me than it does to them," I complained. "I do everything I can for them — early morning workouts, individual one-on-one training, the best equipment. We have great facilities and the opportunity to compete with the best, but I still feel that I'm not able to motivate them completely. They won't make a total commitment. They go 80 percent of the way and then back off. What am I doing wrong?"

My mother reached across the table and rested her hand on mine. She looked at me and began to speak softly of the Great Depression. She said that during hard times people had to develop an "inner need" or determination to survive. Then she spoke of the war and the prosperity of the 1950s and how the memory of not having much made all parents eager to provide generously for their children, to give them all the things that they themselves never had. Ironically, she said, this, along with the emphasis our country placed on external performance at the expense of internal values, has had a crippling effect. My mother often speaks in phrases, and one of my favorites is, "Our strengths are often our weaknesses and our weaknesses are often our strengths." I felt I was beginning to understand her message.

She continued. "Let me explain it this way. When I was a young girl, I would go to my grandmother's farm in Indiana. I would often stay for hours and watch the baby chicks in the incubator fight their way into the world by pecking and struggling to break their shells. Watching through the eyes of an eight-year-old, it took what seemed to be forever. If you've ever watched it, son, the baby chick will peck and peck and work and work, and it always seems that they wouldn't or couldn't make it."

"One day as I watched, one of the chicks got its head stuck popping out. And it just stayed there for the longest time. I was sure he couldn't get out, and as anyone who is kind and thoughtful would do when someone is in a jam, I wanted to help. I asked Grandma if I could help him by breaking him out of his shell. It seemed so easy for me to see and so hard for him to do. She quickly replied with a stern, 'No! You mustn't, and you won't. If you open his shell, he will be too weak and will die. As he opens his own shell, he gains strength enough to survive in his new environment.' So I learned about baby chicks and about life."

As parents and teachers, we have often opened our children's shells for them, and this is the greatest mistake we can make. This story provided a very valuable lesson for me early in my career as a coach, and it came to be my guide as I watched John, my brother-in-law and friend, build inner strength from his struggle with cancer.

Thanks so much to my mother, who shared her wisdom, and to John who proved its truth by helping me to formulate my philosophy for my teaching and coaching.

Tough Love Coaching

In all of my years of coaching, the most extreme example of tough-love coaching was a young man named Cris Robinson during his quest to earn a spot on our team through the Clemson Tennis Morning Madness Program. It was a moment in my coaching career when my heart ached to the breaking point while watching this new freshman struggle to conquer a barrier. The temptation to give him an easy way out was great, but in the end, his hard earned success at that early obstacle in his career was one of the very important cornerstones for a great career. The following story

is now a source of inspiration to many others and its example hangs as a permanent reminder and display on our wall of honor.

> Consider it pure joy my brothers, whenever you face trials of many kinds, because you know that the testing of your faith develops perseverance. Perseverance must finish its work so that you may mature and be complete, not lacking in anything.
> — *James I: 1-4*

Breakdowns Before Breakthroughs

I call it Tiger Pride, my athletes call it Morning Madness; two weeks of 6:00 am running with time trials including a 5:15 mile required to make the team. At the end of the trials, only one boy remained. Cris was smaller than the others at 5'7" and a diabetic. Although he tried valiantly — eight times — his personal best, 5:23, fell short. I was bombarded by the urge to make an exception. If any kid ever deserved it, he did. But on the court and in the world, Cris would not just be competing against small diabetics. I reaffirmed to him the reality that the 5:15 mile was the only way to make the team. He agreed without reservation. I think we both knew this would be the last attempt. With two upperclassmen — Greg and Mike — and a ball of kite string, we made one more try. I tied fifteen feet of string around the waist of each pacer and told Cris, "When you're at the end of your rope, tie a knot and hang on." As they ran, if the string broke, he lost; if he dropped it, he quit. Each pacer would run two laps each with Cris following close behind.

The pacers did their job. One lap and then two, a half mile in 2:31. The hand-off was made to the second pacer. Lap three was the back breaker. This time the string got taut down the back stretch as Cris's pace slowed. "No!" I yelled, "one more tough minute, there's a chance," I yelled inside. As he rounded the final backstretch, I knew he would make it. The stopwatch read 5:11 as he fell across the finish line.

My emotions were high as I coyote-howled and laughed outrageously and ran with Cris on his Victory Lap with the string in hand. This barrier, this stumbling block had been overcome by a strong-minded kid, his coach, supportive friends and thirty feet of string. God is the greatest coach. He allows trials, but he gives us whatever we need to get the job done.

THE COACH: TEACHER OF THE ATHLETE — MOLDER OF THE TALENT

Having a reason to be a coach is probably even more important than having a good philosophy for coaching. The Preface of this book seems a very appropriate time to insert a letter shown to me by a fellow coach. It gives most of us the answer to the question of why we get into this sometimes fantastic and sometimes very painful profession of Teacher of the Athlete.

Dear Coach,

I do not know if you remember me, but I attended your summer camps for four summers. I learned about you and your camp when my family had some of your players stay at our house during the S.I.U.-Edwardsville college tournament that was held in Belleville. I first came to your camp when I was twelve years old (1980). I returned every summer for the next three years spending two weeks there. My friend, Ben, also came with me for three of those years. I remember those camps with so much fondness. I first came to your camp as a pudgy, couch potato type kid with no goals or ambition. The first year of camp was hard work, and I would have gone home at times if I could have, but I stuck it out and made it through. I worked harder during that week than I had at any time during my life to that point. I can vividly remember waking up early to run laps, doing the drills and then running after the drills. This was at first torture, but strangely enough after a time, I began to enjoy the work because I felt that I was improving not just my tennis, but more importantly my ability to dedicate myself toward goals. The goals that I set at first seemed unattainable, but in time I achieved them and then raised some new ones. I put into practice the motivational talk that you gave at your talk on the first night there. When I first came to the camp, I was put on the beginner courts. I slowly worked my way up year after year until I made it to the top of the entire camp three years later. This did not just happen, I worked on my tennis for hours every day and made sacrifices in other aspects of my life. I cannot stress enough the effect that setting and attaining goals has on a person's character and self-confidence. I firmly believe that through hard work, dedication, and sacrifice there are few goals that are not attainable. I have left the most important thing that I remember about your camp for last. You told the whole camp one evening at a talk that you had to humble yourself before the Lord every day in order to do your best with the right attitude. I'd never forgot this. I was involved in church my whole life but I did not have a personal relationship with Christ. Two years ago, I dedicated my life to serving Him and asked him to change my life. I got married on September 19, 1991 and my wife and I had a baby girl two months ago. It does not seem that long ago that I was spending two weeks of my summer at your camp. The time I spent at your camp had a very big impact on me, and I wanted you to know about it.

Very Sincerely,
Bobby

Many times as coaches we cannot see the good that we do. Gratitude is an adult virtue; therefore, we usually will not get thanks from our young pupils. A friend recently told me in regard to coaching that " In any type of teaching or coaching profession, your posterity will usually be much greater than your prosperity."

If you don't do the work you've been called to do, it just may never get done.
— from the musical Christy

INTRODUCTION

· ·

> Quality is never an accident. It's always the result of high intention, sincere effort, intelligent direction, and skillful execution.
> — *The American School, Chicago, Illinois*

HOW DO I REALIZE MY POTENTIAL?

How does a player improve his skills in the very difficult and complex game called tennis? Does he just play sets against better players and hope that some of the skills will rub off? Or does he do drill work, over and over again, simulating the shots and situations that he faces in competition?

What about physical conditioning? What about the relatively new area called mental training? What about strategy and learning what to do and when to do it? Do the necessary skills in this game just evolve if the game is played long enough? Does a player have time to wait for it all to evolve?

Skill Growth

The skill growth curve illustrates growth for most motor skills. At first improvement comes quickly, based on little more than time and effort. As the player improves, his expectations rise, sometimes unrealistically, and it appears that success will be only a matter of working a little harder and longer than the next person. This is true until the player reaches the 50th or 60th percentile of his abilities, when the plateau in growth starts to occur. A player should anticipate later growth to come in small increments. This irregular progress can be frustrating to both players and coaches.

In the early stages, a good system for training must be developed. It is the coach's job to first help the player learn the fundamentals and then to guide his development in specific areas.

Hard work is important, but working harder does not always mean working better. When the plateau in the learning curve occurs, hard work alone will not always bring improvement, so the goal of the coach and the player should be to work hard and to work smart. The athlete must find the ingredient, whether it is physical, mental or emotional, that will facilitate growth. Frustration on the part of the athlete and coach occurs when this solution cannot be found, especially when the athlete's hard and obsessive work produces little result.

Once it's understood that plateaus and barriers do exist, the athlete and coach can plan the next few percentages of improvement. It's exciting to discover that a one percent improvement for the athlete who is at the 70th percentile is a huge jump and may separate him from many other players.

There are many examples of this in tennis. The rapid growth and great improvements that John McEnroe made in 1978 and Boris Becker made in 1985 are good examples. Ironically, both players made the jump as a result of excellent performances at Wimbledon, the most prestigious of all tennis tournaments. It's ridiculous to think that such improvement took place entirely in the space of a few days and a few wins at a big tournament. More accurate is the observation that both players were physically capable of the feat before that tournament, and as they gained momentum from each win, they became confident in their physical capabilities. The next phase of growth, the most critical one, was being comfortable with their new roles and the host of responsibilities that accompanied them. Often players collapse and

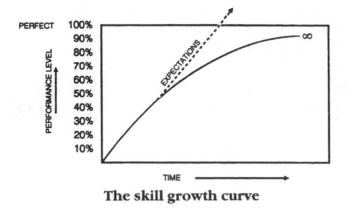

The skill growth curve

retreat after advancing to a new level because of a reluctance to accept all that it takes to stay there; often they cannot deal with the new expectations that success brings them.

What is Total Player Development?

Philosophers, psychologists and teachers all testify to the three areas of human development that are critical to growth: the physical, the mental and the emotional. A tennis player must also develop his whole person in order for his game to benefit. He must be physically capable of the skill, he must mentally recognize and have confidence in that capability, and lastly and most importantly, he must be emotionally comfortable with each new level of play and its new responsibility.

In the early stages of development, the physical skills must be emphasized. They are the foundation without which the other areas cannot be developed. Later, the mental aspect is developed, enabling the physical to become functional. The last area to be developed is the emotional. It either allows the mental and the physical to work together, or, if it is lacking, becomes the monkey wrench that eventually breaks down the machinery.

The coach must be discerning in picking out the area of growth that the athlete needs. He must be able to recognize that, in the learning stages, development must progress from the physical, to the mental, and then to the emotional (outside-in), but that in the functional stage, it must operate in the exact opposite sequence, from the emotional, to the mental, and then to the physical (inside-out). Inside-out performances can be possible only with an understanding that the emotional areas allow the mental areas to function, which in turn, allow the physical areas to engage fully.

Each area has unique components and, for the total development of the athlete, each must be trained. Athletes have a tendency to go through physical motions robotically without engaging the mental and emotional aspects. Too often, the athlete relies on the coach to supply these areas.

Total player development

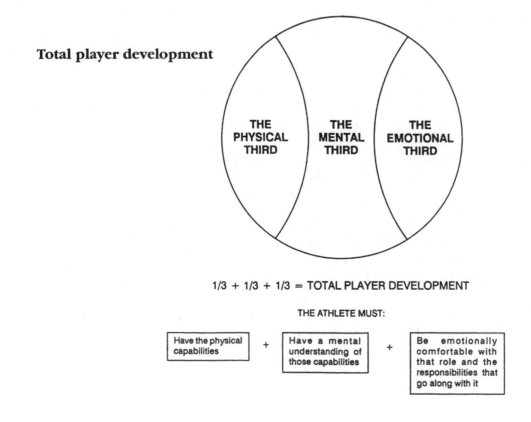

1/3 + 1/3 + 1/3 = TOTAL PLAYER DEVELOPMENT

THE ATHLETE MUST:

| Have the physical capabilities | + | Have a mental understanding of those capabilities | + | Be emotionally comfortable with that role and the responsibilities that go along with it |

The coach, however, must be sure to put the responsibility back on the athlete and make sure that he engages fully in the workouts as well as in matches. It is in this way only that total player development can take place and athletes can grow into champions.

The Recipe for Success

This is the recipe or roadmap that I use as a checklist to keep my players accountable for the growth of their own game. If followed correctly, this checklist represents one complete year of growth.

ONE-YEAR CHECKLIST FOR GROWTH IN THE GAME OF TENNIS

I. IN TRAINING
_____ Mechanics overlearned to point of "unconsciously competent" under pressure!

II. FOR MATCH PLAY
_____ **A. Proper pre-match preparation**
_____ All details and equipment
_____ Proper balance of respect
_____ Something to gain
_____ Total trust in self — "Regular stuff is good enough"
_____ Body language of a champion

_____ **B. Patterns for:** **(*Use Wardlaw Directional Guidelines)**
_____ *1st exchanges
_____ *Meat of point
_____ *Closing of point

_____ **C. Momentum and match flow**
_____ Conversions
_____ Action-reaction
_____ Ahead, behind or even
_____ Match play checkpoints —
Momentum starts fresh at the beginning of each of the six checkpoints
(Best players use checkpoints as benchmarks instead of the scoreboard)
_____ 1. Opening games
_____ 2. Up or down a break
_____ 3. Closing out a set
_____ 4. 1st three games of 2nd set
_____ 5. Up or down a break
_____ 6. Closing out a match

_____ **D. Execution and keeping hands working**
_____ Routines between points
_____ Something to gain — always!
_____ – ⓪ + not ⊖ 0 +

_____ **E. Post-match**
_____ L-FIDO (learn, forget it, and drive on!)

Part One:
The Physical
Third

Chapter 1

TRAIN PHYSICALLY WITH A PURPOSE

●●●

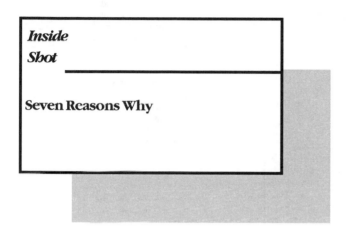

Inside Shot

Seven Reasons Why

For over twenty years, Morning Madness has been a tradition and the initial building block of the Clemson Tennis Program. The ritual is the most well known, talked about, feared and respected part of the Clemson Tennis Heritage. At times, some have looked at it as senseless training, but it has proven to be the cornerstone of many great careers.

The players meet every morning at 6:00 A.M. for the first two weeks of their college careers. Many who attempt the regiment quit soon after the running begins. Those who stick it out get to finally hit tennis balls during their third week. But more importantly, they gain a special sense of pride that they continue to build on throughout their careers and lives. The Cris Robinson story told in the preface is just one of the great examples of character building that has taken place over the years.

The challenge that the athlete faces through basic physical training is important on more than a physical level. The experience tears away the props that are often used to hide any of those initial

insecurities encountered by most young athletcs. The reality check created through the pain of physical training forces the athlete to confront himself; from here, he can begin to establish that foundation which will carry him through an entire sports career. This alone is a great reason for tough physical conditioning, but the benefits are much more far reaching.

I sincerely believe that a tough program of running and physical conditioning is an essential component of excellence for any and all athletic teams.

> There is a close connection between getting up in the morning and getting up in the world.
>
> — *Coach Andy Johnston*

SEVEN REASONS WHY

There are seven reasons why a comprehensive and thorough program of physical training will enhance a player's performance on the tennis court.

1. A rigorous and consistent program of physical training increases confidence in match situations.

If a person is prepared physically for a match, he will be prepared mentally. Mental preparation allows for emotional comfort. An athlete's physical training for a match makes him aware that his body is ready, and he will think to himself, "I have done all I can do — now I am ready to play." This will enable him to perform during the match without pressing, rushing or acting tentative in his play.

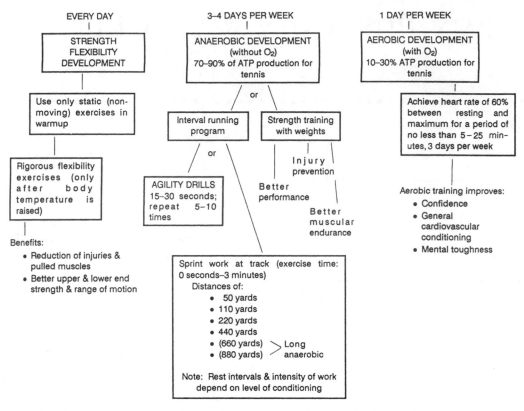

Figure 1-1. A weekly diagram outline of physical training for tennis.

2. A rigorous and consistent program of physical training improves technique, production and power.

Tennis is becoming more and more a strength related sport. Most of the top players are great athletes, and unless a player develops his athletic ability to its maximum potential, he cannot compete at the higher levels of the game.

3. A rigorous and consistent program of physical training reduces the number and severity of injuries.

A tough physical training program should be followed if for no reason other than to reduce injuries. The tennis circuit is so strenuous now, even on the collegiate and junior levels, that the tennis player's body must undergo more strain from competition than ever before. A thorough program of physical training will not only reduce injuries but, in most cases, eliminate them. The training program must follow strict guidelines of flexibility and strength training, and it must also include an adequate running program.

4. A rigorous and consistent program of physical training delays fatigue in competition.

The development of muscular endurance through physical training allows an athlete to participate at a higher intensity for longer periods of time. This enhances performance later in the competition and helps to promote a strong finish in all events.

5. A rigorous and consistent program of physical training promotes a fast recovery after competition.

Muscular endurance developed through a good physical training program enables the body to recover much faster after a strenuous match, allowing an athlete to compete day after day with the same level of excellence in all performances. Most athletes can compete very well early in a tournament, but by the fourth or fifth day their bodies tend to break down under stress. A well-conditioned athlete can go many days in a row and recover quickly after each performance.

6. *A rigorous and consistent program of physical training reduces the number of "tired hours" after training.*

High school and college athletes have to study after practice. An athlete in top condition can recover quickly from workout sessions, no matter how strenuous, and be ready to study. The athlete will also be ready for the next day's activities with a minimal amount of rest.

7. *A rigorous and consistent program of physical training helps the tennis player to become a better athlete.*

Athletic ability is becoming very important in tennis. A strict training program will enable a tennis player to significantly improve strength, flexibility, speed, agility, power and other motor skills. Through the improvement of these areas, the athlete's overall performance will improve dramatically.

Maximum benefit can be obtained from a specific physical training program. Figure 1-1 shows a breakdown of the physical training that a tennis player should undergo in a week. It is essential for a player to follow a good flexibility program every day in order to relax the body before competition, guard against the possibility of injury during the match, and alleviate any soreness from previous performances. Static (non-moving) stretching exercises should be done, but ballistic stretch exercises or any type of bouncing stretch exercises are not recommended. An anaerobic program of training should be followed from three to a maximum of four days a week. It is, however, a good idea for a tennis player to include some aerobic training at least one day a week.

SUMMARY

A specific, comprehensive physical training program will help a tennis player: 1) increase confidence, 2) improve technique and power, 3) reduce the number and severity of injuries, 4) delay fatigue, 5) promote fast recovery after competition, 6) reduce the number of "tired hours" after training and 7) enable the development of a better athlete.

Figure 1-2. Physical training will improve your game.

Chapter 2

TRAIN FOR ANAEROBIC ENDURANCE

• •

Inside Shot

Be Sport Specific

Interval Training

Interval Training Exercises to Train the Anaerobic System

The Step-Out

While doing my graduate studies, I was able to assist with the training of the track team. In that capacity, I observed the unique way in which different athletes train for their individual events. Often there were no similarities at all to their regiments. The head coach would structure the workouts to fit each athletes' specific needs. Distance athletes worked daily on their aerobic capacities with exercises geared to raise their heart rates to a certain level (60% to 70% between resting and maximum) and keep it there for a period of time. The sprinters spent their practices in short explosive activities such as stadium step running, weight lifting, plyometrics and runs of 50 to 440 yards at a pace very close to their maximum. My question to the head coach was, "Isn't running just running for any athlete? Does it really matter that you be so specific?" He replied that he would show me an answer to my question during the next day's practice.

At the next practice, the distance men, who usually ran continuously for 45-60 minutes each day, were assigned a mere 3 times 220 yard sprints at a pace of 24 seconds. He gave them 5 minutes rest between each sprint. I sat in disbelief as I saw all six of these well trained distance men on their knees throwing up after the third repetition.

I asked, "How in the world is this possible?" The head coach replied quite simply. "They are not sprinters, and we just put their systems through a workout that it has not been trained to do. Whereas their aerobic systems are very well trained, their anaerobic systems are not. Similar results would happen if we put the sprinters through a tough distance runner workout." The lesson was learned, and has been an invaluable one for me throughout my coaching career.

BE SPORT SPECIFIC

Most athletes who compete in tennis realize that in order to be fit on the tennis court, they should follow some type of running program off the court. The players who improve their fitness through extra training are usually more likely to prevail in long, grueling matches.

> **P**eople who really get things done in this world are those who drive past the first layer of fatigue.

Many tennis players think that distance running develops the endurance needed to play a long match, and running long distances has been an acceptable training method for quite some time. Many junior, college and professional players run great distances in an attempt to reach the fitness level they hope will give them the strength and endurance needed for long three-set matches. They run long distances religiously without ever asking themselves if distance running is the best way to train. It may be a surprise to many that it is not.

In distance running, the aerobic (oxygen) system is used. This is a different energy system than the one primarily used in tennis. A top-level tennis player must have the capability to replenish his anaerobic (without oxygen) system time after time following several high-intensity work periods. This is not the same as having the capacity to withstand a continuous, low-intensity work load for a long period of time, which is what you get when you run a long distance. A tennis player could run five or six miles a day and still be out of shape to play a match. This is comparable to a dash man preparing for his season by running distances instead of running at maximum intensity for shorter amounts of time with rest intervals between each effort. It has been shown, in Fox and Matthews'

Interval Training, that 70 to 90 percent of the energy expended by a tennis player must be derived from his anaerobic (without oxygen) system. This means that the body, in order to produce the energy needed to play tennis, uses energy stored in the muscles. The chemical names of these energy sources are adenosine triphosphate (ATP) and phosphocreatine (PC), as well as glucose, which is broken down to lactic acid.

Each point in tennis is an all-out explosive type of exercise. Therefore, in order to gain maximal results, a training situation should simulate the playing of a point as closely as possible. The best physical training program for tennis includes exercises with short, explosive movements. Distance running may still be used for weight loss, for general cardiovascular exercise, or for variation in a monotonous training routine. A good way to choose the most effective training method is to ask the question, "Should the physical training be more like a sprinter's or a distance runner's?" Then pattern the training method accordingly.

Table 2-1, from *Interval Training*, lists the extent to which anaerobic and aerobic energy systems are used in a number of different sports.

INTERVAL TRAINING

The concept of interval training is to train at the most efficient intensity of the sport for short periods and follow that with a rest period which allows lactic acid levels to subside. Then, repetitions of the same duration can be done. Figures 2-1 and 2-2, adapted from *Interval Training*, illustrate why the interval method of training is more efficient than conventional training without rest periods.

The amount of work that can be done by muscle tissue depends greatly upon the lactic acid levels within that tissue. If the level is kept down with intermittent periods of rest, more work at greater intensity can be done by the muscle (See Figure 2-2). Without adequate rest periods between exercises, the lactic acid levels soar, thus paralyzing the muscle and preventing efficiency of performance (See Figure 2-1).

After a period of intense interval training, a player can exercise for longer and longer durations with reduced rest periods in between until the intensity is great and the rest period minimal.

SPORT	% ACCORDING TO ENERGY SYSTEMS		
	ANAEROBIC		AEROBIC
	ATP–PC& LA	LA–O2	O2
BASEBALL	80	20	–
BASKETBALL	85	15	–
FENCING	90	10	–
FIELD HOCKEY	60	20	20
FOOTBALL	90	10	–
GOLF	95	5	–
GYMNASTICS	90	10	–
ICE HOCKEY			
a. forwards, defense	80	20	–
b. goalie	95	5	–
LACROSSE			
a. goalie, defense, attack men	80	20	–
b. midfielders, man-down	60	20	20
ROWING	20	30	50
SKIING			
a. slalom, jumping, downhill	80	20	–
b. cross-country	–	5	95
c. pleasure skiing	34	33	33
SOCCER			
a. goalie, wings, strikers	80	20	–
b. halfbacks, or link men	60	20	20
SWIMMING AND DIVING			
a. 50 yds., diving	98	2	–
b. 100 yds.	80	15	5
c. 200 yds.	30	65	5
d. 400, 500 yds.	20	40	40
e. 1500, 1650 yds.	10	20	70
TENNIS	70	20	10
TRACK AND FIELD			
a. 100, 220 yds.	98	2	–
b. field events	90	10	–
c. 440 yds.	80	15	5
d. 880 yds.	30	65	5
e. 1 mile	20	55	25
f. 2 miles	20	40	40
g. 3 miles	10	20	70
h. 6 miles (cross-country)	5	15	80
i. marathon	–	5	95
VOLLEYBALL	90	10	–
WRESTLING	90	10	–

ANAEROBIC	AEROBIC
ATP–PC = Adenosine Triphosphate	O2 = Oxygen
LA = Lactic Acid System	

Table 2-1. Energy system used for various sports activities.

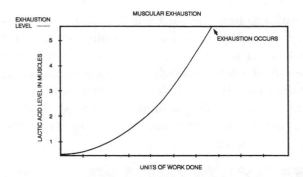

Figure 2-1. Conventional
non-interval training.

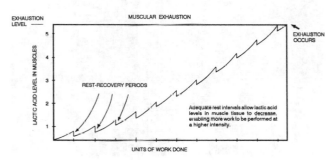

Figure 2-2. Interval training.

Exercise periods must also be at least as equal in intensity as the level of competition that the athlete is training for; otherwise, the training effect will not be adequate for maximal performance. Anaerobic interval training, therefore, is recommended over aerobic training for the tennis player. High intensity sessions with adequate rest intervals are the key!

INTERVAL TRAINING EXERCISES TO TRAIN THE ANAEROBIC SYSTEM: Running Drills For the Track

1. Sprint 50 yards 8-10 times with 1½-2 minutes rest between each sprint.
2. Sprint 100 yards 6-8 times with 2-2½ minutes rest between each sprint.
3. Sprint 220 yards 4-5 times with 3-4 minutes rest between each sprint.
4. Sprint 440 yards 3-4 times with 5-7 minutes rest between each sprint.

Note: Longer sprints should be done early in the training period and the shorter, more intense sprints after the athlete has established a good base.

THE STEP-OUT

The biggest change in footwork technique since the advent of the oversized racquet has been the step-out. It is a technique that facilitates the best preparation for use of the open stance and quick recovery method. When performing the following agility and balance drills, best results will occur with the use of the step-out method of footwork.

The step-out is done from the normal ready position; weight is on the balls of the feet, and the insides of the feet are about a shoulder width apart. From the ready position, the first move to the ball should be made with the foot closest to the ball. The right foot should move first for the right handed player's forehand, and the left for the backhand. This keeps the hips in an open position and allows the player to use his outside dominant leg for loading and leverage. If the ball is close to the player, all that may be needed is a step-out and a load-then-explode movement with the outside leg. If the ball is further away from the player, a three-step move should be made using a normal step-out followed by two more steps to the ball, and finishing with the hips still open and the same loading method used for a one-step movement.

Movement toward balls that are farther away from the player than three steps should always be finished with the same load-and-explode method as used before. It is much easier at first to get the feel of the step-out method when moving to the forehand side. The player will often be tempted to take a crossover step when moving to the backhand upon first learning the step-out. With the backhand, the final move after loading with the outside foot will still be to step into the ball with the foot closest to the net, as is done in traditional footwork technique. The main thing to remember is that the first step should always be made with the outside foot. Pointing the toe on the first step as much as possible toward the netpost will allow for a strong first step to cut off the ball. If a sideways or backwards direction first step is made with the step-out, then the player will probably not be in position to make an aggressive rotation with his hips, and will likely hit a weaker shot. Thanks to Dennis Emery at the University of Kentucky for teaching me this method (See Chapter 5).

Agility Drills

1. Step-out low volley drills: Start in the center of the service box, facing the net. The first step should be made with the outside foot. The hips should face the net. Do not close them with a crossover first step. A split-step is used, a step-out made, and then a crossover movement into the ball keeping the back knee bent low to the ground to simulate proper volley footwork. It is important that good posture is maintained with the upper body for this drill. The athlete should remember to get the back knee down while keeping the back straight. Good posture will lead to very accurate, crisp volleys. You can also run forward and backward or at an angle to get a variety of movement. Do this drill for 20 seconds at maximum rate and then repeat up to five times. Rest for approximately one minute between each execution.

Figure 2-3. Service box drill.

2. Alley touch drill:
For quicker feet, do the same step-out move using the doubles alley instead of the service box. Again, good footwork to simulate the volley should be used. Reach with the right foot when moving to the right and the left foot when moving to the left. Finish the move with a crossover step into the ball.

**Figure 2-4.
Alley touch drill.**

3. Suicide line touch drill: Start at the doubles sideline and sprint first to the singles sideline and back, then to the center service line and back, then to the opposite singles sideline and back, and finally to the opposite doubles sideline and back again to the starting position. Do this drill up to five times with approximately 30 seconds rest between each execution.

Figure 2-5. Suicide line touch drill.

4. Ball drill: Two people are needed for this drill. Once again, use step-out footwork making the first move with the outside foot. One player should kneel down with two balls and roll them, one at a time, to a partner's right side and then to the left side. The partner should retrieve the balls one at a time and toss them back to the other player, always remembering to face him and use good tennis footwork. The crossover step can be made for the last step. Every ball should be picked up with the same hand that ordinarily holds the racquet. This forces body weight forward on the correct foot as though the individual were playing a shot.

Figure 2-6. Ball drill.

Plyometric and Jumping Exercises

1. Bench blasts: Place one foot on a bench (or chair) and keep the other on the ground. Push off as hard as possible using the leg on the bench, come back down, and then immediately push off again. Repeat 20 to 25 times on each leg for one set. Do three sets of exercises on each leg and rest up to one minute between each set. A bench low enough to give good resistance but not so high as to put undue strain on the knee joint should be used. If knee strain or lower back strain results from this exercise, then it should be discontinued. This is a strenuous exercise and should be performed only by the most well-trained athletes.

Figure 2-7. Bench blasts.

2. Loading and exploding with weights or medicine ball: For the forehand loading drill, place the right foot on a platform 6" to 12" in height. The medicine ball should be rotated to the right side of the body, and the athlete's chin should be touching his left shoulder. As the step-up is made with the right leg, the ball and shoulders should rotate to simulate a unit turn for the forehand. The finish should have the chin now resting on the right shoulder. Rapid step-ups with this rotation should be made and repeated up to 20 to 30 times. Make sure the back remains straight so that a horizontal rotation of the hips and shoulders takes place over the vertical axis of the legs.

For the backhand stroke, the left leg is placed on the platform, and shoulders and ball should rotate from the right shoulder under the chin to the left shoulder under the chin. When teaching children the proper hip and shoulder rotation, I'll often tell them to rotate their shoulders under their chin — from "Ike to Mike" — for their forehand and then opposite — from "Mike to Ike" — for their backhand.

Note: See Chapter 22 for illustration and further explanation.

3. Australian double-knee jump: Jump high enough into the air to touch the knee to the chest and then return to the ground. This should be done at maximum intensity 20 to 30 times per set. Complete up to three sets with a 30 to 45 second rest interval between each. This is an advance jumping drill and should only be done by experienced athletes. Landings should be made smoothly and without jarring. If the exercise results in pain or the athlete's shins are irritated by this exercise, then it should be discontinued.

Figure 2-8. Australian double-knee jump.

Genius is 1% inspiration and 99% perspiration. And no one has ever drowned in sweat.

— *Unknown*

4. Power jumping: A weighted jump rope is an excellent way to build anaerobic endurance, muscular endurance and strength. A good work load would be five sets, 50 seconds of jumping with at least 75 revolutions per set, and 45 seconds of rest between each exercise.

Figure 2-9. Power jumping with weighted rope.

5. Speed rope jumping: A speed rope and a weighted jump rope complement each other very well. In the training routine the speed rope should be used for just that, speed. High intensity single or double jumps for periods of 30 to 45 seconds are excellent, and up to five sets should be done with equal rest intervals between sets.

Figure 2-10. Jumping with speed rope.

Table 2-2 is a sample seven-week interval training program for the tennis player. The workouts start with long sprints and middle distance type work. This provides a good base and prepares the player for higher intensity workouts later in the program. In the fifth, sixth and seventh weeks, there are still some long aerobic workouts, but most of the workouts are short, very high intensity anaerobic workouts. These help the athlete to peak in his conditioning for a tournament or competition.

Figure 2-11. Interval training workouts build anaerobic endurance.

SUMMARY

Most of the energy used in playing tennis is anaerobic energy, and therefore it is important for an athlete to follow a good anaerobic endurance training schedule. Interval training — training with high intensity for short periods followed with rest periods — can be used to train the anaerobic system.

Train for Aerobic Endurance

	SUN.	MON.	TUES.	WED.	THURS.	FRI.	SAT.
WEEK 1	Rest	Flexibilities 4x440 @ 75 sec. 2x220 @ 30 sec. 2 min. rest intervals	6 agility drills	Flexibilities 2x440 @ 75 sec. 4x220 @ 30 sec. 2 min. rest intervals	6 agility drills	Flexibilities 6x220 @ 35 sec. 2x440 @ 75 sec. 2 min. rest int.	Distance run 1–3 miles
WEEK 2	Rest	Flexibilities 2x220 @ 32 sec. 3x330 @ 48 sec. 2x440 @ 75 sec. 2 min. rest int.	6 agility drills	Flexibilities 1x880 @ 2 min. 50 sec. 2x440 @ 75 sec. 2x220 @ 35 sec. 2–3 min. rest int.	6 agility drills	Flexibilities 8x110 @ 16 sec. 1 min. rest int.	Distance run 1–3 miles
WEEK 3	Rest	Flexibilities 1x mile for time	6 agility drills	Flexibilities 2x440 @ 70 sec. 2x330 @ 48 sec. 2x220 @ 31 sec. 2 min. rest int.	6 agility drills	Flexibilities 3x220 @ 31 sec. 3x440 @ 75 sec. 2 min. rest int.	Distance run 2–5 miles
WEEK 4	Rest	Flexibilities 880 for time 10 min. rest int. 440 for time	6 agility drills	Flexibilities 5x330 @ 50 sec. 2 min. rest int.	6 agility drills	Flexibilities 2x220 @ 30 sec. 6x110 @ 14 sec. 2 min. rest int.	Distance run 2–5 miles
WEEK 5	Rest	Flexibilities 1x440 for time 5 min. rest int. 1x440 for time	6 agility drills	Flexibilities 6x220 @ 30 sec. 2 min. rest int.	6 agility drills	Flexibilities 10x110 @ 15 sec. 1 min. 30 sec. rest int.	Distance run 3 miles
WEEK 6	Rest	Flexibilities 1x mile for time	6 agility drills	Flexibilities 4x220 @ 30 sec. 4x110 @ 14 sec. 1 min. 30 sec. rest int.	6 agility drills	Flexibilities 5x110 @ 15 sec. 5x50 @ full speed 1 min. rest int.	Distance run 3 miles
WEEK 7	Rest	Flexibilities 880 for time 5 min. rest int. 440 for time	6 agility drills	Flexibilities 5x110 @ full speed 5x50 @ full speed 1 min. rest int.	6 agility drills	Flexibilities 12x50 @ full speed 45 sec. rest int.	Distance run 3 miles

Table 2-2. Seven-week interval training program.

**Note: Times, distances and rest intervals should be adjusted
to the present fitness level of each individual athlete.**

Chapter 3

TRAIN FOR STRENGTH AND FLEXIBILITY

● ●

Inside Shot

Strength Training

Flexibility Strength

Flexibility Strength Training Equipment

Flexibility Strength Exercises

Flexibility Training

Exercises for Wrist Flexors and Extensors

The most often heard complaint about a very tough program of physical conditioning and discipline is, "Why is there so much physical conditioning and running involved? This isn't a track or a weight lifting team." After so many years of dealing with this question, I have developed four basic replies that I use for the inquiries. Besides the fact that the sport of tennis requires so much athleticism in today's arena, these four explanations validate the process of tough conditioning.

Reason #1: Pain Tolerance

The basic fundamental, that one's ability to endure physical and emotional pain leads to an advantage over opponents, is a fact. Many coaches use the saying "No Gain without Some Pain" and "Pain Engages the Brain" to support this fact. Pain tolerance must be learned so that the athlete can develop the ability to enter new and inexperienced levels of discomfort. Technical skills can never hold up unless physical, mental and emotional barriers have been conquered in prior practice situations.

Reason #2: Team Bonding

As athletes train and suffer together, a bond grows between them very naturally. They quickly learn to respect the guy or girl next to them for sharing the same task and pain. Once this bond is experienced, few ties prove as strong or durable during the heat of competition or in the face of tough times.

Reason #3: Ownership of Dreams and Destiny

"The harder that I work, the harder it is to surrender," is a saying that explains why ownership of one's personal effort toward a goal is necessary. If the athlete pays a price in training, he or she will feel the deepest satisfaction for their efforts when the goal is accomplished. The strength to persevere through hardship becomes a conditioned resource that may be called upon throughout life. Likewise, when a person has not worked hard for what they have accomplished, there will often be an unconscious tendency to self-sabotage the very success that's been earned because the athlete is not comfortable with that ownership.

Reason #4: Confidence in Going the Distance

My athletes often ask, "Why does it seem that those athletes who don't train very hard always seem to come up with some big wins? It seems as if they just shoot from the hip in an all to gain situation and pull it off." My answer to them is always the same. I say, "The unprepared athlete can play big at times, but he will never play in the Big Time." This is because to win events, the tennis player must be able to play well five, six or seven times in a row. It's not so much that the championship player is that much better than the undisciplined athlete's best day. It's that the prepared and disciplined athlete's bad day still reaches a level good enough to get him through the rough times. I explain it further by saying that on a scale from 1 to 10, the fly by night athlete may have a range of a "9" on his best day and bottom out at a "3" on his worst day. The athlete who has prepared well has the same "9" range on his best day, but because of his work habits, he only falls off to a level "7" on his worst day. This greatly enhances his

Pretenders versus Contenders: Pretenders can play big at times, but you'll never see them playing in the Big Time.

opportunities to follow through in tournament situations and over the course of a long season. The difference between the "Pretender" athlete and the "Contender" athlete is almost always decided by the degree of commitment in preparation.

As explained in Chapter 1, muscular endurance is a critical element of consistent performance. Strength training is the key procedure for the development of muscular endurance.

STRENGTH TRAINING

For years the prevalent school of thought was that strength training, especially with weights, was not good for a tennis player's development. Many people still believe that weight training tends to make a tennis player clumsy and restricts his movement, hampering the broad range of motion in the limbs necessary to play the game. But, most of what is taught about strength work in tennis has little or no scientific backing. It has been shown that good muscular strength is important for the following reasons:

1. *It reduces the number and severity of injuries and delays muscular fatigue.*
2. *It decreases recovery time from training stress thereby reducing the number of "tired hours" after training. As a result, it is possible to have more consecutive days of good physical performance.*
3. *It increases confidence in athletic ability because it enhances better technique, stroke production, power and speed of movement.*

I have found that strength training has its best results when performed in a workout before drill sessions. The nervous system has a memory and the fine motor skills tend to work better if they're used after weights. I have found that when weights are used after a tennis workout, the player's fine motor skills remember the weight work and not the tennis until the following day's practice.

Consequently, I never schedule weight work within 48 hours of match play and never on days when sets are played in practice. Player's lift only on drill days and do so before practice or during the morning of that drill day.

FLEXIBILITY STRENGTH

Flexibility is defined as the range of motion of any joint in the body — the greater the range of motion, the greater the flexibility. Players today are discovering that the one most important and distinguishing quality that top players possess is flexibility strength. Contrary to some beliefs, strength and flexibility can work together. Strong muscles will not hamper flexibility if they are developed through exercises employing a wide range of motion. The perfect example of flexibility strength is the gymnast, who has the strength of a linebacker and the flexibility of a dancer.

The players winning the most tournaments today are those with proven athletic ability and great flexibility strength. Therefore, the best fitness program for a tennis player's physical development is one that combines both strength training and flexibility exercises. The greatest benefit is obtained if strength work is done three days per week, alternating those workouts with a good anaerobic running or agility program. Work on balance, agility and stretching should be done daily. Figure 3-1 is a sample of a weekly flexibility strength training program.

MON.	TUES.	WED.	THURS.	FRI.	SAT.	SUN.
– Anaerobic exercises – Speed work	– Strength-flexibility training – Optional agility drills	– Anaerobic exercises – Speed work	– Strength-flexibility training – Optional agility drills	– Anaerobic exercises – Speed work	– Strength-flexibility training	– One-day rest or light aerobic workout

Figure 3-1. Flexibility strength training program.

Figure 3-2. Nautilus equipment.

Figure 3-3. Conventional gym equipment.

The most intense periods of physical conditioning should take place in the off-season and the pre-season. After the season starts, the program should be tapered depending upon the physical demands of the player, but the program must never be abandoned. After a base of fitness is established in the pre-season, it can be maintained with timely workouts that are well planned and geared to the schedule and rest periods of the athlete. Optimally, a program of 60 to 70 percent physical work should be maintained in the early season, tapering back to 30 to 40 percent in the late season.

The more that you sweat in Peacetime, the less that you'll bleed in War.
— *Unknown*

FLEXIBILITY STRENGTH TRAINING EQUIPMENT

Nautilus® equipment increases the range of motion of each joint and stretches the muscle properly when exercised. When free weights or a universal gym are used, special attention should be paid to the range of motion and the specificity of each exercise to maintain and perhaps increase flexibility.

The use of a proper weight load is critical for strength development. Too little weight does not give the quality results that heavier weights provide. On the other hand, when too heavy a weight is used, proper exercise technique cannot be executed. Therefore, a weight heavy enough to gain training effect but not so heavy as to inhibit proper technique must be used. (The same principle relates to racquet weight. If your racquet is too heavy or too light, the proper technique of strokes cannot always be executed.) Usually, 8 to 12 lift repetitions work well. Try to follow the interval training guidelines as they relate to muscular work and energy expenditure.

FLEXIBILITY STRENGTH EXERCISES

(If there is no access to weights and equipment)

If a player does not have access to a weight training facility, the following exercises can be used to increase flexibility strength. Notice how many of them have been adapted to increase the range of motion.

Note: In the following exercises quality is much better than quantity for maximum efficiency and strength gain. For example, it is better to do 6 to 10 repetitions at maximal intensity or with a heavier weight than to do 30 consecutive repetitions at a lower intensity or with a lighter weight. The suggested exercise load is two or three sets of 10 repetitions with one-half to one minute rest between sets and three to four workouts per week.

I. Pectoral (Chest) Strength Exercises

1. Men's deep chair aided push-up.

Strokes aided: High forehand and forehand volley.

Description: Unlike conventional push-ups on the ground that only allow half the full range of motion, three chairs can be used to get a greater overload and at the same time a pre-stretch factor and complete range of motion for the pectoral muscles and triceps.

Place your feet on one chair and a hand on each of the other two chairs. Do regular push-ups, making sure to lower your chest as close as possible to the ground between the two chairs.

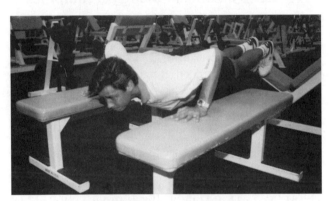

Figure 3-4. Men's deep
chair aided push-up.

2. Women's deep chair aided push-up.

Strokes aided: High forehand and forehand volley.

Description: Use the same method described in the men's version, but keep the feet on the ground instead of using a third chair.

Figure 3-5. Women's deep
chair aided push-up.

II. Posterior Deltoid and Shoulder Strength Exercise

1. Supine lateral raise.

Strokes aided: Backhand and backhand volley.

Description: Lie on a bench or couch on your side so that your right arm comes across the chest and hangs freely to the floor. Hold a small dumbbell or weight in the right hand and elevate it in a backhand motion, using only the shoulder. Repeat on the left side.

Figure 3-6. Supine lateral raise.

III. Triceps Strength Exercises

1. Triceps press or French curl.

Strokes aided: Service and overhead smash.

Description: The exercise will improve power in the serve dramatically in one to two months. The triceps is the primary muscle used for the service motion. Its contraction straightens the arm out. The three joints used in serving are the shoulder, elbow and wrist.

Stand and hold a dumbbell or bar weight in the right hand and point your elbow up toward the ceiling (it may be supported by the opposite arm). Using only the triceps, straighten the arm out and up. Repeat using the opposite arm.

Figure 3-7. Tricep press.

2. Chair dip.

Strokes aided: Service, high ground strokes and volleys.

Description: This exercise aids in development of the triceps for serving and promotes good shoulder strength for many strokes and out-of-position shots. It is often used by pole vaulters to develop triceps strength.

Place both hands behind your back on one chair and place feet on another chair. Using only the elbow joint, lower the body, and then raise it back to the starting position.

Figure 3-8. Chair dip.

IV. WRIST STRENGTH EXERCISES

Good wrist strength is necessary for playing the net. The easiest way to exercise the wrists is to use a tennis racquet that is weighted in the head of the racquet. Enough weight should be used to create an overload situation. The suggested exercise load for wrist exercises is one to two sets of 10 to 12 repetitions with adequate rest periods in between.

Figure 3-9. This low volley illustrates the need for good forearm and wrist strength when playing the net.

1. Wrist curl for wrist flexors.

Description: With the palm of the hand facing up, use only the wrist to elevate the racquet and weight to a fully flexed position, and then lower it. Strength gain will occur in the forearm.

Figure 3-10. Wrist curl.

2. Wrist extension (extensors).

Description: With the palm of the hand facing down, use the wrist only to elevate the racquet, and then lower it. The back of the forearm receives the strain.

Figure 3-11. Wrist extension.

3. Neutral position curl.

Description: With the racquet held in an eastern forehand grip (racquet head perpendicular to the end), elevate the weight using only the wrist. This helps to keep the racquet head up on volleys.

Figure 3-12. Neutral position curl.

4. Wrist pronation and supination.

Description: With the racquet head pointed straight up, use the wrist to twist the racquet to the left and then to the right. This will strengthen your pronator and supinator muscles for added help in hitting top spin on both sides.

Figure 3-13.
Wrist pronation (above)
and wrist supination
(right).

V. Abdominal Exercises

Special attention should be paid to the development of abdominal strength because power for stroke production and athletic performance originates in the stomach. The hyperextension exercises of the abdominal area not only significantly increase the strength of that area, but also increase flexibility of the abdominal muscles for prevention of injuries. The suggested exercise load for abdominal exercises is 8 to 15 repetitions in two to three sets. These exercises are suited for the well-trained athlete who is in top condition. If pain persists, discontinue these exercises.

Figure 3-14. A Roman bench may be used for the following exercises. The Roman bench back raise is illustrated above.

Note: If a Roman bench is not available, the following exercises can be done on a regular bench or table, or with the aid of a partner to hold the legs in position.

1. Roman bench sit-up.

Strokes aided: Service and overhead smash.

Description: Sit at the edge of a Roman bench and lean down as far as possible to extend the abdominal muscles to the point of slight discomfort. Then proceed to do sit-ups.

Figure 3-15. Roman bench sit-up.

2. Roman bench back raise.

Strokes aided: Service and overhead smash.

Description: Using either a Roman bench or with the aid of a partner to restrain your legs, lie face down with lower abdominal area touching the edge of the bench. Go from a flexed position to a fully extended position, arching the back upward.

Figure 3-16. Roman bench back raise.

3. Roman bench external oblique exercise.

Stroke aided: Service.

Description: Using a Roman bench, lie on your side with upper body off the bench. Cross your legs so that firm support can be given by a partner holding your feet. Lower your upper body to the ground as far as possible until slight discomfort is felt in the side abdominal muscles, and then return to the starting position.

Figure 3-17. Roman bench external oblique exercise.

Figure 3-18. The athlete must use abdominal strength in the coiling action of the serve.

FLEXIBILITY TRAINING

Flexibility training should be done daily in a tennis player's preparation for practice or for matches. Two flexibility programs are detailed: a one-man static stretching program that is familiar to most athletes, and a two-man program devised by George Dostal. A stretching program is also recommended after performances to aid in the partial removal of lactic acid from tired muscles which, in turn, helps decrease recovery time.

STATIC STRETCHING PROGRAM: ONE-MAN STRETCHING ROUTINE

To perform static stretching exercises, a joint is held for about 30 seconds in a position that stretches the tissue to its maximum controllable length without undue stress. Static (non-moving) stretching is safer than ballistic (balancing or oscillating) methods because it does not impose sudden stress upon the involved tissue, yet does the work intended. Proper stretching will aid in relieving tension from daily stress.

Static Stretching Guidelines:

1. **Never force a stretching muscle during the exercise to a level of discomfort or pain. Do not overstretch.**
2. **Be patient; work within your limits.**
3. **Stay relaxed in all areas of the body.**
4. **Maintain good posture and body alignment at all times.**
5. **Do not hold your breath—breathe normally.**
6. **Always do some sort of aerobic warm-up exercises before stretching.**
7. **Use equal time intervals between exercises to let the muscles relax (10 to 30 seconds).**

1. Standing hamstring stretch.

Muscles stretched: Hamstring, lower back muscles, upper calf muscle.

Description: Stand in an upright position with knees locked. Bend forward slowly, moving your hands toward the ankles until tightness is felt in the hamstrings. Hold this position for 30 seconds, and then slowly return to the original position.

Figure 3-19. Standing hamstring stretch.

2. Hurdler's hamstring stretch.

Description: Sit on the floor with one leg turned backward (but not so much as to put excess strain on the knee joint) and the other extended forward (hurdler's position). Bend your torso down toward the knee until tightness is felt. Hold this position for 30 seconds, and then slowly return to the original position.

Figure 3-20. Hurdler's hamstring stretch.

3. Sprinter's stretch.

Muscles stretched: Groin area muscles, gastrocnemius (calf), hamstring, quadriceps, upper back muscles.

Description: Stand in an upright position with knees locked. Slowly spread legs apart, forward and backward, as far as possible. Slowly move your hands toward the right ankle until tightness is felt in the hamstring and gastrocnemius. Hold this position for 30 seconds, and then slowly return to the original position. Repeat exercise for the left leg.

Figure 3-21. Sprinter's stretch.

4. Pretzel stretch.

Muscles stretched: Lower back, buttocks, upper shoulder muscle.

Description: Sit with your right leg bent at the knee and upper leg flat on the floor. Raise the left knee and place the left foot flat on the floor next to the right knee. Slowly twist your torso to the left. Place the right arm outside the raised knee to facilitate twist. Hold this position for 30 seconds, and return to the original position. Repeat the procedure on the opposite side.

Figure 3-22. Pretzel stretch.

5. Cobra stretch.

Muscles stretched: Abdominal muscles, upper quadriceps.

Description: Lie flat on your stomach. Push the upper body off the floor with the hands extending up to full stretch. Hold this position for 30 seconds, then slowly return to the original position.

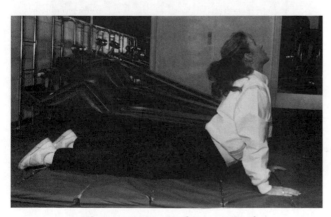

Figure 3-23. Cobra stretch.

6. Static groin stretch.

Muscles stretched: Groin muscles.

Description: Sit down, and pull your heels together toward the groin. Slowly push down on the knees with the elbows until tightness is felt in the groin area. Hold this position for 30 seconds, then slowly return to the original position.

Figure 3-24. Static groin stretch.

7. Hurdler's quadriceps stretch.

Muscles stretched: Quadriceps, shin muscles.

Description: Lie on your back with legs together. Grasp the left ankle with the left hand, slowly pull the ankle toward your waist, and lower your head toward the floor until tightness is felt in the quadriceps. Hold this position for 30 seconds, then slowly return to the original position. Repeat the procedure for the right leg. Note: do not put the knee in a strained position that might put excess pressure on the knee joint. Only the quadriceps should be stretched and not overstretched or strained.

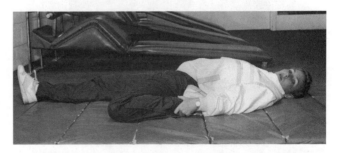

Figure 3-25. Hurdler's quadricep stretch.

8. Sitting shoulder stretch.

Muscles stretched: Shoulder and neck muscles.

Description: Sit down with legs together pointing forward. Place your arms behind your body, with palms on the floor and fingers pointing toward the body. Slowly lean back and increase the angle between arms and trunk until the maximum stretch is achieved. Hold this position for 30 seconds, then slowly return to the original position.

Figure 3-26. Sitting shoulder stretch.

9. Standing shoulder stretch.

Muscles stretched: Front and back shoulder and neck muscles.

Description: Stand with arms straight out to your sides and hold a stationary object. Turn slowly to the left and slowly stretch the shoulder until tightness is felt. Hold this position for 30 seconds, then slowly return to the starting position. Repeat the procedure, this time turning to the right.

Figure 3-27. Standing shoulder stretch.

10. Scissor back stretch.

Muscles stretched: Lower back muscles, buttocks, upper hamstrings.

Description: Lie on your back with legs together and arms extended out at your sides. Slowly rotate the left hip and raise right leg to reach the left arm. Hold this position for 30 seconds, then return to the original position. Repeat the procedure, this time raising the left leg to reach the right arm.

Figure 3-28. Scissor back stretch.

11. Calf stretch.

Muscles stretched: Calf muscle, lower hamstrings.

Description: Stand erect with your feet together and both heels on the ground. Lean forward against a wall or immovable object. Then lean farther until tightness is felt in the calves and Achilles' tendons. Hold this position for 30 seconds, then return to the original position.

Figure 3-29. Calf stretch.

12. Standing shin stretch.

Muscles stretched: Tibialis anterior, shin and ankle muscles.

Description: Stand erect with your back to a wall and feet flat on the ground. Lean backward until tightness is felt in the shin muscles. Turn the toes outward and then inward for different angles (this may be done with one leg or both legs at a time). Hold each position for 30 seconds, then return to the starting position.

Figure 3-30. Standing shin stretch.

EXERCISES FOR WRIST FLEXORS AND EXTENSORS

Pre-stretch position and initial exercise: The following wrist exercises should be done in a contract-relaxation manner and are easily done by one person. The opposite hand should be used as the resisting force to allow the isometric contraction. Extension should be done to the point of muscle tightness and slight resistance. The wrist should then be extended slightly farther and the exercise repeated. Three extensions and contractions should be sufficient for each exercise.

1. Wrist flexor stretch.

Description: The palm of the racquet hand should be facing up. With the opposite hand, pull the racquet hand and the fingers downward so that the muscles and connective tissues of the wrist are then extended.

Figure 3-31. Wrist flexor stretch.

2. Wrist extensor stretch.

Description: The palm of the racquet hand should be facing down. With the opposite hand, press the racquet hand and fingers downward so that the muscles and connective tissues of the wrist are then extended.

Figure 3-32. Wrist extensor stretch.

3. Pronation muscle stretch.

Description: Hold a racquet with the racquet head pointing straight up (12 o'clock position), and rotate it clockwise to a 3 o'clock or 4 o'clock position. At this extended position, provide resistance using the opposite hand and do contract-relaxation exercises. Then, rotate the racquet farther to a 4:30 or 5 o'clock position. Repeat the exercise.

Figure 3-33. Pronation muscle stretch.

4. Supination muscle stretch.

Description: Hold a racquet with the racquet head pointing straight up (12 o'clock position), and rotate it counterclockwise to an 8 o'clock or 9 o'clock position. Provide resistance with the opposite hand, and do contract-relaxation exercises. Then, rotate the racquet farther to a 7 o'clock or 7:30 position. Repeat the exercise.

Figure 3-34. Supination muscle stretch.

5. Neutral position stretch.

Description: Hold a racquet in an eastern forehand grip with the racquet head perpendicular to the ground. Let the racquet head face forward toward the ground, extending the muscles on the top part of the wrist. Keeping the racquet head in this neutral position, add slight pressure for a very gradual stretch.

Figure 3-35. Neutral position stretch.

6. Triceps and service stretch.

Description: Hold the racquet behind your back. The racquet should be dropped straight down the middle of the back for a gradual stretch.

A note about tennis elbow: By strengthening the wrist flexors and extensors and using a good stretching routine for these same muscles, the chances for elbow, wrist and connective tissue injuries are greatly reduced.

Figure 3-36. Tricep and service stretch.

THE DOSTAL FLEXIBILITY TRAINING PROGRAM: TWO-MAN STRETCHING SYSTEM

This contract-relaxation flexibility program combines strength with flexibility. Because strength gain is relative to the joint angle for the muscles being exercised, it is important to follow correct procedure at the proper intensity to develop greater flexibility. It is important to note that before starting this program, the athlete should jog or jump rope to elevate the body temperature to the point in which sweat breaks. This will allow efficiency in the exercise while preventing any injury.

Athletes perform stretching exercises in order to accomplish one or more of the following objectives:

1. **To reduce injuries due to tearing of muscle tissue.**
2. **To increase the amplitude of movements inherent in the activity.**
3. **To promote muscle relaxation.**
4. **To increase metabolism in muscles, joints and associated connective tissues.**

General Procedure for the Dostal Flexibility Training Program

All exercises in the Dostal method should be done using the general procedure described for the hamstring stretch. Mastery of this method is quick, and improvement will be experienced at the initial workout. The exercises should be performed daily for maximum benefit, preferably before specific sport training begins. For added flexibility, the Dostal exercises should be repeated after training.

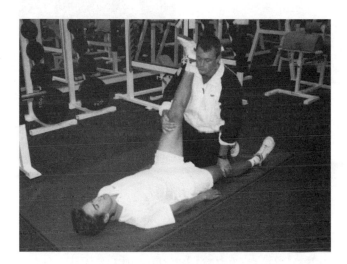

**Figure 3-37.
Pre-stretch, contracted position—
hip extensors stretch.**

**Figure 3-38.
Stretched, extended position—
hip extensors stretch.**

In Figure 3-37, the athlete (P1) lies on his back with the leg to be stretched lifted as far as possible from the floor with the knee extended. The opposite leg remains on the floor throughout the exercise with the knee extended. The partner (P2) is positioned to serve as an immovable object when P1 begins to exercise. With the hamstrings in a lengthened position, P1 begins the exercise by attempting to push his leg back toward the floor. This effort is resisted by P2, who does not permit the leg to move, thus causing an isometric contraction. In the first two seconds of the contraction, P1 gradually builds to a maximum or near maximum effort, and should then sustain the contraction for an additional four seconds. The entire six-second exercise should be counted aloud by P2.

After the initial six-second effort, P1 lifts his leg toward his head by contracting the opposite muscle group. This concentric contraction pulls the leg to a new position as the result of increased flexibility of the hamstrings and surrounding connective tissue. This maneuver should be aided by slight pressure from P2. Slight discomfort may be felt, but if P1 experiences pain, the exercise should be stopped immediately. It is important to note that the isometric contraction should never be explosive but should always involve a gradual increase in effort with the helper only acting to resist and support the contraction — the helper should never apply pressure himself.

In Figure 3-38, P1 moves to a new position as a result of the initial exercise. The entire procedure is then repeated three or four times. This is followed by the same sequence applied to the opposite leg.

1. Hip extensors stretch (hamstrings).

Description: P1 lies on his back, with one leg on the floor and the other raised as high as possible. Both legs remain straight throughout the exercise. P2 gets on one knee, with the opposite foot on the floor and the shoulder against the back of P1's leg. P2 holds the non-exercising leg to the floor. P1 attempts to push his raised leg to the floor. P2 resists this effort causing an isometric contraction. After the six-second contraction, P1 pulls the leg toward his head. P2 assists with light pressure. P1 then repeats this procedure from the new stretched (extended) position two or three more times.

2. Hip abductors stretch I (groin muscles).

Description: P1 sits with his back and legs straight, with legs as far apart as possible. P2 is positioned in front of P1, and holds both P1's legs above the ankles. P1 attempts to bring his legs together, making sure to keep them straight. P2 resists. After the six-second isometric contraction, P1 spreads his legs (abducts the hip joint), and P2 assists with light pressure. P1 then repeats this procedure three more times from the new stretched (extended) position.

Figure 3-41. Pre-stretch position—hip abductors (stretch II).

Figure 3-39. Pre-stretch position—hip abductors (stretch I).

Figure 3-40. Stretched position—hip abductors (stretch I).

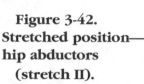

Figure 3-42. Stretched position—hip abductors (stretch II).

3. Hip abductors stretch II.

Description: P1 lies on his back, with legs spread apart as far as possible and raised to form a ninety degree angle with the floor. P2 stands in front of P1, and holds both P1's legs below the knee. P1 attempts to squeeze his legs together. P2 resists. After the six-second isometric contraction, P1 pulls his legs apart as far as possible (abducts the hips). P2 assists with light pressure. P1 then repeats this procedure three more times from the new stretched (extended) position.

4. Hip flexors stretch.

Description: P1 lies prone with his right leg flexed at the knee and raised as high as possible. P2 is behind P1, resting on his right knee, with his left foot on the floor. P2's right hand is placed under P1's raised knee, and the left hand is placed slightly above P1's right buttock. P1 attempts to pull his knee downward to the floor. P2 resists. After the six-second contraction, P1 lifts the leg higher. P2 assists with light pressure. P1 then repeats this procedure three more times from the new stretched (extended) position.

Figure 3-43. Stretched position—hip flexors.

5. Trunk extensors stretch (lower back muscles).

Description: P1 sits down, with legs straight out in front and trunk flexed forward as far as possible. P2 stands behind and slightly to the side of P1, and places his hands on P1's neck and the central portion of the upper back. P2's rear foot should be braced against an immovable object. P1 attempts to straighten up (extend trunk). P2 resists. After the six-second isometric contraction, P1 pulls his trunk down toward his legs. P2 assists with light pressure. P1 then repeats this procedure three more times from the new stretched (extended) position. (Note: This exercise should be performed with less than maximum effort until the athlete is accustomed to it and is confident that no injury will result.)

Figure 3-44. Pre-stretch position—trunk extensors stretch.

Figure 3-45. Stretched position—trunk extensors stretch.

6. Combination: Trunk extensors, groin and hamstrings.

Description: P1 sits with legs spread, trunk flexed as far as possible toward the right leg, and hands stretched toward the right foot. P2 stands behind and slightly to the side of P1, and places his hands on P1's upper back. P1 attempts to straighten up (extend trunk). P2 resists. After the six-second isometric contraction, P1 pulls his trunk down toward his leg. P2 assists with light pressure. P1 repeats this procedure from the new stretched (extended) position. P1 then repeats the entire sequence, but this time reaches down the left leg.

P1 then repeats the sequence again, and this time reaches straight ahead to stretch his middle groin area. These exercese are illustrated in Figures 3-46 and 3-51.

(Note: These exercises should be performed with less than maximum effort until the athlete is accustomed to the stretch and is confident that no injury to these muscles or lower back will result.)

Figure 3-46 & 3-47. Right leg—pre-stretch (left) & stretched position (right).

Figure 3-48 & 3-49. Left leg—pre-stretch (left) & stretched position (right).

Figure 3-50 & 3-51. Middle groin—pre-stretch (left) & stretched position (right).

7. *Trunk lateral flexors (external obliques).*

Description: P1 stands with feet shoulder width apart and left hand resting on the left side of the head. He bends his trunk to the right side. P2 stands on P1's left side, with his left hand on P1's waist, and his right hand holding P1's raised elbow. P1 attempts to pull his body to the upright position. P2 resists this effort to cause an isometric contraction. After the six-second isometric contraction, P1 pulls his trunk downward. P2 assists with light pressure. P1 then repeats this procedure three times from the new stretched (extended) position. Procedure reversed to stretch other side.

Figure 3-52. Pre-stretch position—trunk lateral flexors.

Figure 3-53. Stretched position—trunk lateral flexors.

8. *Shoulder extensors.*

Description: P1 sits down with legs straight out in front, back straight, arms straight up, and shoulders stretched as far as possible. P2 stands behind P1, facing opposite with the back of his legs resting against P1's spine (or P2 can stand facing forward with one foot near P1's body with his knee resting against P1's spine). P2 holds both P1's forearms. P1 attempts to pull his arms toward his legs, keeping the elbows straight. P2 resists. After a six-second isometric contraction, P1 pushes his arms backward. P2 assists with light pressure. P1 then repeats this procedure from the new stretched (extended) position.

Figure 3-54. Pre-stretch position—shoulder extensors.

Figure 3-55. Stretched position—shoulder extensors.

9. *Shoulder horizontal abductors.*

Description: P1 sits down with legs straight out in front, back straight, and arms raised straight out to the sides at shoulder level. P2 stands behind P1, with one foot near P1's body and knee resting against P1's spine. P2 holds both P1's forearms (use of a pad or towel may prove helpful). P1 attempts to pull his arms forward, keeping the elbows straight. P2 resists. After a six-second isometric contraction, P1 pushes his arms backward. P2 assists with light pressure. P1 then repeats this procedure from the new stretched (extended) position.

Figure 3-56. Pre-stretch position—shoulder horizontal abductors.

Figure 3-57. Stretched position—shoulder horizontal abductors.

10. Shoulder internal rotators.

Description: P1 stands erect, one arm raised to shoulder level with elbow flexed to 90 degrees, and shoulder rotated out as far as possible. P2 stands in front and to the side of P1, with one hand on P1's wrist and the other on P1's arm slightly above the elbow. P1 attempts to rotate his shoulder inwardly (throwing motion). P2 resists. After a six-second isometric contraction, P1 rotates his shoulder outwardly. P2 assists with light pressure. P1 then repeats this procedure from the new stretched (extended) position.

Figure 3-58. Pre-stretch position—shoulder internal rotators.

Figure 3-59. Stretched position—shoulder internal rotators.

SUMMARY

A thorough, systematic flexibility program can only aid the athlete. Good sense and judgment should be used, and a consistent program should be followed. The idea behind stretching is to get the muscles to a state of readiness so that they can endure the heavy ballistic action that occurs during competition. It is important to recognize that stretching beyond the normal movement capacity for a joint may be detrimental in many ways to the athlete. Both overstretching and understretching, therefore, should be avoided. With experience, the athlete will learn his own limitations in flexibility training.

Chapter 4

SPEED AND BALANCE: THE EDGE

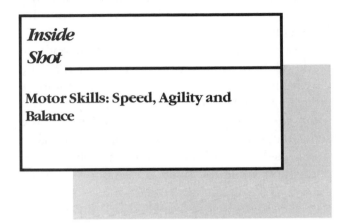

Inside Shot

Motor Skills: Speed, Agility and Balance

We always believed his gifts of movement on the court were a fluke because he was so athletic in other areas. Strength, speed, and anaerobic endurance are extremely important to the success of a tennis player; but the skills of balance and agility along with an overall feel for the court are the finishing touches that the best players have.

MOTOR SKILLS: SPEED, AGILITY AND BALANCE

Tennis is an extremely complex sport, in part because of the many different motor skills that are involved. Speed, agility, balance, reaction time, quickness, power and hand-eye coordination are all important individual skills. But there is not enough time in practice to work on each of these areas alone. Therefore, most coaches try to incorporate a training program that encompasses many of them. Those of primary importance to tennis are speed, agility and balance.

Speed in athletics is defined as "the rate at which a person can propel his body, or parts of his body, through space." When we talk about speed in tennis we are usually referring to a player's foot movement. Can the player move from point A to point B on the court quickly? Can the player run down balls that are out of reach for the average player?

There are several other motor skills involved, however, than just running speed. Every time a tennis player hits a ball, reaction time, quickness

Larry was about the slowest person that I had ever seen in the 100 yard dash. Day after day, he finished last in end-of-practice sprints. His distance running was very poor also. Seldom was Larry able to finish the three-mile run that the coach would have the team do on Saturday mornings. The tennis court was quite a different story, though, for Larry's movement skills.

When Larry played a match, it seemed as if he had magical skills. He seemed to have the unique ability to be precisely in the right place at the right times and from here deliver his very strange shot-making skills. His precision on the court was incredible, and he frustrated multiple opponents on his way to winning four conference championships in four years.

What Larry possessed was more important than merely an ability to run fast. He had great balance, an excellent first step to the ball and very natural perceptual skills of judgment in setting up his shots.

> **Q**uick hands and balance of the feet make for a game that's hard to beat.
> — *Coach Andy Johnston*

and power prove to be important factors. Reaction time, or "the time between the stimulus and the initial response," becomes a key ingredient in any quick exchange of shots. Quickness is a term that refers to an athlete's short spurts of speed. Power is defined as speed plus strength. Power has often been categorized as the greatest individual determinant of athletic ability. But in tennis, the saying, "Power thrills, but speed kills," holds true. Train for both to achieve positive results on the court.

Agility is defined as "the physical ability which enables an individual to rapidly change positions and direction in a precise manner." In tennis, the need for this motor skill is quite obvious, because all stroke production is based on the ability to get from one part of the court to another and then set up, keep on balance and change direction.

Speed agility is a term I use to refer to a player's ability to move as quickly as possible while remaining in perfect balance so that a quick stop and change of direction can be made. Without the ability to get to the ball and set up for a good stroke, refined technical skills are useless. Lack of this combination of speed and agility can prevent a player from progressing to an advanced level.

When starting to lose a match, players often make comments like "I can't feel the ball" or "I don't know why I'm missing the ball." What these players mean is that they're not able to set up for shots, and therefore those shots are not effective. This may result from the player not possessing enough speed.

Professional players' careers falter when they lose speed and balance and cannot make effective shots. In fact, speed is always the first thing to go as a player ages or if the player fails to train. Again, it should be emphasized that speed alone is not what's lost, but speed, agility and balance, the three key ingredients to effective stroke production. Without them, it does not matter what the body is doing from the waist up.

Balance, or "the ability for a person to hold a stationary position," is also a very important ingredient necessary for a tennis player's athletic development. Solid, well-placed shots cannot be made without this important motor skill. The researcher Bass states that there is evidence indicating that the ability to balance easily depends upon the functions of the mechanisms in the semicircular canals; the kinesthetic sensations in the muscles, tendons and joints; the visual perception while the body is in motion; and the ability to coordinate these three sources of stimuli. Balance is very much an inherited skill, but it should be worked on like any other important motor skill in the tennis player's training routine.

All running and agility drills performed in practice should emphasize the need for good balance. Speed is of great help to a player with good balance. In all practice situation stroking work, the reminder, "Head down, and feet on the ground," is critical to proper development of balance for good stroke production. Proper balance allows a player's technical skills to remain effective long into a career.

Figure 4-1. Mitch Sprengelmeyer illustrates how training for speed, agility and power pays off in a match situation.

Furthermore, it allows maximum leverage for stroke production which translates as power and accuracy even if the athlete is not particularly strong.

The following sample 45-minute training routine incorporates many of the components necessary for the development of important motor skills used in tennis. All drills should closely simulate the speed, agility and balance used in tennis. Whenever possible, footwork should be the fundamental tool employed when executing a stroke.

SAMPLE TRAINING ROUTINE

1. Five minutes: Light jog and flexibility (warm-up period should allow the body temperature to rise approximately one degree, or to the point when sweat breaks).
2. Five minutes: 30 seconds jump rope, 30 seconds rest (five times); alternate the weighted rope with the speed rope.
3. Ten minutes:
   a. Box drills and step-out drills: two sets (30 seconds rest).
   b. Bench blasts and loading drills: two sets for each leg (30 seconds rest).
   c. Alley touch drills: two sets (30 seconds rest).
   d. 30-yard sprints: six sets (10 seconds rest).
4. Five minutes: Upper body work; three sets of 10 to 15 push-ups and 10 to 15 sit-ups, 30 second rest periods between each exercise.
5. Two minutes: Jump rope, cool down.
6. Five minutes: Rest break.
7. Two minutes: Loosen up using a jump rope.
8. Five minutes: Lateral court movement drills, ball pickup drills, lateral movement.
9. Three minutes: Power jump rope; alternate 45 seconds exercise, 15 seconds rest.
10. Two minutes: Bench blasts.
11. Two minutes: Jump rope, cool down.

When we talk about speed, its important to understand that strength is a significant component for its development. A misconception was held for years that strength development was detrimental to speed. Research by Zorbas, Karpovich, Wilkin, Masley, Endres and Chul proved exactly the opposite. These educators discovered that strength development, primarily through weight training, significantly improved speed of movement.

> **I**f you are truly striving for excellence, you will only be competing against about 10% to 20% of the people in the world.

Slow Twitch vs. Fast Twitch Muscles

It is also important to understand the relationship between slow twitch and fast twitch muscle tissues. The body's striated (skeletal) muscles contain two types of fibers: dark fibers (slow twitch) and light fibers (fast twitch). Dark muscle fibers have slow contractions but great endurance, whereas light muscle fibers have quick contractions but little endurance.

Figure 4-2. Strength development increases a tennis player's speed.

This relationship is easily understood by looking at a chicken or a quail. Both these birds have dark muscle fibers in the legs and light muscle fibers in the breast. Neither can fly far, but each has strong legs to walk on. A duck's breast has only dark muscle fibers which aid the bird in its long, slow flight to Canada and back. We see this relationship in fish as well. The dark muscle tissue of salmon and trout provides for the endurance necessary to travel great distances upstream to spawn. Bass and bream have light muscle tissue that allows for quick bursts of speed, but both fatigue easily.

In a human being, dark and light muscle fibers are interspersed throughout all the muscles. It may be true that sprinters have a higher proportion of light muscle fibers, whereas distance runners have a higher proportion of dark fibers. Regardless, the training of a tennis player should be geared for both types of muscle tissue. Since tennis is predominantly an anaerobic sport that requires high intensity and ballistic speed, a program of training should be done for the fast twitch muscles.

Exercises like bench blasts, double-knee jumps, sprints, suicide line drills and speed jump rope all work excellent for this. On the other hand, training of the slow twitch muscles is also important for injury reduction, joint and connective tissue strength, and muscular endurance. Excellent slow twitch work can be done with Nautilus equipment, other weight programs or exercises designed to improve strength and speed.

SUMMARY

A tennis training program should incorporate work on speed, agility, balance, reaction time, quickness, power and hand-eye coordination. Drills can be used to develop these skills, and it should be remembered that all drills should simulate actual match play. Exercises should be performed to develop both the slow twitch and the fast twitch muscles.

Figures 4-3, 4-4 & 4-5. Training for motor skills.

Chapter 5

DEVELOP YOUR TECHNICAL SKILLS AND STROKE PRODUCTION

•••

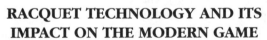

RACQUET TECHNOLOGY AND ITS IMPACT ON THE MODERN GAME

Before any concepts about technique and stroke work can be discussed, it is important that coaches understand just what evolved in the game of tennis during the 1980s and recognize the impact made by racquet technology. The 1980s and early 1990s were very confusing times for anyone in the tennis teaching business. With the advent of the Prince® oversize racquet in 1978-79 and the wide-body super power racquets that followed, playing and teaching techniques would never be the same. Actually the racquet revolution turned careers of players and tennis teachers upside down over night.

Before 1970, the majority of players played with three or four very similar racquets. These produced and required very uniform teaching styles as well. If good technical skills were not used, the player could not produce a consistent or well-struck shot. The hitting surface of these racquets was small, requiring good linear footwork techniques. The better that ones technique became, the better the player he or she would become. Players would therefore devote countless hours to their technical skills as they searched for the perfect stroke.

In the late 1960s, companies began to experiment with steel racquets and a few different shapes. The Wilson® T-2000™ and the Spalding® Smasher™ were two of these novel racquets. Head® also came out with the Arthur Ashe model that many referred to as the "Rug Beater" Racquet. But Howard Head's innovations with the Prince oversized racquet in the mid 1970s really marked the start of the revolution. The game of tennis and the way in which people played it would change forever. During the first years, use of the oversized racquet was treated as a joke. But once the idea caught on, the marketing of new sizes, shapes, lengths, widths, and types of materials was on the way.

It is very interesting that teaching and playing styles did not change immediately because everyone who first started using the bigger or wider racquets had originally learned to play with the small traditional equipment. The real changes in the game started in the late 1980s when a whole new generation of players were coming up who had started out playing the game from the start with the bigger and wider racquets. For many traditional teachers, this was hard to adjust to. A variety of strange stroking styles started to yield positive results in competition. Power more than placement and precision became the norm. Many felt that the entire game of tennis was being changed before their very eyes. Points became much shorter and less interesting to watch, and, to my way of thinking as a teacher and a coach, the game lost much of its art. Point development and strategies became less important than hard hitting and great shot making. I have often stated that the use of higher-tech racquets has made skill less important than the equipment itself; therefore, the sport is made somewhat less fun and interesting to play. The great drop-off of players in the United States in the mid 1990s was most likely a result of this.

Tennis: A Hard Game to Pick Up, A Hard Game to Put Down

I have often used the examples of other art forms like music and painting. There is good reason why the piano remained unchanged throughout history. It is a traditional art that is very hard to master. Therefore people want to play it and are very proud of the skill levels they gradually achieve. Once skill is acquired, that skill is precious and important to the artist. If a person tried to learn music with the electronic keyboard or a less difficult version of musical instrument, the value would not be nearly as great. If the artist could use paint by numbers instead of plain canvas and paints, his skill would not mean as much either. A sport such as racquetball is not nearly as interesting as squash because of much fewer dimensions and less difficulty in playing. The game of professional baseball would not have the same excitement if aluminum bats were allowed because hitting a

> **D**on't ever think expensive equipment will make up for lack of talent or practice.

home run would become so commonplace that it would no longer be valued as such an excellent feat. The examples are obvious in just about every sport and art form. MAKING SOMETHING EASIER DOES NOT NECESSARILY MAKE IT BETTER.

In the case of tennis, I believe the lack of control by the sport's governing bodies has caused great damage to the game forever. Even if making the game somewhat easier to play allows most to experience initial success, it is also the reason why fewer and fewer are captivated by the game enough to want to play it again and again. The game of tennis is great because it is a hard game to pick up, and a hard game to put down.

> **P**ride makes us do things well. But it is love that makes us do them to perfection.

As a child there were two reasons why I took up the game of tennis. First, the sport itself was so challenging that the art of it alone made me passionate about playing. I wanted to spend every moment that I could playing and improving my skills. The second and less important reason that I played was for the sake of the competition. If the sport had lacked the artistic element, however, there is no way that I would have spent so many years in love with it. Simply put, I truly believe that very few who play the game have a love affair with the game. If they did, there would not be so many who quit immediately once their competitive careers are over. I blame the manufacturers and the governing bodies of tennis for not displaying more responsibility to the Best Game Ever Invented.

In this chapter, the technical skills that are described and taught for the most part will be quite traditional, but a lot of consideration has been given to the equipment changes that have taken place in recent years. This chapter should give the reader an excellent base to grow from but enough freedom to develop one's own personal style.

CHANGE OR GET LEFT BEHIND

After the lengthy discussion of what has just happened in the evolution of racquet technology and its effect on the game, it is critical to realize that all coaches and players must recognize that they need to deal with it and go on. I confess that I probably did a very poor job of coaching technique for a five or six year period as I stuck to my very traditional ways. In 1993 I decided that if I ever wanted to be successful again, I needed to change. I took action by visiting a coaching friend, Dennis Emery, the Director of Tennis at the University of Kentucky. Up to that time, it seemed that my players were definitely not able to play as aggressive as others and that I had to be doing something very wrong.

The University of Kentucky teams were known for their aggressive play, and I wanted to know why. They were excellent at using high powered equipment and their shot making was non-compromising. The main thing that Dennis taught me that weekend was how to get critical leverage with the open stance and how to use the very important step-out technique for loading the hips. He showed me some great films of the top pros and how they would use that technique to get to the ball quickly and then recover just as fast.

THE STEP-OUT

The main thing that the players all seemed to be doing differently was that they now played with their hips open and facing the net. They seldom stepped across their opposite leg and locked out their hips. They were excellent at what Dennis kept referring to as the step-out move. The first step to the ball in every case was made with the foot that was closest to the ball. The right foot would move first at an angle to cut the ball off when hitting on the right side of the body, and the left foot would move first at an angle to cut off the ball when hitting on the left side of the body. This allowed the player the ability to load his power on the outside leg and hip so that a circular rotation and hip action could be made for power to be generated. He firmly stated that leverage for all strokes comes from the outside foot and the rotation of the hips into the ball. The instant that the old crossover step is made first instead of this step-out method, the hips get locked out and power smothered. Then, only the arm is left to supply limited power and produce a weak shot.

This meeting with Dennis put me on the right track. I immediately changed my whole paradigm about footwork and the use of the lower body in power production. On shots such as return of serve and volleying, where correct timing and balance are so critical, the step-outs have been incredibly effective. Because of its absolute importance, footwork will be discussed in this chapter first.

The following drills make use of the "Power Groove" (*See Bibliography for more information), an elastic strap-like tool similar to a bungi cord. It is worn to force the player to incorporate his entire trunk and shoulders into the unit turn on shots. These sequences illustrate use of the step-out in teaching proper technique for each of the strokes.

Figures 5-4 & 5-5 (left to right).
Slow feed drill for backhand volley.

Figures 5-6 & 5-7 (left to right).
Slow feed drill for forehand volley.

Figures 5-1 thru 5-3.
Slow feed drills for the groundstrokes: starting position (inset, Fig. 5-1), forehand (left, Fig. 5-2), backhand (right, Fig. 5-3).

LEARN YOUR STROKES FROM THE INSIDE-OUT

I was fortunate enough after college to work for Harry Hopman, who was the Australian Davis Cup Coach for over 20 years. Hopman has been recognized as one of the greatest coaches of all time, and his results with players such as Rod Laver, Ken Rosewall and Roy Emerson may never be equaled in the sport of tennis. Having had little formal tennis training at that point, I approached my new job expecting to learn all the new techniques and mechanics of hitting the ball.

In my first month of working for Hopman, I was shocked, surprised and somewhat disappointed to find out that I was not learning all the fancy schoolbook techniques of the great players that I had heard so much about. Hopman was working with current junior players John McEnroe, Peter Fleming and Vitas Gerulaitis. He would put them on workout courts and make them hit thousands of balls as he ran them from side to side and up and back, the whole time encouraging them to push themselves physically beyond their limits. Very seldom did I hear Hopman talk about certain shot techniques, and when he did, it was always in a way that gave leniency to the player's individual form and style allowing the player to immediately adapt.

Inside-Out Teaching

At first I did not understand Hopman's approach. After three months of working with him, however, I started to realize the genius of this man who knew how much more important it was to train the inner part of an athlete than it was to just train an athlete's technical skills. I think that what Hopman gave topnotch athletes with a bit of rebellion in them (like McEnroe, Fleming and Gerulaitis) was discipline and a tremendous pride that came from their own hard work. Seeing how this pride grew was a great help to me as I developed my own coaching methods.

But I realized that there was much more to his style than just that. I started asking myself questions about teaching and playing styles. Why were the strokes of the top 10 players in the world so completely different? Why were some players baseline players, and why were others net rushers?

Why did almost all the players use different grips to hit the ball? I thought of all the coaches who were teaching structured styles and forcing their pupils to play in certain ways. Then I would watch Hopman. I saw how he could coax the inner part of a player to produce the results that he wanted, but always in a unique way, suiting each player's personality.

During that year, a young Swedish player named Bjorn Borg was quickly coming to international attention. Borg had a revolutionary style that included extremes for stroking on both the forehand and backhand sides. Very few players had ever used a two-handed backhand before, and very few players had ever strayed far enough to use the severe western forehand grip that Borg used. At that point, no one knew the impact that Borg would have on the tennis world. As I first watched him play, I wondered if someone had actually taught him those strokes. Did someone tell him to hold the racquet as he did, to hit two-handed, and to loop the ball with such heavy top spin? Or, did he develop the strokes on his own?

I realized that although certain fundamental skills are important to deliver a ball with the right force, spin and direction, a player's strokes are developed pretty much according to his individual temperament and his own style. This was a revelation for me as a coach, and it gave me new insight in training players. I realized Hopman's genius more than ever.

Forcing a certain structure on an athlete may be confusing to him. It often keeps the outer and inner selves from "meeting," thus preventing the athlete from reaching his full potential. As coaches, we may train an athlete in a certain way and drill the fundamentals into his head. But unless a player develops the inner determination necessary to become the best and allows for his own personal creativity, he will not reach his full potential.

Technical skills are very important as well. I have often wondered what would happen if a coach provided no instruction, but instead delivered thousands of balls to a very coordinated athlete to hit using different strokes. Would the athlete develop into a fine player? My belief is that he would become quite adept at a certain level of play but would develop frustration at a point when his reliance upon technique and lack of good technical skills prevented his further advancement. A comparison would be a pianist who learned to play without instruction versus learning formal classical.

Good basics are very important, and merely hitting balls is not enough. In the early stages of development, strict attention should be paid to fundamentals — helping a player execute the forehand, backhand, serve, volley, approach shot, return serves, passing shots and overhead shots. Only when a player is able to execute these will he be able to develop an individual style of play and shot delivery.

Providing instruction to a tennis player is like providing instruction to a painter or musician. Painters and musicians learn the fundamentals of fingering and brushwork, but artists only become artists when they are able to give physical expression to the world inside themselves. It is the same with tennis players. Athletics is one of the purest forms of art. What a tragedy it is when an individual's inner self is prevented from surfacing either by a coach's inability to let the athlete play according to his personality as he reaches advanced stages, or, at the other extreme, by a lack of knowledge of the fundamentals that should have been learned earlier in the athlete's career!

A coach must understand that each individual will play according to his own personality. If the player is conservative, he will probably have a conservative style of play. If the player is reckless, he will likely have a reckless style of play. It is interesting that in critical match play situations, a player will do exactly what his personality dictates. A coach's most important job is to get the outside of the athlete to work comfortably and confidently with the inside of the athlete and vice versa. This union is the key to reaching maximum potential

> ## A well beaten path is not necessarily the right way.

as a player. The coach should spend about 90 percent of his time in the early stages of a player's development working on technical skills and fundamentals. As a player progresses to a solid base of skills, the coach should work 50 percent on fundamentals and 50 percent on the mental and emotional parts of the athlete. When the player's fundamentals are firmly ingrained, a near complete range of freedom should be given to the athlete to play from the inside-out as his temperament dictates, with the coach keeping a watchful eye on technical flaws that may prevent the athlete from developing his game to the next level.

THE TOOL BOX OF SKILLS: CONSISTENCY, PLACEMENT, DEPTH, SPIN, POWER

I learned a great method of teaching from Ed Dickson, then the tennis coach of Purdue University. He believes that the development of tennis skills should follow a logical progression, beginning with consistency and progressing to placement, depth, spin and then power.

Becoming consistent with the most basic shots is the first step, and placing balls consistently from corner to corner follows. Next is the ability to use both under-spin and top-spin on deep balls hit consistently to each corner, and last comes the ability to hit with power.

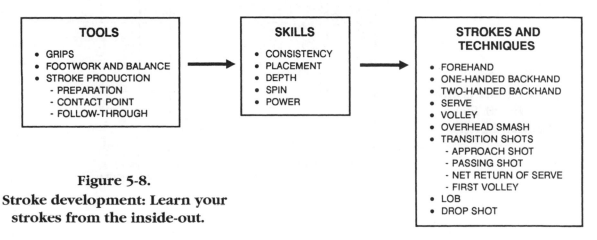

Figure 5-8.
Stroke development: Learn your strokes from the inside-out.

Most players work on bits and pieces of each of these skills throughout their development, but it is important to understand that each skill builds on the previous skills. Many players try to learn power before they learn other ball control skills. This will only work if players are willing to hit hundreds of balls to harness power and maintain consistency. I often tell my players that the key to each stroke is to hit the best shot they can hit without making an error. If you hit a more aggressive shot, you need a safer target. If you hit an easier shot, you can use more precise targets.

Dickson's system of progression is as follows:

Consistency: Repetition is the mother of skill. Consistency is the ability to repeat a skill time and time again. This should be a player's first goal with every stroke as that new stroke is learned. It has become somewhat of a lost art with the large, high-tech racquets and needs to be applied now more than ever. The true measure of consistency comes with how well the stroke holds up under pressure.

Placement: Power thrills but placement kills. Placement is the ability to hit the ball where desired within the court. Doing this gives players the control needed to run the opponent or to direct the ball to a specific place on the court for a point-winning shot.

Depth: Depth is the ability to keep an opponent deep in the court. This increases shot-making options and prevents the opponent from taking the offensive. Controlling depth may also refer to the player's ability to hit short balls and bring the opponent purposely to the net from time to time.

Spin: The ability to place spin on the ball while maintaining control of the shot is crucial and adds a great deal to one's proficiency and skill level. Hitting the ball with top-spin, under-spin or even side-spin opens multiple dimensions of the game. Not only does it enable a player to control a ball hit aggressively, it delivers shots the opponent does not like to hit.

Power: Power is the ability to win points outright and to force an opponent into errors. It is exciting and enjoyable to have power, but it should be the last skill to be developed. The elements that dictate power are speed of the racquet head resulting from efficient mechanics of the legs and trunk along with good hand timing.

TOOL ONE: GRIPS

There are nearly as many ways of holding a tennis racquet as there are people playing the game. Although each player should learn the fundamentals of grip and stroke technique, each person's style and grip will eventually be as unique as his signature.

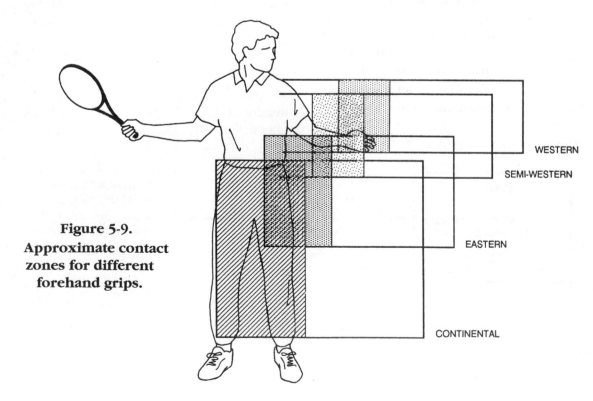

Figure 5-9. Approximate contact zones for different forehand grips.

WESTERN

SEMI-WESTERN

EASTERN

CONTINENTAL

Tennis instructors and coaches are often too rigid in their teaching of grip. Like golf, where different clubs and sometimes different grips and swings are required for each shot, tennis requires some flexibility as well. Different court surfaces and conditions can demand different grips. Clay courts provide a slow, high bounce; hard concrete or asphalt courts provide a medium height and medium paced bounce; grass courts provide a ball that bounces low, skids and dies; and gym floors provide a very low, very fast bounce. For each surface, a different grip and wrist position could be necessary to hit the ball for the best impact and leverage. But each person has learned an individual style and therefore has to make the proper adjustments when playing different surfaces. Sometimes the adjustment is an easy one, and other times it may be very difficult.

It may sometimes be necessary to use different grips for the different balls that are hit at a player on the same surface by the same opponent. Sometimes balls are high, sometimes low, sometimes wide and away from the player, and sometimes close to the player. Some are fast, some are slow and almost all are delivered with a different spin. In order to use the same grip to hit all balls, a player would have to move fast enough to set up for the same bounce every time. This is usually possible on ground strokes because they give a player more time to judge the bounce. A novice player becomes comfortable with a particular grip, usually based on the court surface that he is used to playing on. This will generally remain the fundamental grip used throughout his career. As his skills develop and he must hit balls of different heights and speeds, it becomes necessary to vary this grip in certain situations.

A player should choose a grip that enables him to make contact with the ball in the optimal strike zone. The basic grips are the continental, the eastern, the semi-western and the western. Figure 5-9 shows the approximate contact zone for each grip for the forehand. These basic grips, illustrated in Figures 5-10 thru 5-17, are used by roughly ninety percent of the world's tennis players, including top players. The experienced player will learn that for shots other than the forehand, a slightly different grip and hand position may be used for maximum effectiveness. It is false to assume that only one grip is acceptable at all times for each stroke.

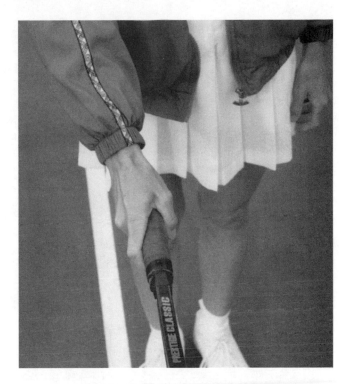

Figure 5-10. Continental grip.

**Figure 5-11.
Continental grip contact point.**

Figure 5-12. Eastern grip.

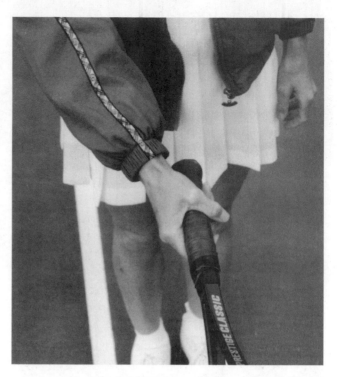

Figure 5-14. Semi-western grip.

**Figure 5-13.
Eastern grip contact point.**

**Figure 5-15.
Semi-western grip contact point.**

Figure 5-16. Western grip.

**Figure 5-17.
Western grip contact point.**

TOOL TWO: FOOTWORK AND BALANCE

Stroking technique and proper grip can work effectively only if a player can get into position to use them. During the player's development, it is important to learn proper footwork and balance when setting up for and delivering each shot.

Proper Footwork

Two things are important to maintain good balance and leverage when hitting any stroke: the head should be kept down and both feet should remain on the ground. The outside foot closest to the ball should be used to load the power. Keeping the head down allows good control over the entire body — if the head comes up, so will the arms, legs and the rest of the body, thereby preventing optimal balance, leverage and weight transfer through the ball. The step-out is critical for maintaining leverage. An in-depth discussion earlier in this chapter explains the step-out method for movement to the ball and should be observed.

Footwork Variations

The two variations of footwork used for all strokes are the closed stance and the open stance. In both variations, the upper body is in the same position, with the shoulders and side turned in a coiled position facing the net. However, in the closed stance both feet are somewhat perpendicular to the net, and in the open stance both feet are more parallel to the net. The open stance is the most widely accepted method and the best to use with today's equipment and style of game. I want my players to always play with their hips facing the net. The step-out technique for movement to the ball should be observed.

Figure 5-18. Closed stance—forehand.

Figure 5-19. Open stance—forehand.

TOOL THREE: STROKE PRODUCTION

Start the Motor and Grab the Steering Wheel

Simply put, I tell my students to use their legs, trunk and body as the motor to supply power for racquet head speed and their hands as the steering wheel to provide direction, spin and placement on the ball. These two components combine to supply good biomechanics for the player.

I have drills that teach players to get effortless power from their legs while attempting to hit balls from one fence to the other fence with a smooth stroke. As their shots start reaching the opposite fence, I tell the players to start using their hands and touch to gradually control the ball and place it on the court while still retaining the same power into the ball.

When players miss, I remind them that the stroke is for power and the hands are for direction; or, the stroke is the motor and the hands the steering wheel. Do not change your stroke as long as you're getting plenty of effortless power through the ball; work to train the hands and establish timing to control the racquet and direct that power.

Hand-timing takes the longest for players to master. Good biomechanics for power should be stressed and locked in as early as possible in the training process to establish a fundamental base.

I believe this simple approach to teaching the strokes makes it easier for players to improve quickly without being slowed by the over-analysis of missed shots. The term "paralysis by analysis" is a very appropriate term for some people. They simply make the game much harder than it should be.

Good stroke mechanics are important, as is the development of a fundamentally sound style. But hundreds of balls must be hit to train the hands and timing skills. These are universal principles.

The point is this: players should keep it simple and play the game according to their unique personality. The mechanics of hitting the ball should be basic and consistent. An instructor can help a player train muscle memory through practice until a stroke becomes automatic. But during competition players must incorporate those mechanics into their own style of play. Remember, all players are No. 1 in the world at their own individual style. They should use it to their advantage.

Preparation

The key to preparation for any stroke in tennis is to turn the shoulders in coordination with the loading action that is done with the legs. The shoulders and racquet should move together like a coil or whip, so that the force can be transferred into the racquet head and through the ball. If a player turns and coils his shoulders properly, the racquet will automatically go back, but leverage on the stroke can easily be lost if the racquet goes back and the shoulders do not turn to coil. When teaching children, I name their shoulders Ike and Mike and tell them that they should be rotated — on the forehand from Ike to Mike and on the backhand from Mike to Ike — signifying one shoulder being under the chin for the start of the stroke to the other being under the chin at the finish. On ground strokes, where leverage for racquet head speed is needed, a player should concentrate on turning his shoulders and coiling his hips to allow the uncoiling action to generate this racquet head speed. Weight should be loaded on the outside leg. For stroke leverage generated from the backswing, the player should move the racquet, then the shoulders, and then the hips. For the uncoiling or swing movement, the player should move his hips first, and then his shoulders and racquet. The open stance provides the most leverage for loading up power from the hips and legs. A linear stance allows the racket to stay on line with the ball but doesn't allow as much racket head speed.

The contact point varies somewhat for each stroke and each grip, but the general principle is the same: it must be the point where maximum leverage can be achieved. In general, though, the ball must be hit in front of or slightly off the front foot or the line of the body. Weight must be shifted from the back foot (loading foot) to the front foot in order to generate force through the ball. The leverage for the racquet head speed comes from the outside leg and hips. A unit turn has to be made with the upper body.

Follow-through

The ball is far away from the strings of the racquet when the follow-through is taking place, but the follow-through should be observed to show how a ball is hit. The important thing to note is the movement of the racquet head, because where it finishes shows where it has been and how it started. A follow-through that is too high shows perhaps too much top spin and a short ball, whereas a follow-through that is too low shows too much slice on the ball. A long follow-through usually indicates a longer stroke that produces a deeper ball. A shorter upward or downward follow-through indicates a shallower shot with more spin on the ball. Whatever the case the follow-through should be very relaxed and smooth to allow for proper feel and acceleration though the ball.

The follow-through also gives a good indication of a player's confidence level. A shortened, jerky or rushed follow-through usually indicates that a player is pressing or is feeling a bit too much pressure. A smooth follow-through shows confidence, control and trust in the stroke.

Figures 5-20 & 5-21 (left to right). Unit turn for forehand—start to finish (Ike to Mike).

Figures 5-22 & 5-23 (left to right). Unit turn for backhand—start to finish (Mike to Ike).

Figures 5-24 thru 5-28. Forehand stroke sequence. Ready position (Fig. 5-24, inset); step-out with foot closest to the ball, shoulders and hips coil and load (Fig. 5-25); closed stance step into the ball (Fig. 5-26); contact point with ball in front of the body (Fig. 5-27); follow-through with good shoulder rotation and balance (Fig. 5-28).

Figure 5-25.

Figure 5-26.

Figure 5-24.

Figure 5-27.

Figure 5-28.

Table 5-1. Physical relationships of the forehand.

FOREHAND VARIABLES

SKILL DEVELOPMENT AREA	THE TOOLS		STROKE PRODUCTION		
	Grips	Footwork	Preparation	Contact	Follow-through
CONSISTENCY (high balls ↔ low balls)	WESTERN: best for high bouncing balls; slow courts SEMI-WESTERN: good for high balls, fair for low balls EASTERN: good for low balls, fair for high balls CONTINENTAL: best for low & stretch balls	Open Stance: requires spin for control Closed Stance: requires a flatter ball	Shoulders & hips to the side	In front on higher balls Even with body on lower balls	Low to high for smooth follow-through Left arm in front for balance Catch racquet on follow-through for balance, to drive shoulder, & to turn through to the ball
PLACEMENT (hit early ↔ hit later)	WESTERN: best for inside court shots, hardest to change direction SEMI-WESTERN: fair for changing direction EASTERN: fair for changing direction CONTINENTAL: best for changing direction and pulling the ball crosscourt	Closed Stance: better for placement crosscourt Open Stance: best for inside-out shots			
DEPTH (shallow balls ↔ deep balls)	WESTERN: hardest to hit deep SEMI-WESTERN: fair for deep balls EASTERN: good for deep balls CONTINENTAL: best for deep balls	Closed Stance: better for depth			
SPIN (top spin ↔ under spin)	WESTERN: best for top spin, hardest for slice SEMI-WESTERN: good for top spin, fair for slice EASTERN: fair for top spin, good for slice CONTINENTAL: best for slice, hardest for top spin	Open Stance: better for spin			
POWER (high ball power ↔ low ball power)	WESTERN: power good on high balls only SEMI-WESTERN: best power EASTERN: best power CONTINENTAL: power good on low balls only	Open Stance: good for circular momentum (spin player) Closed Stance: good for linear momentum (flat player)			

THE JOBS

Discussed in the previous section were the tools or technical skills that build the tennis player. Once a player has a firm grasp of the tools, he is ready to take on the jobs — the physical elements of stroke production.

JOB ONE: THE FOREHAND

The continental and western grips are the most difficult grips to adjust to hit balls of different heights. The continental grip is best suited for hitting low balls and is difficult to use to hit high balls. Conversely, the western grip, which is suited best for high balls, is difficult to use to hit low balls. Both the eastern and the semi-western grips are more responsive to adjustments with low or high balls. A player using an eastern grip has very few problems in adjusting for a low ball and only moderate difficulty in adjusting for a high ball. The player using the semi-western grip has little problem adjusting to a high ball and very minor difficulties in adjusting to hit a low ball. The hardest thing to do is to make an adjustment from the continental range to the western range and vice versa. Table 5-1 lists and describes these relationships in more detail. The execution of the forehand is shown in Figures 5-24 through 5-28.

JOB TWO: THE BACKHAND

Both the one-handed and the two-handed backhands are accepted and used by players of all levels and abilities. The one-handed backhand is easily used in the same situations as the continental or eastern forehand grips. It was developed by grass court or fast court players because it works well with low hard balls or when the player is stretched out. The two-handed backhand is used to hit higher, bouncing balls that are closer to the body and works well for clay court or slow court players. Ideally, players should be versatile enough to use a one-hander for low, skidding balls as well as for balls away from the body, finesse shots, approach shots and drop shots. The two-hander should be used more as an offensive weapon when the ball is sitting up and easier to contact. Table 5-2 lists and describes these relationships in more detail. Figures 5-30 through 5-34 show execution of the one-handed backhand. Figures 5-35 through 5-39 show execution of the two-handed backhand.

Backhand Grips

Figure 5-29. Grip for the one-handed backhand.

The one-handed backhand grip: The one-handed backhand can be hit well with either the eastern backhand grip or the continental grip. The eastern grip allows a wrist angle that favors a ball hit with top spin or hit low to high. The continental grip makes it very easy to slice the ball or to hit a flatter shot. Although some players can generate top spin using the continental grip, proper leverage with this grip is difficult, which can make it quite difficult to control. The eastern backhand grip is the better grip if the athlete can bend well for low balls.

Figure 5-30. Grip for the two-handed backhand.

The two-handed backhand grip: The two-handed backhand is great for hitting the same balls used in the western and semi-western forehand — high balls and offensive shots where the ball is sitting up. With this grip, the left side of the body of a right-handed player does most of the work, so the grip used with the left hand is of prime importance. The left hand should be placed on top of the right hand, and an eastern or semi-western grip should be used. Although the power for the stroke does not come from the right hand or the right side of the body, the right hand should also grip the racquet with an eastern backhand or a continental grip because this grip will help the player when he stretches to hit wide, low and other out-of-position balls that force a one-hander to be hit. The stroke is very similar to the left-handed forehand in that it allows the shoulder to rotate through the ball. It is different from the one-handed backhand where the left side of the body freezes to shift leverage to the right. I often teach this stroke by having players hit left-handed forehands.

Figures 5-31 thru 5-35. One-handed backhand stroke sequence. Ready position (Fig. 5-31, inset); step-out with foot closest to the ball, shoulders and hips coil and load (Fig. 5-32); closed stance step into the ball (Fig. 5-33); contact point with ball in front of the body, strong wrist position, free arm back for leverage (Fig. 5-34); follow-through with good shoulder rotation, extension and balance (Fig. 5-35).

Figure 5-32.

Figure 5-33.

Figure 5-31.

Figure 5-34.

Figure 5-35.

Figures 5-36 thru 5-40. Two-handed backhand stroke sequence. Ready position (Fig. 5-36, inset); step-out with foot closest to the ball, shoulders and hips coil and load (Fig. 5-37); closed stance step into the ball (Fig. 5-38); contact point with ball in front of the body (Fig. 5-39); follow-through with good shoulder rotation, extension and balance (Fig. 5-40).

Figure 5-37.

Figure 5-38.

Figure 5-36.

Figure 5-39.

Figure 5-40.

Table 5-2. Physical relationships of the backhand.

SKILL DEVELOPMENT AREA	BACKHAND VARIABLES	THE TOOLS		STROKE PRODUCTION		
		Grips	Footwork	Preparation	Contact	Follow-through
CONSISTENCY	high balls ⟷ low balls	TWO-HANDED: best for high balls / ONE-HANDED / Eastern: fair for high balls, good for low / Continental: best for low and wide balls	Closed stance: best for consistency	Shoulders & hips to the side	High balls and two-handers to the front. Slice is met further back for more control	Two-handed: shoulders rotate through the ball with high extension, follow-through as if hitting a left-handed forehand. One-handed: left arm & left side of body freeze, shifting the leverage or force to the right side of the body
PLACEMENT	hit early ⟷ hit later	TWO-HANDED: difficult to change direction / ONE-HANDED / Eastern: fair for changing direction / Continental: better for changing direction	Closed stance: best for placement			
DEPTH	shallow balls ⟷ deep balls	TWO-HANDED: difficult to hit deep if stretched / ONE-HANDED / Eastern: fair or good for deep balls / Continental: best for deep balls	Closed stance: best for depth			
SPIN	top spin ⟷ slice	TWO-HANDED: best for top spin / ONE-HANDED / Eastern: good for top spin / Continental: best for slice	Open stance: can be used for under-spin / Closed stance: for top-spin			
POWER	high ball power ⟷ low ball power	TWO-HANDED: best power for high balls / ONE-HANDED / Eastern: linear power for high & low balls / Continental: linear power for lower balls	Closed stance: best for one-handed and linear power			

Although Bjorn Borg and Chris Evert were not the first players to play tennis with two-handed shots, they were the ones who changed the way tennis is taught. We all learned from their success what a big advantage making some shots with two hands could be.

Since the era of Evert and Borg, most players have learned to hit with two hands on at least their backhand side. The two-handed technique supplies a stronger shot for those who have a difficult time stroking the one-hander. Players have also found that two-handed shots can transform a previously weak stroke into a powerful weapon.

The one liability of the two-handed shot, though, has been the inflexibility to hit finesse shots such as the approach shot, the volley and shots requiring underspin. In teaching, I have students learn these finesse shots as one-handed strokes. This has worked well to provide an all-around balance of power and finesse on the backhand side.

JOB THREE: THE SERVE

The serve is the most important shot in tennis — it is used on every point and is the only shot not dependent on how the ball is delivered off the opponent's racquet. Its proper execution can make a person progress to a new level of play. Table 5-3 lists and describes the serve in more detail.

Service Grips

It is very important for a player to learn the fundamentals of the stroke — consistent placement, depth, spin and power. Proper execution takes many hours of repetitive practice. The eastern forehand grip may be used in the novice stages of development, and this grip will allow the player to learn consistency and placement. Once these skills are learned, however, the player should begin to use a continental grip and then an eastern backhand grip, because using these grips will make it possible to learn depth, spins and power. The backhand grip is the best grip to use for the serve. It allows the pronating wrist action to produce the most varieties of spin and also supplies the most racquet head speed for the greatest power. However, the continental grip is suitable for most serves as well, and many advanced and novice players do not advance beyond the use of the continental grip.

Service Deliveries

Most advanced players learn at least three deliveries of the serve: a flat serve, a slice (or side spinning) serve, and a top spin serve. Some also become adept at the reverse action or the American twist serve. The eastern backhand grip allows the wrist action to produce all four of these. Figures 5-41 through 5-46 illustrate the four deliveries.

Figure 5-41 (left). Flat serve—compact delivery, contact made behind the ball.

Figure 5-42 (right). Slice serve—ball is cut with wrist action, contact made at 2 o'clock.

Torque and power are delivered in the serve in much the same way that they are delivered in the forehand and backhand ground strokes. The legs, shoulders, and hips coil and, as they release, the left side of the body freezes to transfer force to the racquet side of the body. Figure 5-51 shows the approximate ball contact point for each delivery.

Figures 5-42 & 5-43. American twist serve—illustration of proper toss location (left), pronation and follow-through (right).

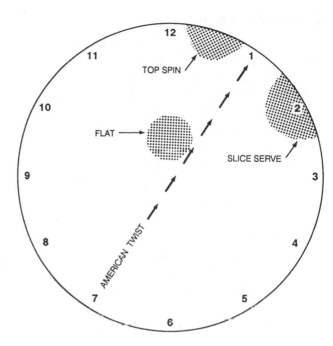

Figures 5-45 & 5-46 (inset).

Top spin serve—contact made by hitting upward at 12:30. (Inset) Kneel down method for learning topspin or kick serve.

Figure 5-51. Approximate contact points with the ball for the four service deliveries.

Service Footwork

The two most accepted service footwork methods are the crossover method and the thrust method.

Crossover Footwork

The crossover method is easier to learn, and it is very good for beginners or for players who lack the strength in their legs to get leverage from them. When serving with this method, the left foot is kept in place, and the right foot pivots to shift body weight through the ball. The crossover footwork method is shown in the serving sequence in Figures 5-47 through 5-50.

Figures 5-47 thru 5-50.

Crossover method of service footwork. (Left to right) service preparation (inset); coiling action and toss; reach and extension to the ball; follow-through with crossover footwork.

Thrust Footwork

The thrust method is better for very good athletes who can thrust by using the coiling action of their legs as an additional power source. When serving with this method, the right foot is brought up behind the left as the ball is tossed and the legs coil. The legs then push upward as the body explodes to the ball. Unlike the crossover method, the left foot leads into the court as the player makes contact with the ball, thus allowing the body to stay sideways as the left side freezes and the force is transferred to the right side and into the shot. Staying sideways also forces the athlete to hit up on the ball to get maximum extension. Figures 5-52 and 5-53 show the thrust footwork method. A smaller person can use a very effective variation to the thrust method by keeping both feet stationary as they coil and jumping into the court with both feet together, again leading with the left.

western forehand grip is vulnerable to flat or low balls moving away from the body. A slice or hard flat serve that pulls this player wide in the deuce court will work very well. In this instance, the receiver can mishit or shank the return.

Serving against the continental forehand grip: The continental grip favors a flat, low ball to the outside, so a high kicking ball to the forehand is often hard for the receiver to handle. The receiver may be able to block back a shot, but he should not be able to hit an offensive return off this serve.

Serving against the two-handed backhand: Reach is the chief liability of the two-handed backhand. If a good wide angle can be hit, the receiver will either have difficulty making a good return or will be pulled wide far enough to allow the server to control good court positioning. But a poor wide kick will allow the receiver to hit a ball perfect for his or her strike zone. Therefore, a low wide ball

Figures 5-52 & 5-53 (left to right). Thrust method of service footwork. Coiling action and ball toss (left); explosive extension to the ball, follow-through with thrust footwork, left foot leading into the court (right).

Read the Receiver and Attack His Grips

It is a good idea for the server to look at the receiver's grip pattern because he can then learn the restrictions and liabilities of the different grips used by the receiver. The idea is to deliver the serve away from the receiver's strike zone. It is comparable to a pitcher throwing away from a batter's favorite hitting zone.

Serving against the western forehand grip: The

would be the best delivery to the two-hander. A serve aimed with some slice into the receiver's body would also work quite well by jamming the two-hander's stroke.

Serving against the one-handed backhand: If the receiver is not very strong, a high ball delivered to the one-handed backhand can often produce a weak or floating return. It is extremely hard for the one-hander to drive the return, and he will often be forced to slice.

Figure 5-54. Backhand serving targets.

BEST AREA WHEN SERVING AGAINST A ONE-HANDED BACKHAND

BEST AREA WHEN SERVING AGAINST A TWO-HANDED BACKHAND

BEST AREA WHEN SERVING AGAINST A CONTINENTAL FOREHAND

BEST AREA WHEN SERVING AGAINST A WESTERN FOREHAND

Figure 5-55. Forehand serving targets.

Table 5-3. Physical relationships of the serve.

SERVICE VARIABLES

SKILL DEVELOPMENT AREA		THE TOOLS		STROKE PRODUCTION		
		Grips	Footwork	Preparation	Contact	Follow-through
CONSISTENCY	easiest to learn ↔ best	EASTERN FOREHAND: easiest to learn; CONTINENTAL: good for consistency; EASTERN BACKHAND: hardest to learn initially	Crossover: easiest for consistency	Good balance. Arms together in front and relaxed	Flat: contact to front & full extension. Slice: make contact @ 1:30 on ball. Top spin: make contact @ 12:30 on ball. American twist: brush ball from 7:00 to 1:00, giving ball reverse spin	Flat: left arm is pulled in across chest. Slice: Left arm is pulled in across chest. Top spin: Left arm is pulled in across chest. American twist: Follow-through is up and out away from body. Keep left arm up as long as possible to insure hitting up on the ball
PLACEMENT	easiest to learn ↔ best	EASTERN FOREHAND: easiest to learn; CONTINENTAL: good; EASTERN BACKHAND: best, but hardest to learn	Crossover: easiest for placement			
DEPTH	fair depth ↔ best depth	EASTERN FOREHAND: fair depth; CONTINENTAL: good depth; EASTERN BACKHAND: best depth	Thrust: gives best lift & depth			
SPIN	least spin ↔ most spin	EASTERN FOREHAND: flat and slice serve; CONTINENTAL: flat, slice, top-spin; EASTERN BACKHAND: flat, slice, top-spin and American twist	Crossover: best for slice, good for flat. Thrust: best for top-spin & American twist			
POWER	least power ↔ most power	EASTERN FOREHAND: least wrist action; CONTINENTAL: good wrist action; EASTERN BACKHAND: most wrist action	Crossover: flat serve is easier. Thrust: best leg action for power			

JOB FOUR: THE VOLLEY

The technique of the volley is much less complex than that of the forehand, backhand, and serve because the movement is less complicated, but it is extremely important to be exact. When hitting ground strokes, there is time to make adjustments in grip, stance, technique and court positioning. Often the volley happens very quickly, so adjustments are harder to make and movements must be more precise.

Volley Grip

The continental grip is the grip most adaptable for both forehand and backhand volleys at nearly all heights and distances from the body. Many top players do use an eastern backhand grip for volleying because it allows a good wrist press for pace on the forehand volley and good leverage for balls below the net. It may be difficult for less experienced players to volley using a backhand grip, however.

Volley Technique

Ball contact should be made in front of the body with a short blocking action, and the racquet head should always be cocked above the wrist. Volleys should be made at eye level. On low volleys, the knees should bend low to keep the racquet head up. The back knee bends to keep the back vertical to the ground.

Unlike ground strokes where the coiling action of the shoulders and hips comes first, the initial movement a player must make in preparation for the volley is to lay the wrist back to prepare the racquet head for contact. The shoulders are then turned, but the racquet head and hands should stay in front of the body. Weight is then transferred to the front foot via a step-out to the ball and a crossover step — contact is made in front of the body. Figures 5-56 through 5-69 show the correct volley techniques for the forehand and backhand.

Figures 5-56 thru 5-58 (left to right). Midcourt low forehand volley sequence. Volley ready position—weight forward, racquet head up and out in front of body; step-out to ball with right foot; step into ball with left foot—low knee bend, good posture, back is up for balance.

Figures 5-59 thru 5-61 (left to right). Midcourt low backhand volley sequence. Volley ready position—weight forward, racquet head up and out in front of body; step-out to ball with left foot; step into ball with right foot—low knee bend, good posture, back is up for balance.

Figures 5-62 thru 5-65 (left to right). Forehand volley sequence. Volley ready position (inset) — weight forward, racquet head up and out in front of body; step-out to ball with right foot; step into ball with left foot, weight forward at contact; follow-through—head is up as stroke finishes.

Figures 5-66 thru 5-69 (left to right). Backhand volley sequence. Volley ready position (inset) — weight forward, racquet head up and out in front of body; step-out to ball with left foot; step into ball with right foot, weight forward at contact; follow-through—head is up as stroke finishes.

JOB FIVE: THE OVERHEAD SMASH

A player's net game is only as good as the overhead smash. When a player is at the net, the opponent will usually try to hit over him. If a player has a good smash, it puts much more pressure on the opponent's passing shot. If a player's smash is weak, the opponent has a definite advantage.

Overhead Smash Technique

Although the fundamentals of the overhead smash are simple and straightforward, it takes a lot of time and practice to develop an effective and confident smash. It is a three-part movement. The first movement a player must make from the ready position at the net is to simultaneously move the racquet head straight back into a cocked position and move the right foot one step backward. This will position him so his side faces the net. Once in this position, the player can move anywhere on the court and be prepared to hit the smash. The left arm should be raised to point at the ball, and it should fall as if it were going to hit the player in the chest or the forehead. A very good drill to help a player learn to position himself under the falling ball is to have the player turn sideways with his racquet cocked and his free arm pointing up at the ball. As the ball falls, the player should reach up with arm fully extended, hand pointed, and catch the ball.

Figures 5-70 thru 5-72 (left to right). Overhead smash sequence illustrating the scissors jump technique. Overhead smash ready position; racquet cocked, right leg back, left arm used to guide ball; scissors jump just prior to contact.

The hitting action is the same as that in the flat serve. The body stays sideways, and the ball is hit from a fully extended position at approximately 1 o'clock. If the ball is extremely high, you should let the ball bounce first and probably slice the overhead for control. If it is low or medium height, it should be hit in the air.

The Scissors Jump

If possible, both feet should be on the ground when the overhead smash is hit. This position provides the best balance and a very solid stroke. When the ball is lobbed too high for the player to stay on the ground, he may need to do a scissors jump. Although this action looks complicated, it is actually a very natural movement that is easy to do with some practice. The athlete must move backward quickly in a sideways position, push off the ground with the right foot, and land on the left foot, moving his legs like a scissors in the process. Figures 5-70 through 5-72 show the overhead smash with the scissors jump and the follow-through.

JOB SIX: TRANSITION SHOTS

Transition shots are shots that allow a transition or change-up in the style of play during the point. The transition shots are the approach shot, the passing shot, the return of serve and the first volley. In each of these shots, except for the return of serve, a transition is made from the baseline to the net by the player or his opponent.

Transition shots are the most missed shots in tennis. Many errors occur because the pattern of play changes and the rhythm of the point is broken up. One of the rules for my team is to avoid

changing the direction of the ball on a transition shot unless it is a very easy shot to do so. The timing is tough enough as it is. Changing the direction of the ball into the open part of the court greatly increases the chance to make a bad error or to deliver a ball that the opponent can easily take advantage of.

Returning the ball back to where it came from (not changing the direction of the ball) allows a player to make a shot that leaves the strings of his racquet at a right angle. This keeps the court closed and forces the opponent to hit a ball that is behind him, tempting him to hit into the open court (or change the direction himself). The Wardlaw Directional guidelines should be followed.

Another rule for players is to always think of hitting two shots when they approach, two shots when they pass, two shots when they return serve and two shots to volley. This makes a player realize that the purpose of a transition shot is to set up the next shot — not to end the point (if the purpose were to end the point, it would be called a put-away shot). When a player starts losing he usually goes for first-shot winners instead of using this two-shot approach.

Transition Shot One: The Approach Shot

In the summer of 1972, I sat as one of a group of summer camp counselors watching the televised Wimbledon final of Stan Smith versus Ilie Nastase. The camp director was Harry Hopman, and he too was present in the room. Mr. Hopman would often make a one-sentence comment about tennis or about life that would be so profound and wise it would carve a permanent place in one's memory.

Nastase, the great shot maker, had just been forced into the corner of the court with a great Smith approach shot. On the dead run, Nastase hit a perfect down-the-line backhand passing shot that left Smith diving onto the grass. One of the instructors commented, "Wow, what a great shot." Hopman responded with, "No, it wasn't, that was the only shot he had." That one sentence taught me more about the importance of proper placement on approach shots than did all the rest of my years of tennis.

Of course what Hopman meant was that players are often physically able to make great shots, especially when they are forced into a position where they have to make them. In the Wimbledon

match Nastase's back was to the wall, and he threaded the needle down the line with the only chance he had. The fact that he made the shot this one time was not a great feat, not any more than would be a basketball player who throws a three-pointer, in desperation, as the shot clock runs down.

I learned from Hopman that day that an approach shot is just that — a shot that a player approaches the net with. The player's job is to handcuff the opponent but also to time the delivery of his shot properly so that he can get himself set up on the net. The ball may be hit short or deep, high or low, to the corner or to the middle, but the main objective is to find a vulnerable area in the opponent's passing shots. The Wardlaw Directionals are great rules to follow for approach shots. But I learned more than this. I learned that many times, if a player is forced into a corner, he can play "spinal chord tennis" — tennis played automatically without thought. Hopman loved the approach shot up the middle because it gave the opponent choices, and having choices is often the undoing of a talented shot maker like Nastase. Hopman taught me that opponents will sometimes make a great shot when a player comes to the net, but this should never deter the player from keeping his attacking game intact. When a player finds the right approach shot to use, the advantage of better court positioning at the net will pay off. Proper execution of the right approach shots may actually be the quickest way to rapid improvement in a player's game.

Technique of the approach shot: As in other strokes, first the shoulders should turn to face the net. As the player moves into position, the anchor foot is planted (left foot on backhand, right on forehand) and weight is shifted from the anchor foot, with force exerted through the ball, onto the front foot. The stroke is similar to the volley but with more backswing and follow-through. Under-spin is recommended to keep the delivery low and to give the approaching player time to get to a balanced and ready position at the net. It is best to use slice or top-spin when approaching the closed court but always hit the ball aggressively when going to the open court.

Note: Top-spin approach shots are best when played up the middle or to the opponent's specific stroke that shows difficulty handling high balls.

Figure 5-73. Illustration of excellent approach shot form.

Transition Shot Two: The Passing Shot

This section should be called "Passing Shots" because it usually takes two shots to pass. The first shot puts the net man off balance and the second passes him with only a small degree of difficulty. A player can go for a great passing shot on the first attempt, but the percentages will not favor it unless that shot is a lot better than the opponent covering the net. To go for the passing shot on the first whack at the ball is comparable to a basketball team that puts the ball up with a thirty-footer immediately after bringing it over the 10-second line. When a player takes the first shot to set up the second or third passing shot, it is more like a basketball team passing the ball two or three times to get a much higher percentage shot. Of course, the best teams can hit the quick 30-footers as well as pass the ball around to set up an easier shot. Likewise, the best tennis player can make a great passing shot when he has to, but understands the importance of being able to hit through an opponent once or twice to get the high percentage final passing shot. Again, the Wardlaw Directionals provide great guidelines for passing shots.

A player's key to passing effectively is to take the first ball early and return it to where it came from. This should catch the opponent off balance and force him to pop the volley up so that it can be returned with an easy passing shot.

Transition Shot Three: The Return of Serve

The return of serve is perhaps the second most important shot in tennis because, like the serve, it must be used in every point of the even or odd games. It is also probably the most boring stroke to practice. It is a shot in which a player is reacting to the opponent, and a good return has very few dimensions. Again, since it is a transition shot, a good general rule is not to change the direction of the ball, thus eliminating many errors that may be caused by trying to make a difficult shot instead of hitting through the opponent. Good returners use their opponent's pace and try to use a short backswing for good weight transfer. They also take the ball early and hit it right back where it came from. The Wardlaw Directionals are great guidelines to follow for hitting the most effective service returns.

Reading a server: Most servers have a serving pattern. For example, the first serve is flat and to the backhand, and the second serve is a top spin serve to the backhand, or the first serve is wide, and the second serve is up the middle. A good rule for a player to follow in returning serve effectively is to watch for the server's pattern in the first few returning games and gauge his returns accordingly. For example, if the server hits his first serve flat to the backhand most of the time, the player should wait with a backhand grip and in a ready position for a backhand shot. If the serve is to the backhand, the receiver can make a short low to high swing and lean into the ball to produce an excellent return. If the serve is to the forehand, the receiver can make a very solid stretch forehand with the backhand grip. The only serve that would really make the receiver vulnerable would be the high kicker to the forehand, and it is unlikely that the server will try this on a first serve. However, most second serves are kick serves. If this is the case, the receiver can either wait with a forehand grip to move around and smack a forehand, or he can slice a backhand from high to low and follow it into the net. If the receiver is successful in reading the opponent's service delivery, he is able to bring the server out of his set pattern. The server then reacts to the receiver's pattern, thereby giving the receiver a better chance of controlling the tempo of the game.

Technique of the return of serve: As the receiver waits for the serve, the lower body should be relaxed and held so that the center of gravity is high. This allows the player to be ready to move a step to the left or right. For many years, players have thought that it was best to wait in a very low crouched position with the knees bent and the center of gravity very low. But the laws of physics show that whereas a lower center of gravity is better for stability (such as a three-point stance for a lineman in football or on all fours for a wrestler), a higher center of gravity is better for a quick movement in any direction. John McEnroe is a player who uses this stance effectively. The best technique for a player is to wait in a low position, come up on his toes for a high center of gravity and readiness to react to the serve, and then lean in to the ball with a wide base that provides stability and allows weight transfer into the shot. A step-out should be done to react to the ball. The upper body movement is quite simple. As the server tosses the ball, the receiver comes up for a higher center of gravity and turns only his relaxed shoulders to the forehand or backhand position. Then he flows forward along the path of the oncoming ball.

High to low or low to high: On a flat, hard first service, it is best for the stroke to flow in a low to high arc. Very often a player will try to slice (high to low) a hard, fast serve. Although this may feel comfortable and safe, it usually either produces a ball in the net or a weak, floating return. A low to high arc allows the racquet to hit along the plane of the ball and lifts it to clear the net. However, on a high, kicking serve, the returner should try to hit the ball with a high to low arc to bring the ball down into the court. He may also want to move around and smack a forehand if able to do so. A quick tip that I often use with my players is to have the index finger move first when driving or hitting over the ball and move the baby finger first when a slice shot is required.

Transition Shot Four: The First Volley

The first volley is considered a transition shot because of its similarity to the approach shot. There are three rules to remember for the first volley:

Rule #1: After the server delivers the serve, his movement should allow him to get in as far as the service line. This will give him a good opportunity to make an effective first volley. Otherwise, a first volley can be popped up and will make it very easy for the returner to pass the server unless the ball can be put away with a winner.

Rule #2: Unless the return is a floater, the first volley should be hit back to where it came from or to the middle of the court, and the finishing volley should be placed into the open court. Then follow Wardlaw Directionals. This rule is very important because if a crosscourt volley is not put away, the whole court is left open for an easy passing shot by the opponent. In general, for any ball that can be put away, the player should go to the open court. If the ball cannot be put away, the court should be kept closed. A reminder to my team when we do serve and volley drills is to call them serve and volley-volley drills. This reminds the players that it takes two shots to volley.

Rule #3: The net should be closed off after the first volley. If the first volley is effective, then the server should be in control of the point. As the ball is in flight, the server should take three or four steps in to the net to close out the point. Not closing off the net is a mistake that gives the opponent an angle to hit a passing shot or a chance to get back into the point.

Figure 5-74. The first volley is an important offensive transition shot.

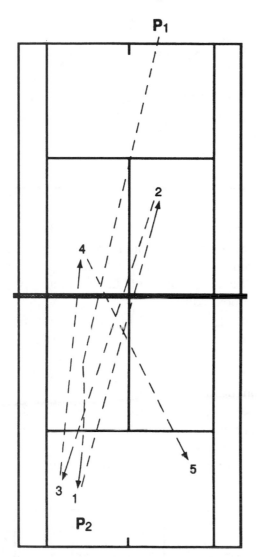

P₁

2

4

5

3 1

P₂

Figure 5-75. The perfect serve and volley point. The server (player 1) makes a first serve to the middle of the ad court (1), moves into the service line, volleys a low ball back to where it came from (2 & 3), closes off the net, and angles the second volley crosscourt (4 & 5).

JOB SEVEN: THE LOB

The lob is one of the best passing shots to use when the opponent comes to the net. There are two kinds of lobs: the offensive lob and the defensive lob. If the opponent's shot can be controlled, the player should hit an offensive lob as an alternative to a passing shot. If the opponent's shot stretches the player or the player is out of the play, he should hit a very high defensive lob.

The Offensive Lob

The offensive lob should be used as an option to a passing shot — out of choice, not out of necessity. The player must have complete control of the ball and be able to disguise the shot until the last second. The arc of the ball's flight should be much lower than the arc of the defensive lob. It is also a good idea to place the lob over the opponent's backhand side, where an overhead would be very difficult.

Players today are quite adept at hitting the top-spin lob, but this shot should be used only when the ball sits up enough to use a full swing and the grip allows extra top spin to be put on the ball.

The Defensive Lob (The Sky Lob)

The defensive lob should be used when a player is definitely out of position and needs time to set up. If the player can get the ball up high enough and back on the baseline, his opponent will virtually have to start the point over. The higher the better on a defensive lob because there is nothing more difficult than hitting a ball that is falling rapidly. When a player is stretched out, it is a good idea to use a continental grip in order to keep a firm wrist to give leverage for a firm ball.

Figure 5-76. Proper balance is a key to hitting a successful defensive lob.

Figure 5-77. The flight paths of the offensive and defensive lobs.

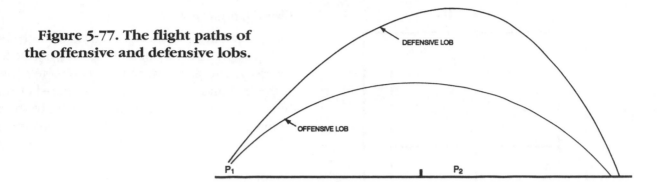

JOB EIGHT: THE DROP SHOT

One principle for controlling the depth of a shot at strategic times is to hit balls short, thereby forcing the opponent to come to the net. A drop shot is an excellent shot to use to do this, but it must be well disguised. It should not be used as a defensive shot but only as an offensive tactic. Placement is very important. A poor drop shot is disastrous in that it allows the opponent to take immediate charge of the point.

Three rules are important to remember when executing the drop shot:

Rule #1: If a player makes a drop shot from the baseline, he should make it crosscourt. This keeps the court closed so that if the opponent does get to the ball, the player will have a shot to pass him on the next ball.

Rule #2: If a player makes a drop shot from the forecourt, he should make it in front of himself, or down the line. This keeps the court closed and gives the player another play on the ball if his opponent runs the shot down.

Rule #3: A player should use the drop shot only as an offensive tactical shot, forcing the opponent to react. As a desperation shot or point ender, it is one of the worst shots a player can choose.

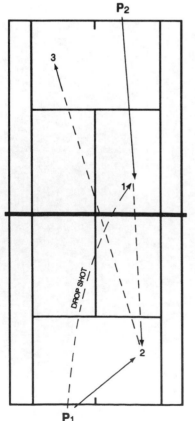

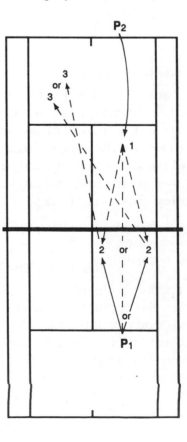

Figure 5-78 (left). From the backcourt, hit drop shots crosscourt.

Figure 5-79 (right). From the forecourt, hit drop shots down the line or in front of you.

THE BACKBOARD: YOUR BEST PRACTICE PARTNER

The beginning player often hesitates to ask people of any level to practice or play out of fear of embarrassment. Fortunately, the best and most reliable practice player is always available: the backboard. The backboard can be any size or surface, as long as it is large enough to provide a suitable target and returns balls with a consistent bounce. Beginning players should use an old ball with a slower bounce to take better control of their rallies.

Figure 5-80. Use the backboard to practice each of the various strokes.

Just about any skill that a player needs for a match can be learned and developed against a backboard. An exception would be handling different spins that may come off the opponent's racquet. A consistent bounce, though, helps a player develop a steady, reliable stroke.

All strokes and most game situations can be practiced alone or with a partner, but the learning progression explained previously should be used. The progression for strokes trained on the backboard is as follows:

1. **Consistency.** This should be the first goal in learning any stroke. Repetitive work done with a stroke is about the only way to develop some degree of confidence in its execution. To improve consistency, emphasis should be placed on hitting one stroke at a time. After a player can execute the same stroke 20 to 25 times without error against the backboard, another stroke can be tried. Players can also develop consistency by alternating between forehand and backhand shots to simulate game situations.

2. **Placement.** The ability to place the ball should be learned immediately after consistency. The easiest way to do this is to give yourself the option of a down-the-line or a crosscourt shot on the backboard.

The down-the-line shot returns the ball to the same stroke. On the next exchange, the ball should be hit crosscourt to the opposite stroke. The following sequence offers a fairly simple progression for developing placement and control of the ball: forehand to forehand down the line; forehand to backhand crosscourt; backhand to backhand down-the-line; backhand to forehand crosscourt; and then repeat sequence.

3. **Depth.** A long stroke produces a deep ball. This skill may be practiced on the backboard by simply moving farther back, stopping at the point where it's still possible to hit the ball to the backboard. Novice players learn quickly that the only way to get the ball to the backboard is with a long, smooth stroke. Repetition of this technique enables one to transfer the stroke to the court. The ball will have to bounce three or four times to return, but this is fine, because here the emphasis is on lengthening the stroke.

4. **Spin.** Top-spin, under-spin and even side-spin shots can easily be practiced on the backboard. Again, it is more easily done with a dead ball that does not return as quickly to the racquet from the wall. This allows time to prepare for each shot and produce the proper spin on the ball.

Spin is one of the most important skills to learn because it enables a player to have more control over the ball and to hit the ball much harder while maintaining consistency, placement and depth.

5. **Power.** After developing consistency, placement, depth and spin, it becomes easy to work on power with the backboard as well. It should be the last skill practiced.

The best way to work on power is to produce a high soft ball off the wall and then set up for a kill shot from the forehand or the backhand. If you are adept enough to keep the rally going, this alternating sequence should be repeated as many times consecutively as possible.

For every stroke learned, it is important to maintain the above sequence.

Hitting the Wall

Most players practice ground strokes first when using the backboard. With practice, a player should be able to move close to the wall and keep the ball in the air with volleys and quick half-volley pickups, shots where the ball takes a short hop at the player's feet.

The serve is also easily practiced by walking off a distance of 39 feet from the wall (equal to the distance from the baseline and the net). From here, the player chooses a target on the wall at which to aim. Good shots and bad shots alike will rebound back to the server for another attempt.

Even the overhead smash can be practiced. By bouncing or hitting the ball into the ground so that it rebounds high off the wall, the player will be able to smash it again in front of the wall.

The greatest advantage of the backboard is that it is a dependable and reliable partner for practice any hour of the day. Players can develop any stroke to any level of competency, as long as they are willing to put in the time. Take advantage of this willing practice partner that never swings and misses, never hits the ball over the fence and never gets tired!

SUMMARY

Each tennis player's strokes are developed according to his personality. It is important that each athlete be allowed to develop these strokes from the inside-out so that he can reach full potential. In the early stages of development, players must learn proper fundamentals — this includes the technical tools of grips, footwork and balance, preparation, contact point and follow-through. These tools can be used to develop the skills of consistency, followed by placement, depth, spin and power. Once these tools and skills are learned, players can put them to use in their strokes — the forehand, one-handed and two-handed backhand, serve, volley, overhead smash, transition shots, drop shot and lob. After these fundamentals are learned, each player will be able to further develop his individual style of play and shot delivery.

Figures 5-81 & 5-82. Backboard drills are a good way to focus on specific strokes or technical skills. The player above practices the forehand groundstoke (left) and forehand volley (right).

NOTES

Figure 5-83. The continental grip works well when you are stretched, and for a forehand on the run.

Figure 5-84. Two-handed players should learn to use one-handed shots on the stretch backhand.

Figure 5-85. Two-handed backhands are a deadly weapon for balls that sit up.

Figure 5-86. Good leverage for torque on ground strokes comes from the legs and hips.

Chapter 6

SUPPORT YOUR TRAINING WITH GOOD NUTRITION

● ●

Inside Shot

Basic Nutritional Guidelines for the Tennis Player

Harmful Foods

The Pre-Game Meal

The Post-Game Meal

One of the most frustrating things that every coach experiences is seeing their players ruin good training with poor diets consisting of soft drinks, chips, cookies and other processed foods. Not only do most young athletes' eating habits hurt their athletic performance, but their poor choices in foods are the start of lasting problems with health, weight control and general well being. All coaches have experienced this; unfortunately, the self-sabotaging effects caused by poor diet often stem from eating habits that do not consciously occur.

Two Months of Training Out the Window

We had been training for six weeks in preparation for our first major tournament at the University of Miami. All details had been taken care of, and the players were in top shape. I was particularly concerned about the heat and humidity in southern Florida and the fact that the players would sweat more in those temperatures than in our cool winter temperatures. So during the week before the tournament, we prepared. Players took steam baths for 10 to 15 minutes every day and, in addition, wore nylon rain suits during workouts forcing them to perspire more than normal.

I thought that I had taken care of all the details, but I had forgotten one thing—I had not monitored the eating habits of my team. We were playing the University of California-Irvine in a morning match. Halfway through the second set, one of my returning All-Americans was playing very poorly and looking sluggish. I walked to his court and asked him what was the matter. He said he really did not know, except that he could not focus properly on what he was doing. At first I was upset with him and told him to concentrate and get going. I said to him, "You've got to get tough. Get your rear end in gear. What the heck is going on here?" As he played another game, I saw a determined but exhausted expression on his face, and I knew he was trying hard to concentrate, but something was wrong. I went over to him at the next crossover. He had his head between his legs and looked totally exhausted. I wondered if I had the guys properly trained. I also wondered if this player had been out on the town the night before, breaking training. Then a thought struck me. I walked over to him and asked him what he had eaten for breakfast. He replied, "pancakes with syrup, a danish, and a glass of orange juice." Then I realized what was happening; he was experiencing a sugar rush from all the sugar he had eaten that morning. It made me wonder if our six weeks of training and preparation for the trip were to no avail because of an order of pancakes and a danish. The match was lost over a very simple detail that I should have monitored.

> **E**xperience is a tough teacher; it tests you first and teaches you later.

BASIC NUTRITIONAL GUIDELINES FOR THE TENNIS PLAYER

A proper diet is essential to athletic performance, but many athletes give little or no thought to their dietary needs. Athletes at all levels should know and follow sound nutritional guidelines.

Food is composed of seven basic substances: carbohydrates, fats, proteins, vitamins, minerals, water or indigestible materials. Each one of these has specific functions in providing nourishment for the body. Athletes should know how each of them affects performance.

Carbohydrates

Complex carbohydrates are metabolized very easily into glucose (blood sugar) to be used for quick energy. Carbohydrates enable the athlete to feel alert, strong and energetic, and they help to maintain proper blood sugar levels.

Carbohydrates provide four calories of energy per gram. The best sources of carbohydrates are fruits, vegetables, pastas, breads and cereal products. Carbohydrates are used up very quickly in the athlete's body and should be replaced often. Sugar, though, is a simple carbohydrate and can be harmful. Too much sugar intake can cause lightheadedness, fatigue and concentration lapse.

Fats

At nine calories per gram, fats provide a long-term energy source. The body uses fat for energy metabolism after carbohydrate supplies are depleted. Fat is also used as insulation and padding for the body's organs. But, fat is much harder to digest than carbohydrates, and too much fat in the diet can cause health problems. Fats are found in many foods such as peanuts, meats, oils and butter.

Proteins

Protein should be an important part of an athlete's diet because it helps tissue grow and repair itself. Proteins are used by the body as an energy source only after carbohydrates and fats are depleted. But protein is very difficult to convert to energy, and therefore should be consumed either on days when the athlete is not competing or a few hours after competition. Carbohydrates, however, are best for immediate, after-match consumption.

> The road to success is not doing one thing 100 percent better, but doing 100 things one percent better.
> — *Unknown*

Protein provides four calories per gram. Meat, fish, poultry, legumes, wheat germ and bean sprouts are good sources of protein.

Vitamins

Vitamins assist body functions and metabolism. They are necessary for cell activity, and are therefore critical to the proper function of the athlete's body. An inadequate diet does not supply all of the necessary vitamins.

Vitamins A, D, E and K are fat soluble. They are stored in the fat, and it is not necessary to eat them every day. In fact, excessive quantities of fat soluble vitamins can cause sluggishness or indigestion.

Vitamins B and C are water soluble. They are not stored in the body and must be replaced as any excess will be removed in the urine. A lack of B-complex vitamins in the body will cause muscular fatigue, cramps, and loss of concentration.

Minerals

As with vitamins, minerals are essential to the proper functioning of the body. They participate in hormone and enzyme production and give structure to the bones and other parts of the body.

Calcium, magnesium, phosphorus, sulfur, sodium chloride and potassium are needed in large amounts. Others needed in trace amounts are iron, selenium, manganese, fluoride, copper, molybdenum, zinc, chromium, cobalt and iodine.

Water

Water is important for every bodily function. In fact, the body of a well-conditioned person consists of about 60 percent water. Water enables the cells to work, and is a component of the blood. It also serves as an important part of the body's cooling system, lymphatic system and nervous system.

Figure 6-1. A proper diet will help an athlete reach his physical, mental and emotional potential.

Almost all foods contain water, but naturally the best way to obtain it is by drinking fluids. Water contains no calories but is primarily responsible for all energy metabolism.

A recent study had an athlete train on a treadmill to the point of exhaustion with no water intake. His endurance was just over one hour. The same athlete then exercised again with two water breaks, during which he was given as much water as he wanted. His time on the treadmill doubled. The third time the same athlete was given frequent small amounts of water, and he was able to exercise up to four times as long as his original time.

The lesson for the tennis player is to drink water early in the day of competition and then frequently from the start to the finish of the match, before thirst occurs. It is also important to drink plenty of water the night before a match — 16 to 32 ounces is recommended.

Indigestible Materials — Fiber and Roughage

Cancer of the colon is now the second most comon type of cancer in America. Many doctors and nutritionists blame high meat and fat diets, preservatives that are added in so many foods and diets that are lacking in fiber-rich foods.

HARMFUL FOODS

Sugar

The harmful effects of refined sugars are far-reaching. Two-hundred years ago, the average American ate about four pounds of sugar per year. Today, Americans eat an average of 129 pounds per year — about 2½ pounds per week. Sugar is added to many processed foods, and consumers should read the ingredient panel on food packages.

Sugar can cause a condition called reactive hypoglycemia, a situation in which the blood sugar level rises quickly, giving a high feeling of energy. The body's balancing system reacts quickly by sending insulin into the bloodstream, which in turn produces a crashing effect that causes depression and reduces concentration. Appetite is controlled by the blood sugar level, so this crash causes great hunger pangs. If these pangs are satisfied by more sugar, an even greater crash results. Appetite is best controlled by eliminating refined sugars and eating complex carbohydrates such as fruits and vegetables.

An athlete who consumes too much refined sugar will experience swings in mood, concentration and performance. The best approach is to avoid sugar intake before or during competition.

White Flour

White flour lacks many of the important nutrients found in wheat. Whole wheat or other whole grain breads are therefore more nutritious than white bread.

Salt Tablets

Sodium, magnesium and potassium are the minerals that are lost through exercise. They are replaced well by fruits, vegetables and fruit juices. The average American consumes far too much salt, and the ingestion of salt tablets can lead to serious dehydration, possible heat exhaustion and stroke.

Alcohol and Beer

Alcohol has a long-lasting effect on athletic performance. One can of beer can lower some athletes' heat tolerance for 24 to 48 hours, and three drinks can reduce heat tolerance for days. Lack of coordination may persist until 24 hours after alcohol consumption.

Juice Supplements

There has been much discussion aout what is the best drink before and during competition. Juice supplements contain varying amounts of potassium, but less than whole milk or orange juice. Milk should not be consumed immediately before or after competition. Perhaps the best drink is a mixture of three parts water and one part fruit juice.

THE PRE-GAME MEAL

The old idea of a steak and potato before the ball game is no longer considered a good one. Protein takes a long time to digest, and meat can sometimes sit in the stomach for hours before entering the digestive tract. Carbohydrates, including pasta, breads, fruits, vegetables and plenty of liquids are the best pre-game meal. Fats are also hard to digest, but are important for an endurance event. It is important to note that small amounts of fat are needed for longer energy burning. Dairy products should not be ingested before competition because the calcium in them may interfere with the magnesium uptake that is important in energy expenditure.

THE POST-GAME MEAL

Athletes are often so hungry after a competition that they run out and grab whatever food they can find. More often than not, they choose sugar-filled foods. There is great harm in this practice because sugar interferes with the body's metabolism and regulating system. The following day the athlete may be disoriented and emotionally sensitive, or experience a heavy feeling in the muscles.

To prevent this practice, a great college basketball coach used to closely monitor the diets of his players after a tough ball game. He would always make sure to have juices, fruits, bread and peanut butter sandwiches in the locker room immediately after the game to help take the edge off the players' appetites so that they would not go out and load up on sugary foods. He discovered, too, that a well-balanced meal made his athletes feel better the day after a game.

SUMMARY

Good nutrition is essential for an athlete's strong performance; diet should be high in carbohydrates, moderate in proteins and low in fat. Athletes should avoid sugar, salt tablets, white flour and alcohol. Fluid replacement on the day of competition is crucial, and athletes should drink frequently in small amounts when competing. The best pre-game or post-game meal is one that is high in carbohydrates.

Figure 6-2. Recognizing the importance of proper nutrition encourages a better performance on the court.

PREVENT AND TREAT ATHLETIC INJURIES

A Costly Injury — It's Okay to Play with Pain but Never with Injury

Jean Desdunes, an All-American in 1982, returned for his senior year having finished a great summer on the satellite tour. Everyone had very high expectations. Actually, he started the year ranked #10 in the U.S. collegiate rankings. Then during our September practices he pulled a hip muscle and was soon unable to do the team running. The tournament schedule for the fall seemed very important at the time. He wanted to both improve his #10 ranking and also try to collect enough wins to be guaranteed a slot at the NCAA tournament that next spring.

The injury was a nagging one, but both he and I felt it was fine for him to compete. As each tournament was played it became obvious that his hip was getting worse. His mobility was drastically reduced, and by the last tournament of the fall Jean was in a great deal of pain. With the Christmas rest coming up, it seemed there would be no problem at all for him to be fully recovered by the time practice

started again in January. He was not. The injury just kept hanging on. His entire senior year became a series of trips to the doctor and the training room, and he never seemed to get to full speed after that. His team role was regulated to playing at a lower position in an attempt to help the team. His chance for a professional career in tennis was for the most part gone.

That entire scenario taught me a very important lesson in coaching. The lesson is that "It is okay to play with pain, but it is never right to play with injury!" If an athlete is injured, it is something to take care of right away and get completely healed. Then a program of rehabilitation should be followed to slowly ease the competitor back into playing shape. The events that seem so very important early in the competitive season are not nearly as important as those later in the year. There is a definite difference between pain and injury. Athlete and coach together must make that distinction.

Know When to Tough It Out

Sometimes an athlete might have to just "gut it out" in a late season championship event, and sometimes he or she may decide to play at other times knowing the consequences for not taking the time to heal. But most of the time, it is the best policy to let an injury heal before going out to compete. Small nagging hurts and pains are a part of sport and an athlete should tough it out through those times, especially when the team needs an individual's contribution. One of the bravest things I've seen as a coach was to watch Ken, a member of our team, vomit for five straight minutes during a tough

> Once you have established the goals you want and the price you are willing to pay, you can ignore the minor hurts, the opponent's pressure, and the temporary failures.
> — *Vince Lombardi*

battle and then return to the court to help his teammates in a big match. The borderline decision between what is injury and what is just nagging pain that can be worked through is one that only the athlete can determine for himself.

bodies, an understanding of injury prevention, management and treatment is of critical importance for both the coach and the player.

TAKING CARE OF THE TENNIS INJURY

Tennis players must compete more than any other athlete. Although a tennis player does not have to deal with the bruises and contusions that hamper athletes in contact sports, the continuous periods of competition cause many stress-and-strain-related injuries. The body's connective tissues, namely the tendons and ligaments, can be affected, and muscle tissue, bursa, tendon sheaths and other lubricating substances of the body are also at risk.

Tennis has become a year-round sport. Most other sports have an off-season when an athlete is able to completely rest and allow the body to heal. But the constant chase of the next tournament or ranking often forces tennis players back into competition before they are ready for full speed play, and this increases the chance for re-injury and further setback. Since tennis players will most likely continue to put excessive stress on their

INJURY PREVENTION

Injuries are very frustrating to the athlete because the training time lost. Thus, it is crucial that a tennis player take action to prevent injuries. The following measures will help in injury prevention and should be part of a tennis player's daily ritual.

Raise the Body Temperature Before Practice

The athlete's muscle fibers and connective tissues can be compared to a rubber band. If a rubber band is cold and is jerked quickly in a ballistic manner, it may tear or break. If, however, the same rubber band is warmed and then slowly stretched without quick and jerky moves, it will be elastic. Likewise, a cold muscle that is put through rapid flexing and stretching may also tear. Raising the temperature of the muscle and then slowly stretching it with static (non-movement) stretching allows for effective flexion and extension. When the body temperature is raised, the speed of contraction and relaxation of the muscles is increased. Light jogging, rope jumping and calisthetics work well to raise the body temperature.

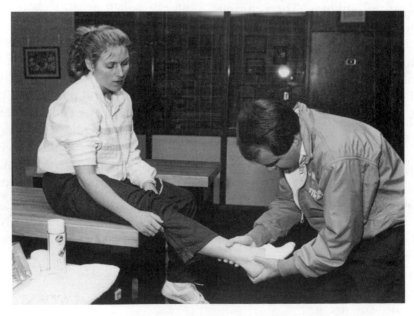

Figure 7-1. Recovery from athletic injuries is dependent upon proper treatment and rehabilitation.

Use a Consistent Stretching Routine

Stretching allows the muscles to relax and allows for a good blood supply and oxygen transport to take place. Flexibility exercises also help to reduce muscle soreness by moving lactic acid out of fatigued tissues. Overstretching, however, may cause damage to ligaments and joints. Therefore an athlete should follow a familiar program every day that includes solid static (non-movement) stretching fundamentals.

These guidelines should be followed in a stretching routine:

1. *Warm up the body by one degree or until sweat breaks.*
2. *Use only static (non-movement) and gradual exercises. Never use ballistic (movement or bouncing) exercises.*
3. *Stretch all muscle groups.*
4. *Do not understretch, do not overstretch.*
5. *Bring the body to a sweat once more before starting workout.*

TREATMENT AND MANAGEMENT OF INJURIES

When an injury does occur, proper methods of treatment and rehabilitation should be used. There are three categories of injuries based on severity of the injury and recurrence. Athletes and coaches should know the proper treatment for each.

Acute Injury

An acute injury is an immediate injury, or an injury that occurs by accident during training. Examples are: ankle sprain, muscle tear and broken bone. The athlete cannot compete with this type of injury.

Treatment: Use ice compression and elevation for the first 24-48 hours. Never, never use heat or aspirin for the first 48-64 hours! Usually a three or four day layoff is required for rest. Consult a doctor if necessary.

Subacute Injury

A subacute injury is an injury that builds up over time to hamper play. Examples are: Osgood Slaughter knee disease and overtired strained muscle. These injuries cause great frustration because although the athlete can participate, performance is usually hampered.

Treatment: Warm up slowly. Use ice after workout and anti-inflammatory medications by doctor's prescription only.

Recurrent Injury

A recurrent injury is usually a joint injury. Examples are: tennis elbow, rotator cuff strain and shoulder bursitis. Recurrent injuries can return very unpredictably.

Treatment: Warm up slowly. Use ice after workout and aspirin and prescriptions under a doctor's supervision only.

Note: Ice constricts blood flow to tissue, and therefore reduces swelling of an acute injury. Heat dilates blood vessels and speeds up blood flow which can make an injury much more severe. Aspirin tends to thin blood, thereby increasing swelling of an injured muscle or joint. When competing with an injury, an athlete should warm up gradually and use ice massage or compression immediately after competition. Never use aspirin immediately after an injury!

REHABILITATION

Rest and proper treatment allow the healing process to take place. But as pain subsides, athletes may feel ready for full-scale competition again. The most frequent mistake the athlete makes is to force himself back into full speed before rehabilitation is completed. The major concern here is that the very rapid atrophy and degeneration of the muscle tissue that takes place leaves the athlete extremely susceptible to re-injury. When re-injury occurs, the entire rest and treatment process must take place all over again. This can start an extremely frustrating cycle for the competitive athlete.

As pain from an injury starts to subside, the athlete should gradually work himself back into practice. Most of the heavy exercise should be done with the stabilizer or support muscles close to the injury, with activities that do not aggravate the ailment. As the injured area becomes stronger, more and more exercises should be done to make the muscle tissue strong and to prevent re-injury. Using athletic tape to restrict movement of the affected area can also be of great help during this rehabilitative period.

Figure 7-2. An effective stretching routine and warm-up period prepares the body for rigorous activity and helps prevent unnecessary injuries.

COACHING NOTES

COACHING NOTES

Part Two:
The Mental Third

Chapter 8

BUILD YOUR BEST GAME

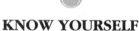

KNOW YOURSELF

Coaches and players alike should realize that people learn the skills of tennis in different ways and at different rates of speed. Coaches often make the mistake of believing that young players should play and learn the game as they did, and these coaches try to mold them accordingly. This is a mistake, because every person is unique and has an individual way of learning and doing things.

> # N
> ever tell people how to do things. Tell them what to do and they will surprise you with their ingenuity. — *General George S. Patton*

This chapter discusses the different ways in which people learn. Hopefully, it will help both players and coaches to understand that there's not "one and only one" way to perform the various skills in tennis. The solid technical fundamentals of the game are of utmost importance, but the manner in which they are learned and executed is an individual matter.

Repetitive Learners vs. Creative Learners

Early in my coaching career I learned a great lesson from two of my players who were very different types of young men and went about things in contrasting manners.

Pender Murphy was a coach's dream both in practice and in matches. He was the first to arrive at practice and the last to leave, and he worked hard while he was there. He would do drill after drill and work on a particular shot over and over until he got it right.

In competitive situations, he was always ready to do his best because he was so well prepared. His strokes always held up; he won many big matches and went on to become a two-time All-American and fine professional player.

Mark Dickson, on the other hand, was a gifted athlete who approached the game much differently. Although he trained hard, repetitive drills bored him; he would quickly lose interest and drift into playing games or creating shots. I was often disturbed by this because I believed everyone would want to do it my way. I couldn't understand that another approach might be just as good.

As I worked with these two players and others on the team, I learned that I was wrong. By the way, Mark also went on to be a great college player and an excellent professional, but he did it in a much different way than Pender.

Pender and I both agreed that repetition was the best way to learn. (One of my favorite sayings has always been that "repetition is the mother of skill.") Mark, however, viewed the game as an opportunity to constantly experiment with new shots.

Psychologist often talk about the difference between left brain (repetitive) and right brain (creative) dominance in people. In learning and playing the game it saves a lot of time and frustration if it is understood which way a player learns best. The manner in which he or she goes about other parts of the daily routine can provide a hint.

If a person is meticulous and prefers a set routine, chances are that he or she learns best through repetition. A more creative person who enjoys doing things differently prefers creative teaching methods. It is important to point out, however, that after a person's best learning style has been identified, the opposite method should also be used to provide balance. The repetitive learner still needs to experiment with shot-making and creativity, and the creative learner needs to perform the repetitive drill work to enhance the reliability of his or her strokes. Both personalities are unique and special, but taken to an extreme they can be counterproductive.

DIFFERENT STROKES FOR DIFFERENT FOLKS

I learned a great deal as a coach from Fred and Florence Littaur's "Whole Again Training Conference and Seminars." Their teachings are invaluable, especially when dealing with young players. Their work has saved me countless hours in heading off problems. It's great to be able to share this material with fellow coaches.

Some youngsters play tennis in the early stages of learning as long as it is fun, some play just so they can be with friends, and others play just because they like the recognition of doing something well, or something that no one else they know can do. As they get older, these individual reasons for playing the sport become factors of motivation. If coaches are aware of this, they will be better equipped to help. There are four different personality types that present different challenges for coaches.

   I. Sanguine

  II. Choleric

 III. Melancholic

 IV. Phlegmatic

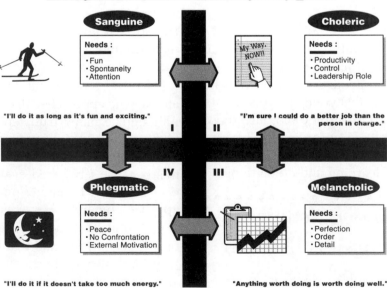

Figure 8-1. Although most people are dominant in one particular personality type, they usually have some characteristics of those personality types that appear adjacent in the diagram. For instance, a sanguine type will generally have some choleric and phlegmatic traits but show weakness in the melancholic area.

Some Just Want to Have Fun

The sanguine personality is driven by the need to have fun and be noticed. This personality also likes spontaneity. A sanguine person is likely to be unorganized and happy-go-lucky. The person might not appear to be serious about learning, but this is not necessarily the case. He or she is driven to learn a skill simply because it's fun to do.

It can be a tremendous tool for the coach to understand what the player needs to learn instead of what they think the player needs to learn. The coach can then structure activities that are meaningful but make sure an element of fun is involved.

A sanguine person who also has characteristics of wanting to be in charge (choleric) can be the best combination for a good leader in a group situation because these individuals have a need to get things done but have fun in the process.

Figure 8-2. Dealing with the sanguine personality—a coach must be strong and detailed.

Some Want to Be the One to Get It Done

The choleric personality has the need to be in control. He or she also wants to get things accomplished. A player with this personality trait makes many decisions for others in many different situations. This person doesn't take on a project without being fairly certain of success.

Coaches and friends might look at choleric players as bossy and pushy, and they often try to subdue or change this trait. It is much more productive to channel the choleric's learning patterns in ways that enable them to have control over the situation. The choleric can be given three or four good choices of what kind of workout to do, or the natural aggression can be used as a tool in dealing with friends.

In a choleric player, the most conflict arises when sparring with another choleric in the peer group. They both fight for territory without even knowing why the tension is there. It is best to give two cholerics in one group different leadership responsibilities and try to teach them to be tolerant of others with similar needs.

Choleric players make great team captains as long as they learn to get along with others in the group. The choleric personality is internally motivated and usually excels in whatever they set their mind to do.

For Some, It Must Be Done Right

The melancholic player has a deep need for detail and a need to get the job done right. Even as young children they have a way of organizing things. They usually do well with repetition and respond well to instruction. These players will carry out the plan of a coach or a parent perfectly and thrive on the fact that they took care of details.

On practice days this works perfectly, but the unpredictability of match situations can cause problems. It might be necessary to give this individual more detailed instruction when preparing for competition. It is important for this player to realize, however, that some of the other players on the team will not care about the details of a situation to the same degree.

Although this player thrives on good organization, it is important for him or her to experience variety in practice.

Figure 8-3. Dealing with the melancholic personality—a coach can be more of a friend but must stay casual and unserious.

Some Learn by Being Part of the Group

The phlegmatic player is usually motivated externally. This person enjoys the process of doing something but does not like conflict or the responsibility of having to make a lot of important decisions. This type of player needs a very detailed program laid out by a coach or parent to get the amount of training that it takes to be successful.

Practice days are difficult for the phlegmatic person because there is no great sense of urgency to get things done. On the other hand, those individuals thrive under certain situations because they keep a cool head.

We All Have Strengths

Each of these personality types has specific strengths and weaknesses in learning and playing tennis. It is also important to note that any strength taken to an extreme can become a weakness, so a wise coach will try to mold a balanced approach for the young player.

> A man does not know his own strength until he realizes his own weakness.

Although a person will have the dominant traits of one of these personalities, he or she is certain to have some of the traits of at least one other type as well. The only personalities that do not mix are the sanguine-melancholic and the choleric-phlegmatic combinations.

After the coach learns the specific learning patterns of a youngster, that coach can be much more helpful to the individual. Athletes should also understand the uniqueness in the manner in which they learn things.

SELECTING YOUR PLAYING STYLE

One of the most important decisions a player must make is choosing the style that best suits his or her ability and temperament. Lessons and coaching can dramatically speed the development of a player's technical skills, but good judgment is critical to developing a game that fits an individual physically, mentally and emotionally. This can save months or even years in development.

Very few people are gifted enough to do everything well, so it is important to understand one's own strengths so that they can be used to their fullest. It is crucial to understand, however, that style must coincide with temperament.

Bjorn Borg's very disciplined and methodical style would not have been successful if his temperament had been like that of Illie Nastase. Likewise, Nastase's flashy, aggressive game probably would not have been successful with Borg's even temperament. Nastase, McEnroe, and Laver were all creative learners. They were all champions, and they were all successful within their styles and their mental and emotional framework. Borg, Wilander and Rosewall all were seemingly repetitive learners, successful in their own ways because of their unique makeup.

Players eventually develop styles that reflect their own personalities. Anyone who attempts to adapt to a playing style that does not fit his or her personality will not enjoy the game as much.

All players should learn the physical skills of stroke technique, but they can concentrate on one of three game styles: the counter-punching game, the attacking game or the all-court game.

STICK WITH YOUR GAME STYLE

Act Never React — Deal On or Be Delt Upon

Over the Christmas holidays in 1983, my team was participating in an indoor tournament in New Orleans. The tournament was to feature a match-up between two of the top collegiate players in the country, each of whom had sharply contrasting styles of play. One was an aggressive serve-and-volley player from Auburn University, and the other was the No. 2-ranked player in the United States, Johnny Levine from the University of Texas.

At first, the match reminded me of some of the exciting Wimbledon matches between McEnroe and Borg in the early 1980s. As the match progressed, however, it quickly became disappointing. Levine won in 55 minutes, 6-1, 6-0. I wondered how a match with such great possibilities could end with such a lopsided score. The reaction of my players and many other bystanders was that Levine was a great player who was very physically and mentally tough and would make a great pro. I was disappointed by their simple reasoning.

Levine's opponent walked up to the lounge area with the rest of the players and his reaction was pretty much the same as those who watched the match. "I don't really know what happened," he said. "I tried everything and nothing worked."

After he said this, I turned to my players and asked, "Who in the world is good at everything?" I told them that I would rather have heard him say, "I played my game. He was just better at his style than I was at my style."

Some players, when their confidence cracks during a match, revert to another style of play. As soon as this happens, the match is pretty much over. Players are never as good at other styles as they are at their own. An old rule of tennis is that you always make changes in a losing game, but not in a winning game. This can be somewhat misleading. What this really means is that you make adjustments to your style without changing your style. I always tell my players, "You are No. 1 in the world at the way you play. The best you can ever be at someone else's style is No. 2."

> **Be decisive even if it means you'll sometimes be wrong.**

You're usually just grasping at straws when you try a lot of different styles. This does not mean you cannot make adjustments in playing different strategies within your style, but the strategy should always be to stick to the style that is most familiar. To try many different options only serves to further confuse a player making it easier for the opponent.

THE COUNTER-PUNCHING GAME

The counter-punching style favors athletes who are relaxed and non-confrontational by nature, but who are at the same time tough-minded. The primary skills to learn are good passing shots and lobbing, a good return of serve and good side-to-side movement on the baseline. Consistency, placement and depth of shots should be areas of concern during practice sessions.

The advantage of the counter-punch game is that it is the easiest style to learn, and it gives the fastest results. A player has fewer decisions to make than with other styles because this one relies on reacting and countering rather than dictating points with aggressive play.

An adept counter-puncher can usually defeat an intermediate player, but experiences problems when facing a skilled, aggressive player or another counter-puncher who is slightly better. This is the best style of play, however, for smaller players, or those who rely on speed. Borg and Michael Chang are probably two of the best counter-punchers in the history of tennis.

THE ATTACKING GAME

The attacking game is suited to a good athlete with an aggressive temperament, or an athlete of large physical stature with a non-aggressive temperament (such as Stan Smith) who doesn't make unforced errors.

The Net Rusher

The skills needed for this style of play include a strong serve, good approach shots, consistent first volleys and a good overhead smash. Errors will be made with the attacking style, but the athlete should always remember to make them aggressively and decisively. Doubt and hesitation are the culprits for the attacking player, so controlled aggression is critical. It is also important that this player take time between points and remain fully aware of momentum swings. John McEnroe and Stefan Edberg are examples of great net rushers.

The Attacking Baseliner

An attacking game can also be played from the baseline, but a high level of confidence in one's ground strokes is critical. Excellent control of spin shots is necessary so that adjustments can be made in adverse situations where timing is thrown off, such as by the wind or an opponent's strange style.

The attacking baseliner takes greater risks than most players from the baseline, but does not give the opponent a quick target like a net rusher does. The attacking baseliner, therefore, can deliver a blow without taking the chance of being passed at the net. Andre Agassi, Jim Courier and Monica Seles are all good examples of attacking baseliners.

All the attacking styles take longer to develop, but can give the player opportunities for big wins. Players who devote themselves to an attacking game will be less consistent at first, and must be patient with themselves even while taking some losses along the way.

THE ALL-COURT GAME

The all-court game is the best style to teach if there is adequate time to train and if the athlete is versatile and well-equipped physically, mentally and emotionally. All the skills that enable the counter-puncher and the attacking player to be successful are needed to lay the all-court game, so this style takes the longest time to learn and requires the most patience.

Consistency, placement, depth, spin and power are needed on all strokes, so the player must have a disciplined temperament and be prepared for occasionally poor performances. It is also critical to master momentum control and understand the flow of the match. Still, mastering this style produces the best results of any style of play.

The following chart shows the skills needed for building a particular style. Once again, the style used should be in balance with the player's unique temperament and personality.

Figure 8-4. Stick with your game style.

SUMMARY

THE COUNTER-PUNCHING GAME	THE ATTACKING GAME	THE ATTACKING BASELINER GAME (Delayed Net Pressure)	THE ALL-COURT GAME
· Best style for limited athlete · Easiest to learn · Fewest decisions to make · Fastest results · Hardest for intermediate player to play against	· For the good athlete · Minimal decisions to make · Somewhat longer to develop · Chance for bigger wins · More inconsistent results	· For small but fast players or big but slow players · Able to hurt opponent without going to net	· For the best and smartest athletes · Allows greatest flexibility against all types of players · Longest to learn · Gives widest base for long-range results · Best results if mastered worst results if not mastered
SKILLS NEEDED	**SKILLS NEEDED**	**SKILLS NEEDED**	**SKILLS NEEDED**
· Consistency · Placement · Depth	· Placement · Power	· Must have a weapon off of ground strokes · Must know and use Wardlaw Directionals · Must develop midcourt volleys · Should have good foot speed	· Consistency · Placement · Depth · Spin · Power
EMPHASIS AREA	**EMPHASIS AREA**	**EMPHASIS AREA**	**EMPHASIS AREA**
· Passing shots · Lobbing · Good movement · Good return of serve	· Good serve · Approach shots · First volleys · Overheads	· Forehand or backhand weapon · Consistency of less dominant stroke · Foot speed and balance · Attacking posture and attitude · Midcourt volley	· All skills and strokes
EXAMPLES OF :	**EXAMPLES OF :**	**EXAMPLES OF :**	**EXAMPLES OF :**
· Michael Chang · Chris Evert · Mats Wilander	· Stefan Edberg · Martina Navratilova · John McEnroe	· Andre Agassi · Jim Courier · Steffi Graf · Monica Seles	· Pete Sampras · Martina Hingis · Boris Becker

Figure 8-5. Building your best game.

CONCENTRATE ON YOUR PRE-MATCH PREPARATION

Being seeded #1 in a tournament was a new experience for Joanne. She came to see me on the eve of her first round and said that she had never been more nervous before a tournament. She explained that she had always looked forward to playing an event when she had the chance to beat a higher ranked player, but in this situation she felt she had nothing to gain and feared that she would play poorly and lose to a lower ranked player. I confirmed that her feelings were normal and very common with all top players. I also told her that until she learned to deal with this new role and the pressures that come with it, she would always feel this way and would probably not make an improvement. "It just comes with the territory," I told her. "The quicker that you can make your butterflies fly in formation and look at this as a challenge, the quicker that you will be able to move on." I also told her, however, that if she backed away from this pressure, it would present itself as a mountain twice as high the next time. I told Joanne there is really no alternative except to take this thing head on and work through it the best you can.

My next job as a coach was to give her the tools that are presented in this chapter to help her work through these new pressures. I congratulated her on the great job she had done to finally be a #1 seed at a tournament after so many struggles on the way up the ladder. I reminded her that as she continued to climb there would be more and more players behind her and fewer ahead. Please understand I said, "This is one of the prices of

The winning tennis player is the one who has become comfortable at being uncomfortable.

leadership in any endeavor. The higher you climb up the mountain, the windier it gets, the steeper it becomes to climb, the more slippery it becomes, the less oxygen there is. You will have constant doubts as to whether your supplies will be enough for the demands of the remaining journey, and the most puzzling thing of all is that those who are not willing to climb with you will most certainly be the ones to criticize, mock and dislike you. That is why there are not many traffic jams at the head of the pack. It is because you will remind them daily of what they cannot do. All of this is the hidden price of winning. Most people decide on comfort rather than the risks that are part of climbing that mountain."

I asked Joanne, "How must it be for the #1 player in the world?" I explained, "Every time she takes the court it is a no-win situation. The only way to deal with such pressure is to evaluate your performances based on your own set of criteria for winning and losing." This takes incredible maturity and is not something learned overnight. It's an evolutionary process few grow to.

The game of tennis is certainly much more than merely the mechanics of hitting the ball more proficiently than the other person. Every situation provides a slightly different pressure. With experience, a player learns that every match presents different problems and different solutions must be found. The game never quite brings you what you expect. Competitors must be flexible enough to adapt, change and to think on their feet. It is not just the mechanical and tactical aspects of the game that constantly change. Mental and emotional situations are always changing as well.

THE RIVER CALLED A TENNIS MATCH

The best analogy I use for my pupils when explaining how to emotionally prepare for a match is that it is much like putting a tippy canoe into a river. It may be an unfamiliar, slightly familiar, or very familiar river. If you have maneuvered down this river before, you were either successful or perhaps you tipped the canoe. If you have never been on this river before, it may be considered an easy one for your skill level, a very hard one for your skill level, or perhaps just about right for your skill level. All of these situations are explained in the "Match Roles" section later in this chapter. When you put the canoe into the river (the match) you must then maneuver down the river without tipping it over. Your destination is two miles (two sets) down the river if all goes smoothly, and three miles (three sets) down the river if things go rough. Regardless of how long it takes you to travel, you have no control over the river (the match). It just takes you where it wants to! Sometimes the going will be smooth. Sometimes it will be very rough. The river may take you along faster than you like, and then go slower than you like. There are unpredictable boulders and rocks in the river that can sink your canoe at any time. There will also be times of peace and confidence when you will falsely feel that you are in complete control of the situation. The only thing that the competitor can do is use all of his wit and cunning to maneuver this river. If he tries too hard to control his path, he will usually turn the canoe over. If he doesn't do enough to control his course, the river will have its own way and run him into rocks and danger.

This is truly what makes the game of tennis so fascinating. Once the competitor understands this analogy he will be in much greater peace as he pursues excellence in the game. This chapter provides valuable tools to help any player identify and effectively deal with the physical, mental and emotional pressures of different matches.

> To accomplish great things, you must not only act but also dream; not only plan but also believe.
>
> — *Unknown*

PRE-MATCH PREPARATION

Preparation for a tennis match can and should start the day before the actual event, if not earlier. Because tennis is an individual sport and so many of the variables leading up to the start of a match can be controlled, consistent routines for pre-match preparation should be developed. Whatever the routine, it should fit the style and personality of the player, and the player should feel confident and comfortable with it. A team routine is much the same. It should fit the image and personality of the team, and have consistent guidelines in order to gain the trust and confidence of team members.

The body, the mind, and the emotions must be prepared for a match: the body should be warmed up, strategy should be reviewed, and attention should be given to emotional balance. The day prior to competition, special attention should be paid to diet and rest routine. Tough workouts should stop 48 hours before the match, and a light physical workout is recommended for the day before. A team's routine for match day might be to meet at the match site an hour before the start. A 30-minute physical warm up period is optimal. The next 15 minutes should be spent in a brief strategy session on what to expect from the match and the course of action to use against the opponent. The last few moments before the match should be spent preparing the emotions for the battle ahead.

PHYSICAL, MENTAL AND EMOTIONAL PREPARATION

The following checklist contains the important physical, mental and emotional considerations to review before the match starts. It begins with the more fundamental and obvious and progresses to greater detail.

> ### *Take Care of All Controllable Details That May Affect Physical Performance*
>
> 1. Follow a consistent routine before the match.
> 2. Be comfortable with a consistent routine to be used during the match between points that have been won or lost.
> 3. Take care of all physical details:
>   a. Eat right.
>   b. Get enough sleep.
>   c. Make sure to have the right equipment.
>   d. Perform an adequate warm up and stretching routine.

MENTAL ASPECTS

Having an Understanding of Your Game Plan and Knowing What to Expect from an Opponent

Understanding game styles of different players and how those styles affect your own performance is one of the most confusing aspects of planning strategies for a match. It is nearly impossible to know what to do in all situations, and it is critical for the player to have a set routine and guidelines to follow in various recognizable situations.

The two defining factors in a match are, very logically, your own play and your opponent's play. The relationship between these factors can be explained by a simple formula:

> ### MW-ME > OW-OE
> MY WINNERS minus MY ERRORS must be greater than MY OPPONENT'S WINNERS minus MY OPPONENT'S ERRORS.

The applications of this formula are many, but it should be remembered that seldom can more than 50 percent of a match's outcome be controlled. It is perhaps the last part of proficiency that a player learns which enables him to force his opponent to play poorly. Therefore, the first priority in a player's strategy is to control those things that he can control, namely his 50 percent. A player's confidence in his own tools will eventually be the factor that dents the confidence of his opponent. All other strategies are worthless if a player's first priority to believe and trust in his game and keep his game intact cannot be accomplished. This does not mean that a player should bullheadedly play only one way, never making adjustments. It does mean that he should control how he wants to play and force his opponent to react to his style. Winners act, and those who react do not win. No matter which style a player uses, this is always the determining factor in the match.

Playing Against a Player with a Different Game Style

One of the best, most easily understood ways that I have learned to determine strategies against opponents is by using player match-up charts. Very simply, I give my own player a basic rating from 0 to 10 (10 being the best) in the three playing style areas: Delayed Pressure, Quick Pressure, and Countering Quick Pressure. An example of this system is found in the charts below. Figures 9-1 and 9-2 rate the great champions Michael Chang and John McEnroe as well as Chris Evert and Gigi Fernadez.

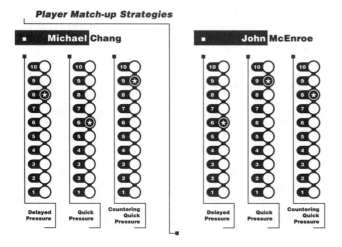

Figure 9-1. Chang versus McEnroe — a comparison of game style strengths.

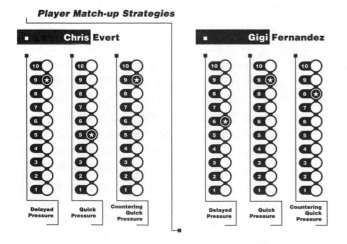

Figure 9-2. Evert versus Fernandez — a comparison of game style strengths.

Of course, the standards for rating are relative based on the level that a player is participating. Each player has strengths and weaknesses that are more directly related to his or her style of play than proficiency in each particular stroke. This results in abilities or deficiencies. By matching up your strengths and weaknesses against an opponent's, a style of play for the match can usually be determined with good accuracy. You will want to decide on a strategy that accents your strengths but also forces the opponent into his weaknesses. This can usually be done quite accurately by devoting adequate time to mental preparation before a match. Figure 9-3 shows how this technique can be used effectively.

In this match my opponent is a great counterpuncher, but he is weak as an attacking player and only fair when it comes to creating pressure while working the ball off the ground in the backcourt. He basically needs a target or his weapons are not that effective. My game revolves around my attacking ability, but because my opponent likes targets, I'll do my best not to give him many targets until the time is appropriate. I will take away his first exchange strength of returning serve by not serving and volleying as much as I would normally like. I will instead use more of what many refer to as "Wide and Glide" tactics, serving and attacking the second ball. In this case I want to create pressure with the serve. This will take away the opponent's ability to hurt me with his great return of serve. Because he doesn't like to play long points and wants a quick target, my objective will be to make him play long points whenever possible, especially on his service game. This will hopefully frustrate him into going to the net more than he is comfortable with; therefore, he will have to use a weak part of his game. If my opponent starts to falter and become frustrated, that is the time to pick up the quick attack and dominate him with my style.

While there are many strategies that can be used to win a match, the most basic and most important to remember is to 1) get locked into the way that you want to play and 2) try to make the opponent play the way he doesn't like to play. The most common mistake in strategy making is not sticking to those things that you like to do while trying to throw the other player off of his style. This can result in match suicide.

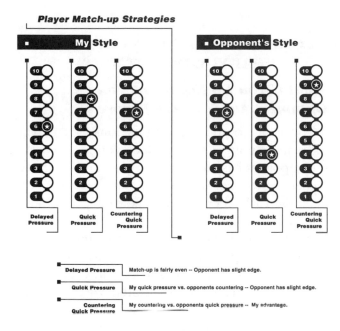

Figure 9-3.

**My style versus the opponent's style —
this simple working procedure can be
helpful in pre-match strategy planning
against just about any style of play.**

**A SIMPLE RULE ON HOW TO BREAK
SERVE**

Forcing the server to come out of the style that he likes to play on his service game is a good strategy to break the serve and cause the server to lose confidence. A player can do this by playing the opponent's style when the opponent is serving. For example, a player would come to the net on returns against a server who is a serve and volley player. This may cause the opponent to stay back on his serve a few points at critical times. Or, it could mean making a baseline player play long and tedious points in order to hold service. This might cause him to get frustrated and rush the net in an attempt to finish points faster. The rule is:

On my serve I play like me, on his serve I play like him! In any case, the objective of the return game is to force the opponent out of the style that he is comfortable with. Challenging him with his own style is a way of doing this.

Playing Against a Player with a Similar Style is a Tougher Task

What about players with similar styles? It was always amazing to see Bjorn Borg beat Guillermo Vilas so badly in almost all of their meetings. Because of the scoring system used in tennis, if two players have nearly identical styles of play, it takes only a slight edge — perhaps only one or two percent greater proficiency — to cause very lopsided scores and results. When the styles are alike, the lesser player has no way at all to attack the superior game, and the player who is a little better will almost always win big. For years, Chris Evert won match after match against baseline players just slightly less adept than she. Her biggest threats were players like Evonne Goolagong, Martina Navratilova and Hana Mandlikova. Against almost all other contenders who played the same type of baseline game, she played nearly flawless tennis for years.

When playing a match against an opponent with the same style, you have two alternatives: you can stick with your style or attempt to play another style. If you are favored, the choice is obvious. If you are the lesser player, abandoning your style violates the first law of strategy, that you must trust your game. The best alternative is to be hardheaded and stick with your game. Remember that although you may have a hard time hurting the opponent, that opponent may also have a hard time hurting you, and the difference between winning and losing may be only a slim one percent. There may be opportunities to effectively attack in a different manner, but it is important for you to remember to stay with your style since it is what you are best at. Even if you copy any one of the best styles in the world to perfection, the best you can ultimately be is no more than a good imitation. I always tell my players that they are ranked number one in the world in their own unique style of play. Again, the charts for rating the proficiencies of quick pressure, delayed pressure and counter-punching abilities will prove helpful in making strategic decisions.

EVALUATE THE SITUATION THAT YOU HAVE TO FACE IN THE UPCOMING MATCH AND DEAL WITH THE PRESSURES OF YOUR ROLE

What is the situation? How might my opponent play? What should I expect? Can I handle it, and am I ready for a tough match? These are all good questions that are certainly worth asking before taking the court against any opponent. Different situations present different pressures and have different effects on performance. A huge mistake that coaches and athletes can make is to either avoid their roles as they enter competition or to think that one situation is the same as all others. Players tend to begin playing without evaluating the situation because of their doubts and their anxieties about dealing with those doubts. Or, perhaps they do not want to deal with the job until they have to. The problem, however, with this approach is that what happens may be totally different from what the player wants or is ready for. This automatically places the player in the role of the reactor in a competitive situation. Ironically, many great players take this attitude and prove to be excellent crisis managers. But it is not a good way to deal with the situation. It leaves the player's coach unable to count on anything. It is better to recognize and prepare for the job at hand.

Match Roles

There are very specific roles that a player can carry into a match. Either a player knows his opponent or he does not know his opponent.

If you do not know your opponent, either:

♦ You are favored.

♦ The opponent is favored.

♦ It is an even match-up.

If you know your opponent, either:

♦ You have played him before and won.

♦ You have played him before and lost.

♦ You have never played him and you are favored.

♦ You have never played him and he is favored.

♦ You have never played him and it is an even match-up.

COMPETING AGAINST AN OPPONENT THAT YOU DO NOT KNOW

What If You Do Not Know Your Opponent And You Are Favored?

This is one of the hardest positions for a player to be in entering a match. Since you are favored, the opponent has something to gain, and you have something to lose. Since you and the opponent do not know each other, it is even more difficult because your advantage carries with it no more clout than hearsay. You should expect the opponent to play fearlessly and perhaps even above his usual level of play. In fact, this is the situation in which most upsets occur. This happens often when playing against players in their first year on the pro tour, their first year in college, or in the initial period after they enter a new level or environment. In all of these situations, the new kid on the block has an all-to-gain, nothing-to-lose situation. The established player has an all-to-lose, nothing-to-gain situation and what's even tougher is that the favored player does not know anything about his opponent.

Preparing for a match in this role, the key is to expect a difficult task. If you have this expectation, you will be able to play close to your very best thereby reducing the chances of being upset. It is important to remember that in tennis the underdog plays with more enthusiasm and less fear, but the favorite usually wins. Upsets generally occur when the favorite either does not prepare properly for a tough match or just plain ducks the pressure of dealing with that specific situation. In this match, the lesser player will keep his game (confidence) intact for a long time, but the flow will usually turn against him with a missed opportunity about three-fourths of the way into the match. The favored player must keep his game intact and be ready to take advantage of the opening when it appears. Failure to do so allows the underdog another chance, and there is nothing that will give the underdog confidence faster than the favorite's hesitation when it comes time for him to take his rightful place as the leader. This work must be done decisively. A fast start helps a great deal and the favored player should always try to show his opponent how hard he will play immediately.

What If You Do Not Know Your Opponent And The Opponent is Favored?

This can and should be the role that is most fun of all. There is much to gain and little to lose in this situation. If the opponent does not know what to expect from you, then this is an excellent opportunity for you to catch him napping. But, even so, anything that appears so good always has its hidden pitfalls.

Beware whenever someone says, "Have fun and play loose — you have nothing to lose!" What you lose is always the match. The balance of pressure that is critical for a good performance is extremely difficult for the lesser player to maintain for an entire match. If the pressure is there only for a good showing, a good showing is all you will get. The underdog role is very enjoyable to play, but the underdog usually does not win. In order to win, a player must perform as if he were the favorite. Therefore, it is critical for a player to approach this match in the same way he would approach the favorite role: expecting the opponent to play well and expecting a tough match. It is essential to prevent a situation that is pressure-free. The right balance of pressure is critical in maximizing the opportunity and getting full growth from a win. It will be a difficult period in the match come when the time arrives to take charge of the match—if you are not comfortable, you will often hesitate when it comes time to lead. No matter how uncomfortable it is you must step up at that time.

What If You Do Not Know Your Opponent And Neither Of You Is Favored?

This is a match nearly free from pressure because there are no expectations for either player. This match should be a test of pure physical and mental skills, nearly void of emotional factors.

Many times the player who gets ahead can stay ahead; therefore, it is important to display good initial body language and appear supremely confident. Remember that the opponent does not know any difference. Sticking to fundamentals and a solid game plan is important here. This is a role that should also be fun. It is best to try to lead early so that you will be comfortable leading late as well.

COMPETING AGAINST AN OPPONENT THAT YOU KNOW

What If You Know Your Opponent And You Won The Last Time You Played?

This can be a difficult role to play if you are not ready, but it is also the most reliable of any for a chance at victory. In tennis, pecking order reigns supreme. The player who won the last time will usually win again if he takes care of the necessary pre-match details. This is because he will be more confident leading at different times in the match and more comfortable winning in the war zones. Again, body language is critical before, during and after the match. You must expect a tough match because if you own just one win over an opponent, the revenge factor will allow your opponent to play with relentless aggression for much of the initial and middle parts of the match. Recognizing this, it is critical for you as the favored player to start out aggressively. You must try to take charge immediately and dent the opponent's confidence. Above all, never let the opponent dictate tempo for extended periods of time. This would allow him to play better and better until he becomes very confident in the leader role.

If a player beats the same opponent twice in a row, he will usually have dominance for some time. It then becomes a true matter of pecking order. Tennis players know their pecking order and, although they may deny it, they eventually become subject to the order until they make a concentrated effort in training and discipline to break out of it.

What If You Know Your Opponent And Lost To Him When You Played Him Last?

Revenge is a negative emotion and a negative motive. A positive cannot be gained from a negative. The revenge factor, although it feels good, always leads to its own undoing. If you lost the match when you played last time, you will naturally be a bit more aggressive and determined this time. The opponent will also naturally have a letdown and not care to face you again. The opponent's tendency may be to sit back and protect those territorial pecking order rites that he has over you. These factors, without the revenge factor, will be enough for a good chance of victory. The critical period will come when it's time to lead — no matter how uncomfortable, you must step up when it's time.

Another determining factor, though, will be how you perform in the clutch at many times. The real truth regarding your confidence, or lack of it, will show when you and the opponent are neck-and-neck at the end of the match. At this point, you will make errors and winners and the opponent will make errors and winners. The key ingredient for winning will be to maintain your confidence and continue to execute confidently as if you were the favored player. The scary thing about the clutch period of the match is that both players fully recognize that they are only an inch away from cracking their opponent or having their own game crack. The player who is proactive always has the definite advantage.

What If You Know Your Opponent, You Have Never Played And You Are Favored?

This role also carries with it the pecking order advantages of being the favorite. There is also a greater advantage in having an element of mystery about you which in itself is somewhat intimidating to the underdog. Strong, confident body language is critical to allow this advantage to help you. "Familiarity breeds contempt" is a phrase for all favorites to remember. The favorite should also be aware that flaws an opponent sees in his personality, training and work habits may be all the fuel that the underdog needs to beat him.

This is one of the most important lessons I learned by watching pro players during their off-court time in my travels as the U.S. Junior Davis Cup Coach. The phenomenon of pecking order permeated even the off-court activities. Players spent their time with those they viewed as equals on the court. The better players associated with the better players, and the lesser players stayed with their own. Bjorn Borg, who was dominating the world of tennis at the time, stayed nearly exclusively to himself and with his coach. This seemed to provide a mystery about Borg that put fear into the other players. Players would even spend time sitting around talking about Borg's greatness, which made him more invulnerable for any underdog who might be trying to challenge him. This mystique is part of the advantage McEnroe lost when he took his long break from the game in 1985. It was not so much that his

game dropped off, but more that the other players did not fear him nearly as much when he returned.

The main point to remember is that the advantage of being the favorite is greatly enhanced if mystery is also kept. This goes for team concepts as well. Everyone fears the unknown. Once familiarity occurs, your opponent's fear can and may become courage.

In the role of the favorite, a strong start in the match is again important. If you are behind, it is important to be confident with all play and actions on the court. Your opponent will always doubt himself at a critical time in the match, leaving an opening for you to take your rightful place as the leader. Your job is to keep your game intact until this opening appears.

What If You Know Your Opponent, You Have Never Played Him, And He Is Favored?

This is one of the more difficult roles because of many of the factors already mentioned. You may be intimidated even before you take the court. You may have placed your opponent on a pedestal at an earlier time and might feel uncomfortable beating him. You may enjoy the lack of pressure, but it may keep you from competing the way you need to in the clutch. Most importantly, if you are aware of these things, you may also be aware that the opponent might not be prepared to play you.

Again, it is critical in this role to control those things that you can control and to execute your own game. A tactic that can also work when in this role is to try to disarm the favorite either by acting as if you are not ready to play beforehand, or to making a statement or two to build up the opponent.

Often players play more for respect than out of desire to win. A mistake college coaches often make is to try to help their teams win in this underdog role by storming in the front door and letting the favorite team know that the underdog team is ready to win. In most cases, all this does is coax the favorite team into preparation of its own and gives them a reason to compete and win. Because of our Clemson team's image, we have always had a hard time sneaking up on the favorite team, and therefore we score infrequent upsets. But, on the positive side, because of our always-ready-to-play image, we have seldom been upset by a lesser team.

Some coaches, however, are masters at disarming the opponent. In 1985, our Clemson team was one of the favorites to win the NCAA's. We had a winning streak of 16 straight matches against the top teams in the country as we rolled into Athens, Georgia on a sunny April afternoon. We were heavy favorites to beat a rebuilding University of Georgia team, and we were resting on the laurels of our successful conquests. We arrived for our pre-match warm up and were greeted by the Southern gentleman coach, Dan Magill. His only words were, "Chuck, mighty good job your boys have done," and with a lower tone, "Hope my boys can stay on the court with them." Not much, less than 20 words, a very sincere statement from a very great coach, but it was enough, even for me. "Yes," I subconsciously felt, "how good that respect feels, how good it is to be recognized for the great job we are doing." My team members were happy and feeling good about themselves and the match that day. I had no doubt, or fear or nervousness about the match.

Thirty minutes into the match, I could see the end. Forty-five minutes later, Georgia had won four straight set matches and our number three singles player was desperately trying to hang on for our last chance. "How can this be happening?" I thought as I frantically rushed from court to court trying to rally the team. It was too late, and it was over quickly. We suffered a stunning 5-1 loss in singles and, even worse, we had never been in the match.

Afterwards, I was so sick I could not go into the restaurant with my team. I went into the parking lot and did some wind sprints and push-ups instead. The pain of the loss would not go away. How could we be so totally dominated? We were such a good team. Why did we play so badly? What did I do wrong? Was I such a bad coach? Finally, one of my players, Craig Boynton, came out of the restaurant to find me. He looked me right in the eyes and said, "Coach, we needed that loss. It'll help us down the stretch when it really counts. We were fat." As he walked back into the restaurant, I suddenly remembered what Magill had said in such a kind, sincere way before the match, and I started to laugh. "That old fox, I can't believe it. He did it again!" My mistake was not to recognize the situation. My mistake was not to acknowledge or deal with the role that my team had entering the match. My mistake was not wanting to deal with such a tough, dirty job. I had certainly not prepared my team for

the match. We were fat, and we needed to lose.

Dan Magill had just given me and my team a great lesson in sneaking in the back door and catching a team with its britches down. I would not forget what I had learned that day from one of the greatest coaches in the history of college tennis.

What If You Know Your Opponent, You Have Never Played Him, And It Is An Even Match-Up?

This situation can produce either the most exciting or the most boring match possible. Both players know each other, and there has not been a pecking order established; hence, both players know fully the implications of winning the match. A win could establish true dominance for one of the players over the other, but at the same time, a loss could cause a serious setback. It is definitely a hinge match or a momentum match for both players. Unlike the pressures of the even match-up when two players do not know each other, this situation presents considerably more pressure because both players are forced to live with the outcome of the battle. If the opponents do not know each other before the match, both players go away less blemished. When the opponent's know each other, and if everyone looks at it as an even match-up, it builds the suspense of any showdown. It's like the Ali-Frazier fight, or the Marvelous Marvin Hagler-Sugar Ray Leonard fight, or like many of the interstate collegiate football rivalries the weekend before Thanksgiving when both teams have had very good years. The winner is allowed "bragging rights for a year" like USC versus UCLA, Purdue versus Indiana, and Clemson versus the University of South Carolina — and the loser has to take it.

With so much riding on the match, what usually happens is that the two very calculating and conservative performers each try not to make a mistake that would give the other player any kind of an advantage. The play remains conservative until a player takes the first lead, which forces his trailing opponent to play more aggressively. At that point, the player who is behind may get himself into further trouble but usually catches up with and often even overtakes the opponent. This forces the initial leader to raise his level of play which usually brings him to the forefront once again. This seesawing of the lead usually occurs because of the lack of pecking order and because each player is uncomfortable being the front-runner or being very far behind. This pattern generally continues until one player is forced to play too well for his capabilities and as a result cracks. There are situations in which a player gets ahead and stays ahead because of the other player's cracking early, but usually the pressure of the situation causes each player's game to rise together at the same rate.

Again, confident body language is critical because each player will have feelings of doubt, and it will be just a percent or two that pushes one player ahead. Being aware of this and dealing with the situations confidently will certainly improve a player's chances of winning the match. A player's best approach is to realize that he cannot control his opponent's ups and downs and therefore stick to his game, trusting his own strengths completely.

Show your opponent the mountain and make him decide whether or not he is willing to climb.

UNDERSTANDING PRESSURE AND PEAK PERFORMANCE

Having a good understanding of pressure and how it relates to performance on the tennis court is basic to understanding the highs and lows and extreme or subtle swings in performance. This concept, spelled out to me while teaching health to college freshmen, has become the presentation for realizing peak performance.

The right level of stress and the athlete's ability to manage the pressure caused by stress are both critical to optimal performance. Throughout the entire match, a balance of pressure must be maintained. Being ahead creates a tendency to take pressure off from yourself while being behind creates the tendency to place too much pressure. Being ahead usually leads to careless play; being behind actually forces a competitor to play well and stay very focused until the burden of being behind becomes too great and the player cracks. I call this situation "when a player's dam breaks." Learning to keep a balance requires an understanding of the benefits that optimal pressure has on performance and demands practice in developing it.

As the pressure curve in Figure 9-4 illustrates, a medial amount of pressure produces the best performance.

The Balance of Pressure

A coach can eventually read his players and recognize when the player or the situation applies too much or too little pressure for optimal performance. As a coach becomes more familiar with each of his athletes, he must develop tools to deal uniquely with each one and help them to feel the right balance of pressure. He should be able to recognize the critical point between too much and too little pressure. Pre-match preparation has a lot to do with finding this balance of pressure, but even after the match starts, it may still be possible to make adjustments.

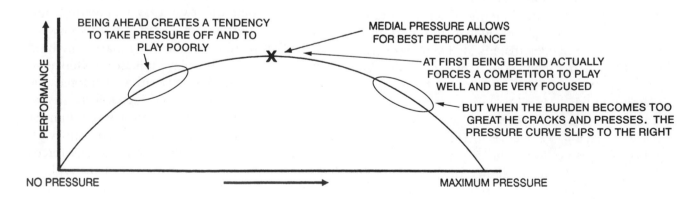

Figure 9-4. The pressure curve.

> A key ingredient of breakdowns and breakthroughs is Pressure — If handled the right way, it can make a diamond of the competitor; if handled the wrong way, it can cause him to crumble.

Being Behind

Although better players perform a bit better when they are behind, being behind, even by only a point, can sometimes lead a player into pressing. A good player will not make bad mistakes when behind unless he is cracking. He will usually play better for a while. The first bad mistake or unforced error that a player makes when he behind should draw the coach's immediate attention, because this is almost always an indication that the player is either pressing or has lost confidence. It is usually easy for a coach to recognize when a player is trying too hard and putting too much pressure on himself; the player will be rushing, and will appear frantic and desperate. At this stage, it is critical for the coach to try to help the player relax. I have always believed that when the player is going off the deep end, the coach must try anything to get him back on track.

A Coaching Strategy Backfires

I had to deal with this situation in a tournament in which one of my freshman players, Chris Munnerlyn, was playing a match against a player that he knew from his state. The situation probably provided a little too much pressure for Chris's best play. As the match progressed, the harder he tried the worse he played. The worse he played, the more negative energy he would put into the situation. It was obvious that Chris was not going to win the match if this cycle continued. I tried coaching him three or four times and nothing seemed to work. Finally, realizing that I had to do something, I called him over to where I was sitting.

Chris is a very strong, athletic person, and his body language always communicates extreme confidence. I thought that a humorous approach might loosen him up, and I thought he would be able to handle my attempt to come up with a joke. When he was close to me, I looked him straight in the eyes and said very plainly and distinctly in what I thought was a joking manner, "You stink!" I waited for a smile or laugh to cover his face, but instead he frowned and dropped his head six inches lower than it already was. I knew immediately that he had taken me seriously. As a freshman, he had no clue that I was trying to say something to loosen him up. I returned to courtside. He looked at me with tears in his eyes and said, "My own coach thinks that I'm a terrible player." I sat there in total embarrassment and told him I thought he was a great person and I was only joking in trying to loosen him up. I told him I would stay with him during the match and try to help him through. But it was too late. He had lost his confidence, and he lost the match. As Chris walked out of the tennis center later that day, I made him look me right in the eyes and say, "Coach, you stink." We both laughed.

Being Ahead

Being ahead, on the other hand, often by only a point, tempts a player to take pressure off himself and allow himself just a bit too much breathing room. This reaction creates a situation that allows careless errors, and even the best players make their bad mistakes when they are ahead. The statement, "When a player is behind, he will make his best shots, and when he is ahead he will usually produce careless play," is one of the most important that a coach can ever learn to understand match flow. Even the great players have a difficult time focusing and playing well when they are ahead.

The physiology behind why players play well when they are behind and play poorly when they are ahead is that when a player's back is to the wall and he must produce, his fine motor skills (his hand talent) work very well. When the player is ahead and doesn't have a sense of urgency to do the job at hand and win, his fine motor skills do not work as well. This is seen in just about every type of sporting event. The basketball team that is behind always seems to come up with the big shot. The team that is ahead often misses free throws and is careless about how they handle the ball and execute fundamentals. The pitcher who is behind in the count when throwing to a batter usually makes good pitches, whereas there is a tendency to make sloppy or careless pitches when ahead in the count.

These tendencies are obstacles that a coach should work hard with his players to overcome. The competitor will start to win a lot of matches once he learns to execute solid fundamentals when ahead and show the resilience to never crack when behind. It is interesting that a program of tough training usually helps the player accomplish the second goal of never cracking first. To be comfortable running forward with leads and to avoid playing sloppy when possessing an advantage in the match takes a bit longer; it is almost always the result of the confidence that comes from winning.

HAVE PROPER RESPECT FOR YOUR OPPONENT

A balance of respect is the key to consistent performances. It is the mistake and the downfall of any athlete to get over-confident or cocky. Likewise, the talented athlete who suffers from under-confidence will prevent himself from ever getting in the ball game. The correct balance of respect for yourself and your opponent is critical for optimal performance. Confidence? Cockiness? Humility? What is best for the pressure curve to be in balance?

> **Definitions I teach my players:**
> *Confidence — belief in self and respect for opponent.*
> *Cockiness — belief in self minus respect for opponent.*

Four things can happen during a point and cause possible reaction or mood swing: 1) you can make an error, 2) you can make a good shot, 3) your opponent can make an error or 4) your opponent can make a good shot. A player's reaction to each is based mainly on his pre-match conceptions of himself in relation to those he has for the opponent.

SITUATION ONE: TOO LITTLE RESPECT FOR YOUR OPPONENT

Here, you beat your opponent badly last time or you are heavily favored (at least you and everyone else thinks so). Often players of individual sports don't want to acknowledge the strengths or accomplishments of fellow competitors. There is an underlying feeling that this affects their own stature or confidence, but quite the opposite is true. It is the confident athlete who can give credit to another athlete and separate performance from feelings. Not having respect for an opponent is one of the easiest traps to fall into. Players tend to try to save their greatest concentration and energy for what they perceive as their toughest battles.

If a player has a lack of respect for his opponent, he is destined to play below his capabilities. Table 9-1 lists the four possible reactions.

TOO LITTLE RESPECT CREATES NEGATIVE - NEUTRAL EMOTIONS

POINT WON/ LOST BY:	REACTION	COMMENTS OR THOUGHTS	LEVEL OF PLAY
My bad shot	Upset (negative)	How can I be playing so poorly against this player?	Down
My good shot	OK; no big deal (neutral)	I'm supposed to make good shots against this player.	Same
Opponent's bad shot	OK; no big deal (neutral)	This opponent is supposed to make errors against me.	Same
Opponent's good shot	Upset (negative)	This opponent is playing over his head; he's so lucky.	Down
State of mind	Upset/disappointed (negative - neutral)	I'm playing poorly and my opponent is playing above his head.	Down

Table 9-1. Too little respect for your opponent.

The fact is that no matter who you are playing, all four of these situations will occur and will probably occur in the first game or two. A player may be able to react positively even when bad things happen against an opponent who is not respected, but the main point to understand is that rarely can anything good come from this attitude. This is true primarily because by not respecting your opponent, you have put yourself into an all-to-lose, nothing-to-gain situation. Having something to gain is a key ingredient to a good performance, and respect for your opponent is a critical element in preparing your mind for a gainful playing situation.

Staying in a Positive-Neutral Emotional Mode

Positive emotions should be maintained from those good things that happen during a match (e.g., my good shot, my opponent's error). If the player is in the wrong frame of mind, he will get upset over the bad things that happen (my opponent's good shot, my own bad shots), and he will only have a neutral reaction to the good things (my own good shots, my opponent's bad shots). An improper reaction to the good and the bad things that happen on the court will lead the hands (fine motor skills) to experience trouble working smoothly and will probably result in a loss. A favorable reaction to the good and the bad that happens will greatly enhance the chance for success.

SITUATION TWO: TOO MUCH RESPECT FOR YOUR OPPONENT

Here, your opponent beat you last time, he is heavily favored, or you hold the opponent somewhat in awe. In this situation, it is easy for a player to have too much respect for the opponent. Because of the pecking order in tennis, all players start in the underdog role. You almost always have to lose before you can win. The transition from being the underdog to being the favored player is a tough one, and this growth usually occurs in cycles. It is extremely difficult to win in the underdog role, especially if you have too much respect for your opponent. Table 9-2 shows the four reactions that can result.

The up-and-down play of the underdog role is what causes confidence lapses at critical times in the match. These highs and lows are caused by a player's reaction to what happens on the court and are difficult to keep in balance.

The underdog role is a fun, non-pressure role to play in a match. You as well as others do not really expect much; unfortunately, not much is what you often get. In the underdog role, the player is destined to react to the favorite. For long periods he may dictate tempo and play with authority, but late in the match or at critical stages, the opponent will take charge of the match, and the underdog will react to that. The winners of matches dictate action, and the losers react to their opponent's play.

TOO MUCH RESPECT FOR AN OPPONENT KEEPS YOU FROM EVER FINDING YOUR RANGE AND A GOOD GROOVE FOR YOUR SHOT MASTERY

POINT WON/LOST BY:	REACTION	COMMENTS OR THOUGHTS	LEVEL OF PLAY
My bad shot	Slight disappointment	My opponent is really good—I'm supposed to make errors.	Down slightly
My good shot	Great!	What a shot—I didn't know I could make that one.	Up; zoning
Opponent's bad shot	Surprised	What a break!	Not reliable
Opponent's good shot	Slight disappointment	This player is really good—he's going to make great shots.	Down
State of mind	Ups and downs	What will happen next? I hope that I can hang in there . . .	Up and down

Table 9-2. Too much respect for your opponent.

A BALANCE OF RESPECT PRODUCES   POSITIVE - NEUTRAL EMOTIONS

POINT WON/LOST BY:	REACTION	COMMENTS OR THOUGHTS	LEVEL OF PLAY
My bad shot	OK—stay tough (neutral)	Stay tough; keep going.	Solid
My good shot	Great—keep it going (positive)	Fine, let it go, feels great.	Up and moving
Opponent's bad shot	Good—that helps (positive)	Fine, this may be my opening.	Up and moving
Opponent's good shot	OK—stay tough (neutral)	Good shot on his part—stay tough.	Solid
State of mind	Good—stay tough (positive - neutral)	I feel great and I trust.	Up and solid

Table 9-3. The proper balance of respect for your opponent.

THE PROPER BALANCE OF RESPECT FOR YOUR OPPONENT

The best attitude to have to maintain the proper balance of respect when entering a match should be: "I know I can win, but I know my opponent can win if I'm not at my best." This attitude puts the athlete in a state of absolute readiness for a tough battle. Many athletes prefer to reject this attitude, however, because giving the opponent respect and recognizing the difficulty of the task at hand supposedly places them in a vulnerable position. Acknowledging this makes an athlete uneasy, but it is this vulnerability and emotional readiness that allows an athlete to have his best possible performance — mentally and physically.

In the case when a player has the proper balance of respect for an opponent, reactions to his good and bad shots and to the opponent's good and bad shots are illustrated in Table 9-3.

The proper balance of respect between you and your opponent also prevents a roller coaster effect from happening. The smart and experienced competitor is always aware that emotional balance is critical for best play. The foolish player fails to respect his opponents, and the inexperienced player tends to respect some opponents too much. The best pre-match preparation is a matter of working to obtain the proper balance. This will enable you to give the opponent credit if he wins and be a gracious winner if you win. Table 9-4 illustrates likely reactions in performance to the different pre-match states of mind.

	TOO LITTLE RESPECT (I'M GOOD, YOU'RE NOT)	TOO MUCH RESPECT (I'M NOT GOOD, YOU ARE)	BALANCE OF RESPECT (I'M GOOD, YOU'RE GOOD)
MY BAD SHOT	↓ NEGATIVE	↑	— NEUTRAL
MY GOOD SHOT	— NEUTRAL	ZONING ↑	— ↑ POSITIVE
MY OPPONENT'S BAD SHOT	— NEUTRAL	↑ OR ↓	— ↑ POSITIVE
MY OPPONENT'S GOOD SHOT	↓ NEGATIVE	—	— NEUTRAL
MY STATE OF MIND	↓ = POOR PLAY	UP AND DOWN = UNRELIABLE PLAY	BEST & MOST RELIABLE PERFORMANCE

− ⊙ +
NEGATIVE - NEUTRAL

− ⊙ +
POSITIVE - NEUTRAL

Table 9-4. Pre-match state of mind (how I view myself, how I view my opponent).

As a coaching tool I have players use a very simple formula to find the correct emotional balance. The pressures that are relative to match play are a) the pressure of the situation and b) the amount of pressure the individual puts on himself in this situation. I have the player use the formula that a + b should equal 4 or (a + b) = 4. Therefore if the pressure of a particular match or situation is level 3 (high pressure), the athlete should only put level 1 (low pressure) on himself. If the match is a very easy one or a level 1 (low pressure) situation, the athlete should then put a level 3 (more concentrated or a bit more pressure) on himself. Of course, those matches with a level 2 pressure (medial amount) are the easiest to prepare for emotionally with a level 2 amount of pressure placed on oneself. Again, the objective is to have a balance in the pressure curve throughout the match (See Figure 9-4). The following diagram explains this method of preparing well emotionally for the upcoming match.

> **Pressure of Situation +**
> **Pressure put on Self = 4**
>
> *3 + 1 = 4*
>
> *1 + 3 = 4*
>
> *2 + 2 = 4*

Figure 9-5 shows the flow and direction that a match will most likely take from the three different attitudes toward an opponent that can be taken before a match.

The best intensity to have to win a two-set match would be similar to the intensity a runner would have in running a two-mile race. He should start out quickly but settle soon into a comfortable stride. He should be solid for the biggest part of the race with few ups and downs and keep enough left over to finish the race.

Respecting an opponent too much is like trying to run too well in this race. It is like a runner who goes out too fast and sprints off to an early lead but collapses quickly when things get close. Tennis players who assume this role often start off by playing all their best shots early in the match. A good opponent is not threatened by great shots early in the match, and often a player who starts this way will not have anything left when the points get critical.

Too little respect for an opponent would be much like a runner starting off the two-mile race in a jog and falsely reassuring himself that he can always catch up and that he does not have to run his best until later. This lack of readiness usually compounds problems and will most likely produce a too little too late situation.

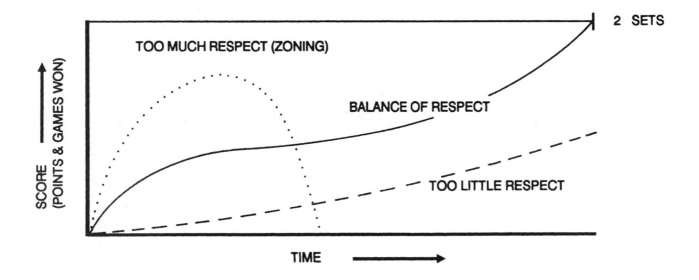

Figure 9-5. Match flow curves as dictated by pre-match attitudes.

SUMMARY

Correct, responsible pre-match preparation is a matter of knowing the toughness of the job and preparing to do it. It is a matter of physical, mental and emotional preparation and the following areas should all be attended to:

Physical

1. Take care of those physical details that are controllable.

Mental

2. Set a game plan and strategy to play.
3. Acknowledge the role in which you are entering the match.

Emotional

4. Work to achieve the right emotional pressure as you enter the match.
5. Have proper balance of respect for the opponent.

Figure 9-6. Player should understand pressure and peak performance.

Figure 9-7. Players must maintain confident body language.

Chapter 10

THE WARDLAW DIRECTIONALS
WRITTEN BY: PAUL WARDLAW

I cannot express strongly enough what it has meant to study, learn and implement Paul Wardlaw's Directional Guidelines. These guidelines represent the coaching tool that I sought for over fifteen years. I always believed that there could be a fundamental approach to shot selection that would allow a player to be proactive rather than reactive to an opponent. I developed a set of "Momentum Guidelines" based on the belief that running the right play held critical importance to the outcome of a point. I knew that a player's ability to keep hand skills working under many changing pressures of the match was critical as well. The tools I used most involved teaching players about the pressure curve and specific routines for maintaining balance in competition; however, until Paul Wardlaw sent me his Directional

Guidelines in 1994, I lacked the concrete tool my players needed to learn solid and accurate shot selection strategies. Believe me, the Directionals represent the most effective approach I have been able to find, providing fantastic results for players — beginners to professionals. Thanks to Paul Wardlaw for introducing this ingenious shot selection strategy to the game of tennis.

— Chuck Kriese

THE WARDLAW DIRECTIONALS

Defending national champion University of California at San Diego was a heavy favorite to retain its Division III women's tennis title. A veteran UCSD team rolled into the 1995 championship match where it would face a young but talented squad from Kenyon College. The upstart Kenyon Ladies bounced out to a 2-1 lead after doubles competition, forcing the Tritons to tighten their singles' attack. Intensity increased with every serve on every court as the singles competition produced a series of nail-biters from beginning to end.

UCSD retaliated with a strong effort that seemed to swing momentum in the Triton's direction as Kenyon trailed 3-2 early in singles. But, a victory by the Ladies' first-year player Ali St. Vincent tied the match, setting the stage for one of the most dramatic Division III title finishes in many years.

Lori Mannheimer, Kenyon's #4 player, lost her first set 6-1. B.E. Palmer, Kenyon's assistant coach, and Lori had tried a variety of strategies throughout the first set with little success. As B.E. related after the match, he had pretty much given up hope of Lori winning her match and was preparing to concentrate on closer but more winnable matches. During the changeover following Lori's first set B.E. knew he had to offer Lori a ray of hope before he left her. But what could he say? With the second set about to begin he finally said, "Lori, follow the Directionals. Just follow the Directionals." Lori nodded in agreement. She was now on her own.

B.E. returned to Lori's court after the first five games of the second set to find Lori leading 4-1. Lori followed the Directionals to a 6-1 second set victory, evening her match at one set all. The third set started out close but Lori continued playing according to the Directionals and won 6-2, pushing Kenyon to within one match of a championship. Moments later, teammate Amy Rowland pulled through an intense match, clinching a 5-4 victory for Kenyon and the Ladies' second national championship in the past three years.

"JUST FOLLOW THE DIRECTIONALS"

What are these Directionals? The Wardlaw Directionals were conceptualized in 1992 and have been a major component of the Kenyon tennis program ever since. The benefits from the Wardlaw Directionals to the Kenyon women's team are clearly revealed by their results since 1992:

♦ The 1992 team finished as National Runners-up, losing 5-4 in the finals.

♦ The 1993 team won the Division III National Championship in decisive fashion, winning all three tournament matches after the singles.

♦ The 1994 team, consisting of only sophomores and freshmen (Kenyon graduated their top five players from the 1993 championship squad), finished 11th nationally.

♦ The 1995 team won the Division III National Championship making a huge jump from 1994's 11th place finish to 1995's first place finish.

♦ The 1996 team finished third at the National Championships, losing 5-4 in the semi-finals in one of the best matches in tournament history. Kenyon had five team match points.

♦ The 1997 team once again won the Division III National Championship. The team looks to repeat in 1998 with the loss of only one player.

The Directionals evolved from my work in 1992 with Kenyon's #2 player, senior Kathryn Lane who went on to earn All-America status in singles and doubles. Kathryn was a solid player with excellent ground strokes. She had limited foot speed but used her aggressive strokes and serve to dictate matches and compensate for her lack of court coverage. Kathryn maintained excellent court position playing on or inside the baseline but she had a tendency to rush points and gave herself little room for error when attacking or closing out points. Most of her errors were wide or in the net. Tactically, Kathryn needed a way of playing which enhanced the following:

♦ High percentage shot selection.

♦ Aggressive attacking play.

♦ Court coverage and anticipation.

♦ Natural stroking — using natural hip and shoulder rotation.

Following Chuck Kriese's premise in his first edition of *Total Tennis Training* that most errors were change of direction errors, Kathryn's tactical decision on each shot became whether or not to change the direction of the ball. At the heart of the Wardlaw Directionals is the question Kathryn learned to ask on each shot, "Do I change direction or do I hit the ball back to where it came form?"

To Change or Not to Change Directions?

What are the advantages of not changing direction? As Kriese points out:

During a point of tennis, a player may choose to change or not change the direction of the ball's flight. Not changing the direction (hitting the ball back to where it came from) allows the player to hit the ball at a right angle. This is very forgiving to slightly mishit shots and also for more difficult shots such as the return of serve, first volleys, passing shots, approach shots and balls placed so that a player is stretched and off-balance or out of position to return them. It is a good rule to avoid changing the direction of the ball on any shot that cannot be controlled.

Changing the direction of the ball (hitting the ball to the open court), on the other hand, is a much riskier proposition. Only a slight change in the angle of the racquet face can misdirect a ball out of bounds or into the net. The temptation is to hit the ball to the open court, away from the opponent. However, this is not always a good idea because of the greater chance for error and because a poorly hit ball will sit up, thereby giving the opponent an opportunity for a put-away on his shot.

Not changing directions has tremendous benefits. However, a major tactical goal is to hit shots which are natural — shots which don't require fighting your body and allow your hips and shoulders to rotate naturally. As you'll soon see, there are some shots where changing the direction of the ball is the more natural and advantageous option.

INSIDE AND OUTSIDE GROUND STROKES

The essence of the Wardlaw Directionals is found in understanding the difference between inside and outside ground strokes. Forehands and backhands are no longer just forehands and backhands. Forehands are either outside forehands or inside forehands, and backhands are either outside backhands or inside backhands.

Outside Ground Strokes

Examples of outside ground strokes occur when two players are in a cross court rally. The ground strokes are called outside ground strokes because the ball crosses in front of a player's body and is moving away or to the outside.

The players in the two diagrams below are in cross court rallies hitting forehand to forehand (Figure 10-1) and backhand to backhand (Figure 10-2). The players are hitting outside ground strokes or more specifically, outside forehands and outside backhands.

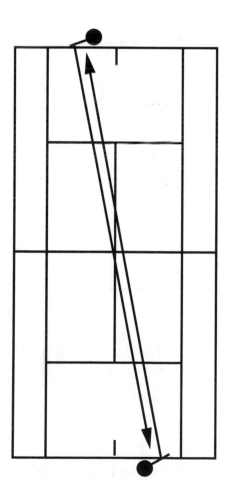

**Figure 10-1.
Outside Forehands.**

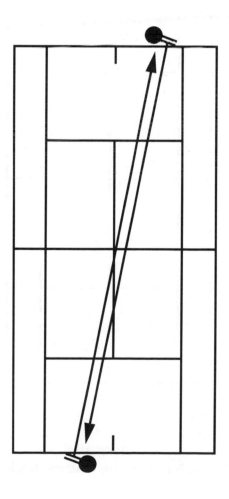

**Figure 10-2.
Outside Backhands.**

Inside Ground Strokes

Inside ground strokes occur when the ball does not cross in front of a player's body. An example of an inside forehand is the following: P1 and P2 are in a cross court rally hitting outside backhands (Figure 10-3) until P2 hits a ball which doesn't cross P1's body and P1 must hit a forehand (Figure 10-4). The forehand in Figure 10-4 is an inside forehand. The forehand is an inside forehand because the ball is coming into or inside the body and doesn't cross P1's body.

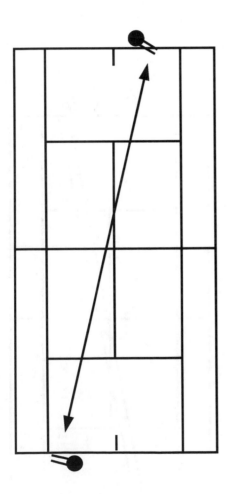

Figure 10-3.
P1 & P2 Exchanging Outside Backhands.

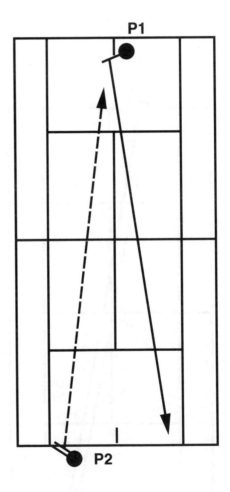

Figure 10-4.
P1 Hitting an Inside Forehand.

An example of an inside backhand is the following: P1 and P2 are in a cross court rally hitting outside forehands (Figure 10-5) until P2 hits a ball which doesn't cross P1's body and P1 must hit a backhand (Figure 10-6). The backhand in Figure 10-6 is an inside backhand. The backhand is an inside ground stroke because the ball is coming into or inside the body and doesn't cross P1's body.

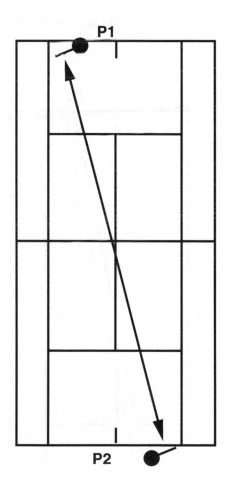

Figure 10-5.
P1 & P2 Exchanging Outside Forehands.

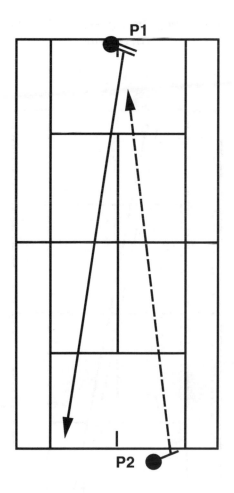

Figure 10-6.
P1 Hitting an Inside Backhand.

DIRECTIONALS: THE BASIC GUIDELINES

The relationship between the ball and the player (not the ball and the court) determines whether an inside or outside ground stroke will be hit. If the ball crosses in front of a player's body then an outside ground stroke will be hit. If the ball doesn't cross in front of a player's body then an inside ground stroke will be hit.

Understanding the difference between outside and inside ground strokes is the novel insight which led to the development of the Wardlaw Directionals. It's important to remember that there are two types of modern players — those who split the court in half (players who equally play forehands and backhands) and those that play with a weapon (players who overplay a strength, usually the forehand). The following three tactical guidelines are for those who split the court in half. Directionals for players with a weapon will follow.

Guideline One: Outside Ground Strokes — No Change of Direction

The most natural and high percentage shot is to hit the ball back cross court by not changing the direction of the ball. This creates a shot that leaves the strings at a right angle. Significantly fewer errors will be made, and your opponents will have fewer openings from which they can attack you.

Outside Forehands — No Change of Direction

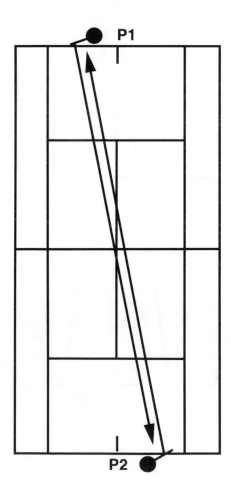

Figure 10-7.
P1 and P2 Hitting Outside Forehands.

Outside Backhands — No Change of Direction

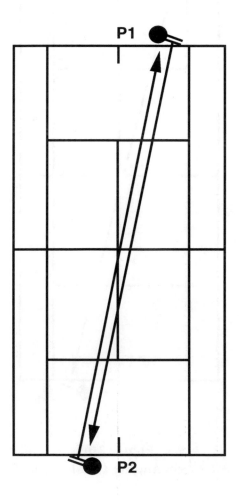

Figure 10-8.
P1 & P2 Hitting Outside Backhands.

Guideline Two: Inside Ground Strokes — *Change Directions*

Because your hips and shoulders naturally rotate, it is far more productive to change directions on inside ground strokes and hit to the open court.

Inside ground strokes are the shots which give you offensive control of the point. Players should be alert to step into the court on inside ground strokes and take the ball on the rise. Court position inside the baseline is the key to taking offensive advantage of an inside ground stroke.

The initial difficulty in hitting inside ground strokes cross court is that this is one of the shots where you cannot see your target as you prepare to hit the ball. Because you can't see your target, mastering inside shots becomes a matter of learning to gain a feel for the court and a sense of the width of the court.

Inside Forehands — Change Directions

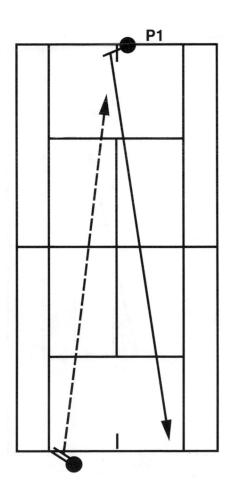

Figure 10-9.
P1 Hitting an Inside Forehand.

Inside Backhands — Change Directions

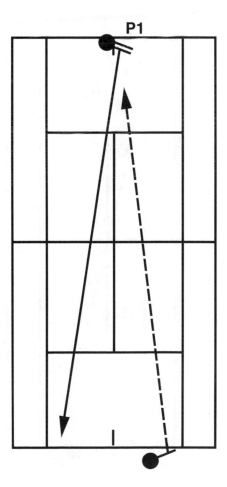

Figure 10-10.
P1 Hitting an Inside Backhand.

Guideline Three: Changing Directions on Outside Ground Strokes — The 90 Degree Change of Direction

Again, on deep outside ground strokes the high percentage shot is to stroke the ball back to where it came from (not changing directions). However, there are times when it's important to be able to change directions on outside ground strokes — the most obvious being on cross court shots landing short.

When changing direction on an outside ground stroke, hit the ball so that it crosses your opponent's baseline perpendicular to the baseline. In non-geometric terms — if you contact the ball three feet from the sideline, the ball should cross your opponent's baseline three feet from the sideline. This is called a 90 degree change of direction (90 COD).

Typically, when players change direction on outside ground strokes they think, "hit the ball down the line." By thinking "line," they aim at the line reducing all margin for error. By changing their reference point from "line" to "90 degrees" the player has room for error and since most 90 degree change of direction shots are forcing, the player has at the very least initiated an attacking sequence without taking a huge gamble. In addition, the player can concentrate on depth as width or angle ceases to be a factor. Increased depth then makes the shot more forcing or penetrating.

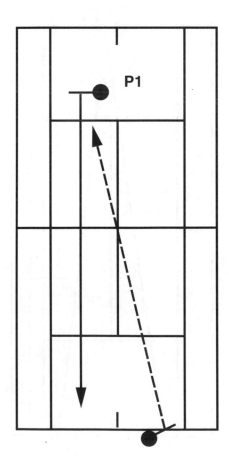

Figure 10-11.
P1's Forehand — 90 Degree
Change of Direction

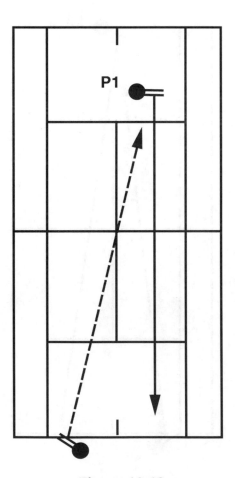

Figure 10-12.
P1's Backhand — 90 Degree
Change of Direction

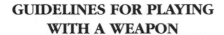

GUIDELINES FOR PLAYING WITH A WEAPON

Besides being the top players in the game, Steffi Graf, Pete Sampras, Andre Agassi, Jim Courier, Boris Becker, Monica Seles, Michael Chang and most professional players all have one thing in common; they all play to their strengths by setting up and controlling points with their forehand weapon. By overplaying their forehands, running around their backhands, and being able to penetrate the baseline with their weapon, top players create many more inside ground stroke opportunities to capitalize on. Two types of inside forehands must be developed and used when playing with a weapon.

Inside Forehand One: Inside-Out Forehand — No Change of Direction

In order to successfully play with a weapon, the player has to be able to hit inside-out forehands. Inside-out forehands are simply inside forehands hit with no change of direction. Inside-out forehands are usually hit off of deep shots and are used to create opportunities for shorter inside forehands from which to attack.

This time the inside forehand by P1 is hit with no change of direction.

Inside Forehand Two: Inside Forehand — 90 Degree Change of Direction

Because the weapon player is playing from the ad court, the inside forehand is hit as a 90 degree change of direction. The emphasis is on depth and penetration rather than width. This shot is usually hit off of ¾ court depth or shorter shots. Having court position inside the baseline is the cue for when to hit the inside forehand 90 degree change of direction shot.

This time the inside forehand by P1 is hit as a 90 degree change of direction.

*Figures 10-13 & 10-14 are guidelines for playing with P1's Forehand Weapon.

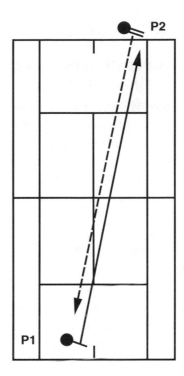

**Figure 10-13.
Inside-Out Forehand —
No Change of Direction**

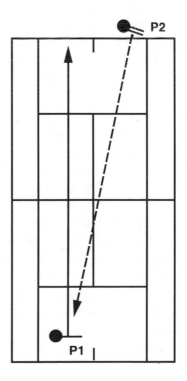

**Figure 10-14.
Inside Forehand — 90 Degree
Change of Direction**

IMPLEMENTING THE DIRECTIONALS

Following the Wardlaw Directionals makes play natural and uncomplicated and creates numerous change of direction temptations for your opponent. As you consistently make correct change of direction decisions, you will find your opponent continually takes the bait by hitting to the open court, making change of direction errors usually on deep outside ground strokes. However, two temptations arise for the player using the Directionals.

♦ Going for too much on inside ground strokes — You've hit three or four outside ground strokes to your opponent and you're finally ready to hit an inside ground stroke. The court is open and you decide to end the point but you miss wide. Inside ground strokes cannot be missed wide! An inside error is equivalent to netting a ball. Inside ground strokes give you control of the point and should be thought of as part of a sequence and rarely a point-ender. Having your inside ground stroke cross the baseline before the sideline will aid in resisting this temptation. Again, emphasis should be on penetration through the baseline, not on width. Don't be tempted to overhit!

♦ Changing directions on deep outside ground strokes — The shot looks easy and the court is open, but you are hitting a difficult, low percentage ground stroke. If you miss your 90 degree change of direction shot you'll either hit wide and out or hit more to the middle giving your opponent an inside ground stroke and control of the point. You must know your limitations and carefully choose when to change directions on outside ground strokes. The shorter the outside ball to change directions on, the better! Don't be tempted by the open court on deep outside shots.

BUILDING A GAME

Putting the pieces of the Wardlaw Directionals together requires a reasoned progression if tactical development is to coincide with technical development and match results are not to be sacrificed. The best way to proceed is by teaching and emphasizing the Directionals in the following order:

♦ Outside ground strokes. (These are the safest to play and the fundamental base)

♦ Inside ground strokes. (These are the offensive opportunity to open the court)

♦ 90 degree change of direction shots. (These are the highest risk because of the angle of deflection, but are important for the high level player to master)

OUTSIDE GROUND STROKES

Points typically unfold in the following manner: Cross court shots are exchanged until an inside ground stroke or a short outside ground stroke opportunity arises. Cross court ground strokes, including the inside-out forehand, are the bedrock of most offensive and defensive games. The first step in becoming a tactical player is learning how to hit outside ground strokes with the emphasis on patience, placement, depth, spin and pace in this order. Even though outside ground strokes are the least offensive oriented shots of the Directionals, hitting deep cross court shots is high percentage tennis and entices the opponent into change of direction errors. You won't hit many cross court outside ground stroke winners, but your opponent will at least have to hit lots of balls and make many more low-percentage winners.

Initially, location and depth are the essential areas

of concern when hitting outside ground strokes. Outside ground stroke rallies need to be diagonal rather than vertical with shots landing out of the middle third of the court (Figure 10-15). The concept of changing the rally from a vertical rally to a diagonal rally is called Shifting the Court (Figure 10-16). Tennis is a diagonal game, not a vertical one. Typically, less advanced play involves vertical rallies — rallies that take place in the middle third of the court. Effective high level tennis requires diagonal rallies, those which take place outside the middle third of the court. Shifting the court is just a matter of hitting away from the middle third of the court. The concept is important in communicating to players that the rally is too vertical. Most importantly, the Wardlaw Directionals are more effective when the court has been shifted diagonally. Playing high level points involves a shifted court where ground strokes are hit through the baseline, not the sideline. Again the emphasis is on penetration, not width.

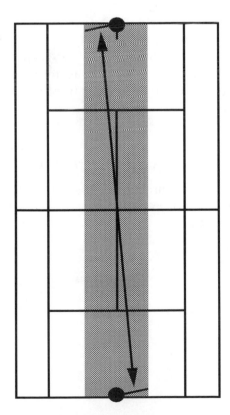

Figure 10-15.
Vertical Forehand Rally in the Middle Third of the Court.

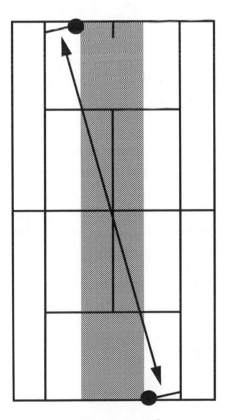

Figure 10-16.
Court Shifted to Diagonal Forehand Rally.

INSIDE GROUND STROKES

Hitting outside ground strokes well will generate numerous inside ground stroke opportunities. The key here is learning to take control of the point and take advantage of these inside opportunities by making your inside ground strokes pressuring shots. The pressure is created by penetrating the baseline and not worrying about width. Also, the inside ground stroke is your opportunity to change directions and hit to the open court forcing the opponent to hit while moving.

As discussed earlier, hitting the inside ball is one of the shots where you can't see the target. Therefore, learning to judge and develop a feel for where to hit the ball is half the battle in becoming proficient on inside ground strokes. Players typically hit inside ground strokes well from the baseline since the inside ground stroke tends to be natural. Inside ground strokes from the ¾ court area are more difficult shots to hit since the ball is hit on the rise and played from unfamiliar court position in no man's land. Establishing court position inside the baseline during rallies and taking the ball on the rise are two areas of development for most players. Again, remember to focus on penetrating the baseline rather than striving for width or angle.

CHANGING DIRECTIONS ON OUTSIDE GROUND STROKES

Hitting outside and inside ground strokes well are really the essentials of a backcourt-based game. The next area to focus on is the 90 degree change of direction shot on short outside shots. The first step is for players to eliminate the mental image of aiming at the "line" when hitting 90 degree change of direction shots. Like inside ground strokes, 90 degree change of direction shots should cross the baseline before the sideline. The emphasis is again on penetration and not width. These shots are usually part of a sequence and not point-enders. The other difficulty here is realizing that hitting from the ¾ court area or shorter requires a different stroke than from the baseline. Players typically make deep errors on approach shots because they fail to adjust their stroke in the midcourt. A baseline ground stroke and a mid-court ground stroke are technically completely different strokes.

Following the above progression will produce a tactically sound player. Individuality will develop as players gravitate toward their particular style as physical, mental, emotional and technical strengths and weaknesses become apparent. Will the player split the court in half or play with a weapon? Will a weapon be developed later? Will the player be an all court player, a baseliner, or a serve and volleyer?

So far only baseline and some midcourt tactics have been discussed. The Wardlaw Directionals have bearing on numerous other aspects from midcourt and front court play to return of serve. The next area to be covered is front court play — the volley.

VOLLEY DIRECTIONALS

The Wardlaw Directionals also apply to volleys with some minor modifications based on the type of passing shot hit.

Outside Volleys

There are two situations that typically occur on outside volleys: 1) the passing shot is hit high or not too hard so that you can control the volley or, 2) the passing shot is hit low or with so much pace that control is difficult.

On outside volleys you can control you have the option to:

♦ Not change direction.

♦ Hit a 90 degree change of direction.

The options here on balls hit above the net which you can control will require you to choose the best shot taking into consideration your opponent's court position, whether your opponent is moving or not, your court position and closeness to the net, and the need for being less predictable (you can't always hit to open court as opponents will begin to cover accordingly).

On low outside passing shots or heavy paced outside passing shots, no change of direction is preferred. You are in essence acknowledging that your opponent has hit a good shot and as you aren't in a position to control the ball, avoiding a change of direction allows you to close farther to the net, cutting down the passing angles. Hopefully, the next shot will present a better volley opportunity.

Inside Volleys

As with inside ground strokes, inside forehand and inside backhand volleys require changing direction.

*Outside Backhand volley options mirror the Forehand examples.

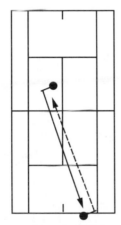

Figure 10-17.
Outside Forehand Volley —
No Change of Direction

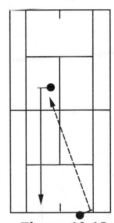

Figure 10-18.
Outside Forehand Volley —
90 Degree Change of Direction

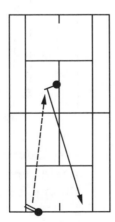

Figure 10-19.
P1's Inside Forehand Volley —
Change Directions

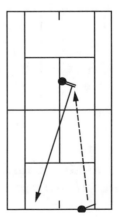

Figure 10-20.
P1's Inside Backhand Volley —
Change Directions

RETURN OF SERVE GUIDELINES

Every point begins with a serve and a return of serve. These first exchanges dictate how points take shape and more than any other area affect the outcome of a match. The importance of serves and returns are often overlooked. In professional tennis the server has a clear offensive advantage and it's understandable why set analysis focuses on breaks of serve — the true measure of server and returner effectiveness. Using the Directionals on returns of serve will give structure to a difficult task and produce higher percentage tennis for the returner.

Return of First Serves

Imagine having to return one of Pete Sampras's 120 mile an hour first serves. With his pace and aim there's no wonder it's difficult to break his serve. As the top professionals show, first service opportunities are the chance for a player to go for an immediate offensive strike.

Because the server has the advantage and typically tries to take the initiative on first serves, the job of the returner when returning first serves is to neutralize the point. Neutralizing the point means that the server does not gain a position in which to pressure the returner off the return.

Deuce Court Returns

On all first service returns, except inside returns, there is no change of direction. By not changing direction you'll create a larger margin of error on a difficult shot and set up a possible inside angle for your next shot. On hard inside returns (serves at the body and to the backhand), a 90 degree change of direction return is best, therefore changing the direction of the ball.

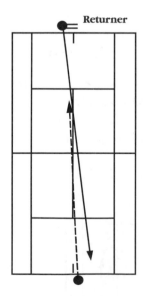

Figure 10-21.
Serve up the Middle, Return with No Change of Direction

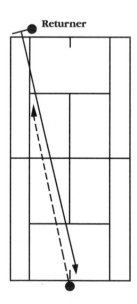

Figure 10-22.
Wide Serve, Return with No Change of Direction

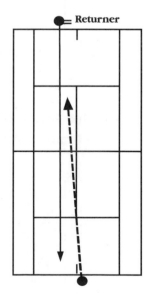

Figure 10-23.
Inside Serve, 90 Degree Change of Direction

Ad Court Returns

On all first service returns, except inside returns, there is no change of direction. Again, by not changing direction you'll create a larger margin of error on a difficult shot and hopefully set up an inside angle for your next shot. On inside returns (serves at the body), a 90 degree change of direction return is best. Ad court returners with a forehand weapon will hit either a 90 degree change of direction or an inside-out forehand on inside returns, therefore keeping the court closed as well.

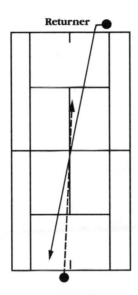

Figure 10-24.
Serve up the Middle, Return
with No Change of Direction

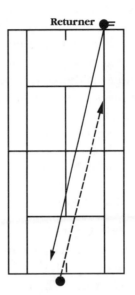

Figure 10-25.
Wide Serve, Return with
No Change of Direction

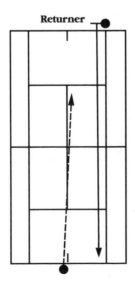

Figure 10-26.
Inside Serve, 90 Degree
Change of Direction

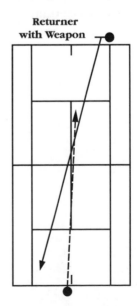

Figure 10-27.
Inside Serve, Inside-Out,
No Change of Direction

Second Serve Returns

When returning second serves, the job of the returner is to take advantage of the reduced pace of the serve and pressure the server by shifting the court (forcing with location) or by pressuring with pace and penetration. Usually the smart play when forcing with pace or penetration is to hit through the middle of the net (the center strap makes an excellent target) with no chance for wide errors. However, if you are going to attack the second serve and come to the net, you will want to either hit the ball aggressively to the open court to take advantage of the opponent having to hit on the run or hit a slice or slower ball which is best placed to the closed court, allowing you have adequate time to get into the net further than a very aggressive shot would allow. If you are not going to attack the second serve, you should get the ball on the outside of your opponent, so that he has to hit his next shot with an outside stroke.

Serving Implications

The server has to be cognizant of the tactical options of the returner when the Return of Serve Guidelines are followed. When serving at the body does the server force the returner to hit an inside ground stroke or an outside ground stroke? As shown above, serving at the forehand side of the body to a player with a weapon in the ad court gives the returner two equally strong options. Likewise, if you serve and volley and serve at the backhand side of the body in the deuce court,

you had better cover your ad court as this is most likely where the returner will pull the inside return. Understanding a returner's best options will make your service game much stronger as court coverage and anticipation improve. The fundamental rule to follow is to serve wide or into the body if you are not going to serve and volley. This will hopefully set up an inside ground stroke for your second shot. You should serve to the body or the middle if you are going to serve and volley. If you serve wide when serving and volleying, you had better close the net quickly to cut off the angle that you have created. If you do so, it will be an effective play. If not, you will be at your opponent's mercy.

APPROACH SHOT GUIDELINES

Approach shots create volley opportunities and should be thought of as part of a two-shot sequence — approach, volley. Approach shots are hit off of ¾ court deep balls or shorter and typically two situations arise — the player approaches off a short outside ball or off a short inside ball. Besides following the Directionals, the key to successful approaching is to remember that baseline ground strokes and mid-court ground strokes are technically completely different strokes (on approach shots the backswing is to shoulder level and the stroke is down and through the ball).

Outside Approach Shots

On outside ground stroke approach shots, hit a 90 degree change of direction with pace or use your slice to go up the middle.

Inside Approach Shots

On inside ground stroke approach shots, players who split the court will change directions. Players with a weapon will either change directions or not change directions on their inside-out forehand.

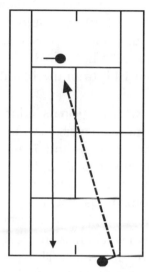

Figure 10-28.
Outside Forehand Approach —
90 Degree Change of Direction

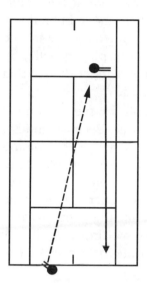

Figure 10-29.
Outside Backhand Approach —
90 Degree Change of Direction

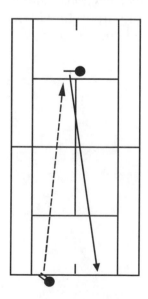

Figure 10-30.
Inside Forehand Approach
— Change Directions

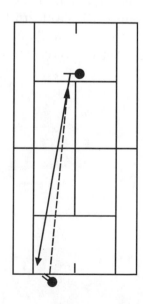

Figure 10-31.
Inside-Out Forehand
Approach — No Change of
Direction

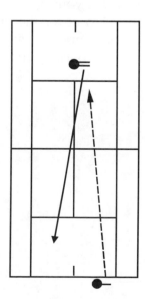

Figure 10-32.
Inside Backhand Approach
— Change Directions

TEACHING ANTICIPATION

In 1993 Kenyon had a first-year player with world class speed based on the USTA fitness testing standards. She could fly on all the standardized tests, but when put on the tennis court her court coverage was average at best. Her problem was not her inability to move but rather her inability to know when to move — she lacked anticipation. Slower, less athletic players with good anticipation covered the court much better than the speedy, athletic freshman.

The question for me became, "How do you teach anticipation?" Because anticipation relies on intuition and experience, the common wisdom has been that the more you play, the better you'll anticipate — exposure to repetitive situations will help you react quicker as these situations occur in match play. While this is true to an extent, there is an option to waiting and hoping for better anticipation. Anticipation can be enhanced and taught.

How do you teach anticipation? Follow the Directionals! The difference now is that you react to your opponent as if they play by the Directionals. You can do this because most players play by the Directionals because the Directionals mirror natural play. If you give your opponent an inside ground stroke, move to cover the cross court return. If you give your opponent a deep outside ground stroke expect an outside ground stroke back. Watch the professionals and you'll see how common these patterns are.

Reading the play, moving and covering certain areas of the court before the ball is hit is the key to developing anticipation. The Wardlaw Directionals give players sound reasons on which to base their court coverage options, and the immediate result is that anticipation improves.

Important Note: In order to adapt your game into the Wardlaw Directional Guideline as quickly as possible, your paradigm must change from the habit of thinking "Where do I hit the ball?", to "What shot can I hit from the ball that has been delivered?"

The Wardlaw Directionals address all these concepts and more. Players learn to make correct decisions immediately and learn to react to situations with minimal thought involved. Once you understand the Directionals, playing points becomes automatic as you simply respond by changing or not changing the direction of the ball.

The Wardlaw Directionals are tactical guidelines. Guidelines are not rules. The purpose of the Directionals is not to make tennis more rigid or predictable, but to instill and establish a base or foundation for players. There is flexibility and freedom in mastering the various aspects and improving and expanding your range and abilities. Ultimately, the Wardlaw Directionals allow players to learn functional and purposeful tactical tennis while at the same time encouraging natural and creative play.

SUMMARY

Benefits of the Wardlaw Directionals

1. Players don't have to think about instant shot selection. By following the Wardlaw Directionals, the only decision to be made is what depth and spins should be used for outside angles before changing direction of the ball's flight. Once you understand the guidelines, playing points become automatic as you simply respond to where the ball is coming from, instead of trying to make shots to different areas of the court from difficult positions.

2. Players don't fight their bodies as the Wardlaw Directionals allow for natural hip and shoulder rotation. Think of a baseball player hitting an inside pitch. The natural reaction for a right-handed batter is to pull an inside pitch down the left field line because his hips and shoulders are rotating in that direction. Going to the opposite field (right field) requires the batter to fight his body on inside pitches. This is especially important on reflex shots and transition shots (first passes, first volleys, returns and approaches). They are also extremely useful when playing on very fast courts.

3. Defensive tennis is played by hitting your opponent outside groundstrokes. The opponent then must change direction if he is going to attack the open court.

4. Offensive tennis is played by waiting for a short ball or an inside angle. By hitting your opponent outside groundstrokes you'll generate numerous inside groundstrokes on which to open the court.

5. Understanding the Directionals allows you to anticipate where your opponent is going to hit the next shot. For example, players naturally hit inside groundstrokes crosscourt; therefore, you immediately cover the open court where the ball is going to be pulled to when the opponent gets an inside ball. You learn to anticipate by following the Directionals! You will considerably reduce the opponent's ability to hit winners and force you into errors.

6. You learn to play percentage tennis by avoiding change of direction errors and by overplaying the opponent's best change of direction options, baiting and tempting them into selecting more difficult shots. Your accuracy and consistency will immediately improve.

7. When following the Wardlaw Directionals, all shots have a purpose during practice and match play.

8. You will never again fear an opponent's weapons because the Wardlaw Directionals give the immediate and correct answer to any shot the opponent tries, no matter how hard it is hit.

9. You can immediately evaluate matches and shot selection patterns of your opponents to make immediate adjustments for yourself under pressure.

Chapter 11

OBSERVE IMPORTANT CHECKPOINTS FOR MATCH PLAY

- -

> ### *Inside Shot*
> **Physical Checkpoints**
> **Mental Checkpoints**
> **Emotional Checkpoints**

It can be confusing for coaches and players, even advanced players, to know exactly what to look for as a match develops. Often a player relies chiefly on instinct, or he may have a tendency to concentrate on stroke production. What are the areas that must be focused on? How much should a player rely on his natural instincts, and how much should he rely on a logical plan of action?

The three aspects of a match — the physical, the mental and the emotional — provide the important checkpoints for match play. In the physical-technical area, the checkpoints are game style match-ups and court positioning; in the mental area, the concern is to make immediate but proper decisions for shot selection and to run the right play; and in the emotional area, the key is to keep a balance of pressure and an awareness of emotional reactions to the good and bad things that happen during the match.

PHYSICAL CHECKPOINTS

What Are the Game Style Match-ups?

As discussed earlier, there are numerous, often complex variables to consider when planning strategy for your particular game style against an

opponent's. Pre-match preparation should be based on an understanding of the tools (skills) available to you and those available to the opponent. Your primary responsibility is to use those tools and execute your game because strategies against the opponent are totally useless unless your own game is in operating order. Often a good strategy fails quickly because a player's tools were not sufficient for the strategy or because a player abandoned his tools early in the match to try an approach that was not within his skill level. A player should always lock in his own style first and then work to derail the opponent. The game style match-up system discussed in Chapter 9 is an important section to review and understand before taking the court. The match-up system can also be of value during a match to expose an opponent's weakness or to find the most effective way to exploit his style of play.

> The confident player looks at himself as a constant and recognizes his opponents' ups and downs; the underconfident player sees himself as the variable and his opponent as a constant. *— Unknown*

Am I Controlling Court Positioning?

Changes in a player's body language, intensity and stroke production are usually obvious, but more subtle changes may occur in a player's court positioning. This is an extremely important physical aspect to watch for. If two players were to rally and hit ground strokes on an open parking lot instead of on a tennis court with all its restrictive dimensions, they would probably discover that their normal shots would travel approximately the same distance every time, perhaps 65 or 70 feet. This is because the player's strokes have been developed within the normal court dimensions (a tennis court is 78 feet long). This rally delivers a ball that falls somewhere in the midcourt every time.

There are many advantages if a player is even one step closer to the net. Taking balls just a step earlier allows several things to happen. First, the ball delivered to the opponent is deeper, which forces his ball to be shorter. This allows the player to be offensive-minded, and it forces the opponent into defensive play. In addition, as shown in Figure 11-1, the angles for court usage are much better.

Good court positioning forces the opponent to make defensive shots, and it prevents the player from having to cover so much court. The greatest benefit, however, is that it rushes the opponent, prevents him from setting up, and thus controls his ability to take charge of the point. To force the opponent a player has two choices: either hit the ball harder or take the ball earlier. It is extremely difficult, if not impossible, for a player to force himself to hit harder instantly while still maintaining control. A much better approach for a player is to take shots a bit earlier and maintain the most confident stroke. This forces the opponent to rush.

The main disadvantage of taking balls early is that the player himself also has a little less time and should therefore hit the ball without changing the direction of its flight. Another disadvantage in taking the ball too early is that a full swing cannot be made; therefore a weak ball is usually produced. A player should hit the ball right back to where it came from, thereby cutting the margin for error. The most obvious advantages to taking the ball early and to establishing good court positioning are apparent in all transition shots, where the benefit of forcing the opponent to rush is even greater.

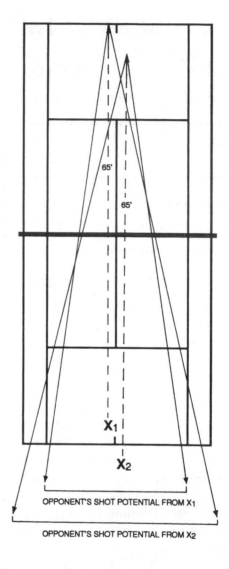

X_1 = SHOT MADE WITH GOOD COURT POSITIONING

X_2 = SHOT MADE FROM COURT POSITION BEHIND BASELINE

Figure 11-1. Angles for court positioning.

> To dream anything that you want to dream...that is the beauty of the human mind; To do anything that you want to do...that is the strength of the human will; To trust yourself to test your limits...that is the courage to succeed.
> — *Bernard Edmunds*

MENTAL CHECKPOINTS

Am I Using Good Shot Selection Strategies?

The ability to instantly make good decisions regarding shot selection and ball placement is truly important to success. To do so makes the player proactive instead of reactive. This combined with an understanding of what play is appropriate to run in a particular situation (momentum control) allows a player to recognize just what he is trying to do in almost all situations. The best shot selection strategy I've ever learned is the Wardlaw Directional guidelines. They are explained in complete detail in Chapter 10.

Am I Controlling the Momentum and Match Flow by Running the Right Plays?

The physical checkpoints of game style match-ups and court positioning are the base for any other strategy, for without these fundamentals other efforts will fall short. Once these are in order, the next checkpoint is a mental or strategic procedure: Which play should be run? In all other sports, the answer is more obvious than it is in tennis. Often,

Figure 11-2. Players must observe the physical, mental and emotional checkpoints for match play.

at the critical stages of a match, tennis players focus on their technical skills or on the trouble they are having with a stroke. This is wrong. Game time is not the time to worry whether or not your strokes are there — you have got to use whatever is in the tool box at the start of the match. Top basketball players do not worry about how their jump shot looks with a minute and a half to go in the game, and a quarterback does not think about his throwing release with the two-minute drill underway. In tennis, though, there is a tendency for players to over-analyze and pick out microscopic technical flaws in their games when they should be thinking only of which play they should run. "Paralysis by analysis" can be a fatal disease for the athlete in the heat of the battle.

EMOTIONAL CHECKPOINTS

Am I at my Optimal Balance of Emotional Pressure?

If a player has chosen the right technical way to play, has worked to control court positioning, and knows which play he wants to run, he has covered the checkpoints for playing a very solid match. The final, key ingredient that lets the whole thing run is making sure that he is in the right "emotional zone" or has the right balance of pressure, as discussed in Chapter 9. It is critical to note that although the physical and mental checkpoints should be taken care of first, this important emotional checkpoint allows everything else to flow and work together.

How Do I React to Points Won and Points Lost?

During the first two or three games of every match, a player will make winning shots and errors, and his opponent will make winning shots and errors. Often a player can judge his emotional state by noticing his reaction to these events.

Usually if a player is in a good frame of mind to compete, he will react positively to his good shots, and his poor shots will cause little or no reaction. His opponent's good shots will not bother him, and he will get a small lift from his opponent's bad shots. When this same player is in a poor state of emotion to compete, he will get upset and annoyed at his poor shots and at his opponent's

...emotional state will give him little ...from the good things that happen. ...starts, it is difficult to reverse. This ...a major checkpoint for emotional balance on the court.

As described in the chapter on pre-match preparation, the player should work to maintain a positive-neutral emotional state and not a negative-neutral state.

SUMMARY

Physical checkpoints:

1. What are the game style match-ups?
2. Am I controlling court positioning?

Mental checkpoint:

1. Am I using good shot selection strategies (Wardlaw directional guidelines)?
2. Am I controlling the momentum and match flow by running the right play?

Emotional checkpoints:

1. Am I at my optimal balance of emotional pressure?
2. How do I react to points won and points lost?

The Ten Do's for Self Confidence

1. Acknowledge your defeats, then let them go.
2. Answer all compliments with "thank you".
3. Constantly affirm your positive self-concept and create a positive system in other people.
4. Actively pursue goals and declare your vision and your mission.
5. Share your vision with friends and coaches.
6. Support your friends who play (verbally and non-verbally).
7. Model yourself after someone successful, especially one who did well through hard work.
8. View negative and destructive criticism as a statement of a critic who may be somewhat jealous.
9. Be a dreamer and dream great successes, harness the unlimited power of your imagination to reach your goals.
10. Constantly acknowledge the fact that the only person you have control of is yourself and you will take your positive and negative qualities wherever you go.

Figure 11-3. Solid returns like this result from attending to the emotional checkpoints of a match.

Chapter 12

USE THE POWER OF MOMENTUM TO CONTROL MATCH FLOW

· ·

In the sixth game of the 1986 World Series, the Boston Red Sox were one strike away from winning their first world championship in years. Anyone would agree that the promise of a seventh game in the World Series would have sounded extremely exciting during that '86 spring training. But a dramatic change of events took place. The result was not only the loss of the Red Sox two-run lead and that sixth game, but also, as was quite obvious to millions of viewers and more importantly to the two teams involved, the loss of Momentum. The series suddenly slipped under the Mets' control. Instead of feeling the jubilation of playing in the seventh game of a World Series, it was likely a dreaded situation for those unlucky Red Sox.

In the 1996 World Series, the Atlanta Braves easily won the first two games in New York to take what appeared to be an insurmountable advantage back to their home field. Their best pitchers were lined up to finish out the job, and the end looked to be only a matter of time for the Yankees. The unbelievable happened once again as the magic of Momentum changed that course and allowed the visiting Yankees to take the three games in Atlanta, then return home to finish off the unbeatable Braves.

Greg Norman had a seemingly insurmountable five stroke lead going into the last round of the 1996 Masters Championship in Augusta, Georgia, until Momentum changed course allowing Nick Faldo to win his third green jacket. Some said that Norman just choked, but what really happened is that the Momentum he had controlled the previous three days was no longer in his corner.

In the 1985 French Open finals, a similar thing happened as John McEnroe saw his two-set lead over Ivan Lendl and the championship slip away. A player the caliber of John McEnroe unable to to win one out of three sets to take a championship? Once again, when the power of Momentum turned there was little he could do to stop the inevitable.

> # There is no heavier burden than a great opportunity.

So what is this force that snatched victory out of the grasp of those Red Sox, Braves, Norman and McEnroe? The power that allows these swings to occur seems almost magical, and no one has seemed to be able to harness it. Sportscasters refer to it on a regular basis, and sports competitors speak of it as if it were both their best friend and their worst enemy. This power is called "momentum" (I refer to it as "MO"), and it is the most awesome power in sports.

All competitive tennis players have experienced the power of the MO. When the MO is with you, it feels as though the match is on the tip of your racquet, as though you are dictating how each point is played. When the MO is against you, you feel like a puppet on a string while your opponent effortlessly puts together one powerfully played point after another.

Tennis, perhaps more than any other sport, is a game of momentum. There is no clock to do the dirty work of finishing off an opponent, and a scoring system based on units makes the flow of the match much more important than any established lead. In sports other than tennis, momentum is also readily recognized and can sometimes be controlled. Basketball coaches are perhaps the most adept coaches at shutting the MO down. In tennis, coaches and players often focus a bit too much on stroke technique instead of concentrating on match flow and sticking to a simple game plan that tells them when to attack and when not to. This is what the best basketball coaches learn to do in their coaching. Sometimes they have their players put high pressure on the opponent; at other strategic times, they have the players let up on the pressure to frustrate opponents into making mistakes.

All too often in tennis, strategy is planned around an opponent's weakness, and too often the match tempo is dictated by how a player is feeling. This would be totally absurd in any other sport, but in tennis the very best players go into matches with the assumption that the outcome rests on their technical skills alone. This is not true. The most important skill that a tennis player can learn is how to be aware of, and learn the skills to apply his or her control over Momentum.

Can This Power Be Controlled?

It is impossible to totally control momentum. There are too many unpredictable, unplanned variables involved in a highly competitive situation. The best that the athlete can do is to use his knowledge of situations to affect the flow of the match and then work within that framework. The upcoming chapter deals with truths about momentum and strategies for use in the heat of the battle to deal with momentum swings.

There are three separate categories explained that give reasons for momentum shifts and how to use them to your advantage.

The First: How to manage momentum based on the score; e.g. Are you leading?, Are you behind?, or Are you tied? **The Second: Action-Reaction guidelines**; deals with managing momentum based on the events leading up to a particular score. (Did my opponent make a winner or an error? Did I make a winner or an error?) **The Third: The Conversion Theory**; deals with the grouping of points to start a flow.

MANAGING MOMENTUM BASED ON THE SCORE

Momentum management based on score has to do with the athlete's ability to: 1) maintain momentum once it has been created (*playing with the lead*), 2) switch momentum once the opponent has it (*trying to come from behind*) and 3) create momentum when there is none (*what to do when the score is tied*).

The basis for momentum management in relation to the score is found in one simple truth: players usually make bad mistakes when they are ahead in a game and come up with their best shots when they are behind. Any coach who has sat through enough competitive matches will tell you that this statement is absolutely true, but the proof to this theory lies in reviewing the pressure curve shown in the chapter on pre-match preparation (See Chapter 9, Figure 9-4). This fundamental should be understood and reviewed whenever necessary.

When you are ahead, there is a great tendency to take some of the pressure off of yourself, and the pressure curve slips to the left; therefore, performance goes down. This happens basically because the lack of substantial pressure keeps the fine motor skills, or the hand skills, from working to their full potential. You get sloppy. This is very obvious in other sports as well. The team that is ahead has trouble hitting the front end of one-and-one free throws in a basketball game, and their shooting percentage goes down. The golfer who is ahead usually will miss the easier putt, and the pitcher who has an 0 and 2 count (no balls and two strikes) against the batter seems to have a hard time getting that third strike across the plate. In tennis we see leads squandered quite often as well — a player lets a 40-love advantage get away, for example. It is not that the player wants to squander the lead, it is merely that the pressure is not great enough when the player is ahead for him to make shots with his hand skills working well.

When you are behind, you will play better and make better shots because basically, you have to! It is crisis management time! It is time to fish or cut bait! This is precisely the pressure that has to be there for the competitor's hand skills to work. The added pressure makes the pressure curve perfectly at the median. A little less pressure and the hands would not work as well. A little more, and the pressure curve would slip to the right too much and the fine motor skills of the hands would press and try too hard. This perfect amount of pressure over an extended period of time is a phenomena that all athletes experience when they are in "the Zone". Great shooters in basketball come to life when their teams are in need of a basket because their hands work. The same shooter usually blows two or three in a row if their team is up by a large margin. In tennis, players will make very good first serves, electrifying passing shots and consistent volleys when they are behind. The same player will miss the first serves, hit the passing shots into the net, and blow the easiest of volleys when he has a service break lead. Basically, when a player is under the optimal amount of pressure, there is a balance that allows the hand skills to work perfectly and keep on doing so for a period of time.

Therefore, the player will usually play a bit worse and make some bad shots when he is ahead, and will play better and make his great shots when he is behind. If the player gets too far behind, he will usually suffer the effects of a pressure overload which will cause him to press. Once the player presses in such a fashion, he's well on his way to

an early handshake at the net with a victorious opponent, because in the game of tennis, your hands have to work. Trying too hard in tennis would be much like trying too hard while playing the piano or painting. This is part of the reason that tennis is such a fascinating game.

The MO Rules

The rules for momentum control based on score have their foundation in these truths listed in the previous paragraphs; therefore, if both you and the opponent tend to play better when behind, and both of you tend to play a bit worse when ahead, this knowledge can represent a significant advantage in deciding what kind of play to run.

KINDS OF PLAYS TO RUN

Quick Pressure Plays

a. Serve and Volley

b. Serve and Attack the second ball to come to the net

c. Hit and charge or Chip and charge off of opponent's second serve

Delayed Pressure Plays

a. Wardlaw Directional guidelines (See Chapter 10)

b. Breakdown patterns (work ball to only one side of the court to prevent movement)

Countering Plays

a. Wardlaw directional guidelines

b. Bring-ins (purposely hit short ball crosscourt to bring opponent to the net to pass him)

Daily practice situations can easily be practiced to simulate points that have to be played by using quick pressure, delayed pressure, or countering tactics. This will help the player to become more confident with his skills when it becomes necessary to run a certain type of play.

Note: It is important for the athlete to know and to understand his skill level at each of these plays and different styles. A simple chart like the one listed in Chapter 9 (See Figure 9-3) illustrates a method of pre-match preparation involving comparison of game styles (My Style vs. Opponent's Style).

MAINTAINING MOMENTUM: WHAT DO YOU DO WHEN YOU ARE AHEAD IN THE GAME?

When you are ahead, your opponent is behind. As you have a tendency to play a little looser, the opponent has a tendency to play a little better. His concentration picks up, he becomes a bit more aggressive, and if he is a good player, he will surely not make a bad mistake. The loss of momentum in this game usually occurs because your relaxed attitude and your opponent's aggressiveness cause the two things that actually change momentum: your sloppy mistake and the opponent's great shot. You find yourself at deuce in the score, but your confidence has slipped and the opponent's has taken a jump. Unless you now respond properly to this switch, your problems can quickly be compounded. As experienced tennis players know, just one improperly played point can start a snowball effect that changes the entire match.

Playing the Breakdown (A Delayed Pressure) Point

When you are ahead by one point in the game (15-0, 30-15, 40-30), your objective should be to play a breakdown point. This does not mean to play tentative though! It means to continue to go after the ball but to give yourself a safer target without providing a quick target for the opponent, whose hands are going to work well. A breakdown point is used to break down the opponent's confidence and prevent him from making any great play that might switch the momentum against you.

There are two common tendencies that players have when they are ahead in a match and want to close it out. One is to rush or press for a reckless outright winner. It is like a basketball team, ahead by ten points, that comes across the 10-second line and shoots 25-footers. No coach would ever allow this to take place. He would naturally want his team to work the ball for a high percentage shot. The other tendency is to play tentatively and try to sit on the lead. This tactic would have you kill off your own momentum by not playing up to the level that you are capable of playing. Neither tendency is good, however. If you rush, or try for a "chain saw killing" as I call it, you will make mistakes. If you play safely and tentatively, you may give the opponent

an opportunity to get back into the match and maybe even take charge himself. The object is to keep control, keep the opponent's confidence low, and try to win the point by forcing the opponent into an error.

Winning tennis tactics are always best when they allow you to force an error from your opponent. This keeps you aggressive, but the error on the opponent's part dismantles his confidence. The best phrase that I use with my athletes when they play a breakdown (delayed pressure) point is to remember, Big Shots and Safe Targets! Another point that I tell my players is to hit a big shot that their opponent can get to. This keeps them from choosing poor shot selections or Checking Out of the point. It gives them the right balance of mind and body. Do not give your opponent a quick target that would play into his hand skills that are now working because he is behind. If he does start playing more aggressively and is experiencing success, you will have to use some aggressive plays to keep the upper hand and to dent his confidence further (see action-reaction guidelines; if he gives you a whack, you've got to hurt him right back). Later, when he is very far behind and pressing, you can also start to run more quick pressure plays. For the most part though, you should think about being deliberate and stingy with points when you are ahead. Play aggressively without giving many targets and continue to execute the fundamentals. At the start of each game in the set, however, it is important to once again establish the upper hand and run a play to take charge. Never play tentatively or too safely at the start of a game when you are leading in the match.

Even if you have a lead in that set, a good opponent will be constantly trying to turn the momentum back in his favor. The first points of the game always involve the least amount of pressure, and therefore the player who is behind will try to accelerate at that point. It is so very important to meet his aggression with aggression of your own, and if you win the point doing so, you will then be able to play more breakdown points and put a few more nails in his coffin. An example of this is the following situation: Your opponent is serving at 1-2, and you break his serve. It is important that you play the first two points of the next game (3-1 with you serving) aggressively to show that you will run with the lead. If you go ahead in that game 30-0, then you can play a delayed pressure point to grind your opponent down a little. A reluctance to step up at that point and take charge could allow a momentum switch back in favor of your opponent. If he responds to your aggressive play and takes a 0-30 lead, that is okay. You may have to fight extremely hard to maintain the service break that you just earned, or perhaps you may even lose the game, but to play tentative after taking the upper hand is asking for lasting trouble. I tell my players that 30-0, after the first two points are played aggressively, is great and the set is probably in the bag. A score of 15-15 is almost a sure thing also. Often, a 0-30 score will allow you to still win the game about half of the time; but absolutely, under no condition, should you play tentative when you have just taken the upper hand in the match. Another example would be as follows: let's consider the case where I am serving at 3-1 and hold serve to make it 1-4, with my opponent now serving. A very good tactic would be for me to attack him if possible off the return of serve during the first point in that next game. If I am successful, I can then play delayed pressure points and grind him down; even if I am not successful in winning that first point, I will maintain the momentum and prevent him from making a Momentum-switch.

The Breakdown (delayed pressure) points are to be played while maintaining the lead and to frustrate the opponent who wants quick targets and quick points to try to get back into the match. A comparison in basketball would be the use of a zone defense when you are ahead by eight or ten points, and there is really no sense in forcing the issue and making the opponent's game rise. Delayed pressure points are not a stalling tactic nor are they meant to be played in tentative manner waiting for the opponent to lose. A good opponent will not go down without a tough fight.

Trying for a Chain Saw Killing

In 1985 we were playing Trinity University at Corpus Christi, Texas. Jay Berger, a freshman, was playing a match against a Trinity opponent who played a great serve and volley game. Jay knew he would have his work cut out for him. Jay played excellent tennis for a set and a half by using his counter-punching ability with tremendous accuracy and speed, keeping the opponent off balance. The serve and volleyer was close to being defeated when all of a sudden at 6-2, 4-1, Jay, who is a baseliner and rarely comes into the net, started serving and volleying on every point trying to get the match over with. The tide turned quickly, and Jay lost two fast games making the score 4-3.

My main concern was not the score, but rather the momentum that had changed because of Jay's impatience and failure to stay with his own game style. Jay's style was to peck away and work every point while trying to break down his opponent's game. As a serve and volleyer, he was just not effective.

At 4-3, I walked onto the court. Jay realized that the momentum had turned, but he wasn't real excited about my having to come out on the court and he did not want to hear any coaching advice that I might give him. I walked over to him, held out my arms, and said, "Okay, hand it over." He said, "What are you talking about?" I said, "Hand over the chain saw." Then he knew what I meant because we had talked so often during the season about the mistake of a chain saw killing when closing out a match. Jay knew that the correct way to close out a match is to do the dirty work, meticulously peck and peck away until the opponent's confidence in his game completely breaks. Jay said, "Okay," and pretended to give me an imaginary chain saw. I stumbled over to the trash can and pretended to dump it in. I then walked back to where Jay was, reached in my pocket, and pretended to pull something out. I said to him, "All right, here's a chisel and ice pick. Peck away at your opponent and work the ball 10 to 15 rallies every point, but keep hitting the ball aggressively." Jay laughed and looked at me as if I were half crazy, but the point was made.

The next game was a difficult one, and it lasted a long time. Jay had problems getting back into his style of working the ball to set up each and every point. He really had to earn his points, but Jay won that game, and the next few games came a bit easier as he went on to win the set 7-5 and close out the match. From this situation I learned that even the best players have a tendency to go for a chain saw killing when they are ahead. Players simply stop setting their points up and try to win points off of the first exchanges. This method not only causes many more errors on the leader's part, but it also forces the opponent into a higher level of play.

The simple chisel and ice pick method of pecking away is a tough one to master when a player wants to finish the match. There is an incredible urge to want to finish it off in a hurry instead of forcing the dying opponent into submission. In the l985 NCAA championships, Mikel Pernfors trailed number one seeded player Jon Levine of Texas 6-3, 4-1 when Levine (who was also a baseliner) started rushing to the net and playing quick pressure. This turned the whole match. Levine started making more errors by rushing and trying to end points too quickly, and this pushed Pernfors hand skills into high gear by having to do so much counter-punching. Pernfors' won this match and went on to beat my player, Lawson Duncan, in the finals to win his first NCAA title. Duncan had beaten him 6-2, 6-1 just three weeks earlier, but did not have an answer for the Georgia Bulldog on that day. He was truly unstoppable after he had survived death in the Levine match.

Remember, the good opponent will not just quit and go away. He will fight to the end with his game in tact and his hands working. Recognizing this fact, the competitor who is leading must treat the opponent like a dying animal, that he must kill and do so decisively and without hesitation. If the job is rushed the momentum of the situation can quickly turn, but if the job is done too tentatively the opponent will escape. It is only when the player gets hold of his confidence that he does the job of winning well.

Playing Tentatively Will Never Finish Off a Tough Opponent Either!

As mentioned earlier, a common tendency for the player who is trying to close out the match to play tentatively. There is nothing more frightening than closing out an opponent and nothing scarier than killing off a wounded opponent. A player can play a perfect match, but, in the closing moments, most players turn their head from the tough and dirty job of closing it out. An opponent who is behind is always going to play better, and the player who is ahead in the match realizes this.

In l997, I had a player who had l5 break points

> F inishing a player off, especially if he is a good player, has to be one of the hardest jobs in any sport.

to beat a top opponent from Harvard, and could not find a way to convert any of them. On six of the points, his opponent made a great play, but on the other nine points, my player missed the return of second serves. He played way too tentative and careful and was far too interested in the result of the score rather than the simple execution of his strokework. He was quite upset at blowing such a good opportunity. I reminded him that his failure to convert those opportunities was a very common scenario for players who were growing quickly and that "Breakdowns usually happen before Breakthroughs." I am pleased to say that this same player went on to become an All-American. It is strange to see that the player with confidence — who is supposed to win — usually does the right thing on break points and gets the job done; whereas the underdog player either presses or pushes, both being wrong.

KEEP GOOD COURT POSITIONING WHEN THINGS ARE GOING YOUR WAY

Timid play and poor court positioning are a few of the worst tendencies for a player with the lead to show. It is court positioning that dictates the ability to control points. If a player merely moves back one or two yards on the court on ground strokes, he gives his opponent the opportunity to take charge and possibly turn the momentum.

In 1987, in an excellently played match against the eventual National Champion Georgia Bulldogs, Craig Boynton, who has a counter-punch game and usually plays long, drawn-out points, was playing against a player named John Boytim. These two players had almost identical game styles, and I felt they were in for an all-day affair unless one player played very well or very poorly.

Craig's strategy for the match was simple: He would maintain better court positioning than Boytim. If Craig could stay up in the court, his balls would fall deep, forcing Boytim's balls to fall short. Craig could then be in charge of most of the rallies, and it was critical that he maintain this control.

Craig played the first set very well and won 6-1. But at the beginning of the second set, I noticed a change. Craig, after a very, very long game which John Boytim won, stepped back from the baseline. He had been standing on the baseline or a foot inside the baseline to take all his ground strokes, but he was now a yard behind the baseline and was running from side to side, frantically trying to run down Boytim's fine-tuned shots. He was being jerked from side to side and dropped point after point. By the time I got down to the court, Craig was way down in the set that Boytim quickly won 6-2. Since the two players had identical games and were identical in just about every way, Boytim had won the set because of his better court positioning. Before the third set, I again told Craig to stand inside the baseline and take balls as early as possible. He did so, and after a couple of very tough games, he was able to turn the momentum of the match to win the set 6-3.

The tendency for a player to play tentatively is hard for a coach to recognize. It sometimes has nothing to do with tentative shots or poor stroke production. Very subtle court positioning is usually the first tentativeness that is seen. The breaking down of strokes and the player's rushing the ball only come after court positioning is given up. There is nothing tougher than finishing off a tough opponent. It takes total concentration and coverage to meticulously do the right things at the end.

Getting Your Opponent to Play Poorly

Winning tennis matches is often not so much a matter of your great play, but more a matter of getting your opponent to play poorly. Tim Wilkison was unable to do this in his match against Boris Becker in the first round of the 1987 U.S. Open. Wilkison, the heavy underdog, was ahead two sets to love and had also a service break lead in the third set. His style has always been to play with reckless abandon and to keep relentless pressure on his opponent until the opponent finally cracks. But this time his aggressive play only forced Becker to employ his survival tactics and go on to play better and better.

Earlier in the match Becker was tight and missing all of his shots, but as Wilkison forced the issue more and more, Becker just got better. Becker got well past the choking phase as he won the third set and the fourth set started. He continued to raise

his level of play until it became obvious to everyone that it was only a matter of time until his victory would be certain. By the end of the match Becker was playing excellent tennis and Wilkison was left without any bullets left in his guns.

Wilkison would have been much better off if he could have manipulated Becker into playing a bit worse by using different styles of points mixed with his best style of relentless attacking. The momentum guidelines would have suggested in this situation to play more delayed pressure points when he was ahead and when he had been successful in using a weapon. Some of the best basketball coaches succeed by using this method. At strategic times they put high pressure on their opponents, and at other times they let up on the pressure to frustrate their opponents into making mistakes. Knowing when to use each is of course the important matter, and that is why the nine points to remember for momentum management are summarized at the end of this chapter.

A Good Time for Playing the Breakdown Point (Delayed Pressure)

When you are ahead or behind by three points, ahead by two points, and sometimes when you are behind by two.

Breakdown points (Delayed Pressure) are played very effectively at 40-0 and 0-40. With a three-point lead (40-0), the pressure really lets up and your hands will not work with great precision. A long point allows you to keep concentration and prevent the possibility of a bad mistake on what seems to be a meaningless point. If you get a mistake from your opponent, it will further dismantle his confidence. Also, there is no reason to rush the last point of the game by putting quick pressure on your opponent, because there is a great chance that his hands will work very well and he will make a great passing shot. This could lift his confidence and make the next point an even tougher one. If your opponent does win the 40-0 point with an aggressive play to make it 40-15, you can follow the action-reaction guidelines and attack him back. If you lost the point with an unforced error of your own, you should play another delayed pressure point to stop the bleeding. There is absolutely no advantage in playing a quick pressure point at 40-0 though.

At 0-40, when you are behind by three points, take advantage of the fact that your opponent will probably relax and that he may give you a sloppy point. You can be sure he does not want to have to dig out a long, long point to win the game. He has probably already chalked the game up and is mentally ready to move on to the next one. But if you can win a tough point on his error and then play an aggressive point at 15-40, you can turn the whole momentum of the game. At 15-40 the action-reaction guidelines should be followed for the next point. If he makes an error, definitely attack. If you hit a winner to get the score to 15-40, then you'd want to play a delayed pressure point again. Winning this game can turn the momentum for the whole match.

Note: The Momentum Guidelines based on score should be used first, but the next immediate consideration should be on how was the new score arrived at. Follow the action-reaction guidelines that are listed to become adept at this.

If you win the first two points of the game to go up 30-0, or if you win two points in a row to go up 40-15 in a game, a breakdown (delayed pressure point) is usually the best to play. You can always play a quick pressure point if you are not successful if the opponent makes an aggressive play to come back in the game to 30-15 to maintain the momentum. (If that happens, Follow the Action-Reaction guideline — If he gives you a whack, you should hurt him right back.)

There are some instances where you are down 0-30 or 15-40, and have just made a bad mistake, the play may sometimes be to run a delayed pressure point to stop your bleeding and also set up the aggressive play at 15-30, or 30-40. Most likely you would opt to attack in an effort to prevent a conversion (three points in a row) by your opponent. This is a decision that you have to make based on where your confidence level is and what you are attempting to set up in later points. If your opponent has just hit a winner to get the two point advantage, you definitely should run an aggressive play to respond.

MOMENTUM MOTTO FOR PLAYING A BREAKDOWN (DELAYED PRESSURE) POINT: *When you are in the lead, be aggressive early in the game and then slowly make your opponent bleed.*

The breakdown (delayed pressure) point guidelines are:

1. Your objective is to keep in charge of the game and tempo while preventing a MO switch.
2. Do not allow your opponent a quick target that could switch MO and give him confidence.
3. Force the error, stay in control of the tempo, hit through your opponent (use Wardlaw directional guidelines) and break him down.
4. Keep good fundamentals intact, and maintain good court positioning.
5. Keep confident and deliberate body language.
6. BIG SHOTS, SAFE TARGETS!!!!!!!!!
7. If your opponent makes a great shot when he is behind, realize that he did because he had to. Simply say "Good shot," and prepare to play the next point aggressively using the action-reaction guidelines.

SWITCHING MOMENTUM

What do You do if You are Behind?

Remembering your opponent's tendency to play a little sloppy when he is ahead is a big advantage. He may have periods of brilliance because of less pressure, but at some point he will play worse as he tries to preserve his lead. His tendencies at this point will be either to rush or to play a bit tentatively. When you are behind, you will play tougher and your shots will work better in order to put pressure back on your opponent. Therefore; attack and take the offensive.

Momentum is never turned by tentative play. All great competitors realize that they must attack or raise their level of play when they are behind. Unforced errors, however, will only put you in a deeper hole if you are behind, so it is essential to attack decisively and, if possible, without errors. You must play within your range as you attack. I usually tell players to use aggressive plays and to make aggressive shots but to aim at big targets.

This helps them to miss less when they use a heavy attacking style. Another coaching tip I offer is hit through the opponent with big shots, and miss long if you miss, but never wide or in the net. Missing long is just a physical error where the hands didn't get the racket head through the ball fast enough — to miss in the net or wide is definitely a mental mistake and an indication that you are afraid of your opponent. This must be corrected immediately to have a chance to win. There is also a tendency to lose confidence in your game when you are losing and to desperately try different things. This is also wrong. It is critical keep your confidence intact and maintain trust in your game.

When behind in the game by one point (0-15, 15-30, 30-40, or ad out), it is very important to run an aggressive play. If you are overly cautious, your confidence will decrease, and your opponent's confidence will increase. Playing aggressively to switch momentum does not mean taking unnecessary risks in your shot making. It means to run an aggressive (quick pressure) play, but to still use safe targets with your big shots. Playing a bit more aggressively mentally and digging into a long point can sometimes also be effective. Sometimes just aggressive and positive emotion can change the course of a match. No one enjoys the process of having to close out an opponent who keeps fighting and attacking.

A good thought to remember about using momentum guidelines properly when trying to close out a tough match when you're ahead versus situations when you are trying to keep from getting beat is the statement "Always win boring by using your stingy fundamentals, and when you lose, always go down in an exciting fashion while taking the attack to your opponent."

Playing the MO-Switch (Quick Pressure) Point

Whenever you are behind, your game plan should be executed aggressively within your own limitations. If you are a serve and volley player, be sure to put pressure on the opponent with your first serve and first volley. For a baseliner, it may again be a matter of being hardheaded and playing with more enthusiasm and emotion. Whatever your game style, be aggressive when you are behind and look for every opportunity to take the attack to your opponent.

Figure 12-1. Run an aggressive play when you are behind.

When a player is behind, he may have a tendency to lie back and lick his wounds and hope that the opponent will just let up and allow him back into the match. This will never work though. Good opponents will close the door, and any progress in the winning direction will have to be made by the losing player himself. Secondly, a player who is behind sometimes stops believing in his shotmaking ability and comes out of his normal game to try and play beyond his limitations. This further complicates the situation by giving away too many free points on errors.

When a player is behind, his game plan should be executed within his limitations. But whatever a player's game style, he must play aggressively when behind, doing his best to avoid making unforced errors that would allow the opponent to gain even more momentum. He must be fearless, and he must dictate the tempo of the points played. Tentative play will never turn a match in your favor unless you are very lucky.

> ### Aggressive is not how hard you hit the ball. Aggressive is a state of the mind.
> — *Carlos Goffi*

A Great MO-Switch

I learned an important lesson at the 1985 NCAA Championships. Kelly Jones and Carlos Dilaura of Pepperdine were playing a team from Harvard in the NCAA Doubles quarterfinals. The Harvard team had played flawless tennis for a set and a half and were ahead 6-3, 4-1. It seemed as if Jones and Dilaura could not get on track. Just when I thought the match was over Kelly Jones started hitting balls as hard as he could right at the opponents and began charging the net with seemingly uncontrolled aggression. Kelly was famous for his "chain saw killer tennis" mentality, and he played this "Go for Broke" kind of tennis very well. He seemed particularly reckless now, and I wondered if he had completely lost control. He hit a couple of returns right at the net man and drilled one overhead ball so hard and with such enthusiasm that I thought he had broken the ball. It was amazing that a game later the Harvard team's every move seemed more calculated and more tentative. Their court positioning moved a few feet back into the court while the Pepperdine team seemed to move in closer on all of their shots. Jones's recklessness also picked up his partner, Dilaura, and they came back into the match winning a close second set and finally a 6-2 third set decision.

After the match I asked Kelly, "What were you doing when you were behind 4-1 in the second set? You seemed almost wild in your play." He answered, "Well, I knew we were going to lose the match and I had to try something. I sure didn't want to go down easy. All I did was play recklessly and try to scare them or throw them off their game." I looked at him and wondered if he recognized his genius as a competitor.

A player's ability to be reckless and fearless when he is behind is his ability to turn matches around at any point on any day. Some players can never be taught this, and some are so afraid of losing that they will never let go even if they know that their style of game will ultimately result in a loss.

A player should win with fundamentals, but he should always lose dictating the action with aggressive play.

Jones and Dilaura went on to win not only the next match, but also the NCAA Championship. It was Jones's second NCAA Doubles Championship in a row. I never forgot that match, and I refer to it when my players are in a tight spot. The lesson is: Be aggressive when you are behind and if you're going to go down, go down swinging and in a fearless manner.

THE MOMENTUM MOTTO FOR PLAYING FROM BEHIND: *"When you're trying to come back, stay very patient with your fundamentals but always be on the attack!"*

> ### The MO-switch guidelines are:
> 1. You must attack—if you are going to lose, lose aggressively, dictating the tempo.
> 2. No unforced errors—stay within your limitations, keep your confidence intact and trust your shots.
> 3. Dictate the tempo between and during shots.
> 4. Use big shots and safe targets
> 5. Appear fearless to your opponent.

CREATING MOMENTUM AT THE TOP OF THE MOUNTAIN

What do you do when the score is tied?

I often refer to these situations as take-charge or bread-and-butter situations. When the score is tied, I tell my players that they are at the top of the mountain — the pressure on each player is about the same. The player who takes charge of the game at that time will usually win not just that game but also create extra momentum for the next game to come. It is important for the player to go with his best and favorite plays at this point. "Regular stuff is good enough" is the term that I use. It is at the top of the mountain or when the score is tied when the confident player does not hesitate to step forward and take the lead. If he is confident taking and keeping the lead, he will also be confident when the time comes to close the match out.

The player who comes from behind to win the last point has a bit more momentum, but each player has the same objective — take charge and create momentum. That player who lost his game-point opportunity may be a bit down or his confidence may be a little hurt, but it is extremely critical that he recognizes the importance of taking back charge of the game. Lock into your style very stubbornly at these times and carry out that style aggressively with confidence.

Playing the MO (Top of the Mountain) Point

At the top of the mountain (when the score is tied), the best play is almost always to go with whatever you have the most confidence in doing. If you are a serve and volleyer, you should serve and volley. If you are an attacking player but do not wish to serve and volley, then serve and get to the net on the second ball (the wide and glide, or the serve and approach method is best). If you are a counter-puncher or an aggressive baseliner, then aggressive Wardlaw Directional guidelines are the best to use. It doesn't matter as much that the play is successful as it does you go with what you want to do. "Deal on or be Dealt upon" is the phrase that I tell my players. Do not wait around for good fortune or for the fairy godmother to award you the lead in a very tough game. You must take it. By taking it with your bread and butter play, your confidence will grow for future close games.

> **I**n planning strategies, be willing to lose a battle in order to win the war.

If you win the top of the mountain point, you will then go to the delayed pressure tactic for being ahead; but if you lose it, you must be willing to risk the whole game and attack from the ad-out position. Even if the play you run does not work, you must be assertive and confident in these critical situations. The confidence that you play with late in the match will be the same as the confidence that you show in early critical situations. Do the right thing! Run the right play! Go with your bread and butter! Don't sell out and play it safe! The top of the mountain is where the confident player shows up, and the other guy goes away.

THE MOMENTUM MOTTO FOR PLAYING AT THE TOP OF THE MOUNTAIN IS: *When the score is tied, the rule is really not tough, always go with your aggressive fundamentals remembering that regular stuff is good enough.*

> *To create momentum, the guidelines are:*
> 1. Take charge with your favorite style.
> 2. Go with your strengths (your bread and butter).
> 3. Dictate match flow.
> 4. Act, don't react.
> 5. Being comfortable taking the lead at each opportunity will make closing out a match easier.

AN ILLUSTRATION OF FUNDAMENTALS OF MOMENTUM MANAGEMENT BASED ON THE SCORE

A story I often use to illustrate the basic rules of momentum control is one about two men who are fighting at the top of a cliff. Both men are in a life-and-death situation and both are desperately struggling to throw the other one over the cliff. The long fall and the jagged rocks below present thoughts of a terrible and painful death.

As the two men struggle, it is easy to see that there are three positions each man can be in: *1) the in-charge position trying to push the opponent off, 2) the desperate, losing position trying to prevent being pushed off or 3) a neutral position, side by side, where neither has the advantage.*

In the first position (maintaining momentum), the only obvious way to mess up is to rush, which could cause a stumble that sends you over the cliff, or to act tentative and turn away from the dirty job at hand, thereby allowing your opponent a chance to regroup and get back on steady ground. Neither the first (chain saw) method nor the second (tentative) method will work. The decisive, chisel-and-ice-pick method of dissecting the opponent with your solid fundamentals is the way to finish him off. Remember — you have the better position, you are in control. Peck away at the opponent, no matter how hard that be, and stay with your game.

At the beginning of each of the next games that you start out leading, it is very important to play aggressively early in the game to keep control of the momentum that you have established. Do not play tentative at the start of any game. Your opponent can switch momentum on you very easily if you back off and try to protect a lead. Again, delayed pressure means that you keep pressure on the opponent, but you don't give him a quick target to use when he is anxious for one to catch up to. These delayed pressure points or breakdown points are always set up by taking control of the situation first and then taking away the targets.

Review of Rule #1 is for when you are ahead: *When you're in the lead, hurt your opponent early in the game and then slowly make him bleed.*

The second position (switching momentum) is a tough one. Your opponent is pushing you steadily back to the edge of the cliff. He is cold-blooded and tough and is neither rushing nor being tentative. You can play possum and act as if you are giving up, but this will work only temporarily. If you are tentative or afraid, you will go over the cliff quickly. You must square off, look him directly in the eyes, and attack him back. Smart aggression is the best, but reckless aggression is better than no aggression at all. You must dent your opponent's confidence. Once you can reverse the position, you must be ready to do your own dirty work

quickly and without hesitation. Letting a wounded opponent survive is dangerous. If you do so, he will become fearless, and it will be even more difficult to finish him off.

Review of Rule #2 is for when you're trying to come from behind: *When you're trying to come back, keep patient with your fundamentals but stay on the attack.*

The third position (creating momentum), where neither fighter has an advantage, is one situation that tests your confidence and trust in your skills. Each fighter spars and trades blows. Back and forth it goes, each fighter trying to gain some kind of an advantage. You have two choices: You either go with your bread and butter and your best tools, or you try something else that you are probably not as good at. Actually, there is no choice. In order to gain any advantage, even against a bigger, stronger or more experienced opponent, you must go with your bread and butter because that is the fight plan you know best. Whatever is your best tool, use it now to take the lead.

Review of Rule #3 is for when the score is tied or it's even-steven going into any critical points and neither opponent has the advantage: *When the score is tied and things are even, the rule is really not that tough. Stay aggressive with your fundamentals while remembering that regular stuff is always good enough.*

Figure 12-2. It is important for a player to always remain mindful of the powerful role that momentum plays in a match.

Climbing the Momentum Mountain
Score Guideline for Momentum

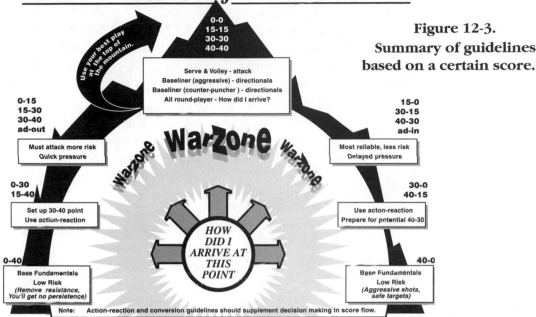

Figure 12-3.
Summary of guidelines based on a certain score.

Note: Action-reaction and conversion guidelines should supplement decision making in score flow.

MANAGING MOMENTUM BASED ON THE EVENTS LEADING UP TO A CERTAIN SCORE

Basketball coaches learn to manage momentum based on the score, but the main focus of their momentum control is on what has just happened and its effect on the flow of the game. Their considerations are like, "Is the other team on a roll? Did my team just make some bad mistakes? Is the other team cracking? Is it time to speed up play? Is it time to slow down play? Should we play a zone defense? Is it time to fast break and pick up the defensive pressure?"

Of course, in basketball and in other sports, the coach can slow down or speed up play by making substitutions, calling time-outs and sending players in from the bench. In tennis, the coach cannot do this, and each player must have a good knowledge and understanding of how to manage this flow.

The tennis player's response to how he arrives at a score and what happened last is an important factor in momentum. Your opponent's good and bad shots, as well as your good and bad shots, should be handled properly as well as those points where no dominance is gained.

ACTION-REACTION FLOW MANAGEMENT GUIDELINES

There are five situations that you as a player must respond to properly during a match:

1. Your opponent has just made a bad mistake.
2. Your opponent has just made a good shot.
3. You have just made a bad mistake.
4. You have just made a good shot.
5. You have just won a long point in which there was no dominance determined.

MOMENTUM MOTTOS

After your opponent's:

♦ Bad shot — challenge his confidence and put pressure on him right away.
♦ Good shot — say "Good Shot" and then attack him right back.

After your:

♦ Bad shot — regroup with your fundamentals.
♦ Good shot — allow yourself to feel good about it and go to your favorite fundamental.

After a long point:

♦ Run the right play according to the score.

If Your Opponent Has Just Made a Bad Mistake

Bad mistakes at critical times in a match are not usually physical mistakes but are often related to nerves. This is especially true on fundamental shots. If your opponent makes a bad mistake when he is behind by a point or errs on a critical game point, this may be an indication that he is cracking and is losing confidence. You should speed up your play a bit by attacking him with quick pressure and see how he reacts. If he responds, it is evident that he is not finished, and you have more work to do. If he doesn't or cannot respond, the start of the end may be right there. Even if it is early in the match, a show of confidence and a take charge attitude at this time can cause your opponent's confidence to be damaged early.

MOMENTUM MOTTO AFTER YOUR OPPONENT'S BAD MISTAKE: *If your opponent makes a bad mistake, a quick point you should try to take.*

If Your Opponent Has Just Made a Great Shot

The tendency here, of course, is to get a bit scared. After your opponent's great play, you may begin wondering if the opponent is really that good or if you can stay with him. Many players feel like retreating and licking their wounds, but this is definitely the wrong response. The attack must be taken back to your opponent.

After an opponent's basket, good basketball teams are trained to get the ball inbounds and down the floor as quickly as possible and attempt to score to negate their opponent's score. If they do not get the quick score, they then set up a calculated and well-planned play, but they always try to neutralize the opponent's success. In tennis, the proper response to an opponent's great play is to take the attack right back at the opponent. This prevents any confidence gain by the opponent and keeps your confidence from being damaged as well. If it does not work, you can then regroup and run a play based on the score guidelines to switch the momentum.

> # B
> e quick to take advantage of an advantage.

Giving a Whack Back

In the 1987 ACC Championship football game between Clemson and Maryland, the most important play of the ball game was just such a situation. Clemson was favored, but Maryland was a tough opponent. Clemson was ahead by three when the Maryland quarterback hit his tight end over the middle with a strong pass and a 78-yard touchdown. This put Maryland ahead 7-3. On the next series of downs, I sat in my seat watching with the hope that Clemson would try to hurt Maryland right back. This Clemson team was definitely a running football team and seldom used the pass. I was not quite sure what the Clemson coaching staff would do, and as I watched three consecutive running plays, I was disappointed. Although Clemson had gained a first down, trying for a long drive with Maryland in the lead could have dangerous repercussions. If they stopped Clemson's drive, they would be in control of the momentum, both offensively and defensively. Then it happened! On the first play of the second series, the Clemson quarterback faked a hand-off up the middle and dropped back quickly to find his own tight end open across the middle. A well-delivered pass and a 65-yard run gave Clemson the lead and a major MO switch.

This dampened Maryland's confidence greatly and from then on Clemson dominated. It ended 45-10 in a blowout. I wondered as I left the ball game what might have happened if Clemson had played tentatively after they had been hurt by Maryland's great touchdown. In tennis and most other sports, countering your opponent's good play with a good play of your own is an important aspect of momentum management. The consequences for not being aggressive right back may allow the opponent to steamroll you with his confidence.

MOMENTUM MOTTO WHEN YOUR OPPONENT HAS JUST MADE A GREAT PLAY: *If he gives you a whack, you must hurt him right back!*

If You Have Just Made a Bad Mistake; How to Regroup

Most athletes and coaches recognize that after a bad mistake it is critical to take time to slow down, to regroup, and to prevent things from snowballing against you. If possible, it is time to call a time-out. Even so, the human tendency is to want to make up for the mistake right away. Too often, however, this leads to another bad mistake and the start of the snowball effect which must be prevented.

A golf coach once told me that it is not your bad shot, but rather the shot after the bad shot that is critical. Sometimes a series of bad shots occurs because a player panics over a miscue. Knowledge of momentum along with the insight to run the right play can help the athlete think rather than react to his emotions in this situation. The best thing to do after a bad shot, therefore, is to slow down and think about the play to run instead of following the emotions. The first priority should be to stop the bleeding and then move forward again. A description that I use with my team for this situation is to ask them to imagine falling down a mountain that they are trying to climb. When they are falling, they must first stop the negative fall, turn around, and then start back up the mountain with little steps first. Only after they stop the negative can they start moving toward their goal again.

MOMENTUM MOTTO AFTER YOUR OWN BAD MISTAKE: *If your bad shot has you in a fret, regroup with your fundamentals, and don't start until you are set!*

If You Have Just Made a Great Shot; How to Keep the Flow Going

Like tennis, golf has a way of keeping a person humble and helping him keep things in perspective. One day, after a short year of playing this game, I drove a ball from the second tee some 230 yards straight down the middle of the fairway. What a shot! The Best Tee Shot of my short career! It felt so good. I just knew that I could do it again, even though I was still 220 yards from the cup. I lined up with the same stance and same club that I had used for my great tee shot. Without hesitation or doubt, I lined up and let my swing rip toward the ball that I knew would carry to the green. The rest is obvious. What could have possessed me to use my driver off of the fairway? What kind of stupidity was that? The only green that my ball found was the forest of trees way to the right of the out-of-bounds. The next three shots were even more stupid as I tried to recover with high risk attempts. My potential birdie turned into an eleven. I was trying to play out of my limitations. The right play would have been to use my 5-wood, which I hit very well, and make a routine approach shot to the front of the green.

The lesson for tennis is the same. There are times during a match when your shots feel so good that you think you can do anything at all with the ball. The natural tendency is to try to play better and better and better, but instead your game collapses. One of the things that I remind my players of is that the loser of a match often plays great shots right before he finally collapses. He stops playing the game and tries to win everything back in a hurry with desperation first exchange winners. This tactic may be successful for a short time, and may scare you, but it usually is the start of the end for that player. He is usually his pressing to play above his limitations.

Therefore, after you hit your best shot, keep your play at a high level, but remember that you have to still keep playing the game. You cannot rely on first exchange winners alone to win. Good shots will be there during a tough match, but even so, it is solid fundamentals that wins tennis matches. Simply accept a great shot and run the next appropriate play. Staying within the upper limitations of your fundamentals is the way to achieve consistent results. Do not be afraid of physically playing well when it happens though. Let it go and trust your shots. Do not consciously try to "Zone or Tree" though.

MOMENTUM MOTTO AFTER YOUR GREAT SHOT: *After you've hurt your opponent and he's started to bleed, delayed pressure to fester the wound is what you really need.*

High Tech Equipment Teases Players into Trying to "Zone"

It is very interesting to me as a coach that since the advent of the super-rackets in the mid-l980s, players do a very poor job of understanding and knowing where there mid-range or average game is at. The High tech equipment fools them into thinking that their norm is much better than it usually is. I believe that they therefore try very stupid shots because they just don't have an accurate barometer for their shot making abilities. Many players never really learn what they can and can't do with the ball consistently. Coaches complain these days continually that players neither have the will nor the know-how to develop fundamentals that will hold up under pressure. I believe that this is one of the real tragedies of the equipment revolution and is a prevalent problem for learning in any sport whenever equipment becomes more important than the skill level that is involved.

If You Have Just Won a Long, Tough Point, and Neither You nor Your Opponent Gained Momentum

After a long, tough point, you should expect another long, tough point. No dominance or momentum has been established, so running the right play based on the score is the best approach to take. These points are comparable to grinding out tough third down conversions in football or making a tough basket after seven or eight passes on the basketball court. No real momentum is established other than scoring the point. Many of these points must be won during the course of the match.

SUMMARY OF WHAT TO DO BASED ON ACTION-REACTION GUIDELINES

The example that I often use to summarize what to do to control momentum based on what has just happened is to have two players act as if they are boxing. Your opponent's good and bad shots, as well as your good and bad shots, should be reacted to properly. I'll have one player act as if he lands a punch, and the other player will counter-punch. *(If he gives you a whack, you should hurt him right back.)* I'll then have the first player swing and miss with his punch, and then have the second player come in from the other side with a punch to his off-balance opponent. *(If he makes a bad mistake, A quick point I will try to take.)* The third scenario is for the player to throw a punch that misses its mark, and I have him immediately retreat one step and cover up until he regains control of his skills before his opponent can take advantage of his mistake. *(If my bad shot has me in a fret, I should regroup with my fundamentals and don't start until I'm set.)* The last scenario has my player landing a very good offensive punch, and then going in for short jabs to solidify that punch and keep the upper hand while preventing a counter-attack. *(After I've hurt my opponent and he's started to bleed, delayed pressure to fester the wound is what I really need.)*

THE CONVERSION THEORY OF BOB LOVE: THE FINISHING TOUCH ON MOMENTUM CONTROL

An important concept in momentum management was taught to me by Bob Love, a good friend and one of the few people in America today to have done research on psychological momentum. He has studied momentum in Tennis but also likes to study how flow changes in volleyball as well because of its very noticeable up and down cycles. When he learned of my work with momentum management and I of his, we got together to share notes and ideas. His conversion theory was an exciting concept to me because in nearly every case, it correlated perfectly with my work on momentum control.

A conversion is defined as winning three consecutive points. Bob Love's conversion theory states that the key to winning tennis matches and controlling match flow is to focus on two objectives: 1) make conversions for yourself, (trying to win three points in a row) and 2) to prevent your opponent from making conversions. (Try to keep him from getting three points in a row.)

The scoring system in tennis dictates that whenever a player is behind by a point (15-30, 30-40, and ad-out), he has to win three points in a row to win the game. The wisdom of this theory is more far reaching than this fact though. The most important aspect of the theory to me as a coach is that the favored player is usually very comfortable winning three points in succession at any time in the match. For the underdog, one point well played and won is very common, whereas two well-played points in a row usually satisfies his appetite, and winning three consecutive points is usually uncomfortable and too much of a burden for him. The underdog always reaches his comfort level of achievement long before the favored player does. It is helpful to realize this to understand why the underdog usually does not win in tennis and in many other sports. With this realization, and the recognition of the importance of making and preventing conversions, the following two rules can be established.

MOMENTUM MOTTO FOR BOB LOVE CONVERSION THEORY: *Three in a row starts the flow!*

> 1. To make a conversion: After the second point won in a row, do not slow down between the points, therefore preventing your opponent from regrouping. Win the third point with solid fundamentals and try to force the error from your opponent.
> 2. To prevent a conversion: After your opponent scores the second point in a row, take time between points to regroup. Tie your shoe, go back to the fence, or do whatever it takes to give you time to decide exactly which play you want to run. In trying to prevent the third point, play an aggressive MO-switch point. You must regain confidence and try to dent your opponent. Above all, do not allow your opponent to stay on this upward flow.

Bob Love's conversion theory fits almost perfectly into the momentum control guidelines based on the score of the game. In using both concepts together, a player can see when the conversion theory dictates that an aggressive (momentum) point should be played (after losing two points in a row the score is either ad-out, 15-40, or 0-30). The same is true when the conversion theory specifies to play a breakdown delayed pressure point. (After winning two points in a row, the score is usually ad-out if your opponent is serving, and ad-in if you are serving. The only exception is at 30-0 and 40-15, where a momentum (top of the mountain) point is specified.)

The player who can use the momentum control concepts has an invaluable edge during competition. All three concepts — momentum control based on score, momentum control based on the events leading up to a certain score, and momentum control using the conversion theory — can be used independently or together. The more adept the player becomes at using all three, the greater the advantage he will have in controlling this seemingly magical power that greatly affects all sporting events.

HOW TO USE THE TIME BETWEEN POINTS TO HELP MANAGE MOMENTUM

A very obvious reality that most players fail to capitalize on is the fact that there is considerably more time between points than the actual time spent playing points. The average point at Wimbledon is now about 4 to 5 seconds and the average point at the French open has been reported to be right around 10 seconds in length. The time that is allowed between points is 25 seconds and there is one minute thirty seconds allowed to the players for changing sides of the court. Therefore, it is extremely important to recognize that what a player does during that time between points and between games has much to do with his or her performance and the ability to manage momentum of the match. The best players all have very definite routines that they use to help them during these times when they are not actually hitting the ball.

I explain to my players that there are four different scenarios to respond to after the completion of a point. They are:

I HAVE JUST MADE A BAD ERROR: In this case, my players' routine is to put their racket in their opposite hand and to walk back to the fence and to touch it. Touching it signals the end of the previous point and that they should move on to the next point. I ask them to try to control their breathing and their eyes; perhaps to look at their strings or their shoes. Do not let the eyes wander outside of the court. Get a narrow focus for the eyes. I tell them to then take as much time as possible and to think about the Momentum Play that they want to play on the next point. (Follow momentum guidelines for score and for action-reaction) Show confident body language and start the next point.

I HAVE JUST MADE A GREAT SHOT: In this case, my players' routine is to turn away from their opponent and to allow themselves to feel good about their good play. It is O.K. to say something like "Yes," or "Way to go," or "I'm the Man," as long as it is never directed toward the opponent and is not obnoxious. It is important to feel good and confident when you do good thing. I again ask my players to walk back and touch the fence to signal to themselves the end of the previous point and to get ready for the upcoming point. A couple extra seconds should be taken to decide what play that should be run according to momentum guidelines (follow momentum guidelines for score and for action-reaction). Show confident body language and start the next point.

MY OPPONENT HAS JUST MADE A BAD ERROR: In this case, it is important to recognize that the opponent's confidence may be slightly hurt, and it is a great opportunity to take advantage of the situation. I have my players turn and walk back to the baseline to start the next point an say to himself, "O.K., this is my chance to take the attack to my opponent and take the upper hand." I want them to accelerate the tempo slightly between the points and to show confidence with their body language. Run the right play according to the momentum guidelines. Do not hesitate. This could be the opportunity to open up the match. If the opponent responds, then you will just have to continue on until the next opportunity.

MY OPPONENT HAS JUST MADE A GREAT SHOT: In this case the first response is to say "Good Shot" or "Well Done" or to say something that takes the pressure off of yourself. Doing this shows confidence to your opponent and keeps you in a something-to-gain situation. This simple act is one of the most useful tools that I have ever discovered in a player helping himself to keep the proper balance of pressure on himself during a heated battle. You should then walk briskly back to the baseline without taking much extra time and say to yourself, "Now it's my turn to whack him back." Always run an aggressive play under the momentum guidelines for score and action-reaction for the next point.

In summary, after your own great shot or bad shot, you should take as much time as necessary to regroup and then run a good fundamental play. I have my players go back to the fence and actually touch it before they start the next point to signify the end of the previous point and the start of the next. After your opponent's great shot or bad shot, you should take a bit less time and then run a more aggressive play. The time between the actual playing of the point is a critical period of time to manage if momentum is work for your benefit.

POINTS TO REMEMBER ABOUT MOMENTUM MANAGEMENT

1. Don't sell out. In the long run winning the point is not as important as controlling momentum.

2. It is essential to manage momentum in each game, but be aware of momentum swings within each set and throughout the whole match. Major momentum swings are often a result of crises situations, such as bad line calls, equipment problems, unnecessary delays, injuries, or rain. Take extra time when these things occur to regroup your thoughts.

3. When the momentum is definitely against you, take time to do whatever it takes to regroup your thoughts. When you start the point again, remember that your objective, more than winning the point, is to turn the momentum by dictating what should happen during that point.

4. Your opponent's great shot should never prevent you from executing your own game plan and dictating the flow, nor should your bad mistakes keep you from dictating your game plan as well. Run the right play, regardless of whether or not you are winning points by doing it early in the match. It will pay off late in the match.

5. Never let your confidence "dam" break when you are behind. Stay in the match mentally until the momentum swings back to you again.

6. Your opponent should never feel like he played well against you in victory or defeat. Controlling the momentum will prevent this.

7. Be able to recognize your opponent's checkout winners or checkout losers. Checking out of a point means his concentration is waning or that he feels too much pressure. It is a way of not dealing with the pressure and not taking care of the ball. The opponent just slaps the ball haphazardly. These checkouts should never worry you. It should only give you confidence in thinking that your opponent is about ready to crack.

8. The correct flow of the match is very much like running a three-mile race: Start swiftly, but then settle into your own pace and comfort zone. Finally, keep enough left to sprint or to play your very best at the finish line. Starting too fast is like sprinting the first one-half mile; you will fade at the end, whereas starting too slowly puts you so far behind that you will never generate the tempo to be in a position to win the race.

9. Breakdown break games: This type of game should be played when you are already ahead by a service break and working for the second break. Although you should be aggressive on the first point of the game to keep control, the rest of the game should be primarily made up of breakdown points to prevent your opponent from making any great shots and gaining momentum. The exception is to prevent a conversion if your opponent does get momentum.

FINAL MOMENTUM CONSIDERATIONS

When first learning the momentum sequences, it is helpful to learn the conversion theory first, then the momentum based on the events leading up to a certain score, followed by the momentum based on the score. This is the most practical sequence for learning how to control momentum.

The Tournament

You will seldom go through an entire tournament without poorly played matches and close escapes from disaster. Almost all tournament champions have to come from behind more than once during a tournament. Take your bad matches in stride. Kick the ball over to win if you have to when you are playing poorly. Remember, when you cannot be pretty, you need to play gritty.

The Match

Remember that you will always have to either get ahead and stay ahead, or come from behind to win matches. You must be comfortable and be able to execute in each role.

The Set

Regardless of the games you lose, always play the game point the way you want to play it. You dictate momentum. Never give up the momentum to win a point, a game, a set or a match. It will haunt you later. Execute! Execute! Execute! No checkouts, no checkouts, no checkouts!

SUMMARY

1. Basic momentum guidelines. When you are even, play a MO point; when you are ahead, play a breakdown point; when you are behind, play a MO-switch point.

2. Action-reaction guidelines. How you arrive at a score is as important as the score. It is important to know what to do after your opponent's bad mistake or good shot, after your bad mistake or good shot, or after winning a long point where no dominance has been established.

4. Bob Love's conversion theory. Try to win three consecutive points and prevent opponents from winning three consecutive points. Know how to prevent and make conversions.

Take Time to Evaluate Your Match

• •

evaluate. After a loss, the athlete is usually reluctant to go back through the pain that comes with analysis of the event. Most opt to forget about it and try to move on. The problem with that approach is that most likely the same mistakes will continue to happen time and time again. I call this the "Groundhog Day Syndrome" named after the movie "Groundhog Day." In that movie, the main character, Bill Murray, had to keep living the same day and the same events over and over again until he made some corrections. He was only able to move on to the next day after he got the process for his approach to life worked out in an unselfish way. And so it is with the game of tennis. The failure to take advantage of the opportunity to learn from a loss will nearly always retard growth of one's potential.

> **I**f you make a mistake and fail to correct it, you have already made another mistake.

The emotional pain that results from losing is an extremely important part of the learning process and often avoided by the athlete. Randi Mani, a top teacher in the New York area, once stated that "Pain is not the enemy; pain is the only thing of value that is given to the athlete for free."

I have a formula called L-FIDO for my players which means "Learn — Forget It, Drive On!" The learning part usually cannot happen without some pain and accurate evaluation. Losing is an absolute reality of tennis. Bobby Blair, a top U.S. coach, stated in a seminar that my team attended that "In tennis, you must lose; your main goal should be to figure out how to lose less."

Most people are usually down on what they're not up to. One of the hardest things for a coach to do is to convince an athlete of the importance of accurate evaluation after a match. After a win, the athlete usually does not have a keen sense of urgency to

While watching a collegiate event together, a father of one of the opposing players once said to me, "You know, most of these players have spent as much time playing tennis and trying to perfect that skill as a brain surgeon would have spent at medical school. Then why is it that you see them continuously repeating mistakes that are always going to be losing scenarios for them? It just doesn't make any sense that some don't learn at a faster rate." His statement has remained with me for a long time and has taught me the very important lesson of accurate and immediate feedback for the player after competition.

What happens after a match can be just as important as the procedure before the match. Since a lot of time and preparation have gone into planning for and playing the match, it is important for players to receive immediate and long-term feedback after wins and losses. The way the coach handles this situation can often hasten or delay the athlete's growth. In addition, the coach must address the player's physical, mental and emotional needs. The right timing and approach to these areas is important. Chapter 19 includes a detailed description of the use of positive and negative feedback as well as a discussion of long-range affirmation guidelines.

POST-MATCH CONSIDERATIONS FOLLOWING A LOSS

Some losses are harder to take than others. The sting of some losses is just a little worse and lasts just a little longer. There is always a fine balance that a coach looks for in an athlete's reaction to a loss. The extreme reactions of discouragement and despair are not positive, nor is it positive to minimize a loss or avoid dealing with it at all.

In some situations in which the athlete has invested a great deal in his training, the loss will hurt more than if he were casual about his preparation. The player who takes a loss hard may make the mistake of not training well or not making a full commitment to his preparation for the next match. Usually, the greater the commitment the greater the pain in losing. At the same time, without commitment the chance of succeeding is much less. Losing to an underdog can be painful, and in team match play, losses bear an added stigma because others rely on you to perform. Sometimes an athlete feels it is better not to try his hardest rather than to risk committed failure once again.

Whatever the reason, the coach must be aware if the athlete withdraws energy before, during or after the competition and performs less than his best. This is an obvious defense mechanism and must be dealt with. Lack of commitment to a match and/or to the game of tennis itself is common, especially in more talented athletes. The coach should always remember that the athlete does care or else he would not have spent hundreds of hours working at the sport. As a coach, though, you always wonder, "Can I get this player to care and to make a commitment?"

Another situation is one in which the athlete takes his loss very hard and stays in a depressed state for a long time afterward. This reaction to a loss can be equally counterproductive. Some athletes always seem to take losses hard and will

often replay the critical parts of the event over and over in their heads. As a coach, you want a player to care a lot, but you also recognize that this attitude may hurt later performances and could affect his whole concept of competition.

The coach wants the athlete to separate the match he has just lost from his feelings of self-worth. A coach once said to me about Kent Kinnear, a player on my team, "When you win against Kent, you merely beat his tennis game, you never seem to beat him." Kent's approach to competition is very mature and is hard to learn, but it is one that the coach and athlete should strive for. His longevity on the tour is proof of his great balance of character.

Figure 13-1. When the true competitor suffers a loss in tennis, it is the match alone that is lost — not self-confidence.

Figures 13-2 and 13-3 illustrate the effects of losing confidence and I often show them to my players. Figure 13-2 shows the athlete whose confidence is totally determined by winning and losing and its upward/downward swing. Figure 13-3 shows the athlete whose confidence grows from a win, but stays the same in a loss. Winning should be a chance for confidence, and losing should be a chance for growth.

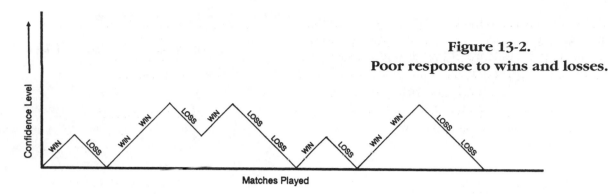

**Figure 13-2.
Poor response to wins and losses.**

The physical, mental and emotional aspects of the athlete must be dealt with after a loss beginning with the emotional aspects. Usually the athlete needs a few moments to himself. Nothing concrete can be accomplished until the emotions have settled. The coach must be able to read the situation immediately and then administer to the athlete's needs with a scolding or encouragement.

A scolding should be given only if the coach is certain that the athlete did not give his best effort. If, on the other hand, the athlete has given his best effort, a loss is the coach's opportunity to build his player up. The coach should compliment the athlete on his effort and on the positive things that took place in the match. The coach may appear disappointed, but he must not look as if he has doubts about his player. Another good practice is for the coach to help the athlete give credit to the victor. This shows class and allows the player to get on with his own growth.

> A man must be big enough to admit his mistakes, smart enough to profit from them, and strong enough to correct them. — *Unknown*

GO BACK TO THE COURT NO MATTER HOW HARD IT IS

One of the best things to do after a tough loss is to go right back on the court and work out for a period of 20 to 30 minutes. Some of my team's best practice sessions have taken place immediately following a crushing defeat. This practice does two things. Primarily, it is a great way to release anger, aggression and any negative emotions from the loss. Secondly, it allows the player to leave the tennis court that day in a positive frame of mind while putting an end to the possible negative effects of the loss. It is difficult to go right back to the court to practice after a loss. Both players and coaches alike would rather do anything than hit tennis balls. It is the best possible form of release, however, and should be considered a constructive alternative after a tough loss. Again, L-FIDO (Learn — Forget it, Drive on) is an important philosophy to use.

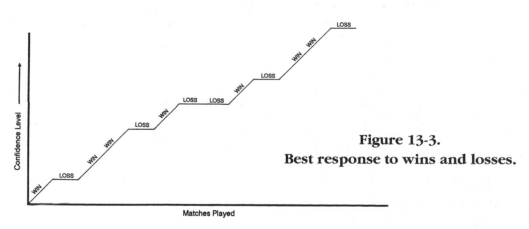

**Figure 13-3.
Best response to wins and losses.**

The mental perspective on what happened cannot be discussed until the emotional and the physical are taken care of first. It is always best for the coach to approach the strategic and technical part of the match after the player's emotions have calmed down, when what is discussed can be evaluated and made most helpful to the player. This might even be the next day. It is usually best for the coach to do this by asking questions so that the player himself has to search for the answers.

POST-MATCH CONSIDERATIONS FOLLOWING A WIN

"Winning is a chance for confidence, but losing is sometimes your only chance for growth." Just as a loss sometimes needs to be treated as a win so the coach can point out positive things in his player's game, a win gives the coach an opportunity to point out the negative. In this way a player can always keep a proper perspective. In other words, after a loss the coach should help raise the player's spirits, and after a win the coach should help keep the player from flying too high. The key to a good performance each time out is to keep this balance, and never get too high or too low. Helping the player to achieve this balance is something that takes great coaching wisdom and sensitivity.

The coach's job is and always should be to help players perform to the best of their capabilities. The coach's feedback is perhaps more important than that of anyone else. Good judgment must be used to discern what each player needs in the way of positive and negative feedback. This is often difficult because the coach's own emotions will usually be high or low following a win or loss, especially if the match was an important one. It is important for the coach to remember that the player will often get a lot of praise from friends, parents and fans. Therefore, the coach can and should be the countering balance for the player without hurting the player's confidence. Again wisdom in providing balance is up to the coach.

Taking care of the finer details of anything is the difference between average and excellent.

Guidelines for the Coach's Feedback

1. *Deal with the physical, the mental and the emotional after a win or loss.*

2. *Losses are good opportunities to reinforce the positives in a player's game and to identify what skills need further growth.*

3. *The time following a loss can be a good time for a short and intense workout session.*

4. *Wins are a good time to be critical of a player, but never in a way that would hurt the player's confidence or slow the momentum that he or she has built from the victory.*

5. *Never reward a mediocre performance, regardless of its outcome.*

6. *Wait until the emotion of the match has settled for effective analysis.*

7. *The coach's job is to help the player keep perspective in both winning and losing.*

CHARTING SYSTEMS FOR MATCH PLAY

Knowing what your objectives are before you chart a tennis match is critical to the effectiveness of a charting system. Charting a match, though, is one of the best ways possible for the coach and player to analyze the performance on the tennis court since emotions can often prevent them from seeing what is really happening.

A match chart can:

1. Analyze the strokes used.
2. Identify the areas of the court that are producing missed shots.
3. Analyze the amount of aggressive or forceful play used by a player in relation to the opponent.
4. Study match flow.

The following three charting systems can be used to study these areas:

The Paul Scarpa Charting System

This charting system is an original system developed by Paul Scarpa, the tennis coach at Furman University. After charting hundreds of matches, Scarpa determined that in an average game a player's game points were usually made by: 1) hitting one winner, 2) making one unforced error, 3) forcing one error from the opponent and 4) accepting one error from the opponent. The fifth point and those thereafter pretty much tell the story. Hitting two winners in a game is good, and making two unforced errors is bad. This system can be used to show winners, errors, forced errors, opponent errors, the stroke used to win or lose the point and the running score. The column that shows the forced errors is the most important, because the player who wins the match usually has a larger tally in this column. This category has the same importance as the line-of-scrimmage in football; or the area under the basket called "in the paint" in basketball; or the tally of body punches in boxing. The objective for the perfect match would be to have a "Zero Ratio" or " A plus ratio" between the error - winner columns and then control the area of forcing errors out of the opponent. Figure 13-4 is a sample Scarpa charting system tally sheet.

The Bob Love Flow Charting System

Bob Love's simplified flow charting system may be one of the easiest and most practical systems devised. Its main emphasis is the measurement of the flow and momentum of the match. In addition, it shows points won and lost, the stroke used to win or lose the point, the running score and conversions. Figure 13-5 is a sample Bob Love

Player 1　vs　Player 2

ERRORS	WINNERS	FORCED ERRORS	COACH'S COMMENTS	SCORE	ERRORS	WINNERS	FORCED ERRORS	COACH'S COMMENTS
F	S	S B		1-0	F	V$_1$		
B BR	FA	F		2-0	B V B			
F B V$_1$ S				2-1		BR		
	FB			3-1	B B	S		
F S*		B	*Double fault-game point!	3-2	F		B F	
	V			4-2				
	V S	V V		5-2		FP		
F B F FR*			* Poor game	5-3				
S	S V1	V		6-3	FR BR	O		
14	9	7		TOTALS	12	5	2	
				SET 2				

KEY

F = Forehand	S = Serve
B = Backhand	BR = Backhand Return
V = Volley	FP = Forehand Pass
V$_1$ = First Volley	FR = Forehand Return
O = Overhead	FA = Forehand Approach

Figure 13-4. Paul Scarpa charting system tally sheet.

charting system tally sheet. This charting system is the best to use with advance players who have already mastered a consistency in their competitive performances. Those who have used the Scarpa charting system for a while would find the flow charting technique the next step in getting great evaluations of their matches. It is easiest to use this charting system with the aid of graph paper.

The Harvard Skills Inventory

Match evaluation is an extremely important tool that can be used to focus on a player's strengths and weaknesses. It is difficult to tell just what is happening on the the court without it since players rely on feel and emotion so much when under pressure. Accurate analysis makes practices much more productive and saves time. Without it, players have a tendency to work on only their strengths — shots which are hit comfortably and consistently. Players are often reluctant to address their weaknesses. "We are usually down on what we are not up to" is an appropriate phrase when it comes to addressing the pain that comes from facing flaws in one's game. Post match analysis is critical.

At practices, time is often wasted when players go by feel and emotion alone. A self-analysis sheet such as the Harvard Skills inventory is invaluable for players who seek to improve match play by assessing their technical skills. Doing so provides a "shopping list" for the player that helps highlight areas that are essential for extra work in practice. I will often have each player evaluate himself, and I will make my own seperate evaluation. We then compare our results and establish an understanding of those areas that should be emphasized in workouts.

I really believe that the Harvard inventory system set up by Dave Fish and Peter Mandeau is an excellent coaching tool. It can guide any player onto the necessary course of improvement. Figure 13-6 is a sample Harvard skills inventory sheet.

SUMMARY

Post-match analysis is critical for the growth of the player. It is also critical for the coach to determine what actually happened during the match. The player's confidence and growth often depend on the method and system used for this analysis. Day-to-day analysis is also important for effective practices.

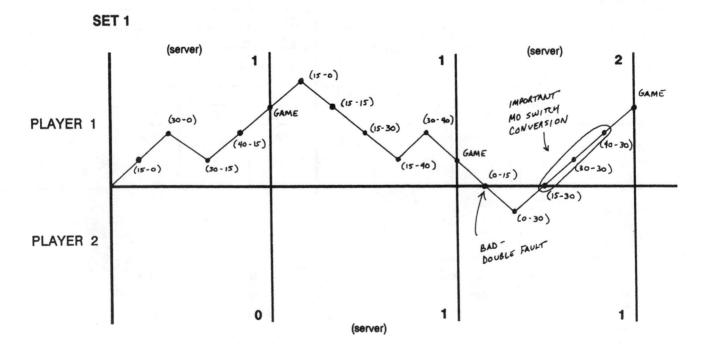

Figure 13-5. Bob Love flow charting system tally sheet.

Figure 13-6. Dave Fish and Peter Mandeau skills inventory tally sheet.

HARVARD MEN'S TENNIS SKILL INVENTORY

NAME:

DATE:

In order to determine specific goals for your development it is helpful to assess your PRESENT strengths and weaknesses. Please rate yourself in each category below using the following scale as a guide:

l0-World class/NCAA national top 10 player (Major strength-almost never breaks down)
9-NCAA national top 50 player (Solid strength-rarely breaks down)
8-NCAA top 100 player (Strength-sometimes breaks down)
7-NCAA regionally ranked player (Often breaks down)
6 or below-Needs work (Usually breaks down)

MENTAL
___ Confidence (present)
___ Resiliency
___ Ability to stay calm
___ Ability to focus for an entire match
___ Desire
___ Motivation
___ Anticipation of where ball will be
___ Ability to deal with less than perfect conditions
___ Ability to turn things around when you arc having a tough day
OVERALL MENTAL SKILLS:___

___ Ability to win close matches
___ Ability to be aggressive through entire match
___ Confidence (general)
___ Body language
___ Mental toughness
___ Ability to focus for an entire tournament
___ Commitment to your development
___ Ability to close out a match
___ Anticipation (Returns)

PHYSICAL
___ Endurance
___ Balance (close balls)
___ Balance (on the tun)
___ Balance (return of serve)
___ Balance (passing shots)
___ Strength (upper body)
___ First step explosiveness
___ Hands
OVERALL PHYSICAL SKILLS:___

___ Upper body flexibility
___ Lower body flexibility
___ Overall speed
___ Lateral speed
___ Forward speed
___ Ability to get to lobs
___ Strength (lower body)
___ Recovery explosiveness
___ Ability to change directions

GROUNDSTROKES
Forehand
___ Consistency
___ Depth
___ Ability to deal with pace
___ Ability to deal with high balls
___ Ability to hit down the line on the run
___ Ability to downshift
___ Disguise (drive, dip, loop or lob)
___ Ability to take balls on the rise
OVERALL FOREHAND RATING:___

___ Accuracy
___ Topspin
___ Power
___ Ability to deal with slice
___ Ability to hit crosscourt on the run
___ Ability to hit angles
___ Run around forehand
___ Ability to restart when pressured

Backhand
___ Consistency
___ Depth
___ Slide
___ Ability to deal with pace
___ Ability to deal with high balls
___ Ability to hit down the line an the run
___ Ability to downshift
___ Disguise (drive, dip, loop or lob)
OVERALL BACKHAND RATING:___

___ Accuracy
___ Topspin
___ Power
___ Ability to deal with slice
___ Ability to hit crosscourt on the run
___ Ability to hit angles
___ Ability to hit balls on the rise
___ Ability to restart when pressured

SERVES
First Serves
___ Consistency of technique
___ Power
___ Serve and volley
___ Disguise
___ Deuce court T
___ Ad court T
___ Ad court wide
OVERALL FIRST SERVE RATING:___

___ Consistency under pressure
___ Variety (top, slice, flat)
___ Serve and stay back
___ Court wide
___ Deuce court body
___ Ad court body
___ Other _____

Second Serves
___ Consistency of technique
___ Power
___ Disguise
___ Deuce court T
___ Ad court T
___ Ad court wide
OVERALL SECOND SERVE RATING:___

___ Consistency under pressure
___ Variety (top, slice)
___ Deuce court wide
___ Deuce court body
___ Ad court body
___ Other _____

RETURN OF SERVE
___ Consistency of technique
___ Ability to handle pace
___ Ability to generate pace
___ Deuce court (wide balls)
___ Deuce court (T)
___ Deuce court (body)
___ Ability to hit to targets
___ Chip lobs
OVERALL RETURN OF SERVE RATING:___

___ Consistency under pressure
___ Ability to handle heavy topspin
___ Ability to handle slice
___ Ad court (wide balls)
___ Ad court (T)
___ Ad court (body)
___ Ability to downshift
___ Chip and charge on second serve

VOLLEYS-FOREHAND
___ Consistency of technique
___ Accuracy
___ Handling low volleys
___ Handling pace
___ Half volleys
___ Ability to finish point
OVERALL FOREHAND VOLLEY RATING:___

___ Consistency under pressure
___ Depth
___ Handling high volleys
___ Generating pace
___ Transition volleys (first volley)
___ Drop volleys

VOLLEYS-BACKHAND
___ Consistency of technique
___ Accuracy
___ Handling low volleys
___ handling pace
___ Half volleys
___ Ability to finish point
OVERALL BACKHAND VOLLEY RATING:___

___ Consistency under pressure
___ Depth
___ Handling high volleys
___ Generating pace
___ Transition volleys (first volley)
___ Drop volleys

APPROACH SHOTS-FOREHAND
___ Consistency of technique
___ Accuracy
___ Generating pace
___ Taking balls on rise
OVERALL FOREHAND APPROACH RATING:___

___ Consistency under pressure
___ Depth
___ Drop shots
___ Dealing with loppy balls

APPROACH SHOTS-BACKHAND
___ Consistency of technique
___ Accuracy
___ Generating pace
___ Taking balls on rise
OVERALL BACKHAND APPROACH RATING:___

___ Consistency under pressure
___ Depth
___ Drop shots
___ Dealing with loopy balls

PASSING SHOTS-FOREHAND
___ Ability to use combinations
___ Generating pace
___ Topspin lob
___ Crosscourt
OVERALL FOREHAND PASSING SHOT RATING:___

___ Angles (red rollers)
___ Drop shots
___ Defensive lob
___ Down the line

PASSING SHOTS-BACKHAND
___ Ability to use combinations
___ Generating pace
___ Topspin lob
___ Crosscourt
OVERALL BACKHAND PASSING SHOT RATING:___

___ Angles (red rollers)
___ Drop shots
___ Defensive lob
___ Down the line

COACHING NOTES

COACHING NOTES

Part Three:
The Emotional
Third

Chapter 14

USE YOUR ABILITY, DESIRE AND OPPORTUNITY

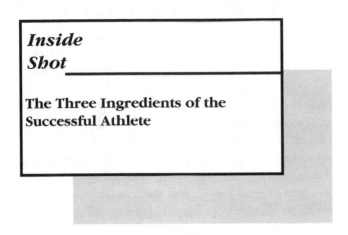

Inside
Shot

The Three Ingredients of the Successful Athlete

THE THREE INGREDIENTS OF THE SUCCESSFUL ATHLETE

You cannot do it on your own, but neither can anyone else do it for you. Three ingredients are necessary for success in tennis and in most other sports: ability, desire and opportunity. Many unsuccessful athletes have had two of these ingredients, but all three are essential to reach peak performance in any endeavor.

Ability

Ability is the God-given component of an athlete's makeup. Basically, what you see is what you've got. If you are born with a four-cylinder engine, then you cannot run on six or eight cylinders. Your size, speed of movement, strength, coordination and sport sense are some of the attributes you're born with, and each has a maximal capacity for development. These gifts may be great or small, and are usually somewhere in between.

Their development is based on the athlete's desire and opportunity. It is the responsibility of the athlete to do the best he can with whatever he has been given.

Desire

Desire is the athlete's job, for it is his choice whether to develop or to neglect the ability he has been given. In the early stages of training, parents, teachers, coaches or friends can coax the individual into developing some parts of his skills. Ultimately, the athlete determines this development himself. Desire is the basis of motivation. Knowing how to desire is a mystery that is rarely solved, but in the end it is always up to the individual athlete.

Opportunity

Opportunity is relative but necessary for the tennis player. A tennis player needs to know how good he has to be. Tennis is so bound by the pecking order and ranking philosophy that, without opportunity and exposure, a player's growth can easily stagnate. Exposure keeps a player hungry by helping him answer the questions, "How good do I need to be? What do I need to work on? Who do I need to be able to beat? What do I do to get the necessary workouts and practice?" In other sports, athletes are usually rated on their athletic motor skills rather than on how much exposure they have received, and it may be detrimental that rankings carry such a heavy weight on the pecking order of tennis players. But in tennis, the player needs exposure, and his growth comes from knowing that he can perform. Without opportunity, this is impossible.

> **W**hat I am is God's gift to me, what I become is my gift back to God. *—John Wooden*

Opportunities are plentiful for tennis players in the U.S. Many of our young athletes have a problem that's difficult to recognize — too many opportunities available to them with little or no effort.

Parents and coaches, aware that opportunity is an important element in the athlete's growth, often supply them freely before the athlete has paid his dues. I have actually found that when grooming players the best results come from making sure to schedule matches that allow the opportunity for bad losses as well as good wins. This teaches the player to deal with a variety of emotions, including the uncomfortable feelings associated with playing as a favorite.

Remember the story about the chick hatching from the egg. In America we are so enthusiastic about providing opportunities that we often prevent a person from making his own way, thus crippling our best talent. The following stories illustrate this point.

I got a tremendous amount of mileage out of the chick and egg story because it taught me the fundamental truth that there is no shortcut to development as a tennis player and an athlete. As a coach I would like to protect my players from the hardships they experience, yet to do so would often hurt their development. The self-reliance, inner strength and pride they develop by knowing that they can do it themselves is what makes them great athletes. After my mother explained the story to me, I told it in a team meeting. The reaction of the players was very ho hum, and I didn't think anyone had listened.

The very next week, our team was participating in a tournament that would qualify the two finalists for the National Indoors Tournament. That year, one of my players, Rick Rudeen, automatically got a tournament bid because he was a returning All-American. I also had an outstanding freshman player named Lawson Duncan, who later that year went to the finals of the NCAA Tournament. In the draw, though, my hope was that Richard Matuszewski, a blossoming sophomore, would have the opportunity to play well and perhaps even be in a position to make the finals. As the tournament progressed, he knocked off seed after seed en route to a semifinal meeting with Rick Rudeen. In the other bracket, Lawson Duncan had advanced to the finals and was waiting to play his next match. It then dawned on me that I might have three Clemson players in the National Indoors Championships. This would only be possible, of course, if my young sophomore could beat the All-American, Rick Rudeen. I thought about having

> # Many fail to recognize opportunity because it usually comes disguised as hard work.

Rick default or perhaps not play quite as hard as he should, giving the younger player a chance to go to the Nationals. After all, Rick was already assured of a spot in the tournament, so why should he have to win the match? Similar thoughts enter every coach's mind in the middle of a competitive situation. I guess it's a normal tendency to want an easier way for the players. But I realized that this would be a bad decision, and I dismissed these thoughts immediately. It would have been wrong to have Rick take a dive. Having him play less than his best would compromise his integrity as a player and wouldn't be fair to the promising young sophomore. He needed to open his own shell.

The match was played, and seniority and experience determined the outcome. When the match was tied at 5-5 in the first set, the younger player played tentatively and the older player took charge. The final score was 7-5, 6-4. Rick Rudeen won his spot in the Nationals, and the younger player was sent to the showers. On his way there, I tried to console him and tell him that his timing was not there yet. I tried to make a joke by telling him that he was not quite ready to turn pro. This was small consolation. Tears formed in his eyes and his voice trembled as he talked to me.

It is a terrible feeling to see your players hurt when they don't accomplish something they want so badly. On the ride back from the tournament, I was still so upset that I pounded my fist on the dashboard, waking up Lawson Duncan who was in the back sleeping. He said, "Coach, what's the matter?" I said, "I don't know if I did the right thing. I could have had Rick default his match and we'd have had three players in the Nationals." Lawson said, "Oh, I never thought about that. You could have done that, I guess." Then he said, "Wait a minute! That would have been like opening Richard's shell for him." I threw my arms in the air, let out a yell, and said, "That's great! You guys really were listening the other day when I told that story."

Richard Matuszewski did not make Nationals that year. The next year, though, he played number one and number two on the team, making All-American the hard way by beating three tough players at the NCAA tournament and gaining selection, as a result, to the junior Davis Cup squad. In addition, he won three tough qualifying matches as well as a main-draw victory at the U.S. Open and was ranked on the computer. He and his doubles partner, Brandon Walters, won the National Indoor Championships that year as well.

Richard's senior year was even better. He again made All-American and again went to the finals of the National Indoors Doubles. Richard then went on to a fine professional career highlighted by his final sixteen showing at Wimbledon in 1991. His professional ranking reached as high as #49 in the world.

I know that had I manipulated the situation and given Richard the shortcut, pushing him into the National Indoors, it would surely have hindered his growth as a player and as a man. By making him go the long haul and letting him earn his way, he ended up a far better player than he ever could have been if the situation had been manipulated for him. I'm glad I did not open his shell.

A similar situation occurred when I forced Lawson Duncan to go through a long qualifying event at the Nike All-American Championships as a freshman when he could have gotten into the tournament as a wild card. After four tough rounds, I told Lawson that I had indeed gotten him a wild card into the event, and he looked at me, eyes flashing with anger, and said, "Why did you make me go through those four tough rounds when I didn't have to?" I said, "Lawson, tomorrow you play the number two seed in the tournament's first round. How do you feel? Do you think you can win?" He said, "Shoot, yes! I know I can win!" I said, "Well, you just sweat through four tough rounds and that's given you a lot of confidence. What if you had to play the number two seed in the tournament without having fought your way into this position? I know you'd be excited to play, but do you really think deep down that you would feel like you had an opportunity to win?" He looked at me and said, "No, I guess not. I really feel now that I have a chance to win this whole tournament." Lawson went into the tournament and won three tough rounds, making the semifinals, and finished fourth in his first big national collegiate event. Once again, I think there's no way he would have gone on to have such a great freshman year and a chance to play professional tennis if I had given him the shortcut without making him earn his own way. That is the first great rule of coaching: Never open your players' shells. Make them bust out on their own and earn every step of the way.

SUMMARY
ABILITY + DESIRE + OPPORTUNITY = ALL THAT I CAN BE

(God's Job) + (Player's Job) + (Parents', Teachers' & Coaches' Jobs) = All That I Can Be

The coach and athlete should both recognize the critical ingredients to reaching potential. Ability, desire and opportunity are all essential for the athlete's growth. But the responsibility of each comes from different sources. Ability is the job of God, desire is the job of the athlete, and opportunity is the job of the parents, teachers or coaches.

Figure 14-1. A player must take advantage of opportunity.

DEVELOP YOUR MOTIVATIONAL PROGRAM

THE QUESTION OF HOW TO MOTIVATE

"Please motivate my child" is the most often heard phrase by coaches these days. Parents seem to believe that the coach who has the right magic bullet will do the job. Unfortunately, even with our sophisticated, high-tech methods and equipment, the problem of motivating individuals remains much the same. Motivation is very much an individual and unique issue for each human being. I am convinced there is no magic bullet other than these two old reliable truths: You must have the Passion to work for something and then the Patience to wait for the fruit of your labor.

> **P**assion to care & Patience to wait for the fruit of your labor. — *Unknown*

After more than 25 years of coaching and teaching, I believe that the Ability + Desire + Opportunity guidelines are very accurate. If an individual does not have high achievement needs in his personality to begin with, the coach's job becomes incredibly difficult — sometimes nearly impossible. When the individual starts with high achievement needs, he does not easily derail. The coach becomes a steering wheel for the athlete, his job to guide the player's determination. There are three motivational tools that a coach can use in those tough situations. I call them the 3 P's of Motivation: Peers, Pain, and Pleasure.

First of all, the coach's best bet is to surround the athlete with the best friends or peers possible. Secondly, the coach can apply negative reinforcement and punishment (Pain) to the athlete when he has messed up. Thirdly, the coach can use positive reinforcement and rewards (Pleasure) when the athlete is successful with a given task. Good coaches know just how to use these tools, and they do so without reservation because they realize that such tools are really the only methods to use if the athlete is not a self-starter.

THE PROBLEM: MOST WANT COMFORT MORE THAN THEY DESIRE EXCELLENCE

I worked side by side with my top player for six weeks to prepare him for a great opportunity against the #2 ranked player in U.S. College tennis. Our player was recruited from the junior ranks and the #19 ranked player in the United States. Interestingly, he started this particular season as the #19 ranked player in the United States collegiate ranks as well. These were the highest rankings of his life — he had never been further up the ladder than #19. As a coach, I truly believed that this particular match would be his big breakthrough match, and he would finally enter the ranks of the elite players of the U.S. college scene.

Match day was upon us. Everything seemed ready. The training was complete; his equipment was in top condition; pre-match warm-up was good; we went through an effective strategy session on how to win the particular match; it was a beautiful day to play with many fans in the stands, and, and, and, ...HE TANKED THE MATCH!!!!!! I hung on the fence screaming at him, "Tanking is not an option in the Clemson program. You'll run until you drop." But, to no avail, he threw in the towel anyway. I was devastated as a coach. I told him to turn in his uniform, and put him on immediate suspension. I told him to report to me the following Monday for a meeting regarding his future with the team. When the Monday meeting took place, the main thing on both my mind and those of the players was why, oh why, after so much training and preparation would tanking ever become a possibility in such an important match. Also at the meeting was my volunteer assistant coach, Bill Brown. Bill, who had worked in management for many years with the business world, looked at both of us in the eyes and merely said, "It looks to me like the Black Door Fear Syndrome." "What is the Black Door Syndrome?" I asked. Bill then went on to explain to me a very important principle that has helped me immeasurably to in turn help players clear emotional barriers and make breakthroughs.

THE BLACK DOOR

A Persian General has the enemy spy placed against the wall as the firing squad takes aim and readies themselves to shoot upon the given order. He slowly walks up to the spy and says, "I'm going to give you a choice about your fate." You can take the firing squad that is ready to carry out your sentence, or you can take what waits for you behind that Black Door." The spy asks, "What is behind the Black Door?" The General replies, "I can't tell you. It is your choice." The spy starts to imagine the possibilities of a long and painful death. Perhaps there are tigers on the other side of the door that will tear him to shreds, he wonders. Perhaps it will be snakes, or a death that is very frightening. After much contemplation, he confirms to the general that he is ready to take the quick and simple method of execution of the firing squad. And the execution is carried out swiftly. Afterward, a young corporal who had witnessed the whole thing walks up to the General and asks, "What is behind the Black Door?" The General very calmly replies to him, "Why, it's Freedom. But, no one has ever chosen it. It seems that most people would rather choose a death that they are familiar and comfortable with than to risk the unknown."

In my player's situation, he was secretly afraid of the possibility of moving into a ranking area that he had never been. He had never reached any higher than #19 in the rankings, and to be higher meant that he could look forward to facing entirely new responsibilities and a very unfamiliar situation. His performance was totally a subconscious response to a situation that he was uncomfortable with and not quite ready to take on. Withdrawing energy from the competitive situation was the response that was chosen over the threat of the unknown. And so it is with many who are confronted with "Black Doors" to travel through. Most people secretly want the comfort of a familiar situation more than they desire excellence if pursuing excellence means dealing with the unknown.

> The athlete secretly wants comfort more than he needs excellence.

Give All in Practice; Risk All When You Compete

Understanding the concept of the "Black Door" has played a significant role in my efforts to help players move past emotional, mental and physical barriers. Once a person recognizes the black door, it becomes much easier to take on the challenges ahead. I have a sign in the locker room that reads, "Most want comfort more than they desire excellence." Another sign reads, "To get all, you must give all everyday in your training, and be willing to risk all every time that you compete." Both signs have helped a great deal. The coach and players must always be aware that giving all in practice is much easier than risking all when they compete.

As a learning tool, I use the following diagram to explain and to teach the Black Door Syndrome.

The Black Door

Figure 15-1. The black door.

Once through the Black Door, you are through it for good. You may fail in the process but you will never have to go through that same passage again. Gradually, confrontations with new Black Doors become less and less intimidating as the person starts to recognize the challenges for what they are.

GETTING THE ATHLETE TO RISK

The objective of any motivational program or technique is to help a person reach the point at which they make a commitment. Most people know that success is difficult to come by without a commitment, so it would seem logical that everyone would be eager to make one. This is not the case, however. Commitments are difficult to make because to do so means that a risk must be taken. Many competitive tennis players play the sport for years without ever making a commitment to the game or to themselves.

He who has conquered doubt and fear has conquered failure. — *Unknown*

Taking the risk of commitment is like walking on thin ice. A 100 percent effort brings elation if the effort succeeds, but many athletes fear that failure after making a commitment will result in real damage to their self-esteem. They therefore choose to make only a partial commitment. Ideally, the athlete wants the elation of winning while risking only moderate disappointment to protect esteem in the case of a loss. A partial commitment seems to eliminate risk. Thus the athlete tries to preserve his self-image by settling for a mediocre job.

The most frustrating and difficult thing for a coach to do is to try and induce his athletes into making a total commitment. "Why doesn't he try harder?" or "He has so much talent, why doesn't he use it?" are questions every coach wishes he could answer. Teaching athletes the value that is inherent in the risk of a commitment is often the greatest gift a coach can give his players. The ability to make a commitment will stay with them throughout their lives — on a job, in a marriage, or in adherence to a religion. In America today we can satisfy 70 to 80 percent of our needs and achieve 70 to 80 percent of our potential without ever making a commitment. But the last 20 to 30 percent — that portion of effort which brings total success — is dependent upon commitment. In short, "a prosperous society allows us hesitation in taking the risk of commitment."

Oftentimes a player tries to delay making a commitment by relying more and more on mere athletic talent. The greater the natural ability of the player, the longer he will generally procrastinate in this fashion. Less talented athletes, on the other hand, make a commitment more easily. If they do not commit, they cannot experience success and cannot stay at their desired level of competition.

THE THREE D'S OF EVERY CHALLENGE

A method I use with tennis players to help them overcome the fear of commitment is to tell them, "There is no heavier burden than a great opportunity." I try to teach my players the 3 D's of every challenge: first, they must have the Dream; following that, there will usually be Disappointment; then, there comes either Discovery or Discouragement. For anything of value, "a breakdown usually occurs before a breakthrough." This is an important truth for an athlete. His job is to decide on the reaction that will yield growth.

EXTERNAL AND INTERNAL MOTIVATION (OBSESSION VS. INSPIRATION)

Indirect or external influences — such as coaches, parents, and peers — are usually prime motivating factors early in a player's development. Tennis is a difficult game to play, let alone to become proficient at. Many failures and setbacks occur, and every level of competition presents new and more frustrating obstacles. External motivation from parents, coaches and friends is necessary, therefore, to help a player work through difficult times.

In order for maximum growth to take place, internal motivation is essential. As described by the skill growth curve in the introduction to the book, a player's growth in the initial stages of training is relative to his amount of work. At some point, however, growth slows, and a player reaches plateaus and barriers in development. These may have a positive effect and bring about a commitment, or they may have a negative effect and cause frustration. Eventually, though, a commitment must be made or growth will stop.

When an athlete finally decides to make a commitment, he can make it either by obsession or by inspiration (externally or internally). A commitment made by obsession is final-result directed. This does not mean that the athlete's motives are wrong, nor does it mean that he will not be successful. But it does mean that his drive and determination are caused by a deep need that stretches far beneath the surface.

The award-winning movie, Chariots of Fire, told the story of two quite different athletes as they prepared for the 1924 Olympics. One of the athletes was motivated by obsession. His actions were well planned and goal directed, and he drove himself with one thought in mind — winning the gold. He was so obsessive about winning that when the time came to compete, after all his planning and training, fear of both failure and success engulfed him. He completely used what he accomplished as an athlete to validate who he was. Only a very wise coach could help him to perform his best and become an Olympic champion. The other athlete in the movie was motivated by inspiration. His drive came from within. For this athlete, running was not a mechanism for success as it was for the other athlete, but rather, it was a way of expressing his inner self. Training and competing seemed to be joys instead of burdens, and success and medals seemed to be natural outcomes of his pursuit and not ends in themselves. He, too, became an Olympic champion.

A coach might learn from this great movie that athletes can be successfully motivated by either obsession or inspiration. When the athlete who is motivated by obsession is successful, he feels relieved and expects rest and relaxation until the next competition. His successes or victories are usually not as fulfilling as he had hoped. Competition presents anxiety and nervousness — fear of a negative outcome is a constant threat. Defeats or setbacks produce anxiety and discouragement. More importantly, they produce tremendous fear of further competition in this case. The athlete who is inspired from within, in contrast, finds satisfaction and happiness in his successes. His fulfillment is magnified as the depth of his inner spirit is realized. A failure brings disappointment, but it also brings an eagerness to compete once again.

> **F**ailures are only temporary tests to prepare us for permanent triumphs. — *Unknown*

Tough Love Coaching

I thought of these two kinds of motivation as I searched for a way to help one of my team members. My number five singles player, a freshman, was not playing up to his ability. I tried everything I possibly could to help. I felt that reasserting my confidence in him and explaining to him that things would come around if he just kept trying were the best things to do. But the longer I tried, the worse things got. It wasn't that he was not trying hard. He continually played close matches but would somehow eventually find a way to lose. Whether out of fear or frustration, he just was not coming through at the crucial points. Every time he would get close in the third set, he would miss balls for no apparent reason and come away losing.

The solution to the problem came from a conversation with my parents three days before a very tough match against the number three team in the country, SMU. I explained the situation to them and my father immediately said, "Son, have you told the boy how much you care for him and reminded him of all these things?" But before I could answer him, my mother said, "The heck with that stuff. Pull the rug out from under the kid and see if he can fly on his own." It sort of shocked me the way my mother talked, but trusting her as I did, I thought she could be right. I had tried everything I could think of and nothing had worked. In light of this, trying her idea couldn't possibly have any worse results. So I resorted to the last straw — I decided to yank him from the lineup.

The next day I spent extra time after practice with this talented freshman to work on his volleys and to make sure they were well tuned. Right after the workout, I walked up to him and said, "This is a tough decision, but you are not going to play tomorrow against SMU." He looked at me in disbelief. Before he could say anything, I said, "You're a good player, but you're not playing well. You're going to have to get it together if you want that starting position back." With this, I walked away from the tennis court. Fifteen minutes later I looked to the court from my office, and he was still sitting there. I thought to myself, "He's going to quit the team now. He's definitely going to give it up." The player got up and walked away.

I knew that he had one of two choices to make: he could take the negative route and feel sorry for himself, or he could work to improve. As coaches, we often hesitate to put a player in a position in which he has to fish or cut bait, because our feelings tell us to be gentle with the player's confidence. But if we don't let a player make his own decisions, we prevent his growth. In this player's case, he responded beyond my highest expectations. For two weeks straight, he worked out extra in the early morning and I made sure that he knew I was there to support him. I've never seen a player more determined than this freshmen was during the next two weeks. Of the last eight matches of the year, he dropped only one and went on to have an exceptional summer. He came back in the fall and earned the number one position on the team. This growth spurt, I am convinced, was caused by the fact that this burden was completely placed on his shoulders; it was his responsibility to improve or to stay out of the lineup.

> There are two types of people who compete in sport, Winners and Quitters.
> — *Bear Bryant*

I truly feel that sometimes the smart move for the coach involves putting the more talented athlete in a failure position to spur his development and commitment. Remember that the only true coaching tools that the coach has at his disposal are the 3 P's. Figure 15-2 illustrates an athlete's commitment making process.

The fear of giving 100% and then perhaps still losing is what keeps all athletes from totally releasing from the heart. The partial holdback that happens is a subconscious or sometimes even a conscious effort to protect oneself. Therefore, the athlete has the feeling that if he doesn't give his whole heart to this endeavor, he will be protected from pain if things don't work out.

I explain that the only two rewards possible through competition are the Process (the learning and internal rewards of the experience) and the Product (the material or outer rewards from the competition).

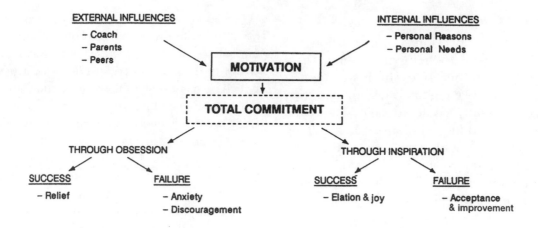

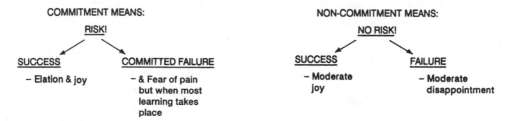

"If you don't commit totally, losing may not hurt as much but winning will never feel as good either." — *Dick Vermeil*

Figure 15-2. Motivation and commitment.

The four scenarios that are possible, I explain are:

1. To give your whole heart and win.

2. To give your whole heart and lose.

3. To not give your whole heart and win.

4. To not give your whole heart and lose.

The rewards from each of these scenarios are listed in the following box.

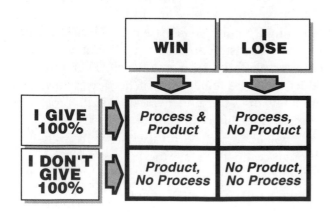

Figure 15-3. Product and Process.

Of course, all athletes would like to get both the product and the process for their efforts, and all would of course like to avoid the "No Product, No Process" scenario. The telling tale of the athlete who will improve and grow through competition is the one who makes a decision to pursue the "Process, No Product" scenario (I will give my best even if it is in a losing cause) over the "Product, No Process" scenario (I want to win, regardless of doing the right long-term things or not.)

The order of the four scenarios (best to worst) should be:

1. Achieve the Process and the Product.

2. Achieve the Process and not cash in on the Product this time.

3. Get the Product but sacrifice the Process in getting it.

4. Get no Product and get no Process.

The athlete can achieve either #1 or #2 every time he or she competes with the correct outlook.

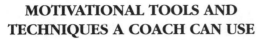

MOTIVATIONAL TOOLS AND TECHNIQUES A COACH CAN USE

As stated earlier, the coach's best three tools to use for motivation are the Role Model (good peers), the Positive stimulus and Negative stimulus (Pain and Pleasure).

Role Modeling and Mentors

My mother used to say that "If you hang around with dogs, you're bound to wind up with some of their fleas." Likewise, "association breeds assimilation" in the positive direction as well. The fastest way to teach young children or newcomers in any arena, is to associate them with those role models or mentors who you'd like them to emulate. No matter what the desired needs of the group, people will bind themselves to the chemistry and system of whatever group they're placed. My main focus with the rookie members of any team is to place them with those older role models who will teach them and guide their efforts constructively. Unfortunately, if the leader is a bad one, a good ship can go down in spite of all the good effort in the world.

> Character and ideals are catching. When you associate with men who aspire to the highest and best, you expose yourself to the qualities that make great men.
>
> — *Unknown*

The Christian men's group "Promise Keepers" has a great concept about mentoring. As described in some of their programs, each person should have three types of friends in their lives: a Paul, a Barnabus, and a Timothy. This means that for the most growth to take place in one's life it is important to have someone good above you as your teacher (this is a Paul). It is equally important to have someone important in your life who is on an equal status and will hold you accountable for doing the right thing even when the pressure is on (this is a Barnabus). He is an equal whom you have given permission to straighten out your way of thinking and doing in the case that you start to do things that are harmful to your life. It's called Tough-Love Friendship, and we all need it because sometimes our vision gets foggy on the way up a tough mountain. Finally, we all need to consider the importance of being a teacher ourselves and passing on to someone under us the very important truths that are critical for success and a good life. We need to pick someone who we mentor to also (this is a Timothy). These three people — Paul, Barnabus and Timothy — are all taken from scripture and illustrate a fantastic concept for learning at any level and for any challenge.

Always Go to Dinner with the Best Putters

There is a great story that was relayed to me in the earlier days of my coaching career about the great golf coach Harvey Pennick and one of his greatest pupils at the University of Texas, Tom Kite. It had to do with finding mentors and good people to be with when times get tough. In the story Tom Kite went to his coach and asked him, "Coach, I'm going out to play professional golf very soon." Is there something that you can give me to hang onto when the going gets tough. I realize that it will be very lonely out there and not a lot of those other guys will be wanting to help me out." The wise old coach looked at his star pupil and merely said, "Tom, remember to only go to dinner at night with the best putters." Of course, the coach was telling him to hang around those people who are going to the top and who would be good mentors for him during his quest. Tom Kite obviously took his coach's advice as he has become one of the great golfers of all time.

I speak continuously to my players about mentoring and the necessity of finding good role models. As they climb the very steep and rocky mountain of success, it helps tremendously if they have someone's shirt tail to hang onto a little bit as they ascend through those unfamiliar passages. "The higher that one climbs up a mountain, the steeper, the more windy, the colder, and the more frightening it becomes." I really don't believe that anyone can make it to the top of the mountain without good people around for support and guidance.

Pain Avoidance

Players will find their level of expectation for themselves. They will do just about anything to avoid uncomfortable emotions and pain. If a loss at a certain level is painful, they will usually win. If the loss is not that bad in respect to the level where they see themselves, then they'll lose more easily. Thus, the "pecking order of expectations" is quite a reality and becomes a huge factor (See Chapter 16). Once again, comfort is usually desired over excellence. The subconscious may actually work harder in its attempt to run from pain than the athlete's own consciousness works to try and seek out a win. The best illustration of this is an experience at "Morning Madness" training for a freshman on my team named Guma.

Although all rookies were notified during the summer prior to entering school that a 5:20 mile would be required for them to make the team, Guma showed up for the first morning session in poor condition. His first attempt at this 5:20 barrier was only a 6:07, some 47 tough seconds off of the time needed. I looked at the Clemson hopeful and said, "Son, 47 seconds is a long way and a lot of pain away from being able to start hitting tennis balls at the court." Are you really sure that it's worth it to you to go through all that is necessary to get your time down in order to make the team?" Guma was a very strong-willed and strong-bodied athlete and he answered right back, "Bring on the training." He said, "I want to make that time and the team very badly, and I won't just make the time, I will destroy it and set a new standard." Part of the reason I always liked Guma so much was because of his strong personality and his confidant stature, but I don't really believe that he knew the new pain thresholds that he would be going through during the next three weeks of training. I really think that he believed he could accomplish this very tough feat on determination and guts alone.

> # Pain and pleasure are the only true stimuli for motivation in any endeavor.
> — *Anthony Robbins*

He got sick nearly every day as he pushed his body beyond its normal comfort zone. He improved his 440-yard run time by doing interval training, and he made daily progress. After an extremely painful three weeks, he proclaimed that it was time for him to knock down this barrier and move through this Black Door. My thought was, "Is this young warrior-in-the-making really ready for the pain that it will take to run this 5:20 mile after just fifteen workouts? He said that he was and that he would will himself through the pain of the challenge.

His pace was excellent for the first two laps and then and he started to struggle down the backstretch on lap three. I knew that the attempt would be very close. His stride began to shorten, and as he rounded the corner for the homestretch on lap three, you could tell that the pain was forcing him to back off. He managed to fight through the last lap, and as he came down the homestretch, I was yelling out 5:13, 5:14, 5:15, 5:16, 5:17............5:21 read my stopwatch as he came across the finish line. His run was one second too slow.

Guma was extremely upset with himself and with me because he wanted to believe that there was some way that I had fixed the time to purposely keep him from being successful on this try. I assured him that there was no way that I would do that and that I only recorded the times. It was his job to make the time. The very interesting point about this Black Door and all barriers that people try to break through is that when so much effort, commitment and pain are invested in a failure, the tendency is then to pull back and not give as much the next time. This was the case for Guma in his next attempt to make the 5:20 mile.

His next attempt was one week later, and all that he was capable of running on that day was a 5:39 mile. He invested very little pain this time. It took a very calculated and planned routine of training to bring his pace back up in his training. His confidence was noticeably shaken, and he considered many times whether or not making the team was worth the whole procedure that he had to go through. Four attempts and three weeks later — on a day that I felt he may give up for good — he broke through with a 5:16 run. On this particular try, there was not much said at all, but there was a deep confident passion in his eyes. There are few more rewarding times to a coach than to see the face of an athlete after he has conquered a frustrating obstacle. As I presented Guma with his team uniforms and equipment in front of the rest of the team, the look on his face said it all as he seemed to understand exactly what he had accomplished in these weeks of pain and challenge.

This event taught me a tremendous amount about bringing people through Black Doors. Being aware of the approach-avoidance way that people react in competitive situations to pain and obstacles is extremely helpful in saving athletes time on their way to their goals and dreams.

> The credit belongs to the man who is actually in the arena, whose face is marred by dust and sweat and blood, who knows with great enthusiasm the great devotions and spends himself in a worthy cause...who in the end at best knows the triumph of high achievement and worst fails while daring greatly, so that his place shall never be with those cold and timid souls who know neither victory or defeat...
>
> — *Theodore Roosevelt*

Seeking Out Rewards and Pleasure

The third motivating force that a coach can use involves helping the athlete look forward to the pleasure of success and all of the rewards that it may bring. It is only the very mature individual who understands that by "being all that you can be" the internal rewards will eventually far outweigh any material reward. The coach should therefore use any bait that he can to get the athlete to see how much better the situation is on the other side of the mountain. Material rewards such as rankings, publicity, praise in front of team members, and any other symbols that represent the athlete moving up are helpful. Even if the athlete acts as if he doesn't enjoy the attention, it's almost certain that he or she secretly does. In the long run, the only important rewards will be those that are internal — actualized by the athlete himself. The small perks along the way merely make times of struggle more bearable. I am very outspoken to my players in regard to insisting they take time to enjoy victories and accomplishments. I tell them that the game of tennis is just too hard not to enjoy the good times and that it's extremely important to see and taste the fruit of their labor. But I always make sure that they focus in enough time to prepare for the next competition.

In order to move away from poor or mediocre performances, it is important for the athlete to recognize a strong personal distaste for losing. Competitors should never be afraid of losing, but the best must dislike a loss to the point that it's uncomfortable and painful. In order to move toward positive results and develop the ability to beat the better players, it is also important for the athlete to realize the importance of allowing himself to enjoy the rewards for his successes. This will lead to a subconscious desire for more of these victories as well as allow the athlete to feel comfortable in the winner's circle. It is quite interesting that even though these seem to be very simple tasks, most athletes are confused by the balance that is necessary to progress.

The following chart shows four different types of athletes in relation to how winning and losing affect them. No one really wants to hurt and go through pain, and most of us want to feel the joy of a job well done, but you will be able to see the differences among athletes that you know by studying this chart.

Pleasure

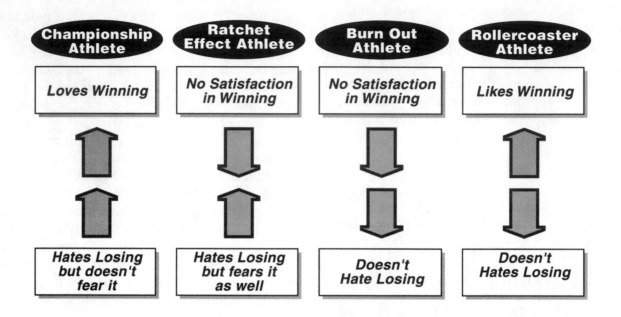

Pain

Figure 15-4. Coach's stimuli chart for motivation of the athlete.

MOTIVATIONAL TOOLS AND TECHNIQUES FOR THE PLAYER

Put P.E.P.P. into your Motivational Program

In planning a motivational program, it is important for an athlete to construct a well thought out and specific plan of training and then stick to it. The program should be thorough, and it should cover all bases of training. PEPP is a plan that can give direction and guidance to the athlete in his training. PEPP can be used as a plan for other jobs, whether it be in the training of an athlete for a specific event or the work of another occupation that takes discipline and direction. PEPP covers training from the planning phase through the actual execution and success.

P (PREPARATION): THE ATHLETE'S FIRST OBJECTIVE

Bob Knight, coach of three NCAA Basketball Championships at Indiana University, said it best in a television interview, "More important than an athlete needing the will to win, he or she needs the will to prepare to win." Without preparation and planning in the physical and mental areas, an athlete has little or no hope for success in his sport.

Preparation is the base that has to be laid before an athlete steps onto the court or playing field. An athlete's preparation must be detailed and thorough. It must include complete programs of training for the body, the mind and the spirit so that at its conclusion the athlete is mentally, physically and emotionally ready for the job at hand. A well thought out plan of training gives tremendous confidence, but without a well-designed program of preparation, success on the playing field is almost totally left to good fortune or chance.

Your success in tennis is limited only by your desire to achieve excellence.

— *Peter Mandeau*

Preparation Step One: Have a Burning Desire

Nearly every person involved in athletics will say that he has a desire to be successful. But simple desire is very different from burning desire. It is the intangible difference between the two that draws the distinction between good and great, between okay and super, between just another day at the ball park and one that is remembered for years. A burning desire cannot be manufactured. It must come from within, and each person must obtain it on his own. The athlete who has a burning desire will endure his training and the hardships and setbacks that take place along the way.

Preparation Step Two: Set Specific Goals

Most coaches and athletes agree that setting goals is very important to success in competitive sports. Nearly all athletes and coaches set goals. Some goals are never realized. Others are always reached. Some direct the athlete toward maximizing talent. Others never help the athlete achieve beyond the level he or she would have reached to begin with. What, then, is the key to setting effective goals?

Working toward achieving maximum success for the athlete depends on not just setting goals, but rather on setting the right goals. The conflict in goal setting is that when goals are set too idealistically, few are reached. Goals infrequently reached tend to make an athlete lose enthusiasm for his work and to forget about the objective. And, although it is important to dream, there is a danger that success will remain a dream and never become reality. On the other hand, when goals are set too realistically, all may be reached. In this case, there is essentially no challenge and performance remains far below potential. The key, then, is to set goals that help an athlete strive for the maximum use of his gifts while still allowing him to reach a moderate amount of the objectives set. Goals that are set properly should be reached only about 50 or 60 percent of the time. Proper goal setting can be done by a person comparing what might be totally idealistic goals with what might be totally realistic goals and then finding the point midway between the two.

Goals should be constantly reset and redirected. It is best to set three goals for an objective: a long-term goal that is the ultimate objective (the thought of which keeps the flame of desire bright), an intermediate goal that is a year or so away (to keep on course toward the main goal), and short-term goals that constantly provide smaller successes and failures (to keep enthusiasm and learning stimulated for the ultimate objective).

There is a high correlation between athletic success, intellectual success and social success. Goals should, therefore, be set in other areas including academics, family areas, social areas, spiritual areas, career planning and finance. Success in each of these areas supports and aids the development of the others.

Preparation Step Three: Make Your Work Constructive and Positive.

Working hard is necessary to achieve goals, but it is not a guarantee of success. Hard work increases the chances of success and gives one peace of mind in knowing that he has done everything in his power to ready himself for the task at hand. It also keeps you knocking at the Black Door. Thinking that hard work deserves success distorts motives for competing and can lead to frustration.

Many people work hard for the wrong reason: they are result-oriented and think only of the reward. I call this "outside-in" work. This work is not productive because it is not inspired or creative. It results in frustration, and the successes that are sometimes achieved may not be fulfilling. Athletes or coaches who do their jobs for the wrong reason find their successes more of a relief than an elation.

On the other hand, working for the love of one's work, or pursuing a calling as an expression of one's self (what I call "inside-out" work), will inspire countless successes. "Great athletes compete to express, not impress." Athletes should work hard, sacrifice, and pay the price, but they should do so positively and for the right reasons. Love of one's work and enjoyment of the accomplishments that might result from it are the keys to longevity in a career. Working from the inside out rather than the outside in keeps the motivational fires burning for a long time.

Preparation Step Four: Take Care of Details

Often both athletes and coaches alike have thrown away months or even years of hard work by neglecting the simple process of taking care of details. An athlete may have a burning desire, may set the most specific and appropriate goals, and may work in a dedicated fashion to prepare for a match, but all can be wasted by neglecting seemingly insignificant details. An athlete should pay attention to simple concerns such as eating properly, sleeping properly, having a sufficient supply of quality equipment at courtside, taking the time to have a good warmup, and starting the match mentally prepared.

Preparation Step Five: Acknowledge Fear and Nervousness and Their Benefits

One of the best things the athlete can do prior to performance is face the fact that he will probably experience some fear and nervousness before and during the event. Fear can be looked at as a prelude to the positive emotion of courage, because courage occurs only when fear is first present. Again the Black Door Syndrome must be recognized. It is important that the athlete recognize this fact and, when fear is present, acknowledge it so that it can be dealt with and used productively. Disregarding fear allows it to grow, and leads to the negative emotions of doubt, worry, anxiety and frustration, all of which can prevent the athlete from having his best performance.

There are instances when fear in competition does not exist. Children usually are not very susceptible to the negative effects of fear until they reach the age of 10 or 12. This is about the age when pressure starts to become noticeable and when children can start reasoning logically about the rewards or consequences of their behavior. Sometimes both direct and indirect outside pressures can create a situation that is more than the youngster is capable of handling. For this reason, the pressures involved in competitive sports should increase gradually along with the young athlete's ability to understand and deal with them.

Another no-fear situation occurs when the athlete completely ducks away from the pressure of the event and convinces himself that he doesn't much care about the outcome. But if the event truly were not important to him, then the fear wouldn't exist. This is one reason why athletes who are greatly talented do not all show commitment to their sport. They feel that if they don't risk, then they don't lose. But unfortunately, in most cases if an athlete does not risk, he does not gain either. It almost appears that many athletes would rather have success come their way by good fortune or chance than by taking an active role in making it happen.

E (ENTHUSIASM): THE FORCE BEHIND PERFORMANCE

The word "enthusiasm" comes from the Greek *en theos*, which means "the spirit of God within." The meaning of the word describes its importance to the athlete or anyone working in a creative field. Inside-out or true enthusiasm is inspired, whereas outside-in or false enthusiasm is forced. The latter is seldom helpful. The former should always benefit the performance.

Athletics is perhaps the purest and most expressive of all art forms. Through sports, the inner self can be totally released in a creative manner. Athletes often inhibit this inner creativity and hold back their opportunity to express the inner self through performance. The most outstanding benefits of enthusiasm are:

1. Enthusiasm projects the athlete's confidence in his own abilities, and true confidence in one's own skills will always overcome the fear that may exist in competition.

2. True enthusiasm often makes the opposition fearful. Most athletes will not counter with enthusiasm when confronting an enthusiastic opponent, but rather they will remain passive and fail to meet the challenge. Many matches are lost for this reason.

Enthusiasm is difficult to generate as a job becomes routine. Even the most exciting experience has a tendency to become drab and boring after it's done a number of times. The true test for an athlete, therefore, is his ability to keep enthusiasm for his job day in, day out, long after the novelty has worn off. Great players and coaches are usually able to perform their jobs each year with the same eagerness and enthusiasm as they had during their first year, and consequently they are able to grow and attain higher levels of development. Enthusiasm coupled with the experience of a veteran makes a great combination.

P (POISE): THE QUALITY OF
THE EXPERIENCED ATHLETE

Poise is the ability to execute one's skills on the court or playing field regardless of the pressure of the situation. It is an important skill to have, and great athletes are able to execute under pressure time and time again. In fact, poise must be learned by experiencing many pressure situations in different athletic contests.

It is difficult to teach poise, but there are a few directives that will enable the athlete to develop poise in the heat of the battle:

1. The athlete should know that growth occurs only when there is adversity and tough competition, and athletes should train themselves to look forward to these situations. Each pressure-filled situation can only better prepare the athlete to become less fearful in more important matches or games in the future.

2. The athlete should know that creativity in any area of life comes from within only when a person is in a relaxed state. Creative talents are never forced to the surface. Writers, artists, and musicians often retreat to a hideaway so that their creative talents can flow and surface within their work. Players should use adverse situations to bring their creative talents to the surface.

The key to continuous growth in athletics is to treat success and failure in the same manner. This helps an athlete develop poise and confidence. The normal tendency after an episode of success is to let the emotions run sky high. Likewise, the tendency after a setback is for the emotions to bottom out in grief, anxiety or discouragement. But the athlete should learn never to get too high over a win and never let the emotions run too low over a loss. This is not to say that one should not be happy over a win or disappointed over a loss. Any athlete who cares will have these feelings, but a balance between the two is critical for development. If excuses are not made, if losses are accepted as the athlete's own responsibility, and if positive qualities are recognized, maximum growth occurs. "Winning is a chance for confidence; losing is a chance for growth."

An athlete must learn to maintain a balance between enthusiasm and poise to achieve his best performance. This balance can be obtained by practicing concentration. The optimal situation — a rookie with the poise of a veteran and a veteran with the enthusiasm of a rookie.

P (PERSEVERANCE):
THE DURABILITY OF COMMITMENT

The greatest athletes in the history of sports and some of the greatest people in the history of the world became great for no reason other than the possession of this one trait. Perseverance in all situations, and the ability to face all adversity and keep trying, is the finest quality all great athletes must possess.

Many people see only the glory and glamour of the successful star athlete. It is difficult to see the hardship and struggle they had to go through at every level to achieve that greatness. But actually, it is the hardships and the setbacks that mold the great athletes. Through their determination to keep trying, they learn to conquer overwhelming odds along the way. The confidence that is obtained from those struggles is what propels them to greater and greater heights. They fear little because they have faced and conquered much.

Many people give up after two or three unsuccessful attempts. They cannot see down the road any farther than the immediate reward they are supposed to gain from their effort. What is not taught often enough is that it is not the immediate reward from the effort that is important, but rather the wisdom and experience that is gained from the process of pursuing a goal. Deferred gratification is the true reward that enables a person to take advantage of a much greater opportunity when it becomes available. One can only imagine Thomas Edison's perseverance as he failed and failed again in his attempt to make an electric light bulb. Each time a player has a setback on the tennis court, it is like Edison's light bulb that flickered and then went off again and again, until one day, after much perseverance, the player finds a way to keep the light bulb lit.

One of my favorite quotes for understanding the importance of growth through never quitting is a phrase of Winston Churchill's that states, "To each man there comes a time when an opportunity presents itself that is specifically designed for those talents and gifts of the man. What a tragedy when this time comes and finds the man unprepared to take advantage of them."

In developing perseverance, a few reminders are helpful:

1. Remember that breakdowns always happen before breakthroughs.
2. Setbacks are the clay from which all great people are molded.
3. Each person has his own unique timetable for success. Never compare your own successes with another person's, for this leads only to frustration. Keep working at your own rate.
4. Another person's accomplishments never make you look bad. Jealousy is a negative emotion and nothing positive can be gained by it. Be happy for others' successes, and you will find all your creative talents working in a positive way.
5. Be disappointed but never discouraged.
6. Know the difference between quitting and changing directions. Quitting is running away from a threatening situation and avoiding the responsibility involved. Changing directions is moving in a new direction that will improve the situation and be a benefit to one's life. A person may change direction in a field a hundred times during his lifetime, but he should never quit.

Figure 15-5.
Compete to express, not impress.

SUMMARY

PREPARATION

Train the body, mind and emotions for the trials of competition.

♦ Decide what you desire
♦ Set specific goals
♦ Work constructively
♦ Take care of small details
♦ Acknowledge the presence of fear

ENTHUSIASM

From the Greek *en theos*, meaning "the spirit of God within."

♦ Total release performance
♦ Enthusiasm can make the opposition fearful and builds your confidence
♦ Confidence in your abilities will always overcome fear you may have for the opposition
♦ True enthusiasm is inspired; false enthusiasm is forced
♦ Be a go-giver, rather than a go-getter
♦ Compete to express, not to impress
♦ Veterans must have the enthusiasm of rookies

POISE

Remember: pressure can make you shine or crumble — it's up to you!

♦ Rookies must have the poise of veterans
♦ Love adversity and close situations: that is when the growth occurs
♦ Remember #2 level of arousal during the heat of battle (See Table 17-1: Optimal Arousal Levels)
♦ Creativity only occurs in a poised and relaxed state
♦ Most growth occurs when success and failure are handled in the same way

PERSEVERANCE

NEVER GIVE UP — BELIEVE IN YOURSELF

♦ Breakdowns always happen before breakthroughs
♦ Setbacks are a key to the molding of any great person
♦ Be disappointed, NEVER discouraged
♦ Learning and personal growth are the keys
♦ Every person has a unique timetable for success

CHAMPIONS HAVE P.E.P.P.

PREPARATION

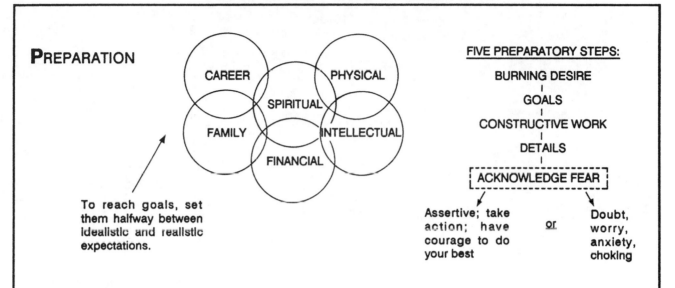

To reach goals, set them halfway between idealistic and realistic expectations.

FIVE PREPARATORY STEPS:

BURNING DESIRE
|
GOALS
|
CONSTRUCTIVE WORK
|
DETAILS
|
ACKNOWLEDGE FEAR

Assertive; take action; have courage to do your best

or

Doubt, worry, anxiety, choking

ENTHUSIASM

From the Greek <u>en theos</u>, meaning "the spirit of God within"

- Total release performance
- Enthusiasm can make opposition fearful and builds your confidence
- Confidence in your abilities will always overcome fear you may have for the opposition
- True enthusiasm is inspired; false enthusiasm is forced
- Be a go-giver, rather than a go-getter
- Compete to express, not to impress
- Veterans must have the enthusiasm of rookies

POISE

- Rookies must have the poise of veterans
- Love adversity and close situations: that is when the growth occurs
- Remember #2 level of arousal during the heat of battle (see Table 17–1: Optimal Arousal Levels)
- Creativity only occurs in a poised and relaxed state
- Most growth occurs when success and failure are handled in the same way

Remember: pressure can make you shine or crumble — it's up to you!

PERSEVERANCE

- Breakdowns always happen before breakthroughs
- Setbacks are a key to the molding of any great person
- Be disappointed, NEVER discouraged
- Learning and personal growth are the keys
- Every person has a unique timetable for success
- NEVER, NEVER, NEVER GIVE UP — BELIEVE IN YOURSELF

Figure 15-6. The P.E.P.P. system.

Chapter 16

EXPECT YOUR BEST AND UNDERSTAND PECKING ORDER

● ●

Inside Shot

What You Expect is What You Get

The Pecking Order and Expectations

When Your Opponent Plays Above his Head

WHAT YOU EXPECT IS WHAT YOU GET

In 1978, in my third year of coaching, I learned that the coach's expectations can easily become the player's expectations if the coach does not let the players know the difference.

We should never have won the state collegiate tournament that year. My number one player, Mike Gandolfo, had a shoulder injury and was unable to compete. To make matters worse, our top freshman player was unable to play because of a disciplinary action. I was left with a much weaker team, and we had to face very strong opposition from the best teams in South Carolina. The team that I would field for the tournament consisted of three freshmen, two sophomores, and only one player who had much playing experience at all. As I evaluated the situation, I knew that we were going to get killed. There was no way in the world that I could expect this team to finish in the top three, and to think they could win the tournament was out of the question.

> **A**dversity causes some to break, others to break records.

I realized that I had two options. First, I could expect nothing out of my team and be pleasantly surprised if they did well. My second option was to flat-out lie to my players and explain to them that we had our best chance to win the tournament anyhow. The tournament would be held on the clay courts of The Citadel in Charleston. I rationalized to the team that the two players who had to sit out were hard court players and we now had our best clay court team entering the tournament.

I told my players that champions are made from adversity and that because we had this adversity we would be in a prime position to win the championship. I explained to them, though, that the job was going to be very tough. I set a specific goal for the first day of winning at least eight matches out of the nine flights. Regardless of how our team did, though, I told my players that one other team would play great the first day and win all nine flights. Our goal for the second day would be to have another solid day. Another team would also play great the second day; we would be on the money rounds, and on the third day the best-conditioned team would win. Because our training had been tough, this was the day that our conditioning would have a chance to pay off. As I told the guys these things, I thought to myself, "This is the biggest lie I have ever told in my life. There is no way in the world that these guys can win." But then again, I thought about my two options and felt this was the best one.

My players actually believed me, and that fact taught me how important my expectations for them were. It also taught me that young people trust a person who is in a position of authority, especially if they respect that person. I was learning that my job as a coach and a role model was a very important one.

The team meeting the night before the tournament was much the same as previous meetings. I told the players what they would be up against the next day and that one team would play great. I told them that we would have to fight through some very tough matches and accomplish our goal of having a solid first day. To my disbelief, a few of the players who should never have won matches came through in the clutch, and we ended up winning eight matches the first day. South Carolina had a day equal to ours, and Furman won all nine of their matches and took an early lead in the tournament. That night, I told my players that we had accomplished our goal for the day and that the second day would be a very tough one. Our goal for that second day was to have another solid performance. Again I looked at my team in disbelief and wondered how I could tell them that we were going to do such unrealistic things.

The second day was a poor one for the Furman team, the South Carolina team won eight matches, and our team won seven matches. Once again, I was surprised to have so many wins. That night in the meeting, I congratulated the players on reaching their goal for the day and explained to them that this was the way it was supposed to be. We were now in a position to win on the last day which had been our goal all along. I told them that we had worked hard enough to be in better condition than anybody else and that the long matches on the clay had worn out a lot of the other players. I also told my players that none of the matches would be easy, that it was clutch play from this point on.

Even after two days of solid performance, I still felt as if I were lying, and I did not really give my team much chance of winning on the last day. My expectations for my team were low, but somehow I faked positive comments and actions. All of the matches were tough. In fact, five of them were three-setters, and three of those ended up 7-5 in the third. But the players came through in the clutch every time and when they walked off, instead of happy jubilation, they took the wins with a matter-of-fact attitude as if they were supposed to win. As we won the deciding point to win the championship, I caught myself before I could let out a yell. I immediately walked a hundred yards away, stood behind a tree, and let out a scream. I thought about how I had lied to my players and how I had so much less confidence in them than

they had in themselves. We were certainly not the best team in the state tournament that year, and their confidence had merely come from the expectations that I had expressed to them. The bottom line, though, was that my players thought they were the best team and that is why they won. I walked back onto the courts and did everything I could to contain my happiness, because I realized that if I were to celebrate outwardly too much, I might kill the momentum that we could develop as a team from that point on.

THE PECKING ORDER AND EXPECTATIONS

Tennis is a tough sport because of its ranking system. The pecking order is quickly established, and players discover what achievements they are comfortable with. The pecking order is so rigid that I firmly believe if a player is not favored to win at least in his own mind, he usually cannot and will not win. On the other hand, it is fun to play the underdog role because it poses the unthreatening situation of having something to gain and nothing to lose. But it has been my experience that when a player plays a match with nothing to lose, he usually loses the match.

A tennis player playing a match with an absence of pressure usually begins by making many great shots and points. The problem with this overextended play early in the match is that it usually cannot be kept up for long. The favored player usually catches up to the underdog late in the first set and then cruises for an easy second-set victory. It's as if the player who plays above his head uses all the shots in his tool box early on, and when he does not have anything else to use, he collapses.

The scoring system in tennis dictates that a player has to win a minimum of 48 "battles" or points to win one match. To close out the other player, a player must be better by two points every game. It does not matter whether a player is a whole lot better or more spectacular on point 21 or on point 37. The bottom line is that unless a player's great shots scare his opponent and dent his confidence, he still has to play better than his opponent on the last two points of the match to finish him off. The ingenious scoring system of tennis makes it difficult indeed to score upsets.

A match is lost when a player is challenged time after time and has opportunity after opportunity stripped away. Positive reactions that the player had experienced early in the match after hitting good shots turn neutral, and the neutral reactions that had accompanied early errors turn into discouragement. The player has already thrown everything he can at his opponent, but the opponent still has not cracked. This up and down swing in emotions usually cracks the lesser player. Upsets can occur, but the favorite player usually wins.

Because playing as a favorite is such a critical position, it is important for the coach to help a player believe that he should win, not just that he could win. One attitude produces a win, while the other produces a good chance to play close before ulitmately losing. In nearly every endeavor in life, people will seldom achieve more than they expect to achieve. Many books have been written about positive self-concepts, positive thinking and success attitudes, and they all seem to contain a similar message: How a person perceives himself and how comfortable he is with that perception determine what he will be.

Academic endeavors provide good examples of the effects of expectations on performance. For example, one student is and has been an A student for quite some time. He makes A's again and again with little or no surprise or excitement from teachers, parents or himself. His success is expected and accepted, so his reward is also sometimes neglected. However, it takes the same work and dedication as always to get the A's. When a B is made, it is a tremendous disappointment to the student, his teachers, and his parents. The student's feeling of failure is great.

Another student has a C average. He is quite comfortable in his role as a C student, and his expectations are to make more C's. On one grading report this student makes two or three B's, and everyone sings the praises of the great job done. What different reactions for the same job done by two different people, and all because of the expectations placed on each of them.

One semester the C student changes his behavior and studies more diligently than ever before and makes straight A's. Everyone is thrilled; he is praised by all and is the most elated he has ever been as a student.

The next semester he makes straight C's again. He and everyone else wonder what happened. Expectations are an indication of what a person is comfortable and not comfortable doing or achieving. If someone achieves beyond his own expectations, he may retreat to the level that he is comfortable with.

A coach can have a tremendous impact on a player's self-concept by helping the player to feel comfortable with higher expectations. The scary thing is that along with achievement and higher expectations comes a more difficult job and additional responsibility. Therefore, it is obvious why many players remain in a safe position of mediocrity.

> **U**nless a man undertakes more than he can possibly do, he will never do all that he possibly can.
>
> — *Unknown*

Pecking Order in Tennis and How to Overcome It

Since my first day of team coaching in 1975, I have recognized the power of group motivation for individuals who are trying to accomplish goals. I have seen young men and women accomplish things beyond their potential many times when the group itself was highly motivated. Conversely, I have seen excellent talent underachieve because of poor team attitude. It is absolute to me, after so many years that the expectation level of the group will usually dictate the achievement of the individuals of the team.

The importance of good team leaders is absolutely critical. High expectations and ideals of the best players teach the lesser players exactly what Pecking Order they should fall into. At higher levels of competition, this power of the Pecking Order dictates the level of performance for a player more than his or her ability to hit forehands, backhands or serves. Pecking Order is the expectation of the outcome or result that the competitor has and is comfortable with.

The Power of the Pecking Order

Just as baby chicks line up to follow each other back to the hen house, people will line up to achieve only the level that they are comfortable achieving. A story related to me recently by a basketball coach describes the belief that you will usually accomplish what you expect to accomplish The story goes:

A man found an eagle's egg and put it in the nest of a backyard hen. The eaglet hatched with the brood of chicks and grew up with them.

All of his life the eagle did what the chickens did, thinking that he was a backyard chicken. He scratched the earth for worms and insects. He clucked and cackled. And he would thrash his wings and fly a few feet into the air.

Years passed and the eagle grew very old. One day he saw a magnificent bird far above him in the cloudless sky. It glided in graceful majesty among the powerful wind currents, with scarcely a beat of its strong golden wings.

The old eagle looked up in awe. "Who is that?" he asked.

"That's the eagle, the king of the birds," said his neighbor. "He belongs to the sky. We belong to the earth — we're chickens."

So the eagle lived and died a chicken, for that's what he thought he was.

And so, the way a person thinks of himself also has a great deal to do with the way he performs in a competitive situation as well.

In team sports, the Pecking Order is not as definite and upsets happen more often than in an individual sports. In the sport of tennis upsets just do not happen very often at all. In no other sport is the pecking order more pronounced. At every major tournament it seems that the same seeded players make their way through tough draws to the final rounds. With so much parity of talent today, this does not seem logical. At critical times of the match, the favorite player always seems to take charge and make exactly the right plays. The underdog seems to play well for a while but then presses or becomes tentative at those same critical times. This internal and personal ranking that we all have for ourselves during competition is extremely powerful. This Pecking Order will usually determine the outcome.

Teaching My Players About the Power of the Pecking Order

The most interesting experiment that I've ever done with my team to try and teach them the influence of the Pecking Order was at our morning running sessions during fall training in 1992. Each morning we would meet at 5:45 A.M. for a workout that always started with a mile run. For six consecutive days we started the workout in this way and for six consecutive days, the same team member, Frank, would win the race and another player, George, finished last (14th position). More interestingly, after day three, all of the other athletes consistently finished daily in the same respecitve positions with few exceptions. It was almost as if the players found their "pecking order" and so fell quietly into their designated spot. Of course, for me as a coach who was trying to motivate his athletes to reach higher performance levels, their resignation to a set position day after day was very upsetting. Their response — to my disapproval — was that the results were based totally on their running ability and not the pecking order. I disagreed.

I decided to try an experiment to prove my point. At the next mile run, I put the players at the starting line in reverse order. George, who finished last every day would start first. Frank, who had won every day would start last. Each of the remaining players would then have a head start based on how many seconds they finished behind their personal best time. For example, George whose best time was 5:15 would start four seconds ahead of Mike, whose best time had been 5:11. Frank's best time of 4:40 would give him a starting place 35 seconds behind George. The race was started with each player handicapped accordingly. Theoretically the race should have ended with all players side by side or tied at the finish line. If each runner were running to the best of his ability, then the resulting times should have wound up dead even. Instead, to everyone's surprise except mine, the race finished in just about the same order that it had every other day. Frank again won, and of course George finished last for the 7th straight time. If the Pecking Order had so much control in such a basic event as running, then how much more powerful must it be in the more sophisticated psychology of a sport such as tennis.

> For every person to climb the ladder of success, there are usually ten who are still waiting around for the elevator to show up. — *Unknown*

I have always known that this power was strong because I'd seen it at work so many times in tennis matches. The favorite almost always wins in tennis. That's fine if you're the favorite, but what if you're not. I've found that hard work is usually the main tool against it. It seems that the harder someone works, the more pride that they develop. This pride gives them an attitude that they are ready and deserving to win. It keeps them always knocking at the Black Door. The teachings on momentum and match flow management were developed as a tool for use against the pecking order. I have also found that scheduling easier matches before a big event can help to prepare the player to win. Regardless of these efforts, the Pecking Order still seemed like a huge invisible force that decided the outcome of most matches anyway.

Only recently have I learned the reason for its power and been able to give my players some practical ways of combating it.

The Howler Monkey Story

At a recent coaching convention, a high school coach shared with me his knowledge of the howler monkey, which demonstrated perfectly the phenomena of the Pecking Order and territorial protection by a species. These monkeys get their name from the tremendous shriek that they give off when someone from the outside tries to invade their territory. They are small in size but have the best environment when it comes to food, water and protection from outside enemies. It would be quite accurate to say that they had the best level of living when it comes to the Pecking Order of the monkeys of the jungle. Their neighboring monkeys often try to come into their territory to gain some of the benefits of the better environment, but are always met with strong resistance in the form of screeching and howling by the inhabitants. Instead of

persisting, the sometimes larger monkeys retreat to their lesser territory where it is safe from the shrieks. The safety becomes much more important to them than the prospect of a better life.

Border Disputes

Of course, the greatest conflict always happens along the border of their territory, where the screeching is violent. The coach referred to this border territory as the Conflict Zone. I have renamed this conflict area as the "War Zone" for my team. Just as the howler monkey will screech and fight to keep an envious outsider out of his domain and area, so does the favorite player fight with all of his might to keep an upset-minded opponent out of his area. As a match starts with a favorite and an underdog opponent, things may go smoothly, but very quickly conflict occurs when the lesser player tries to step up and take command of a match. Initial battle starts with a long game that goes from deuce to ad-in or ad-out many times. I call this game a mini-battle and tell my players that this is their first encounter in the war zone. It is quite interesting that if the favorite player wins the first mini-battle, he usually wins two or three quick and uncontested games, therefore establishing his leader role and pecking order. If the underdog wins the first mini-battle, he is usually uncomfortable and plays sloppily for the next few games and gives the lead right back up. An upset usually happens when the underdog player is allowed to lead three or four times during the course of a match and then eventually becomes comfortable with his role. If the favorite player will fight the underdog for the leader role every time that a mini-battle happens, the conflict usually breaks down the will of the underdog and he resigns himself to the much safer and comfortable territory.

It has always amazed me that many players are sometimes happy with close losses. The thing that they don't realize is that the next time that they try to beat that same player, it will be even harder to overcome the conflicts that they will experience in the war zone.

What's more discouraging is that the underdog will be even less comfortable trying to overcome the Pecking Order because a trend has been established and the favorite will fight even harder to preserve it the next time.

Coaching Implications

As a coach, certain tools are necessary to help the athlete in both the role of the favorite and the role of the underdog. If my player is the favorite, I tell him to do nothing to motivate the fighting ability of his opponent and to make sure he looks extremely confident on the outside. It is critical to fight very hard for the early war zone. Try immediately to take a lead and establish command of the match. This can sometimes be enough to keep an underdog opponent from becoming a real threat. If you loose the early mini-battles and war zones, keep your poise, play hard and be aware when your opponent starts to feel the burden of the leadership role.

If my player is the underdog, I tell him to stay aloof and away from his opponent so that he won't buy into the comfort that the favorite's actions might bring. I also tell the player to do nothing before a match that might fire the opponent up or cause him to play harder. In other words, try to sneak in the back door and catch him with his britches down. This attitude also helps prepare the competitor for the extremely difficult battles that will take place in the war zone. I want my player to be very aware of the fact that during the attempt of an upset of another player, it is not going to be a comfortable situation. All good opponents will have fought long and hard to establish their territory. Getting a player in the habit of winning makes it much easier to overcome certain barriers because when they get in the conflict area (the war zones), they will be much more comfortable moving through it.

When a contest is an even match-up, it is easiest of all to prepare for the player who already knows that he will be in many war zones and will be quite ready for the conflict there. Since there is not a favorite or an underdog, there is not as much pain nor apprehension in the transitions.

> The best coaches handle every player differently but treat everyone the same.

Many coaches have told me that they just tell their players in all situations that they are the better player and that they are supposed to win. My argument with this is that it is untrue. Sometimes my player will be the favorite, sometimes he will be the underdog, and many times he will also be an even match-up for the other player. I believe that the best approach in trying to get good results is to acknowledge the role that the player has coming into the match and then to give my player the tools that he needs emotionally to overcome this tremendous power of the Pecking Order. (Also see Chapter 9 on pre-match preparation).

The Pecking Order of tennis is similar to the Pecking Order that we also have in our daily lives. Some people are always going to be successful, no matter what their field of endeavor. It is in some people's nature to have high achievement needs and to be winners. Likewise, some people will always have trouble feeling comfortable with achievement and will retreat from the border disputes that could potentially take them to a higher level.

My father used to tell us as children that we should learn to lead, to follow, or get the heck out of the way. You cannot change people's nature, but perhaps you can change their attitude . The Pecking Order is very ingrained in our personality. Some players need no help at all in learning how to win, whereas others need every tool that a coach can teach them.

OVERCOMING THE PECKING ORDER

The role of the favorite has definite advantages in a tennis match. The problem is that no matter how well a player is prepared mentally, physically, and emotionally, the opponent may be better and he may be the underdog. What are a player's options in this case? Not to play? Concede that he will probably lose, but play the match for experience anyway? To go for broke and hope that magic happens?

Figure 16-1 gives some guidelines for overcoming the Pecking Order of tennis. A player should remember that 50 percent of the match outcome has to do with how his opponent plays. It is critical for a player to try to maintain his best play while staying within his limitations and using the tools in his tool box. A player's goal then is to get his opponent to play at his lower limitations.

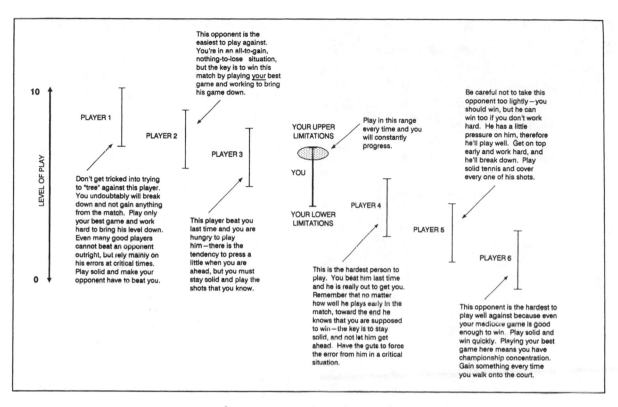

Figure 16-1. Overcoming the Pecking Order.

Follow the guidelines given and stick to and believe in a basic game plan:

A. In Training

1. Remember that hard work and smart training techniques are the best tools to prevent bad losses and to help you through Black Doors.
2. Use visualization and mental relaxation techniques to become comfortable at higher levels of play.
3. Small victories are important in becoming comfortable winning — schedule easier matches leading up to a bigger one.
4. In practices, learn how to play the role of the favorite in winning as often as possible and try to prevent bad losses.

B. At Match Time

1. Use only your tool box of skills.
2. Keep good court positioning.
3. Make good decisions about shot selection regardless of the pressure (follow Wardlaw Directionals).
4. Run the right plays (use the momentum control system).
5. Keep emotional balance and proper reactions to the ups and downs in the match.

Have a Method for Goal Setting

"The person without a goal is like a ship without a rudder," as the saying goes. Every athlete and coach understands the importance of goal setting in trying to achieve potential. It is critical to set proper individual and team goals and work toward them. It may be easier to accomplish tasks in a group situation.

As discussed in Chapter 15, long-term, intermediate, and short-term goals should be made by both the team and the individual. The long-term goal might be two to four years in the future; the intermediate goal might be six months to one year ahead, and short-term goals might be one week to three or four months ahead. These goals should be constantly evaluated and reset as they are accomplished. The athlete should write down and post his goals in a place where he will look at them regularly.

Seedings and rankings are what others think of you. Results are what you think of yourself.

Figure 16-2. Setting goals will help you reach your potential.

WHEN YOUR OPPONENT PLAYS ABOVE HIS HEAD

In all sports, it sometimes happens that an athlete performs better than he usually does. This phenomenon is not the norm for competition or training, but players should recognize it as something that may have to be dealt with in playing an opponent. In tennis, "zoning," "treeing," "laying out of your mind." and "playing above your head" are all terms used to describe this phenomenon, and in other sports, the terms "the Cinderella team," "the home court advantage," and the "rookie sensation" are used to describe the same phenomenon. Whatever the label, in no other sport is this phenomenon seen more than in tennis.

When a player plays above his head, he is not playing above his physical abilities, because he must possess these abilities to do what he does. Rather, he is merely playing above his mental

expectations because he is involved in an emotional situation. Most athletes have experienced the emotional high that allows such a performance to take place, and most athletes have also played an opponent who is going through such an experience. To compete against someone who is zoning is frustrating, and sometimes the usual pecking order falls apart. Physical educators and sports psychologists have recognized and labeled three distinct situations in which this emotional phenomenon takes place. They are: the novelty effect, the experimental effect, and reminiscence.

The Novelty Effect

The freshman year, the first year of the tour, playing up an age division — in each of these situations there is a good chance for an above-average performance. Perhaps the enthusiasm level plays a large role. Perhaps the lack of pressure in an all-to-gain and nothing-to-lose-situation allows it. It may have a lot to do with the fact that the veteran opponent who plays the newcomer plays poorly in this more-to-lose-than-to-gain situation. This is called "the novelty effect," and it has been the reason for many great performances by newcomers at every level of tennis.

The Professional Tour is marked by many cases of first-year players who have zoomed to a high first year ranking only to drastically drop in their second year after the novelty wore off. In college the second year is often referred to as the "sophomore blues" year, describing the deflating of the high-flying freshman year.

If a player is competing against a rookie or a first-time performer, it is important for him to be aware that his opponent will compete without fear and will make some above average shots. He should be ready for a tough, emotional match and be should be aggressive and enthusiastic. If he can get ahead early and dent the rookie's confidence, he should be able to win comfortably. The longer the newcomer stays in the match, the better he will play and the greater will be the pressure on the favorite.

The rookie should use this situation to his advantage, but he should remember that initial good results do not necessarily mean that he has arrived as a player. The player who makes it is the one who keeps working hard after the initial enthusiasm has worn off.

The Experimental Effect

The home court advantage; a one-chance tryout; mom, dad, and girlfriend in the stands watching — all these situations provide what is called "the experimental effect" that can allow a person to play above his assumed capabilities.

The experimental effect presents a situation that allows the home team to play at a consistently high level in which bad play does not dent confidence, and good play creates momentum. The opposing team is put into a situation in which good play provides very little or no upswing in momentum, and poor play provides a definite downward cycle. It takes a very disciplined and well-trained athlete to win against this phenomenon of experimental effect.

The experimental effect situation means that a player and a team are on display. A player who is competing against the home favorite should be ready for and expect the opponent's great play. He should expect the home team's confidence to stay intact regardless of the score, because even when the home team is behind, there is a chance of them coming back. In addition, he must maintain confidence in his skills throughout the entire contest. This is one of the toughest situations to win in. In many cases the fine motor physical skills, as well as the mental processes so necessary for playing tennis effectively, are overridden by the emotional effect of this situation.

There are many examples of the experimental effect in collegiate and professional sports. In the 1987 NCAA Tennis Championships, a major issue was made out of the fact that the University of Georgia had used its home court advantage to score major upsets on the way to its second championship in three years on its campus. The situation prompted a movement by coaches and NCAA officials to consider neutral or rotating sites for future championships. The NCAA Soccer Championships in 1987 saw nineteenth-ranked Clemson come from the bottom of a tough field to win that National Championship at its home site. The Boston Celtics' phenomenal record at the Boston Garden is an example of how experimental effect plays a big factor in professional sports. The examples are numerous in sports of all types. The advantages of experimental effect need to be recognized by both the athlete whom it helps and the athlete whom it hinders. It is truly a powerful force.

Reminiscence

A golfer plays three days a week for a year and averages in the low 80's. He does not play for three months during the winter months, and he shoots his best ever 75 on his first time out following the layoff. The basketball player who has been out for five weeks with an injury amazes everyone as he scores 25 points in his first game back. The tennis player lays off two months only to win his first tournament outing.

Perhaps it is the fresh enthusiasm and eagerness to compete, or perhaps it is the low expectation placed on the competitor that caused these above normal results. This phenomenon of superior physical performance immediately following a period of non-participation is called "reminiscence." It happens often, and it can sometimes fool the athlete into thinking that a program of steady and consistent practice is not important.

The problem is that the effects of reminiscence usually last for only a very short time. The elated golfer finds that his second and third rounds drop from that 75 to 95 and 96. The basketball and tennis players experience similar crashes in performance. Usually, though, their performance improves in each subsequent outing until they get back to their normal results. Because of its inconsistency, reminiscence should never be counted on for consistent performances, nor should it be a substitute for a solid training routine.

SUMMARY

The tennis player should recognize that the Pecking Order is an extremely powerful force in tennis and one that must be dealt with. Players should be familiar with the phenomenon of playing above their usual level, but this phenomenon should be recognized for its fleetingness and unreliability. Players should also be aware of the three situations in which this phenomenon takes place; the novelty effect, the experimental effect, and reminiscence. An understanding of each of these three situations allows the athlete to better plan for and deal with the up and down performance swings that can be caused by them.

Chapter 17

SOME TOOLS FOR COMPETITION

● ●

Inside Shot

Different Arousal Levels at Different Times

Eliminate Excuses and Defense Mechanisms

Legitimate Defense Mechanisms

Focus on What Tennis Really Teaches

As I grew up and competed in tennis and other sports, I believed that the harder I tried, the more successful I would be. If I lost, I felt guilty that maybe I had not tried hard enough. Sadly, many athletes feel the same way and constantly berate themselves for laziness when things go poorly. Sometimes the athlete's self-image and confidence are torn down.

Can someone try too hard? As a youngster, I used to play my best friend, Lester, in match after match. I tried so hard and got extremely fired up for each attempt at beating him. But, even so, each of our 15 or more meetings in the Junior rankings turned out the same — close straight-set losses to Les. The thing that always got to me was that he always appeared not to be trying. In a relaxed way he would move smoothly from corner to corner threading passing shots, always getting one more ball back until I would crack. I always responded by saying to myself, "I'll just work harder and try harder." My level of arousal when I competed was about the same as that of a pro football lineman, and Les always acted as nonchalant as someone sunbathing on the beach.

I was 24 years old and taking a course in graduate school when I learned about the optimal levels of arousal for different sports. Was I really trying too hard? I had not thought that was possible.

I thought an athlete should always try 110 percent. My emotional level was so high when I competed that I would physically tie up and choke. This high level of arousal also hampered my mental processes, and I was unable to think clearly, making myself subject to the rollercoaster ride of my emotions.

Table 17-1 is a listing that was shown to me in a graduate school class, and I have kept it to help athletes who do not focus their concentration properly in the heat of the battle. It is from an article by Joseph B. O'Xendine, called "Emotional Arousal and Motor Performance. It has been invaluable to me as a coach of such a delicately balanced sport.

LEVEL OF AROUSAL	SPORTS SKILLS
5 (EXTREMELY EXCITED)	Football (blocking and tackling) Performance on the Rogers' PFI Test Running (220 yards to 440 yards) Sit up, push up, or bent arm hang test Weight lifting
4	Running long jump Running very short and long races Shot put Swimming races Wrestling and judo
3	Basketball skills Boxing High jumping Most gymnastic skills Soccer skills
2	Baseball (pitching and batting) Fancy dives Fencing Football (quarterback) Tennis
1 (SLIGHT)	Archery and bowling Basketball (free throws) Field goal kicking Golf (putting and short irons) Skating (figure eights)
0 (NORMAL STATE: NO EMOTION)	

Table 17-1. Optimal arousal levels for some typical sports skills.

DIFFERENT AROUSAL LEVELS AT DIFFERENT TIMES

Two different personalities prevail in competitive sports: the diligent hard worker and the person who is loose-as-a-goose. The former is obsessive and driven, and he practices skills again and again until he does them correctly. The latter is a cocky competitor who thinks he can do it all.

The athlete with the driven temperament has obvious advantages, and most coaches love to work with this type of athlete. The problem is that on game day this athlete usually tries too hard and often chokes. The cocky athlete does a lot of good things on game day and always appears as if he can and will pull it off, but because of his lack of repetitive work, he often does not come through in the clutch and cannot be counted on for consistent performances.

Bill Moore, a sports psychologist, helped our team by explaining that the levels of arousal for practice day and those for match day should not be the same. It would be best if a player's personality

Figure 17-2. Athletes should focus their concentration properly in the heat of battle.

were a combination of the two personalities — someone who is driven on practice day to do everything possible to polish his skills and who on game day is able to approach the competition with a confident or even cocky attitude. But athletes tend to be one way or the other and often find it difficult to change arousal levels from practice day to game day.

For your best performance on game day, it is best to use shots that are your medium risk shots or those that you are comfortable with. Pressing to play better than you are or to make high risk shots over and over will most certainly make your performance very poor and extremely inconsistent. My advice to my players as they prepare for a big match are statements like, "Regular stuff is good enough" and "Try soft. Not try hard" or "Don't want to win more than you want a total release performance."

There are exceptions in every sport to the optimal level of arousal theory. Even if an athlete knows what level of emotional arousal produces the best performance, he may not be able to compete comfortably at that level. Each athlete must find his own individual level of arousal and work to find that zone of emotional balance for competition.

Figure 17-1. Each tennis player must find his optimal level of emotional arousal.

Figure 17-3. Learn to take responsibility for your own play — use no excuses.

ELIMINATE EXCUSES AND DEFENSE MECHANISMS

One January evening after wishing my mother a happy birthday, I told her that I was upset with my team for making excuses and failing to accept responsibility. "Young people nowadays," I said, "have the brashness to take a stand on anything, but few have the guts to accept responsibility. Why can't people just say, 'I screwed up, I'm sorry?' Why are there always 40 reasons why it happened?" My mother calmed me and said, "Human nature is the same as it's always been. The only difference now is that society has provided people with reasons. Let me put it this way: Mrs. Brown who lives next door is an old battle-ax. Nowadays we look at Mrs. Brown and say, 'Poor Mrs. Brown, isn't it sad that her husband is an alcoholic, her daughter ran off with her teenage boyfriend and her son is taking drugs? Poor Mrs. Brown. She's upset. She's nervous. She's got troubles.' But, hey! The bottom line is that Mrs. Brown is an old battle-ax whatever the reasons!"

I thought of the old woman who lived next door to our house when I was a child. There were six kids in our family, and the old woman would yell at us and steal our ball whenever it went into her yard. I knew what my mother was talking about. Perhaps today we might have found an elaborate way of giving this old woman some excuse for her behavior. I remembered thinking, though, "Wouldn't that be the wrong thing to do?" After all, it seemed that the role of battle-ax was something she was good at and almost enjoyed. Why rob her of it by giving her excuses for her actions? I also thought, "Hey! If we had looked hard enough, we could have found reasons for a lot of old women on the block to be battle-axes."

This story made me understand that one of the toughest jobs in coaching today is to get young players to take responsibility for their actions. Tennis is a difficult game to play. It is even more difficult to play well, and it is one of the hardest games to learn to win. But the biggest frustration that I have as a coach is not that the physical and mental aspects of the game are so difficult to learn, but that it is so difficult for the players to take the responsibility for their own play. It seems that usually the better the player, the more sophisticated is his excuse for coming up short in a match. The temptation to make an excuse will always be with a player, because tennis is such a hard game to play. Name it, tame it, but don't blame it — identify the excuse mechanism but remember that using the excuse will prevent you from knocking on Black Doors.

> A man may fall several times, but he is not a failure until he starts saying that someone pushed him.

LEGITIMATE DEFENSE MECHANISMS

Sigmund Freud stated that sometimes a failure situation is so painful for a person that he may need a defense mechanism in order to preserve self-esteem. Unfortunately, though, a defense mechanism can seriously hinder an athlete's growth because it keeps him from working to improve his skill level. I tell my players that once they take the court, there is no reason for a loss other than, "He played better than I did." That's all there is to say. If something is bothering you, don't take the court.

A player should be humble in victory and give full credit to his opponent in defeat, no matter how tough that may be. If, however, the loss is just too unbearable, I tell my players that they should at least know the clinical names for their excuses. Each year I give each of my team members a list that is taken from the book *Life and Health* by Grawunder and Steinmann.

1. **Repression** is "forgetting on purpose" — pushing a shameful or distasteful experience or thought out of one's consciousness and pretending that it does not exist. Repression, which is usually an unconscious process, is the most fundamental of the defense mechanisms.

2. **Compensation** is trying to make up for failure in one area by success in another area. For example, a person who is in sports may become a successful team member or sports writer.

3. **Displacement** is discharging an emotion on something other than the situation that caused it. For example, a teenager questioned by police for being out at 5:00 A.M. might kick a neighbor's trash can in lieu of kicking the police officers.

4. **Sublimation** is transforming "unacceptable" impulses into acceptable ones. For example, a person who feels the socially unacceptable desire to be aggressive may enter a highly competitive career field.

5. **Escape** is running away from problems through daydreaming, fantasy, books, movies or even excessive sleep. Children who have intolerable home conditions, for example, have been known to construct elaborate fantasy worlds.

6. **Regression** is reverting to behavior more appropriate to an earlier stage of life. A woman whose husband yells at her for breaking something might revert to baby talk and call her husband "Daddy" as a way of avoiding responsibility for her actions.

7. **Reaction formation** is replacing a negative feeling with its opposite. For example, a parent who feels hostility toward a child may react to that unacceptable feeling by being overly nice to the child.

8. **Identification** is choosing another person as an ideal and then trying to emulate that person. A teenager might identify with a famous rock star in order to share vicariously in the star's successes, even to the point of dressing like the star and keeping a scrapbook of his career.

9. **Rationalization** is providing a substitute reason for an occurrence. It is an attempt to cover up one's failures or mistakes, to soften the blow. Common rationalizations include: "I would have done better if only I had more time," "The game was rigged," "There were too many distractions...That professor doesn't like me," or "I was just testing you to see if you were listening."

10. **Projection** is shifting one's negative emotions or problems to someone else in order to maintain self-esteem. A person who accuses others of lying, cheating or bigotry is often projecting.

11. **Avoidance** is staying away from situations that produce anxiety or bring repressed feelings to the surface. An insecure person may avoid demanding tasks. A person who is unsure of his sexual identity may avoid the opposite sex. A person whose self-concept is tied to family life may avoid traveling or other situations that bring separation.

12. **Denial** is refusing to perceive or accept some aspect of reality. A heavy smoker will deny scientific reports on the dangers of cigarette smoking. People who are vain about their appearance may deny the fact that they are growing old.

When the athlete decides what he really desires with all his heart and the price that he is willing to pay for it, he stops worrying about the small pains, those things that the opponent does, and any other stumbling blocks, and he focuses on the job at hand. — *Vince Lombardi*

The point to be made about excuses is generally well understood and usually winds up being a lot of fun for the players. They are quick to pick up on another team member's attempt to make an excuse, even if it is a valid one, and to label it with the clinical name. In nearly all of these cases, it serves to make a positive situation out of a painful loss.

On the more humorous side, Bill Bos, a former collegiate coach and currently a tennis pro in Dallas, wrote this list of excuses used by tennis players. I remember that this list was a big help to me as a college athlete. Here are examples of some of these excuses:

For the Tennis Player Who Runs Out of Excuses

1. Ate too much lunch.
2. Did not eat enough.
3. Favorite racquet broke.
4. Balls too heavy.
6. Net was too high.
7. These strings just don't give me the power I need.
8. How can I be expected to play my best on these courts?
9. This injury keeps me from playing well.
10. I just couldn't get into it today.
11. Opponent was ranked.
12. Opponent didn't play tennis, just hit the ball back.
13. Opponent was so bad I couldn't play my game.
14. I didn't realize opponent was left-handed until the next-to-the-last game.
15. Tournament director didn't seed me.

My dying brother-in-law once read to me "Rockne's Prayer" by Knute Rockne as I fretted and hurt during an impending defeat. Now, the words of the prayer are with me always as I go into competition. It reads:

Lord, in the struggle that goes on through life,
We ask for a field that is fair,
A chance that is equal,
With all this strife,
And the courage to strive and dare.
But, if we should win,
Let it be by the code,
With our honor held high.
And if we should lose,
Let us stand by the road,
And cheer as the winners go by.

FOCUS ON WHAT TENNIS REALLY TEACHES

"I'd give anything to be able to play golf like you," the fan said to the professional golfer as he watched him hit balls on the practice tee. To which the golfer replied, "No you wouldn't, or you would have spent over 10,000 hours practicing just like I have."

Lesson 1: Develop a Strong Work Ethic

So many people in our society, especially our children, don't understand what it takes to excel in sports. Not everyone is meant to spend thousands of hours at the practice tee, or hitting tennis balls against the backboard. One must have a tremendous love for a sport to devote that much time to it. Many people believe that all it takes to be good at something is natural ability.

I once heard a professional basketball player remark during a speech at a coaching conference that even his own sons, ages 15 and 16, had fallen victim to the belief that talent is enough. He explained that his boys would say, "Dad, we should be able to do as well as you at playing ball. After all, it's in our genes. We're talented...just like you."

"They had heard so many sportswriters tell of my talent and jumping ability that they thought all they needed to do to be as good as me was to lace up their sneakers and take the court," he said.

"Talented? I don't know. What I do know about my jumping ability that is never told is that I used to practice it every day of my life as a youngster, running errands for my mother. You see, we lived on the fourth floor of an apartment building, and twice a day all my life I would play this game of seeing how many steps I could jump up at a time.

When I was six I could only jump up two, but when I was sixteen I could jump up the entire flight of seven stairs, take a step and jump up seven more, and so on all the way to the top.

"Now I don't really know if it was just talent that allowed me to be a great jumper, or if, just maybe, all of those thousands of steps, over so many years, might have had something to do with it."

Young people must understand that a strong work ethic and a passion for what they do is more important than talent. Talent is relative and an individual has no control over his natural gifts. To believe that talent alone is enough, to believe in the "microwave mentality" of our society which promotes the idea that everything can be done quickly and with little effort, is not a healthy attitude for athletes. Sports are a great vehicle for learning the values of hard work and persistence. Young athletes should not be denied this opportunity.

Tennis, like other sports, can offer great training and preparation for life. The four foremost lessons young participants can gain are as follows:

Lesson 2: Find a Dream and Go After It

It has been said that the greatest bankruptcy in the world is a man who has lost his dream. Dreams start with a vision and then take shape in the form of goals and objectives.

These goals should be pursued with structured and disciplined action. We are often too practical about our dreams; we might think that something is just too hard, too unrealistic, too impossible. The successful athlete must have no limitations to his or her thinking. After a dream is identified, the athlete's subconscious is set into motion, and many goals can be accomplished.

In reality, the physical differences between the fair and the great athlete are not that great. The primary difference is the unlimited power and focus that comes from having a dream. The dream takes shape in the form of a commitment, which leads to goals and objecties, which leads to action, and finally to the reward of accomplishment.

Setbacks and disappointments are bound to occur, but the committed athlete has the desire to overcome them. As the old saying goes, "The world steps aside for the man who knows where he is going." Dreams provide purpose and direction. Tennis is a great vehicle for training the young person to find a dream and go for it.

> **S**ome complain about the bricks that are thrown at them during their pursuits of excellence, others use those bricks to build with.

Lesson 3: Learn that Setbacks and Successes are Both Helpful

"Breakdowns usually happen before breakthroughs," the saying goes. I am absolutely firm in my belief as a coach that any time an athlete is going through a hard time, there is some bigger and better success just around the corner. Setbacks serve to teach us perseverance and humility.

Our last match of the 1986 season was against the University of Tennessee. It was a very dramatic match, with all of the suspense that would help prepare our players for the NCAA championships to take place one week later. With the match tied 4-4, the outcome came down to the performance of our No. 2 doubles team of Kent Kinnear and Vince Vangelderen. Every shot of the match had the fans and the players from both teams on their feet cheering. In a very dramatic but heartbreaking conclusion, Vince netted an overhead in the tiebreaker of the third set that gave Tennessee the victory. It was disappointing for the team, but much more painful for Vince! Kent and the rest of the team tried to console him.

As a coach, you occasionally see one of your players in such pain that you wish you could rescue him from it and take the hurt away. This was one of those moments. He said, "It hurts so bad, I don't think I can ever play again." In a situation like this, a coach finds himself trying to say the right thing, never really knowing if it will make a difference.

As much as I would have liked to show him how sorry I felt for him I couldn't or he would have just curled up inside his self-pity and quit. I looked him right in the eyes and said slowly, "You can quit if you want to, and if you really believe what you just said, then that is the right thing to do. But if you do, be man enough to know that it is over and don't be looking for somebody else to pick up the pieces of your broken heart. In situations like this, you have two choices, and they are to quit or to try again. I can't make that decision for you. Either give 100 percent again the next time out or hang up the racquets."

> A true reality of competition is that the worst times usually come before the best times.

two choices. You can quit or keep trying. Believe in what you do best and do your best to execute it."

I knew that Vince wouldn't quit, but I certainly didn't think I could expect much productive play from him at the NCAAs the next week. As fate would have it though, the second round of the doubles championship found he and Kent paired against another University of Tennessee team — this time the No. 1-seeded team in the entire tournament. The match was incredibly dramatic, and to the surprise of most everyone, Kent and Vince came away with a three-hour victory that proved to be the upset of the tournament. Kent and Vince acheived All-American status with the victory and went on to reach the final four of the tournament.

In one week's time, Vince had gone from the verge of quitting tennis to the pinnacle of his collegiate career. I looked at him after the match with tears in my eyes and said, "Breakdowns truly do happen before breakthroughs." Once again, a young man had grown through the adversity of the pain of losing. By taking the next crucial step of trying again and again, he had learned a great lesson — not just for tennis, but for life.

Lesson 4: Make Perseverance a Habit

Perseverance is a virtue that enables athletes to never quit, no matter how great the adversity. Athletes must be willing to hang in there and keep trying long enough to see the fruits of their labor.

One of the best examples of perservance I've seen in college match play was a match that Kent Kinnear played during his junior year in college. I had seldom seen a player getting dominated worse in my coaching career. The player from the University of Tennessee was playing great tennis that day, and Kent managed only six sporadic points in the first set. In 25 short minutes, Kent lost 6-0. He was not playing poorly, but his opponent was playing so well that Kent was clearly outmatched. As he lost another game and went down a service break in the second set, he shook his head in disgust and said, "I don't know what to do." My reply to him was, "You really only have

Kent did somehow hang in long enough that day for the momentum to change. It started with a few small things going right, and little by little the momentum began to shift. When it did, his opponent gradually became frustrated until, by the end of the match, a complete reversal had taken place with Kent going on to win. When he came off the court he said to me, "All I was trying to do was to do the small things as well as I could, such as making first serves and being in the proper position. Climbing back into the match was like moving back up the mountain an inch at a time. When I was losing, it felt like I was sliding down the mountain ten yards at a time. Things were just going so fast. It was so discouraging that I really felt like quitting. I'm so glad that I didn't."

When things are going poorly it is so hard to keep trying, but through perservance the competitor gains courage. Even the best competitors feel like quitting when they face difficult obstacles.

Figure 17-4. In the game of tennis, perserverance builds champions.

Lesson 5: Seize the Opportunity

The ability to take charge of a moment is something all athletes must eventually learn. The previous three lessons have emphasized the athlete's strength of character and the ability to deal with adversity. The ability to take charge of an opportunity is a somewhat different challenge, however.

The moment to take control of a match presents itself very quickly in competition, and the habit of doing so must be automatic. In a tennis match, these moments might present themselves only one or two times, and the athlete must recognize the importance of seizing the moment when they do appear. If these opportunities are allowed to pass by they may never come back again.

A Big Opportunity Missed

My favorite story about the importance of taking hold of an opportunity comes from an interview I watched on a talk show with a top executive. The businessman was being proclaimed as one of the best in his field, and after his accomplishments were read, the host asked him for the catalyst for his success. His story is one that I often use when talking to young people.

He said that the greatest lesson in his life came from the greatest disppointment of his athletic career. He explained, "As a senior in college, I had achieved an excellent sports career in the pole vault, and at the start of the 1975-76 season, I had set a school and conference record — just four inches short of the world record! It had always been a dream to one day represent my country in the Olympics, and now it looked as if I would have my chance. I was ecstatic when I received an invitation to the Olympic Trials.

"The Olympic Trials of 1976 were approaching quickly. Although excited about this once-in-a-lifetime chance, the fear of the approaching dream and the responsibility of finally laying it on the line seemed like a larger-than-life burden to me. I felt almost somewhat relieved when I pulled my hamstring during training six months before the trails were to start. Of course there was a lot of sympathy and concern for me, and much speculation as to whether I would be back to top form for the trials. For whatever reason, my training to regain form was much less than adequate after my leg healed. My attitude was poor, and I made many excuses for my poor training routine and my physical conditioning. My social life picked up, but my training did not. I blamed others around me for not doing more to get me ready for the trials, and I took no responsibility for my poor condition. Looking back, I know that it was fear on my part that gave me this poor attitude.

"When the Olympic trials arrived, complaining was all that I was really good at. I didn't even make the cut for the team. I was disappointed, but in a way I felt somewhat relieved; after all, I would now have four years to really get ready for the 1980 Games without so much pressure. I vowed to be ready for that appointment.

"The next four years of training were excellent, and through sheer work and determination I finally regained my championship form. I was ready, and finally, at age 26, I would realize my dream."

"When the word came of President Jimmy Carter's boycott of the Moscow Olympics, I was devastated and stunned to the point of disbelief. How could this be? This is so unfair! This is my time and my chance! I've trained my whole life for this, and now they tell me it's gone. The next Olympics were in Los Angeles in 1984, but I knew that I would be past my prime, and that for all practical purposes my athletic career was finished.

"I often look back upon that time when my fear and doubt held me back from trying. That fear must have been very powerful to keep me from

> To every man there comes a moment when an opportunity is presented to him that is perfectly designed and suited for the talents and ambitions of that man...What a tragedy when the moment arrives and finds the man unprepared to take advantage of it.
>
> — *Winston Churchill*

putting my best foot forward. In the toughest lesson of my life, though, I learned that there are only a very few special moments in life when we truly have that chance to 'go for it.' No matter how much I wanted that chance back again, it was gone forever. I was in the prime of my career, and only four inches separated me from the world's record.

"So you ask me, what motivates me in all that I do today? It's very simply the lesson I learned about the very small difference between being good at something and having the chance to be the best. The hard part is crashing through the barriers of fear in the pursuit of this small difference."

Then he very calmly, but dramatically, raised his shirt sleeve to reveal his wrist watch and said, "And here wrapped around my watchband I have a four-inch piece of leather that reminds me — each time I look to get the time — of that small difference between being good and being the very best. I will follow through in all that I do the rest of my life because of the very tough lesson I learned in my sports career."

This wonderful story should help teach tennis players that it is important to pursue goals and dreams. More importantly, it should help players to seize the moment — dreams and goals can be made, but action must be taken when the time comes to take advantage of an opportunity.

I consider this ability to take charge to be the finishing touch on the foundation for competition. This fundamental will probably take more time to harness than the other three. It is also an unfortunate fact that some athletes never become comfortable with this role, regardless of their skill level.

In summary, the foundation of the athlete must start with the vision of what he or she wants to accomplish, in the form of a dream. Secondly, setbacks and hard times must be accepted, and even welcomed, as fundamental ingredients for growth. Thirdly, perserverance must become a habit. And finally, the athlete must become comfortable at seizing the moment when it's time to take charge.

These four lessons are great tools for life.

SUMMARY

Having a proper perspective in winning, losing or competing is a must to handle the emotions that accompany each. Growth can only occur for the athlete if he faces up to the responsibility of his performance and does not look to any reason other than his performance and that of his opponent's, crediting that opponent's performance in victory or defeat.

Figure 17-5. Levels of emotional arousal should be different for practice and competition.

Figure 17-6. The ability to automatically seize control of a match given the slightest opportunity is what makes the good tennis player great.

COACHING NOTES

COACHING NOTES

Part Four: Individual and Team Coaching Considerations

BUILD A TEAM IN AN INDIVIDUAL SPORT

● ●

Coaching team tennis may be the most complex and unusual type of coaching there is. The paradox is that tennis is an individual sport, and each player's game must be developed at an individual rate. It is the coach's job to develop a plan for each player's growth that is specifically designed for the needs and talents of that player.

At the same time these individuals, who are all growing at independent rates, must mesh their skills, talents and interests into the common goal of team direction and unity. Although this contradiction can make team tennis coaching very difficult, the situation allows valuable growth to take place for all involved with the team family.

THE ANALOGY OF THE TEAM WHEEL

It was mid-season in the spring of 1987, and our team had suffered more losses than in any previous year since 1978. We had done very well early in the season by reaching the finals of the National Team Indoor Championships, but that was about it. We were in a mid-season slump. A few of the team members were starting to get down on themselves, and I feared a snowball effect. We still had fourteen tough matches ahead of us including our conference season and the NCAA Championships.

I called a team meeting in hopes of reversing the momentum. I spoke briefly about where we were in the season, the job that was ahead of us as a team, and some goals that we needed to reach to follow through for a strong season. The players seemed bored and unfocused. Then, instead of saying anything more, I walked to the chalkboard and drew the picture illustrated in Figure 18-1.

I told my players that each one of them was a spoke in our team wheel. When the road is smooth the wheel can get by, even if a few of the spokes are not strong and are not doing their part. But on a rocky road, like the one that was ahead of us, a weak spoke may allow the road to bend the wheel and cause a breakdown. The team wheel is only as strong as its weakest spoke or member, and each spoke must do its part, no matter how insignificant that may seem.

No prize won for self can compare to the great feeling of accomplishment and pride that's shared in victory among those who've suffered side by side for a common cause.

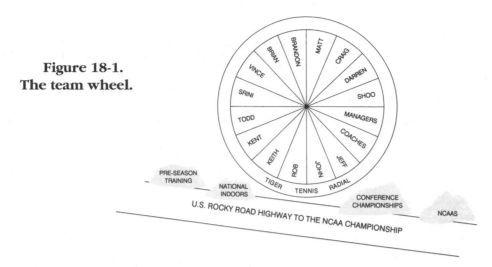

**Figure 18-1.
The team wheel.**

A basketball coach once told me early in my career that it does not matter how small or large a team member's role is. What is important is that each person involved in the organization has a role and knows that it is important to the team. The coach should remember that the number 14 player's life is just as important as the number one player's life. In ten years' time, the significant thing will be that the two players worked side by side to reach a common goal and that they learned about themselves and about life.

DIFFERENT PERSONALITIES FOR TEAM STRUCTURE

It is important to have a variety of personalities on a team. When I first started coaching, I felt it would be best to have a team made up only of self-motivated, hard-working members. I thought this would produce a team with few discipline problems that would always be a contender. I am now convinced that the team should be a melting pot of different personality types. Each personality type contributes in his own way and grows because he is surrounded by different ideas, different ways of doing things, and the unique styles of the other team members. More importantly, a team made up of a variety of different personalities allows each team member to grow independently without having to compete for his own personal space on the team. I have also come to realize that 20 different personalities can easily work together for a common goal, and that when all the parts work together, there are few things more exciting to experience as a coach.

The personality section in Chapter 8 gives great insight into the different personality types that may go into the melting pot called a team. The coach should understand that the attributes of all these unique personalities are together what is necessary to build the best team.

NICKNAMES FOR TEAM MEMBERS

Many great coaches and athletes have been known and called by their nicknames more often than by their birth names. There is something very special and important about the confidence and identity that a nickname can give an athlete.

> Learn to sacrifice for others. Learn to feel for others. Learn to take pride in your team and teammates. Learn to cheer for them to succeed.

It seems that a team structure provides an appropriate setting for nicknames to emerge and be used. Even if team members act as if they do not enjoy a nickname, they probably do. Nicknames provide many positives in a team structure — but the coach should make sure that positive names such as Warrior, Thunder, Terminator, Scrappy and Rocket are used instead of negative, derogatory names like Stinky and Porky.

THE FOUR-YEAR DEVELOPMENT OF A TEAM MEMBER

The development of a team member in his four-year high school or college career can be compared to a person's development from birth until he is 18 years old.

The Freshman Year: The Year of High Enthusiasm and Fast Learning

As the young child needs the constant caring and direction of the parent, so a freshman responds to and needs the same from the coach and the team. Most of the successes that come to a freshman are based on the combination of high enthusiasm and very little pressure, but always accompanied by a great deal of support from his new family of team members.

Often a player starts his career in a blaze of glory. It is good for an athlete to have early successes as long as he keeps a proper perspective and builds a strong foundation of fundamentals. The lack of proper fundamentals makes for a quick rise and a quick fall, and this scenario is all too common in American society. An athlete's career must be built on a foundation that will enable growth to continue after the initial enthusiasm has worn off. The coach must remember that the late show is always the great show in an athlete's career, and he must plan for the long term and not for the immediate rewards that seem to be fast-coming initially.

The Sophomore Year: The Sophomore Blues or the "What-Am-I-Doing-This-For?" Year

Like the second lap of the mile run, the sophomore's initial enthusiasm is just not there any more, and his destination is not yet in sight. Sometimes the sophomore year goes very smoothly and the athlete is able to make steady growth, but more often it is a year of confusion and questioning. The coach should try to spend as much time as possible with a player during this year to help keep him focused on his goals. Individual workouts and frequent feedback are helpful.

The Junior Year: The Year of "I Can Do It on My Own"

Just as the 15-year-old reaches the stage when he rebels to some extent against his parents, so too the athlete will usually go through a similar period of rebellion against the coach or the team structure. Team meetings and the coach's structure and guidance were exciting for the freshman, but what the coach has to say does not seem to carry much weight with the player during the rebellious junior year. Much of this simple rebellion comes from the first glimpses of seeing the end. This rebellion is very natural and should be taken as a positive aspect of the athlete's maturing process. It usually passes quickly as the player finds and better understands the direction he wants to take with his tennis and his life.

A Junior Who Finally Started Calling His Own Shots!

Teaching and working with Richard Matuszewski as a freshman and a sophomore was any coach's dream. He was pure, soft clay readily accepting any and all molding. With each step of his development, I would feel great pride that I had something to do with his improvement. He seldom said a word, usually letting me make the decisions. And so it went, until that turning point when I felt that he really made the turn for true ownership of his own tennis game.

We were playing SMU at Clemson. Richard was playing Richie Reneberg and the match was very tight. I went out onto the court and started coaching him nearly every point.

Overcoaching is more what I was doing. After all, I felt I needed to call the plays to help him through. At the start of the third set and out of the blue, Richard walked over to me on the side of the court and said to me, "Dammit! Would you please let me do it on my own. I know how." I looked at him fairly stunned because this was so much out of character for him. He looked at me in a terrified way as if he'd just talked back to his parents for the first time. I was shocked, but smiled from the court. I said to myself, " It's time, He's ready to fly on his own." I never took offense to his acting this way because of the kind of person Richard was. Now he was a man.

I have heard that the two greatest gifts that a parent can give are "roots and wings". I think that wings are often the harder of the two to give, and they usually grow about the junior year.

The Senior Year: The Year of Leadership and Direction

The reality of the approaching end is all that most seniors need to help them focus on the job at hand. The realization that it is the last time around is usually a tremendous motivator. Senior team members, the same members who were rebelling a year before, often take charge of the younger players on the team. Those players who do not take a leadership role should become very focused and goal-oriented. A team composed largely of seniors will almost always be successful because of its members' maturity level and because of the concentrated focus on what must be done for success. On the other hand, if the team has senior members who have poor character and do not set good examples, a team can be quickly destroyed.

If the coach recognizes these stages in the four-year evolution that his players undergo, he can provide great help in handling problems and in making players aware of the things to expect along the way.

> The strength of the wolf is the pack and the strength of the pack is the wolf.
> — *Warren Forney*

DEVELOPING STRONG TEAM UNITY AND PRIDE

Although a coach can help his team develop unity and pride, these bonds are primarily developed as team members share common goals and experience the struggles, hardships and disappointments of working toward those goals. Unity can be developed only through the ups and downs of shared experience. Pride comes only from successes earned by paying the price for achievement. The common bond that a team must develop in order to be successful is something that cannot be forced — it comes in its own time and only after enough interaction occurs between the team members.

The Coach's Job in Developing Team Unity and Pride

The coach's work with a team in developing unity and pride must begin on the very first day of practice. The coach should make practices tough, and he should challenge the members of the team daily. He should set a standard that requires and demands physical, mental and emotional strength. Often a coach can be misled by an athlete's talent or by his own expectations for promising young athletes.

Figure 18-2. The 1981 U.S. Junior Davis Cup Team.

Our armed forces have a tremendous concept in developing pride and group unity. Young people enter the service from every walk of life. Whatever a recruit may be — rich, poor, tall, short, black or white — each and every one starts at base zero. The young men's heads are shaved, and the recruits are forced to go through six strenuous weeks of boot camp where they are pushed mentally, physically and emotionally. In a sense, they are isolated from the rest of the world. They share common oppositions, and they have one common goal — to make it through boot camp. By the time boot camp is finished, this group of young people that was so diverse has become a unit bonded by pride and respect for each other and for themselves. Under totally adverse conditions, they have overcome the obstacles put before them, and they have learned a great deal about themselves and each other in the process.

In a team structure, or within any group of people that must work together, the same concepts apply. If they go through a struggle together, they will develop a bond. A friend of mine related a story that illustrates how this bonding takes place. At girl scout camp there was an obstacle course, and on it was a wall that had to be climbed. As a girl scout arrived at the wall, she realized that there was no way in which to get over the obstacle alone. She had to have other campers boost her, and then once on top she in turn had to help out the last girl over from the bottom. What a great way to learn how to deal with the obstacles that occur in life.

During my first nineteen years of coaching, I never cut a player based on his playing ability alone. I wanted players who would build a strong team spirit through hard work, loyalty and pride. That is why is I set up the Morning Madness program.

Morning Madness

Morning Madness begins a player's tennis career at Clemson — no matter whether he is ranked or unranked, recruited or not recruited, each new player has to meet at the track at 5:45 A.M. for a workout. The players are encouraged to quit if they want to, and many do. A tryout squad of 40 or 50 is reduced to 10 or 11 after the first two or three days. After a week, usually everyone has quit except those individuals who have a burning desire to be a member of the team. These few people grow more determined every day until they reach a point where nothing in the world would make them quit.

One of the highlights of my coaching year comes on the day that I walk up to the athletes at the start of a workout and say, "I would be very proud to have you as a member of this great team. Congratulations." It is breathtaking to see the elation of the new team members as they walk back to the dormitory arm in arm. I usually give them an inscribed T-shirt that says "Morning Madness Survivor," "Tiger Tough," "The Few, The Proud" or something similar.

From that day forward the struggles that those players have will seem very controllable, especially with the help of the other team members. After that it does not matter whether or not they are good tennis players. They will make a contribution to the team, and they will have respect for each other and for themselves.

DEVELOPING TRUST

Mitch Sprengelmeyer was one of the best students a coach could ever hope to have. He was only ranked #127 in the U.S. Juniors when I recruited him and did not make the Nationals that year in singles. His improvement was never dramatic but always steady. He exemplified the saying "inch by inch, it's a cynch" for when he finished his senior year, he left as a two-time All-American and won the National Senior Player of the Year award which is one of the highest honors of recognition given in collegiate tennis. He also set many records over the course of his Clemson tennis career.

The most frequently asked question that I've had to answer about Mitch is "What made him special?" or "What was his secret?" or "How could he have improved so fast?" My reply is always very simple — I say "Basically, nothing was special with Mitch except he seldom wasted time, he used all of the tools that our coaching staff threw his way, and most importantly he trusted the coaches and players around him." Consequently, his development was always a steady push forward with very few slowdowns.

Figure 18-3. Trust in your game, your teammates, and your coach.

Teaching the Players to Trust Your Teaching

I tell my players over and over that they need to trust me to make the right decisions regarding their game and future. "You cannot see yourself, you can only feel yourself," I remind them. "Your path is often blocked by your fears, doubts, and the mystery of what lies ahead. At other times, confidence, faith, and trust may help you along. But feelings should not be the guide for your progress. Trust the coach for guidance and maintain faith in your skills."

I often use the analogy of climbing a mountain. I tell players that they must climb the mountain wearing a blindfold, hanging on to the belt buckle of the one in front of them, keeping trust in God, their team, and their coach. The reason that every team needs good leaders is to teach the younger players to trust as they climb. The leaders have already been up the mountain and know how it's done. But, if your older leaders are not good teachers then they can do more harm than good. In that case the coach should remove them from the process or the team will never grasp onto how to climb the mountain.

Faith is believing without seeing; trust means to allow those whose eyes have already seen to be your vision on the climb. This is very difficult in a sport like tennis where individual ego and pride play such a large role in personal success. The following tool has been very helpful in getting players to buy into that trust and faith.

I begin by explaining that there are four stages to every learning process. You are:

First - *Unconsciously Incompetent; you are not aware that you are not good at carrying out a skill.*

Second - *Consciously Incompetent; you recognize what skill you are not good at.*

Third - *Consciously Competent; you have the skill but not automatically.*

Fourth - *Unconsciously Competent; you have the skill automatically.*

I then tell the player that he must trust me as his coach, trust me when I tell him that I know the recipe. As a coach, I will not look to take credit for the player's success. I only want for the player what the player wants for himself. I encourage players to trust the eyes of the teacher.

I show players the basic Johari Window from Psychology 101 that was adapted and given to me by Coach Sam Shrivastava. It clarifies the logic behind the necessity of player trust in the coach's judgement.

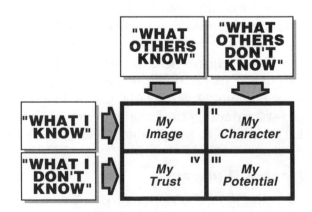

Figure 18-4. Coach Sam's Johari window of coaching.

The window explains the relationship between what we do and do not know about ourselves and what others do and do not know about us. Those relationships create four different scenerios:

> ### The Relationship Between Ourselves and Others: The Johari Window Panes
>
> **<u>Window Pane I</u>** - What we know about ourselves and what others know as well
>
> **<u>Window Pane II</u>** - What we know about ourselves and no one else knows; what we keep private
>
> **<u>Window Pane III</u>** - What others know or see but we are unaware of ourselves
>
> **<u>Window Pane IV</u>** - What neither we nor anyone else knows or sees about us

Window Pane I (This is our Image). This seems to be quite important to most athletes of this generation, but in truth it is the least important and least reliable window. Of course, a good image is important, but it must not be the primary focus in one's development. It should only be the result of the good work and growth in areas of character and skill. I remind my players often, "Do not sell out your work ethic or your growth to chase an image that seems popular at the moment.

Window Pane II (This is our Character). The cornerstone of every athlete is his or her character, integrity and humor. This pane represents all that goes on which no one else knows about. It is our hidden self. The athlete should receive maximum encouragement and nurturing in these areas.

Window Pane III (This is our Trust). Faith is believing without seeing. Using someone else's eyes whom we trust to guide our way through rocky times is a must. This is particularly difficult for the headstrong athlete. The truth, however, is that only by trusting others can the athlete hear what is needed to reach his potential. This is the ingredient that I work hardest to convince players and parents of.

Window Pane IV (This is our Potential). That which we cannot see and others can't either is our potential. Only God knows our full potential and, therefore, few ever reach it completely. The hunger to realize one's potential is what really motivates us to strive for our dreams. The normal boundaries of our minds can be exceeded if we understand that potential is a gift from God to all of those who dare to believe.

The Role of the Parents in the Trust Process

No matter how much trust the athlete has in the coach and others for guidance in his or her career, all is wasted without the support and trust of the athlete's parents as well. In many cases, the parents who do not support the coach or teacher tear down all that is being built in the athlete.

Because pain and hard times are very necessary in the growth process, many parents make the terrible mistake of running interference or protecting their children from the pain of tough times. During those adverse times, the coach must communicate with the parents constantly to lead them through the process.

Early in the player's career the coach must teach and remind the parents how important their support and trust is to both the player and the coach. They should never interfere with the process any more than they would interfere with a doctor, a lawyer, an engineer or any other professional.

PRACTICE SOUND COACHING FUNDAMENTALS

We live in a world of fast cars, fast food, fast service and microwave ovens. Is it any wonder that we also look to the quick success some athletes have as the the standard by which we judge ourselves? A common belief is that talent alone determines the early success of an athlete, and talent is all that must be nurtured. This is absolutely wrong.

> A leader has two important characteristics; first he is going somewhere; second, he is able to persuade other people to go with him.
>
> — *Unknown*

The Child Prodigy Syndrome

During the past fifteen years we have been bombarded with child prodigies in tennis. We see younger and younger stars who are promoted as the standard instead of the exception. Many boys and girls are now turning professional in their mid-teens, and many teachers support the popular belief that tennis is a game for the teen years. In truth, to reach tennis maturity as a teenager is rare. The tragedy is that this belief causes many youngsters to hang up their racquets — along with their dreams — long before the natural union of the body, mind and emotions takes place. Many tennis academies and teachers prosper by promising to make children "immediate champions." Unfortunately, many buy into this sales job.

The media and manufacturers love the younger champions because of the public interest aroused by their extraordinary success. Young stars are good for sales and excitement, but they are not the standard, and they should not be the model to follow when planning a career.

As stated before, female athletes do not mature mentally, physically and emotionally until the early twenties. For males, it is a few years later. The optimal years are probably between the ages of twenty-four and thirty. Therefore, young players should slow down and enjoy learning all aspects of the game and solidify their base fundamentals. I have two rules I try to use in developing talent.

RULE ONE: GROW SLOWLY

I coached the U.S. Junior Davis Cup Team in 1980-81. That year we had a youngster named Jimmy Brown, who, at the age of 17, dominated the Junior schedule. When he announced that he was turning professional at the end of the summer schedule, I was shocked to hear another 17-year-old on our team say, "Darn it, I'm so upset that he beat me to the professional circuit." I cornered this young man immediately and said, "I never realized that you were racing. Your timetable for growth is totally independent of everyone else's."

This mentality, I discovered, is common among the players and parents in the junior tennis scene. The quest for "keeping up with the Joneses" drives the thinking and behavior of many people in tennis, but should be avoided. Everyone has his or her own timetable.

Diamonds vs. Rhinestones

We get fooled these days. It's disappointing that our sports world and society as a whole can't seem to tell the difference between what is quality and what is superficial. I believe that much of the disrespect young people show toward authority in our society stems from the fact they really don't see or understand the work ethic that is the prerequisite for real success. It is possible to get some things quickly that, on the surface, appear to be just as good as those things that take time and effort. We are often confused by what is truly a great man, a great system, or a great work.

We often have a difficult time seeing the difference between a true diamond that was formed through time, effort, and tremendous pressure and the rhinestone, which is a quickly-made, inferior copy. The rhinestone shines just as brightly, looks just as attractive and can pass most tests of the untrained eye. We have the best of fake diamonds, fake art, fake music and fake anything that looks good and is easy to get. The sad thing is that so many people can't tell the difference anymore.

Just as the true test of quality for the diamond is the test of time, so it is with one's tennis or athletic career. The true champions, like diamonds, stand this test because they have been formed slowly and carefully and have withstood all of the pressures that have faced them. The lessons and values that can be taught by tennis also stand the test of time. Young players and their parents should keep this in mind when selecting a coach. The ideal coach does not promise quick success, but offers a base of fundamentals for the long run.

Train the Root System First

I learned a wise approach to player development at the Tennis Training Center while lecturing in Japan. I will use it for as long as I coach.

On the wall of the Japanese Youth Training Center, I saw a picture of a flower, including its stem and root system. I asked the director of the center about it and he said, "The first priority for the athlete is to train his root system; this part, which is underground and not seen, is the base for the plant and for the athlete. It represents his attitude, his heart, his work habits, his integrity, and all of the qualities that don't get immediate attention by others, but are critical for success that endures the test of time.

"The stem, which represents the physical condition and athleticism of the athlete, is the second priority. We see athletic ability as we see the stem of the flower, even if it doesn't attract attention as the bloom of the flower does. Just as the stem of the flower is the critical link between the roots and the flower, the physical ability of the athlete is critical to final success.

"The flower, the third priority, represents the players' strokes. We are initially attracted by the appearance of the strokes, but they can succeed over a period of time only with a strong root system and a well-working stem."

These ideas reinforced very strongly the beliefs and ideals that I try to teach my team. I tell my players that confidence is equal to self-concept and self-respect, nothing more. And, you see your opponent as you compete, but you feel yourself. Your opponent sees you, but feels himself. Therefore, a player's self-concept, which is only developed by the root system, is always the first priority in a long-term training program.

Think of the quick-growing corn stalk that is impressive for one season and then dies. Its roots are very shallow and easily ripped from the ground. The Dutch tulip bulb is completely opposite. Its blossoms are pruned early and often, each time sending nourishment back to the root system, until that bulb is large enough and strong enough to produce year after year. The strong oak tree — with as many roots underground as it has limbs above ground — is another example, taking years to develop.

In training, players and coaches should remember that although growth may be underground and out of direct sight, the root system requires the greatest emphasis and care to produce beautiful blossoms and success season after season. A good teacher understands the great importance of character development early in a youngster's career.

> **S**ow a thought, reap an act; sow an act, reap a habit; sow a habit, reap a character; sow a character, reap a destiny.
> — *Unknown*

RULE TWO: EARN WHAT YOU GET

Because many of us often can't recognize the difference between "diamonds" and "rhinestones," it is human nature to seek to accomplish things the easy way. Shortcuts are always tempting.

My #1 player in 1992, Greg, was questioning our university's academic learning center director in the following way: "Why does Coach Kriese make us take the tough road on everything about our training." He wondered if it really was worth it to do so.

Bill D'Andrea, a former member of Clemson's football coaching staff, calmly stretched out his hand to Greg and said, "In 1986, we won our conference championship. Do you see this championship ring that I wear? The pain and the tough times were many in earning it, but now I have few more prized possessions in my life than this ring."

He continued, "Now, let's suppose that I had been given this same ring or I had found it. What if I had a chance to sell it for two or three hundred dollars? If that was the case, I could easily part with it. But because I have earned this ring, I wouldn't part with it for all the money in the world. It means too much to me because of the investment that I had to make to earn it." Greg's eyes opened wide as he stared at Bill's golden ring.

Society often tries to teach youngsters that the bottom line or end result is what matters, and that if they can get something more quickly, then all the better. We need teachers who continue to teach the root system philosophy for long-term growth.

HAVE ORGANIZED TEAM PRACTICE

Tennis team workouts are difficult to structure because there are multiple variables involved with each individual player, and, at the same time, the team as a whole needs work on doubles, conditioning and match situations. Meeting these needs is critical to running a complete and thorough practice.

In the daily routine, the more boring and repetitive work should be done early in the practice. Then the intensity should build in the practice with drill work that simulates match situations (See Chapter 21). Competition is best at the end of a workout because it allows the

SAMPLE WORKOUTS

Drill Day: Two-Hour Workout

15 Minutes: Total body warmup, light hitting and flexibility work

3 Minutes: Movement drills and agility work

30 Minutes: Individual weaknesses and fundamental training

3 Minutes: Movement drills and agility work

45 Minutes: Match simulation and intensity drills

3 Minutes: Conditioning sprints and agility work

20 Minutes: Competition/match situations — optional individual work

Drill Day: Three-Hour Workout

15 Minutes: Total body warmup, light hitting and flexibility work

5 Minutes: Agility and movement drills

40 Minutes: Individual weakness and fundamental training

3 Minutes: Agility and movement drills

1 Hour: Match simulation and intensity drills or station drill work

50 Minutes: Competition and match situations

10 Minutes: Conditioning work — optional individual work

concentration and intensity to stay at a high until the end. Sprints or agility and movement drills at three or four different intervals throughout the workout help to keep a high intensity as well. Below are two sample practice schedules that incorporate these concepts.

On some days it is recognized that a practice schedule may need to be set up with different objectives than a normal drill day situation. Approximately two days per week should be set aside for match play. Team drill work is more helpful if matches are worked into the weekly schedule. If strength training facilities are available, they should be used two to three days per week with one day between each training session for rest and the alternating days for sprint work or movement conditioning.

DRILL WORK VERSUS MATCH PLAY

How much drill work should a team do? How much match play? What are the advantages of each? Individual team players would probably opt for more drill work than match play. Drill work is fun and pressure-free. The body can perform without interference from the mind and the emotions.

Drill work sessions are effective if players can work on grooving particular shots and learning new ones (shining existing tools and adding new ones). But, if only drill work is done, only the physical one-third of the player is used. With the many fine facilities, teaching devices, ball machines and teaching pros in America today, many players have become great rallying machines. They are able to duplicate most of the shots that the pro players hit, but often with little or no understanding of how to use them. All the tools and materials to do any job are there, but there is often very little of the practical know-how, mental concentration or perseverance to be successful. Because of this, the coach should do the best job possible to make his athletes work mentally and emotionally as well as physically.

In match play a player is forced to test himself and learn how to use the skills and tools that are already in his tool box. Moreover, he learns to win and to lose and, most importantly, to compete. The best shots in the world will not help a player if he has no knowledge of when and how to use them, and that comes only from match play. Ideally, the coach should schedule both drill work and match play in a timely way so that the player benefits from both and grows at a maximal rate.

The price of success is hard work, dedication to the job at hand, and the determination that whether we win or lose, we have applied the best of ourselves for the task at hand.

— Vince Lombardi

**Figure 18-5. Players can work on grooving shots
and learning new ones in drill work sessions.**

ADMINISTER DISCIPLINE

Everyone wants discipline and love, and administering discipline is the most sincere way of showing concern and love. "Tough love," as counselors and psychologists often refer to discipline, simply implies taking the time to do what is necessary to provide a person with a system of parameters and restraints. This provides a point of reference from which a proper interpretation can be made in a given situation. What a tragedy today that this very basic human need is often neglected.

Kids Really Want to Be Told No!

On one of my recruiting trips, I sat on the plane next to a counselor for youthful drug offenders. After we had talked for awhile, he asked me why I thought kids from wealthy or parentless homes become involved with drugs. I replied, "I guess because they have too much time on their hands, too much money." But he said, "No, the real reason is that the child is crying out for discipline." Discipline is a parent's way of showing love. In caring enough to punish a child, a parent cares enough to be involved in what is happening to the child, and the parent cares enough to make a decision that the child is not yet equipped mentally or emotionally to make. Basically, the parent who takes the time risks having the child dislike him. The child whose parents do not take these measures will look for ways to attract the discipline that he wants and needs. Sometimes the youngster will resort to drinking or drugs or breaking laws as ways of looking for the restraints that are supposed to come from somewhere. It is very sad that so many people feel that it is best to let youngsters make decisions for themselves without giving them specific guidelines during their formative years. These youngsters are neither equipped nor ready to deal with such responsibility. Like horses, children want to know their parameters. The first thing that horses do when they are put into a new pasture is to run to every corner of the field to find out the boundaries. Only after they have done this do they settle down and become content.

I saw the application of this truth from what took place at the home of a good friend of mine who has a 16-year-old daughter. In South Carolina it is quite the social thing for high-schoolers to go to Myrtle Beach for spring break. I watched a very interesting scenario unfold as the mother denied her daughter's request to make this trip with her friends. It started with the girl's saying, "All my friends are going." The mother replied, "I don't care what your friends are doing." The daughter responded with, "How can you be so unfair? I hate you, I hate you," and the door slammed behind her as she rushed upstairs to cry. The mother looked at me and said, "It's so hard. I feel I'm doing right, but I hate to see her hurt so." Five minutes passed, and the young girl returned down the stairs and telephoned her friend, and said, "My mother won't let me go. I hate her. She's so mean, and I'm so mad. " As she hung up the phone, I saw her look directly at the wall and breathe a large, peaceful sigh. She walked calmly upstairs to do a reading assignment. I thought, "Oh, my gosh, this girl is really happy that she's not going. She knew that it was an opportunity for trouble, and the bottom line is that her mother took the responsibility of having to go against her friends off the girl's shoulders."

Young people need responsibility, and more importantly want discipline. The easiest way out of a situation that they know is wrong for them is to say, "I can't do this or my mom will kill me — or my coach is a jerk and he'll make me run."

Saying No Gives the Person a Safe Way Out of a Bad Situation

One of the most dangerous episodes I've ever encountered which illustrates this point occurred during a boat ride with my son one summer afternoon. Upon our return home, we traveled under a 200-foot-high railroad bridge. I looked up and saw a group of six young boys walking out onto the trestle. The two boys leading the way were shouting commands to the other boys to hurry up and to not be cowards. The four boys following the ring leaders were obviously terrified and wanted no part of the adventure to cross this dangerous bridge. Seeing this, I quickly turned my boat around and yelled to the boys above us, "Hey, you Kids! Get off of the bridge! I'm a game warden; the police have been called and they'll be here in five minutes!" The leaders shook their fists at me and made some obscene gestures as they yelled,

"Sure thing, buddy! You're full of it." But the four boys in the rear turned and ran, yelling, "Come on guys, let's get out of here! The police are on their way!" The ring leaders reluctantly followed them, yelling obscenities at me the whole way.

My son looked at me with big eyes and said, "Dad, you told a whopper to those kids. You're no game warden." I laughed and said, "Son, all I did was give the boys in the back a way to get off of the bridge and out of a dangerous situation, without having to stand up to their more aggressive friends. It worked this time, and I'm glad." My son still looked at me in a funny way that seemed to say, "Who is this weird person I have for a father, anyway?"

Players Who Feel Guilty Will Sometimes Get in Trouble on Purpose

After my conversation on the plane with the youth counselor, I came to realize the importance of good discipline within a team structure. No matter how players fight it and no matter how often they deny it, their greatest need in a competitive situation is discipline. It takes personal discipline to excel on the practice court, in match situations, and in the routine details that no one enjoys. The coach provides the discipline of structure and the administration of punishment, and this sometimes dictates that he set down unpopular requirements and restraints and punish or correct players when their actions are wrong.

In 1986 I learned a great lesson about the need to discipline players when a team rule has been broken. We had just lost a tough 5-4 match to Pepperdine, the number two ranked team in the United States. Two of our players, the number one and number five men on the team, had lost tough three-set matches to Pepperdine players, and both those matches were pivotal for the team. After a tough loss like the one we experienced that day, we would usually go through a very intense drill session for about 15 minutes so that we not only took some of the sting off the loss, but also were able to go away from the courts with confidence. After this particular match, though, we had to leave immediately to catch our flight back to the East Coast for two more matches. I gave a talk to the guys about how proud I was of their effort and sorry that we had come up short. At the airport I checked the bags and rode the escalator up to where my team was waiting. As I got to the top of the escalator, I could not believe what I saw. Sitting at the bar directly ahead, for me and the whole world to see, were my number one and number five players — drinking a couple of beers. I am very strict on trips and never allow drinking, and this rule is well known by the team.

I stormed into the bar and screamed at the top of my lungs for the two players to get out into the hall. All the people in the bar immediately stopped drinking and talking. The players slid out into the hall, sheepishly acting as if they had not done anything wrong. I continued to yell. I screamed, "How could you do this to our program? How could you break a rule so flagrantly? Get out of my sight, just get out of my sight!"

It was still about an hour and a half before the flight took off, and I went to the farthest place in the terminal to brood. "How could my players be so stupid?" I thought. My mind was made up, though, and as soon as we got back to Atlanta to change planes, I sent those two players back to Clemson on a bus. The rest of the team and I went to the Washington, D.C. area to play two conference matches. This was very tough because we now had a crippled lineup and had to use two freshmen in critical positions. Fortunately, though, we succeeded in barely winning the two matches. This situation had actually strengthened our team because we had developed great confidence after winning in spite of the absence of two starters.

The two players were very remorseful when we returned. They walked into my office and sat down for a meeting. My first question to them was, "Why did you drink beer right out in the open knowing you were going to get caught? You could have gone to any other bar in the airport and gotten away with it. You could have put the beer in a plastic cup and sat in the back of the bar, and I wouldn't have known the difference. Why did you so blatantly break a team rule?" The older player looked at me and said, "Coach, I don't know why we did it. Right before you walked up the steps, John said, 'Hey, Coach will be here soon, and we're going to get caught. It was as if we both knew we would get caught." As he said this, it dawned on me that these were the players who had lost two very tight three-set matches in our battle against Pepperdine. Could it be that they felt guilty and wanted to be punished? Could it be that they felt that they had let the team down but could not admit it? Had they sabotaged the situation so they would be caught? I asked them if they had ever heard of self-sabotage. I explained it to them, and they looked at each other and were quiet for a minute. I told them that as long as they gave 100 percent effort on the court, they would never let the team down. But their reaction to losing was wrong, and if they wanted to play on the Clemson team that year they would have to meet me at the track the next two days and run Dawn Patrol. They took their punishment and the incident was forgotten, but a great lesson was learned not just by the players but by me as well.

When people fail, they feel guilty and feel the need to make things right, sometimes even punish themselves to clear the slate. It was not bad or wrong that these players lost, but they felt that they had let the team down. After they caused the situation to occur, they felt it was critical that they be punished. Without some form of punishment, they would have to carry their self-imposed guilt inside for a long time, and that would destroy their confidence. If I had said, "It's all right guys, I'll have a beer with you. It's not a big deal. We had a rough day today," it would surely have hurt the team, but most importantly it would have hurt these two players. They wanted to be punished even though there was no reason for it. Subconsciously they planned a situation out of their guilt over what they had perceived as a failure.

After realizing this, I saw the importance of having a workout after a tough loss so that the players can get out some of their negative emotions. It is bad that 18 and 19-year-old young men and women carry around guilt because of their failure in performance, but it is hard for some of them not to, because so much emphasis is placed on

success and failure. Only after a lot of maturing can a person walk away from a setback without carrying some of these feelings around.

METHODS OF DISCIPLINE

Team Discipline

Once the team policies are established, the rules and disciplinary actions for rule infractions should be handed out and explained in detail to the players at the first team meeting of the season. The rules should be specific and enforceable. They must be enforced, or they cease to be effective. If there are too many rules, it can be impractical to enforce them. The well-respected coach Tom Parham once told me, "If you've got them, you better enforce them," and he continued, "I've got three rules for my team — no drugs, no drunks, no bums — and that covers it all. I enforce these and things work out pretty smoothly."

The coach does not have a lot of flexibility in enforcing the team policies — he must make sure that the rules are followed by every member of the team. It is a good rule for a coach to treat everyone the same and handle everyone differently. Problems can quickly arise when allowances are made for different team members because team members will suspect preferential treatment based on a player's rank. In fact, the coach may want to make a special effort to be even a bit tougher on the top players on the team. Once the players know what is expected of them and know that the rules will be enforced fairly, they will almost always respond favorably. Establishing these parameters takes considerable pressure off the players and gives them the chance to train wholeheartedly.

A coach should set team policies in the following areas; he can add rules in other appropriate areas:

1. *Academic standards*
2. *Team image*
3. *Conduct on court and off*
4. *Competition standards at home and on the road (dress, routines)*
5. *Training (on court and off)*
6. *Lineups, practice schedules, use of equipment*

> A good coach has the ability to get people to do things that they don't want to do in order to have things that they want to have.
> — *Tom Landry*

Individual Discipline

The purpose of discipline is to help each player reach a point where he can achieve self-discipline. All team rules will be bent or broken at some time, thus forcing the coach into the position of having to discipline a player or players. There is always an initial testing period in which even the most cooperative players will sometimes break a rule.

This usually happens three or four weeks into practice when the newness of the training has worn off and the players have become familiar with the coach. The coach's role is a tough one, because he must be distanced enough from his players to administer discipline, but close enough to show a lot of concern for each person.

If a rule is broken by a team member, immediate disciplinary action must be taken. A good procedure is to have a progression of disciplinary actions for repeated infractions. For example:

Disciplinary Action—Slight Infraction

1. Talk to player, inform him of his infraction.

2. Have player do Yard Patrol (yard or maintenance work).

3. Have player do Court Patrol (have him pick up balls or do the manager's work instead of playing during practice hours).

4. Have player do Dawn Patrol (meet the player at 6:00 A.M. for a morning running workout).

5. Sit the player in the stands to watch practice.

6. Have the entire team run stadium workout or sprints for the infraction of the individual player while having the individual sit out of the running.

The only two infractions that I give immediate dismissal with no reprieve are for stealing or use of drugs.

Disciplinary Action—Serious Infraction

Suspend the player indefinitely from the team, and as a last resort, dismiss him completely. A good coach will always feel bad about having to discipline a team member. But if players are treated in a consistent manner early in their careers, then by the time they become juniors or seniors, they are often a helpful resource in training the younger players on the team.

Give More Freedom As They Learn

Athletes, especially very talented ones, are like thoroughbred racehorses. If left alone with no reins or restraints, they might run around the track on their own, but more likely, they will trot over to the pasture and graze in the sweetest grass they can find. The coach's job is to supply the reins and this may at first be like dragging a bucking bronco stubbornly down the turns of the racetrack. But as the athlete becomes better trained, the coach can gradually decrease the pressure on the reins until finally he throws them down and says "Run, baby, run." As bad as failing to guide the untrained thoroughbred, however, is the case of holding back and overly restricting the thoroughbred that is ready to run on its own. The best coaches know when and how to hold back and when and how to let the athlete go. They recognize the point at which the athlete can take to his own wings. The journey to that point begins with discipline.

Figure 18-6. A player should gradually develop those qualities that lead to self-discipline.

Use On-Court Coaching Whenever Permitted

Although most team or individual matches prohibit on-court coaching of players, it is allowed in some situations, such as the Davis Cup play and college team matches. Although most of the coaching must be done before the match begins, a coach may use some of the following guidelines if he is allowed to coach during the match:

1. If it's not broken, don't fix it. Too often the temptation for the coach is to overly advise instead of letting the player win on his own merit. The coach needs to read the situation void of his own emotions.

2. Leave the player alone until the emotion from the start of the match has settled. Usually this lasts for the first set. Nothing will register with the player if the emotion of the match is controlling his thoughts.

3. Knowing when to coach:
   a. Watch for the first bad mistake when your player is behind. This is an indication that the player is starting to crack.
   b. Watch for the first (checkout) wasted shot when the player is ahead. This is an indication that the player does not want to take care of the dirty work ahead.
   c. Watch for initial changes in body language. This is the first indication that the match is in trouble.
   d. Watch for bad decisions in shot selection. This is an indication that the player wants out of the pressure of staying in points.
   e. Watch for poor court positioning — winning is very hard without it.

4. How long to coach:
   a. Stay with your player during a loss. This is when your player needs help. Do not let him go down alone.
   b. Try not to be on the court when a player wins. The win should be to his credit and on his own doing. This will give confidence.

5. What to look for and correct:
   a. Is the player's shot selection good?
   b. Is the court positioning good?
   c. Is the player running the right play and controlling momentum?
   d. Are the errors aggressive ones and not tentative? I encourage my players to miss long balls, but never wide or into the net. I stress that a long miss is only a physical mistake, but a ball wide or into the net is a mental mistake.
   e. How is the player reacting to his and his opponent's winners and errors.

6. Priority for player to execute:
   a. The first priority is for a player to have confidence in his own game.
   b. The second priority is to break down the opponent's game.

7. Coach's reaction to a player and the coach's body language:
   a. Maintain confident body language on the sideline and appear to be in control of the situation.
   b. Reinforce and confirm effort after loss of a point. Positive reaction to the player's hustle and effort when he loses a point keeps his confidence at a good level.
   c. Save giving too much praise until the match is over; although constant encouragement is very important. This is often hard to do, but not reacting to good shots in the middle of a match keeps the player in balance to continue execution. Congratulations can be given after the match is over.

8. Other guidelines:
   a. Wait until after the first game of the next set to coach. There is usually too much emotion, high or low, for anything to make much sense immediately after a tough set.
   b. Do not upset MO or cause overreaction through untimely coaching. Ask yourself, "Is this exactly what the player needs, or is it a reaction to my emotions?" A few timely words are all that are usually needed.
   c. When in doubt, do something to change MO. When the player is definitely going to lose, if he continues in the same routine, try for a MO switch. Do not give up. The scoring system in tennis allows the chance of a MO switch at any point. Most of the time if you can get your player to relax, the match can turn.

Figure 18-7. Use guidelines for on-court coaching.

Some Unusual Coaching Techniques

It has always been amazing to me that in the heat of the battle, it matters very little at all to have certain strategies or tactics if the emotions of the athlete are not in balance. I've seen coaches use some very strange and funny tactics to try to relax their players during the course of a stressful period of a match.

In 1977 we hosted a fall tournament where North Carolina State was a participant. J.W. Isenhour, the Wolfpack coach, was very frustrated as his coaching efforts were having little or no impact whatsoever on his #2 player who continued to play worse and worse during the match. I watched as J.W. jumped down from the stadium seats to court level and motioned for the player to come to the fence at the change-over. As the player did, I saw J.W. reach into his pocket and get out a hand puppet from a fast food restaurant. He ducked down below the level of the six-foot windscreen and put the puppet into the player's view. He moved the puppet and in a very high voice said, "Make your first serves to set up your second shot." His player couldn't help but laugh. Basically, it was a great coaching tactic as it helped the player to relax and consequently go on to play a better match.

Also in the late 1970s, I watched Kent DeMars who at the time coached Southern Illinois University at Edwardsville (SIU-E) help his player to completely change the momentum of a match

at the Rice Invitational in Houston. After the reversal and victory, I asked Kent what it was that he said to the player. He answered, "Oh, I just asked him if he got a date with that beautiful girl back at school last weekend." I said, "What!" and Kent went on, "He was way past the point where strategy was going to work. I had to somehow try to relax him so that he could make shots again."

At the 1987 NCAA Tournament, I coached a doubles team of Craig Boynton and John Sullivan. They were playing a very tough first-round match against the number eight seed from Cal-Berkeley. Our team was explosive and capable of beating anyone on a given day.

Sullivan-Boynton jumped out to a quick lead and won the first set. The second set was a struggle, but they finally got a service break and went up on the team 5-3 in the second set, serving for the match. John Sullivan, a sophomore at the time, was very excited about being in his first NCAA event. He had played extremely well, but as it came time to serve the match out, I saw the signs of his pressing and the balance of pressure changing. I was certain that he was going to have a hard time with this service game. Sure enough, a double fault and an overhead into the net left the team down 0-30, and the match seemed to be changing. A missed volley and double fault later, and Boynton-Sullivan had just lost a love game. They crossed sides to receive serve, still leading 5-4, with a chance to win the match.

I recognized the shift in momentum and realized that the next three games would be lost very quickly unless something was done. I walked over and tried to talk to John and Craig, but they did not want to hear a thing I had to say. They brushed me off and said, "No problem, Coach. We have it under control." I said, "Guys, you really don't. You're pressing and you're really not doing the things you need to do." They replied, "No, coach, we're really fine, just leave us alone." As I got up to walk away, I realized my talk to them had been totally ineffective. I knew the next three games would be lost, and I knew the momentum switch would cause a quick third set to be lost also. I thought to myself, "There is no way I can walk away and let this happen."

At other times, I may have been more aggressive verbally and yelled at the players to shake them up. But this time I walked to Sullivan, picked up his water, and dumped half of it on his head. He turned around and gave me a long, silent stare and I said right then, "You guys played like crap that game, get yourselves in gear!" Sullivan kept looking at me in surprise and disbelief, and then he let out a laugh, and as he did it seemed that his whole body let go and relaxed. I walked off and stood about 50 yards away.

The California team had been ignited and played extremely well, but the most important thing that happened was that the Sullivan-Boynton team, so shocked at what I had done, maintained their level of play. Although they did not break serve, they arrived at 5-5 with their game and emotions intact and a good chance of winning the match in a tiebreaker or the third set. As it turned out, the match went to 6-6 and Boynton-Sullivan won a tough 7-5 tiebreaker.

Looking back, I am still surprised at the tactic I took, and I still do not know what motivated me to pour the water on John. I just knew I had to do something. In no way did I want to degrade a player or lessen his self-respect, but I figured there was no other way in the world to get him out of his panic. The hope of any coach is to learn the best way to get a player's attention. When in doubt, it is far better to do something rather than nothing at all and watch your players disintegrate because of their inability to keep the right balance of pressure on themselves throughout the match. I hope it can be a much more conventional and acceptable move than the one I used.

Although all of these examples were very unconventional, the purpose was the same in all cases — to get the player to the emotional level where he could perform to his ability. Great communication must exist for any coaching philophy or technique to be successful.

The longer I coach, the more I understand that there is no magic formula to coaching — there's only doing what you feel is right and caring for your players. Recognize this and the correct tactic will follow soon after.

SUMMARY

There seems to be no harder job in coaching than getting individuals to function as a unit. In an individual sport such as tennis, the variables are many. A team of talented individuals cannot be successful, though, unless they bond together. The coach's job is to guide the individuals through many tough obstacles to accomplish goals; then, little by little, bonding will take place.

Administering discipline, holding team practices, providing on-the-spot coaching, and working for the total development of each of the individuals are all details that are critically important. Although different methods and approaches may be used, the objective should be to allow each spoke of the team wheel to do his job to the best of his abilities.

Chapter 19

Use Timely Positive and Negative Feedback

● ●

> ### *Inside Shot*
>
> **Positive Feedback**
>
> **Negative Feedback**
>
> **Long-Range Motivation for Player Development**
>
> **The Coach's Confidence in his Players**

When to praise, when to criticize? We would all be great leaders, motivators and coaches if we knew just when, where and how to do each. For years the popular conception was that coaches gave only criticism and negative feedback to their athletes. Perhaps this is still true in the early part of a coach's career because it is usually easier to see what someone is doing wrong than knowing how to help him do it right. Since the 1960s, however, the use of positive feedback has increasingly become the rule rather than the exception for coaches with the unfortunate result that, all too often, mediocrity has been rewarded and acceptable standards of performance have been lowered. In the 1990s it seemed that we became more interested in youngsters having good self-concepts than we were in promoting excellence. Some states even began using non-graded criteria in their schools. What a disaster — I call this approach the Doctor Feelgood society. It brings about more mediocrity in our educational system, and encourages a nation of result-oriented rather than process-oriented people. Educators are now realizing that learning and growth do not occur by placing an emphasis on results, but rather from the process of working toward a result.

So where is the balance between positive and negative feedback that a coach should use with his team? A coach should not beat down his players, nor should he reward mediocrity.

Once again pain and pleasure are two of the only tools a coach can use to motivate (See Chapter 15). Everyone knows the importance of reward, but the teacher, leader, and coach are often misunderstood by others when they discipline their students or subordinates. They will usually agree that it is not the winning or the losing that is the subject of discipline, but the accompanying behavior. The wrong message is sent to the youngster when poor effort and mediocrity are not addressed. It is ironic that if the pupil is not disciplined for what he does wrong, he or she will usually feel unloved or not cared for. This was expressed in the previous chapter. Discipline and punishment are just as much a part of saying "I care" as offering reward. If a player is not punished when they need it, he or she will self-sabotage something else to get that attention or care that all desire and need.

Wise and proper use of the carrot and the stick is so very essential for the coach. I hope that the following guidelines for positive and negative feedback prove effective. Always remember that each situation is unique and may require special handling.

POSITIVE FEEDBACK

Positive Feedback Should Be Used Before & During Competition

Before competition, positive feedback should be used exclusively. The day before or the day of competition is definitely the time to reinforce a player's strengths and emphasize the good points of his game. Overly analytical pre-match discussions of technique only serve to point out minor flaws that really cannot be corrected at such a late stage.

This realization should help the coach treat his player like the trainer treats the prize fighter. The coach should emphasize that the opponent will be tough but that his player is ready, sharp and looking good. A player must respect his opponent, but at the same time he must have complete trust in his own strengths and skills. This is not a time for building the opponent's strengths in any way because discussion of the opponent's good points only makes him a tougher foe. Whatever the coach may be feeling, he should offer only positive reinforcement to his player on game day and the day before.

Although Sometimes Needed, Positive Feedback Should Be Used Less at Practice Sessions Than on Game Day

The practice session is the time to be a perfectionist with the athlete. At practice sessions, the coach should be picky when analyzing the athlete's game, and he should not accept anything but the top effort and performance from the athlete. The coach should be selective in the timing and amount of positive feedback he gives each athlete. Unlike pre-competition periods, practice sessions give the athlete time to regroup from this criticism and develop a tough exterior that will prove helpful under match pressure. It is a good idea for the coach to let his players know that practice has to be the toughest time and that here he'll continually expect high intensity and an excellent performance. If the coach allows a weak performance in practice, he will get a weak performance in matches.

The ability to tell the athlete what he needs to hear and not what he wants to hear is an important one for the coach to acquire. This is tough to do because of the coach's very human need to be approved of and liked. From the outside it is easy to say, "Why isn't that coach tougher on his athletes, or why does he give in to all their whims?" The fact is, it is very hard to carry out the tough assignment that makes players unhappy, even though a coach's best coaching instincts tell him it's what they truly need. Players often look away, frown, grumble or even walk away when the coach gives tough instructions. But the bottom line remains — the coach should have the athletes do what they need to do, not what they want to do. When these interests become the same, the coach is on the way to developing great players and a great team.

Positive Feedback Should Not Be Used for Mediocre Performances

What a coach praises in a player is usually the performance that the player will give the next time. It may be difficult for a coach not to get excited and praise any accomplishment of a team member, especially if that player is a low achiever. The coach must have a good perspective on what is truly a superior achievement for the individual as opposed to what is a mediocre achievement. This is hard to judge because what is mediocre for one athlete may be superior for another and vice versa.

The athlete himself is ready for any type of praise after a win, whether it is warranted or not. Again, what he needs and what he wants may be two completely different things. A coach's praise at the wrong time can make the athlete too comfortable, whereas withholding a compliment at the wrong time may be discouraging for the athlete.

Neither the coach's need to give positive feedback nor the athlete's need to receive positive feedback should override what the athlete truly needs for his growth and development. Again, the coach's perception of what his player needs is the most important factor for productive use of positive reinforcement.

Positive Feedback Should Be Used More with Less Experienced Players

Just as the newborn is sensitive to his new environment, so the rookie athlete is sensitive to his new situation. Veterans have tougher exteriors and are usually better able to handle the coach's criticism. Veterans also have a track record and the confidence to persevere through tough times. The young player will surely have obvious doubts from time to time. No matter how confident the rookie may appear, he'll need positive feedback to make it through the initial tough times. The job of the coach is to help the young player get through this transition period without babying him along. The tough job is to be objective about successes, failures and improvement areas, while giving as much sincere positive feedback as possible.

Positive Feedback Should Be Used in the Presence of Others

To praise in public and criticize in private is one of the first rules of leadership. Sometimes a negative revealed to the athlete's peers can do a lot of harm.

On the other hand, team meetings or other public occasions are good times to give sincere, truthful praise of a team member. People, especially young people, tend to express and develop the qualities that are affirmed in them. When done in front of peers, positive affirmation has an even better effect.

Everyone works for and truly enjoys recognition. Positive recognition in the presence of others is an excellent coaching tool.

Positive Feedback Should Be Used After a Loss (If the Player Played as Hard as He or She Could)

Positive reinforcement can be difficult to give when both the coach and player are emotionally involved, especially if the match is an important one. Often the coach's disappointment is directed toward the player. This frustration must be vented, but the most available target is not always the best target. After a tough loss, the athlete and the coach need to have some time for their emotions to settle.

In almost all cases, the athlete who has diligently prepared for a competition will care enough to give 100 percent. He may at times withdraw energy when in a losing situation, but in more cases than not, the athlete who has trained hard will also play hard. It's a shame so many people equate losing with poor effort. The belief is that if someone tries hard enough, he will win. This is not always true, especially in a sport such as tennis where creative skills, talent and confidence are so important.

As difficult as it may be, the time after a loss is an excellent time for the coach to praise the positive aspects of the player and to rebuild confidence in his skills. No matter how self-assured the athlete may appear, inside he will be shaken up. To achieve his best performance, an athlete must find the balance between his confidence, the acceptance of his own shortcomings, respect for the opponent, and trust and belief in himself and his humility. When a tough loss or great win upsets this balance, it is the coach's job to boost the wounded ego or bring down the high-flying ego.

> **A** word of encouragement during tough times is worth more than a dictionary of praise after success. — *Unknown*

Positive Feedback Should Be Used Less Often After a Win

A player will not be short of pats on the back following a win. Parents, teammates, girlfriends and friends will sing the praises. The compliment that comes from the coach always means the most, but it is not always essential for the coach to praise the athlete. A coach should point out the good things in the player's game, but the period after a win is an excellent time for him to be critical about areas that need improvement. The coach must be the judge of how much positive feedback to give. Sometimes a coach can slow the player's progress by over-rewarding what should be a routine success. Even a big, exciting win may be put in a different perspective by considering the player's total development. Early celebration and an abundance of praise may prevent the athlete from performing up to his ability the next time out. A football team has a week between games to go through the whole process — win, celebrate, come back down to earth, work hard, prepare for next ball game, take care of all pre-game details. The tennis player sometimes has only an hour or a day to go through this entire process. If he needs praise and celebration after a win, these must be short so that preparation for the next match can begin.

Recognizing these facts, the coach should be very selective in his praise of a player immediately after a win. Credit should always be given, but the balance should be there as well. It is very important, though, to enjoy your victories; otherwise motivation will likely suffer. I usually will tell my players to enjoy their victory until a certain time, and then refocus for the next match.

NEGATIVE FEEDBACK

A good example of negative feedback is the stereotype of a drill sergeant who never gives praise and continually berates his recruits' confidence and self-image. Although the drill sergeant's approach is appropriate for the needs of military recruits, badgering or belittling does little good for athletes; however, the timely use of negative reinforcement can greatly help them. How to use it, when to use it, and which players to use it on are the keys to its effectiveness.

Negative Feedback Should Not Be Used Before Competition

If it has not been taken care of before you get to the battlefield, it is probably too late. There is no sense in pointing out the small wart on the pretty girl's face right before the beauty pageant. Bringing attention to flaws and weaknesses in a player's game before he takes the court serves no good and can actually do a lot of harm. It would be like the manager of a boxer who says something like, "We should have worked more on your left jab before the fight. I hope it will hold up," or the coach at the Super Bowl who says "We've got to hope they don't throw the ball a lot, our secondary just isn't ready."

Pre-match tension is enough to cause the athlete to have some doubt. This is the time for the coach to say, "We're ready, the hay's in the barn, and the horses are at the gate. It's exciting to play today, and your game looks sharp,"; or the boxing manager to say, "You're fit, you're fast, you're sharp, and there's none better."

> A good leader does not walk behind his people with a whip; He walks in front of them with a banner.

Negative Feedback Should Not Be Used Immediately After Competition

Nothing said in the way of criticism immediately after a match will work positively. After a loss the player is so scared and vulnerable that it will probably only do harm to point out his flaws. The best thing for the coach to do is to wait until the emotion of the situation has settled and then talk to the athlete. Specific points should be made in a constructive manner and in a way that does not attack the player's own self-concept. If there is enough time, the day following the match is the best time to point out flaws and weaknesses in the player's game. If there is not enough time, the coach should wait at least for an hour or so to let the emotions settle.

Negative Feedback Works Well in Practice, but Maintain a Positive Attitude While Using It

Practice is the time to expect and to get perfection. Since there is no opponent to supply pressure, the coach should provide it. In the pressure-free environment of practice, play can appear to be good without really being good. Great coaches nit-pick in practice so that in a match situation when real pressure exists, the player can execute.

It is easy for a coach to be lulled into a false sense of security because his team performs well in a practice situation when there is no pressure. A good rule of thumb for the coach is to be very fired up and emotional, and to always expect perfection during practice sessions. On game day he should be more relaxed and accepting and allow his players' creative juices to flow. Ideally, practice days should contain repetitive, obsessive work, and each athlete should be pushed hard by himself or his coach. Match days should be easier, and the coach should cultivate a creative and inspired atmosphere that allows the creative and inner talents of each athlete to surface. The coach should maintain a positive and helpful attitude toward each individual making it visibly apparent and even obvious that he is correcting actions, not dressing down people.

Negative Feedback Can Be Used More with the Older Team Members

The veterans of the team are more resilient and tough and will best handle negative reinforcement from the coach. Familiarity with the coach's methods prevents the older athlete's confidence from being damaged as easily as the younger athlete's. But it is a tough job for the coach to always obtain maximum effort from an older member of the team. That is because the motivation provided by the coach in the early part of a player's career must lead ultimately to an inner motivation on the part of the athlete. A good method of keeping motivation is to give responsibility to the junior or senior team member. With this added responsibility, the team member senses trust from the coach and will better understand the coach's negative feedback and tough criticism of the weak areas in his game.

Negative Feedback Should Be Done in Private

"Don't hang out your dirty wash in public," as the saying goes. The rule to praise in public and criticize in private can once again be applied. People tend to become what we label them. Scolding or criticism of a player should take place in the office or in another private area. This allows the athlete to avoid being put in a defensive position in front of his peers, and it preserves his ego and self-esteem. In a disciplinary situation, the privacy of an office allows the athlete a chance to state his opinion and to get things off his chest. In front of a team this might not be appropriate and might make the coach defensive. Coach-player confrontations that occur in front of the team will (and must) be won by the coach because he has the designated power and authority. Often a situation that could have been taken care of in the privacy of an office is allowed to escalate when handled in front of others.

Negative Feedback Can Be Used After a Win if the Effort Was Not What the Coach is Looking For

Remember that your players need important pats on the back. The fun and praise of winning is one big reasons and is why we all play tennis; but, the time immediately following a win is an excellent time to critique your player and be picky about his tennis game. The player is probably flying high and, once again, one of the coach's jobs is to bring the player's emotions down to a workable level. The performance, and not necessarily the win or loss, is what should be analyzed.

After a win, a coach may have a tendency to praise the athlete and to feed that emotion that the athlete wants fed. But if winning is a chance for growth and confidence building, the coach must be objective enough to reward or punish the player's performance and not just the result.

Good Judgment Should Be Used When Giving Negative Feedback After a Loss

This is a delicate situation because the athlete is already vulnerable and sensitive. If his game is criticized, it must be done in an objective manner. Again, it is best to wait until the emotion of the situation has settled — usually an hour at least.

Once again, the older members of the team are better equipped than the younger members to handle criticism following a loss. The coach must use good judgment and timing in the use of negative reinforcement after a loss. Remember that we all need positive feedback, but negative feedback hurts. Always address the issues and not the substance of the player.

When Using Negative Feedback, Always Build the Player Back Up Before Dismissing Him

Just as a surgeon never performs an operation without closing the incision, so a coach should never punish, criticize or overly critique an athlete without building him up again. A good method is to say something like, "Your actions stink, and I expect more out of you. This is not up to your standards and quality. You really messed this job up, but I believe in you and know that you will get the situation corrected." Or, "The team and I want you on this team because of your good qualities, and I know you will be able to handle this tough situation." Ideally, the action and the person can be separated, and the player can leave with his self-esteem intact, knowing that he has to do to correct any problems.

LONG-RANGE MOTIVATION FOR PLAYER DEVELOPMENT

Affirmation is the key word in confidence development. Ultimately, a coach's trust and belief in his players as people and athletes will overcome any short-term ups and downs that occur. In the four years that a coach works with a player, immediate positive and negative reinforcement must take place and, in addition, the overriding tone and the underlying current provided by the coach must be filled with trust and confidence.

Just as the player must believe in the coach, so must the coach believe unconditionally in the player. The player usually accomplishes what the coach expects him to accomplish. He seldom accomplishes more, and he usually accomplished less. Positive affirmation of positive qualities and acceptance of those qualities that cannot be changed must be the long-term goal for the coach.

Figure 19-1. A good coach will know the appropriate times to use positive and negative feedback.

THE COACH'S CONFIDENCE IN HIS PLAYERS

There are some players a coach finds it easy to have confidence in and others with whom it's more difficult. But, sooner or later, there comes a critical point when a coach has to let go of the reins completely and say to the player, "You're on your own." As mentioned earlier, it is like training a thoroughbred racehorse. First, you pull the reins tight in order to get the stallion to move in the direction you want. Little by little, you let go of the reins until at some point you drop them completely and let him run. If you hadn't been strict and pulled the reins tight at first, the stallion would do whatever he wanted and react only on instinct.

Like thoroughbred racehorses, the best athletes need to have their energies directed positively. Emotion plays a big part in the development of a lot of top athletes. The coach must discern the direction the athlete needs to go in and give him guidance. Some athletes never seem mature enough to allow the coach to give up the reins completely. Usually these are the quiet or shy athletes who look as if their confidence is always close to breaking.

During the 1980 season, I had a player named Dick Milford who was our number six player and played number three doubles. At this point in my career, Clemson had never won the conference championship and we had just moved into a national ranking for the first time in the history of the school. My tendency then as a coach was to be tentative and calculate all moves so that we would not lose what we had gained. Dick's Junior year had been difficult — he had a lot of trouble with self-confidence, and some of the other players on the team had started to lose confidence in him as well. After a player's first year or so, when the initial enthusiasm of being a college athlete has worn off, he will often go through a slump.

Dick's slump started his junior year and went on for eight or nine months. Both he and I had worked very hard in overcoming the trouble he was having and in trying to pull him out of this slump. It was truly not a matter of hard work, though, because Dick was one of the hardest workers I have ever had on a team.

I learned a great lesson about having confidence in a player during an early February tournament in Arkansas, in a match against Brigham Young University. We were down in a team match 4-2 after singles, and when doubles play started it looked as if we had a good chance of making the match a close one. We then won number one and number two doubles. The entire team match came down to the number three doubles match, in which I really felt we were outmatched.

Dick's partner was a player named Mitch Mitchell, and they were totally dominated in the first set 6-2. As the second set started, I knew the only chance we had was to play much more aggressively. Dick usually chipped all of his returns, making it easy for the other team to gain control of the point. Early in the second set, I walked to the court and told Dick to hit out on the ball aggressively even if the balls went into the fence. If we were going to lose, I wanted us to lose with aggressive mistakes and not by trying to place every ball. Mitch Mitchell played the ad court and almost never missed a return of serve, thereby allowing us to take this gamble in the deuce court. Dick followed my instructions and hit the first two balls into the backstop, but I kept insisting that he hit out on the ball. Somehow, Dick finally connected with a few balls, and the change of play and his aggressiveness got us back into the match. At 5-5 of the second set we got a service break and held on to serve out the set.

In the third set our team made some early mistakes and got behind 4-2. The BYU team went ahead 5-3 and we held serve to make it 5-4. On the next return game, with no ad scoring, it came down to a single point, which we won to make it 5-5. I, of course, instructed Mitch to take the sudden death point, and he made a fine return. Then at 6-6, we went into a tie-breaker. At that time we played nine-point tie-breakers, which meant that at 4-4, one point decided the whole match. Dick's play had been sporadic. Sometimes he made contact with the ball, sometimes he didn't, so the safe play was to allow Mitch to take the 4-4 point if we got to it. The BYU team served to make the score 4-3 with two more serves coming up. Mitch made a fine return to make the score 4-4. Six hours of a very tough team match had come down to a single point. The suspense was both exciting and terrifying.

The obvious coaching decision at this point was to have Mitch take the return. I knew he would put the ball in the court, and I knew he would put tremendous pressure on the serving team by returning the serve. This was the calculated and best play. But there were other considerations in the decision that I had to make. One was our best opportunity to win the team match. But I also knew that Dick had been struggling with his confidence for some time. I knew that if Mitch made the return, winning or losing the point, Dick would be in the same dilemma in future matches. I knew what I had to do if I truly cared for Dick's development. Both players looked up at me and said, "Who should take it?" Without hesitation, I said, "Dick, you take the return." He looked at me in surprise and then turned around and looked to where the rest of the team was sitting. As he did so, the team stood up and cheered for him saying, "Go Dick! Do it, Dick!" Then I saw a big smile come across his face and saw any fear he might have had turn into courage. He spread his legs wide and got a good base as he readied to return serve. Although Dick had been hitting out on his return the entire match and had done fairly well, I felt that at this point he should go with his bread and butter and what he did best. I called from the stands, "Dick, chip and charge the way you like to do it." I had not let him chip a ball the other two sets and now I was asking him to do it at the biggest point of the match and probably the biggest point of his career.

> **The hardest victory is victory over oneself.**

Dick had been chipping and charging for the ten years he had been playing tennis, and he seemed confident that he would make the return.

The BYU player missed the first serve, which made it easier for Dick to chip and charge on the second. The second serve bounced up high on Dick's backhand. Dick sliced from high to low to put the ball down at the server's feet and closed off the net. The server made a good first volley, but Dick was already on top of the net, and he drilled a volley between the players for the match win.

I have never had a more exciting moment as a coach. The players cleared out of the stands and grabbed Dick into their arms. I was thrilled not only with Dick but also that I had elected to go with the boy's confidence and the thing that would be better for his growth. It is something I have always remembered, and any time I've been in a similar situation, I've always gone with the decision that was important for the growth of the player. The wins, I feel, will always take care of themselves. The players have few such growth opportunities.

Four more times in that season (the best season in the history of Clemson tennis) the team match came down to Dick's match. One was against Georgia in Athens, and Dick hit the shot that let us beat the Bulldogs for the first time in over 10 years. Another was our first NCAA Tournament victory over Princeton, in a dramatic come-from-behind match that we won with another 7-6 in the third. In each of these, when the match got close, Dick played aggressively, assertively and without fear. I know for a fact that if I had not given him the chance to return serve and win that team match, not only would his game not have come around that season, but our team may not have either. Perhaps even the Clemson tennis program would have been delayed in becoming a nationally recognized program for a year or two more.

Later, after Dick's graduation, I received a letter from him that meant more to me than just about any letter I have ever received from a player. It talked about my trust in the players, and how I set high expectations for them, and how even though we had not won the national championship his senior year, in the end, there was not one member of the team who truly did not believe that the team could accomplish such a goal. He stated that it was truly amazing that a group of guys who started out in last place in the conference as freshmen had accomplished so much. The team had experienced a great victory in the tremendous growth that the team members had made.

SUMMARY

The coach's use of positive and negative feedback in the proper manner and with the proper timing is critical to a player's growth. Immediate feedback is essential, and the coach should try to incorporate positive and negative feedback in the daily work with his players. When mistakes are made, they should be made with sincerity and with the right purpose in mind. These will be interpreted in the right way by the team members even if what the coach does is not exactly the right thing. In many ways the wrong action is better than no action.

A coach's belief in, and affirmation of, positive traits in the athlete is the only way for a player to develop long-term confidence. The coach's trust must exist through good times and bad.

Figure 19-2. It is important for the coach to help the player put a match into perspective, win or lose.

Figure 19-2. Individual players will react differently to positive and negative feedback.

TRAIN YOUR TEAM'S DOUBLES SKILLS

In team tennis, doubles becomes one of the focal points of concern in the training routine. Most of the pressure of a team match is in doubles because that is where the climax of the match usually occurs. The whole point is to arrive at the season finale with three well-tuned teams.

In college tennis, players keep the same partner for two to three years. In the junior ranks and also in the pro ranks, players often switch partners and doubles routines because of the logistics of different schedules and because of the many different training sites. Regardless of whether your partner is a regular one or not, most of the same basic principles for good doubles play still apply.

With four people instead of two to cover just a bit more court than in a singles match, the doubles match relies more heavily on court positioning than on shot-making. Shot-making seems to be of greater importance in singles play because there a player can be forced off balance and out of position much more easily. In singles, the court position to shot-making ratio could be rated at about 65 percent to 35 percent; in doubles it is probably just the opposite, 35 percent to 65 percent.

The doubles game is also more repetitive than singles, and the doubles player finds himself playing the same type of point again and again. In singles it often seems that no two points are the same. Playing good doubles, then, is a matter of taking care of fundamentals over and over while being flexible enough to make subtle changes when needed.

The coach's first task is to teach his players their specific jobs and responsibilities at each position they play on the court. Each player will play about one fourth of his points as the server's partner, and one fourth of his points as the receiver's partner. If each player knows his responsibility at each position, the doubles match can be played with much more confidence.

The specific jobs of server, server's partner, receiver and receiver's partner should be worked on at every doubles practice until players understand them and can effectively carry them out. They are the fundamentals for playing doubles effectively and, if learned well, establish a firm foundation that can be built upon.

THE FUNDAMENTAL POSITIONS

Server and Receiver Fundamentals

The positions of server and receiver must be played well for a doubles team to be effective. It is critical that the server master the fundamentals of a good second serve and a solid first volley. Equally important is a solid crosscourt return for the receiver. These skills are so important and basic that I spend the first two months of the fall season playing one versus one (invisible partner doubles), or crosscourt serve and volley matches where records are kept and results used to rank the players for later doubles pairings. Also, the players are only allowed one serve when they are ahead which helps them learn an

237

**Figure 20-1. The doubles match relies more heavily
on court positioning than on shot-making.**

effective second serve under pressure. The players
get tired of playing the same crosscourt game over
and over, but after the second month they are
skilled at second serves, first volleys, crosscourt
returns and quick volleys. Figure 20-2 shows the
boundaries for these games. (My thanks to James
Wadley, tennis coach at Oklahoma State University,
for helping me to establish this approach to
teaching doubles.)

THE SERVER'S JOBS

Job One: Make the First Serve

This is the most basic job because the receiver
naturally thinks defensively on the first serve,
whereas on the second serve he thinks offensively.
A big first serve about once a game works well to
keep the receiver off balance and out of a groove,
but a high percentage of first serves is critical to
be successful.

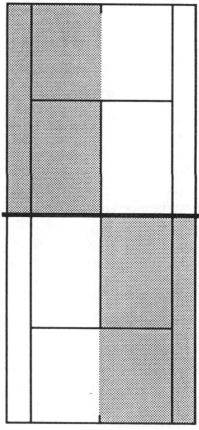

**Figure 20-2. Boundaries for half-
court serve and volley games.**

Job Two: Serve to the Middle of the Deuce Court and to the Player's Body in the Ad Court

The angle of possible return that the receiver has is critical to holding serve effectively in doubles. A wide serve opens up the court for the receiver to hit a sharp angle back or to go down the alley past the net man. In the deuce court, a serve to the backhand of the middle of the court keeps the court closed and allows the net man to poach effectively to help the server hold serve. SD on Figure 20-3 shows the best place to serve in the deuce court. In the ad court, the server may be concerned with a serve to the middle because the receiver gets to hit a forehand. A serve wide to the backhand still makes the alley vulnerable, and it allows a sharp angle crosscourt return. For the best serve into the ad court, the server should aim at the receiver's left leg to deliver a ball into his body. The angles are kept close, and the receiver's stroke is jammed. A wide serve can be used effectively, but it must be used with the right timing. Even though aces will be hit in doubles even more than in singles, the purpose of the serve is to set up the second shot. Smart placement of the serve makes holding serve much easier (SA on Figure 20-3).

Job Three: The First Volley Should Go Down the Middle

For the same reasons that a wide serve should not be used very often, so the first volley should not be angled unless it can be hit for a winner. A first volley to the middle again keeps the angles closed and prevents the receiving team from making an offensive shot. If the first volley is close enough to the middle of the court, the receiver will probably lob, which is what two players who are on the net would favor (See Figure 20-4).

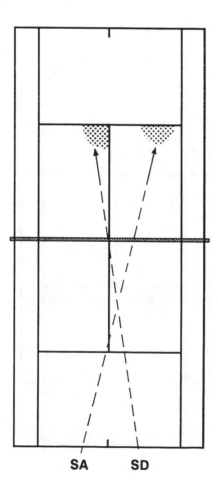

Figure 20-3. Target areas for serve to the deuce and ad court.

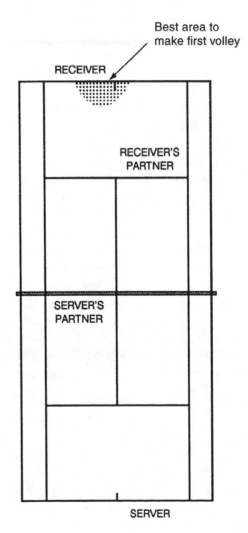

Figure 20-4. Target area for the first volley.

Job Four: Move in as Close to the Net as Possible to Make the First Volley

The difference between hitting an offensive or a defensive first volley is the server's positioning close to the net. An offensive or put-away volley is possible on high returns if the server can move in quickly. A low ball will have to be dealt with more conservatively, and just a few feet can make a big difference.

Job Five: The Server Should Assume Responsibility for All First Volleys to Allow the Net Player to be Aggressive

Miscommunication between the server and partner is often what causes a break of serve. The most common scenario is when the server's partner starts to poach on a floating ball at the net and then changes his mind, leaving the server unready to make the volley and upset at his partner for not taking the ball. This only has to happen once for the server's partner to become either tentative or overly aggressive the next time in trying to make things happen. Miscommunication can be prevented with the simple rule that unless a planned poach is called, the server is responsible for all first volleys. If the server's partner rushes across with a swing and a miss, the server still backs him up. This allows the poacher at the net total freedom to move on any ball that floats, making him a significant threat. The server is the backup man, and his partner is the cutoff man. The partner should cut off any ball that he can reach, but if he cannot hit a solid volley, he should allow the server to play the first volley. When the server knows that he is responsible for all first volleys, he is able to put the right amount of pressure on himself to allow him to hold serve a bit easier. The net man should feel free to attack the receiver's poor returns with total aggressiveness.

Job Six: Use the I Formation for Change-up

The I Formation (sometimes called the Australian Formation) can be used as an excellent tactic when a receiver is in a groove and not missing any returns. Even if this formation does not make him miss returns, it will at least change his groove and perhaps change the flow of the returning team's confidence. The I Formation forces the receiving team to change the direction of the ball on the return in order to go down the line instead of crosscourt. This changing of direction usually causes errors on the service return.

One seldom-noticed advantage of the I Formation is its ability to handcuff the receiver's partner and prevent him from making any poaches. It works very well to take away this element of a receiving team.

A good idea on service placement is to realize that wide serve allows the receiver angles to hook the ball down the line, pinning the net man down. The serve to the opponent's body is best, but the serve to the middle of the court can work well also. The I Formation should be practiced often so that the doubles team is comfortable with it in pressure situations.

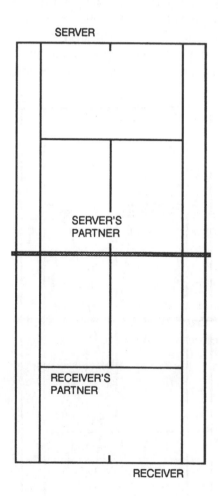

Figure 20-5. The I formation.

THE RECEIVER'S JOBS

Job One: No Returns Wide or in the Net

This is the only what-not-to-do in this section, and it acts as a reminder that the return should be hit over the net and through the opponents. It is a good idea for the receiver to completely block the poacher out of his mind as if he were invisible or nonexistent. It is best not to change directions on the return, as this reduces the percentages for an error (see the section on transition shots in Chapter 5). The rule is basic, but it should be ingrained in the player's subconscious. A ball hit wide or in the net is an immediate loss of the point and the mortal sin of a returner. Most returning errors in doubles are a result of pressing or trying to make the shot be too good. The player's "regular stuff" is good enough, as long as the rule "No balls wide, no balls in the net" is followed.

Job Two: Determine Which Formation to Use and Which Play to Run

Option One: Move into the net behind a weak serve. Controlling the net is a big advantage in doubles, and when a receiver can take the net away from the serving team, it becomes easier to break serve. The return does not have to be hit hard, only deep into the court so the point can be won on the next volley. If the serve is weak, the receiver's partner must be sure to move in also.

Option Two: Return low at the server's feet, allowing the returner's partner to cross for a winning poach. This is an advanced play that can be used effectively with the combination of a good returner and a good volleyer as the receiver's partner. The idea is to hit low and aggressive returns that will force the server to pop the first volley up. The receiver's partner can be intimidating to the server by leading him to press and make errors at critical times in the match.

Option Three: Play both players on the receiving team back and try to take the net off the first weak ball. Dan Magill, tennis coach at the University of Georgia, uses this formation exclusively, and until my team was defeated by his team's use of this style at the 1986 NCAA Championships, I would seldom use it. The objective is to take a bit of pressure off the receiver in having him make a great crosscourt return every time. With two players back, the serving team has a tough job to put away the first volley. As soon as the first volley is made, the receiving team hits through the serving team until the serving team pops up an easy ball that creates an easy winner for the receiving team. The offensive top spin lob is also thrown in to keep the serving team from closing the net too tight. Of course, the serving team gets its share of winners, but they also make many errors from being forced to handle so many volleys. This formation does take practice, but if mastered it can beat any opponents who are not good volleyers. The best doubles teams, though, will usually beat a defensive doubles team which uses this both-players-back formation. Top-flight doubles is won at the net and players should definitely learn offensive tactics as well. The optimum would be to use the both-players-back receiving formation at strategic times. The coach's job is to judge the ability levels of his players and to decide which formations to use.

Figure 20-6. Good communication on the court is one key to a strong doubles team.

THE SERVER'S PARTNER'S JOBS

Job One: Direct the Server's Placement of His Serve

Much as a catcher does in baseball, the net man can give a signal that dictates the type or the placement of the serve. This is a very simple combination that works well in holding serve. If the server is directed to serve to the middle, then his partner knows to move a step toward the middle with or without the fake of a poach. There are other combinations that can also be used.

Directing the serve with signals works better than calling poaches with signals because once the poach is called, the net man is forced to cross even if the server has hit a poor serve. When the server's placement is planned, the server's partner can watch for that specific serve and react accordingly. Poaches can still be planned, but it is recommended that they be called verbally so as not to have any mistake in communication. To be effective, signals must be kept simple and specific.

Job Two: The Starting Position Should Be a Step Farther Back with Weight on the Inside Foot

The starting position should be a position that allows the net man to be able to move quickly on any floating ball. The weight should be on the inside foot, and the net man should position himself a step or two farther back to be able to lean in as the receiver makes contact with the ball.

Job Three: Move for a Poach on All Floating Balls

An important key to holding serve more easily is for the net man to move on any ball that floats. This aggressive play will often take the receiver's concentration off making a solid return and help score many points for the serving team. If the server's partner is tentative and does not move, the receiver has a great opportunity to get into an excellent groove on his return. The server's assumed responsibility to cover the first volley allows the net man great freedom to aggressively hunt for floating balls.

Job Four: Poach with a Step Out and Lateral Movement

Poaching with sideways or lateral movement gives the net man good balance for reaction to a ball that may be hit behind him or in an awkward position. The poacher often makes the mistake of running through a poach out of balance instead of moving laterally for the poach.

Job Five: Stay Aggressive at the Net

The server's partner should not stand still, but should either fake or cross. His job at the net is to distract the concentration of the receiver through his aggressive play. This helps his partner tremendously in holding serve. Even making eye contact with the receiver can sometimes help tremendously. He should look for and poach on any floaters. If nothing else, he should draw fire from the receiver. Holding service is always done with the help of a good partner at the net. He should stay active and make things happen.

Figure 20-7. The partner at the net position must play floating returns aggressively.

THE RECEIVER'S PARTNER'S JOBS

Many players do not recognize the importance of the receiver's partner. But, if this position is played well, it can be the game breaker and the difference between a good or a great doubles team. The receiver's partner has specific jobs in helping to break service.

Job One: Start at the Service Line and Square Off Facing the Server's Partner

If the receiver's partner is at the service line, it will:

1. *Allow him to help make the service line call.*
2. *Put him in a position out of the way of the return of serve.*
3. *Most importantly, give him an opportunity to react to a poach that the net man may make.*

The primary reason for squaring off toward the net man is that the net man has the first play on the ball after the return. Therefore, the receiver's partner's attention should be focused on this position, allowing the best opportunity to negate a poach through the middle. Once the ball has been returned past the net man, the receiver's partner should then take care of his next job.

Job Two: Take Three Steps to Close Off the Net

Immediately after the ball is returned past the net man, the receiver's partner should take three steps straight in to close off the net. This puts pressure on the server's first volley and allows the receiving team to take advantage of a good return of service. Staying at the service line rather than moving in does nothing except put the receiving team in a crippled situation.

Job Three: Inside-Inside or Outside-Outside Coverage

Once the receiver's partner has closed off the position on the net his other attentions should be directed to the server's first volley. If the ball is returned low and to the inside of the court, the receiver's partner should move to the inside lane to cut off the first volley. This puts tremendous pressure on the server's first volley. The server can try to hook a backhand volley from the inside

to the outside behind the poaching receiver's partner. This will force the server to change the direction of his first volley that will very often lead to the serving team's errors at critical times in the match. If the receiver's return goes to the outside or the server's forehand, the outside or line must always be covered.

Job Four: Play Both Back for a Change-up or a Different Look

As explained earlier, it is often a good tactic to play both back for a different look to the servers. This should be done at strategic times according to the type of pressure the serving team needs to have put on them.

> A great partnership is determined by the degree to which each partner benefits from the influence of the other.

WORKING AS A TEAM IN DOUBLES

How to Pick a Partner

Before choosing a partner, it is important to understand what makes a good doubles team. There are countless examples in the professional ranks of two fairly good players who, when combined, make a great team. A good doubles team should be put together with a player who can attack and put balls away (the hitter) and a partner who makes few or no errors (the setter). The setter allows the hitter to do his work, and the hitter provides the element of recklessness and aggression that the setter cannot. Two setters together would fall prey to a more aggressive or a more consistent team, whereas two hitters on the same team would be hot or cold, either scoring great wins or very bad losses. The combination of a good hitter and a good setter works well if the two players get along with each other.

The temperaments and personalities of the doubles partners should complement one another in the same way that the game styles do. (See "Different Strokes for Different Folks" section, Chapter 8). Two aggressive choleric personalities do not work well together because they may end up fighting. Two passive phlegmatic personalities usually cannot make up their minds. Although neither personality must be overbearing, a comfortable mesh between them works well.

Figure 20-8. The personalities of doubles partners should complement each other.

Who Plays Which Court?

The decision of who should play the ad court and who should play the deuce court is based on who returns best in each court. Another important factor is that the best returner should play the ad court since that is where most of the big points are played. With the exception of scores at 40-15 and the 15-40, games are always won or lost in the ad court. Positioning the better returner in the ad court helps very much in keeping the pressure on a serving team which leads to service breaks.

What About a Left-Hander?

A left-hander on a team usually adds a positive dimension to the team's effectiveness. The left-hander's shots provide different spins and force opponents to deal with a variety of additional stategies.

Although some teams prefer to have a lefty play the ad court for crosscourt returns, my preference is that the lefty play the deuce court, allowing both player's forehands to be in the middle for ground strokes and for poaching. Of course, both players must be able to handle the wide serve to the backhand well.

MOVEMENT AND TRACKING FOR THE DOUBLES TEAM

It is often said that two players moving well as a doubles team appear as if they are connected invisibly as they flow in unison from side to side and up and back.

The Inside-Inside/Outside-Outside Rule for Tracking

Tracking, or the ability to cover the opponent's possible shots at the net, can be done effectively by following the rules of inside-inside/outside-outside for your doubles team. The rules basically hold that if your shot goes to the outside (your opponent's forehand in the deuce court or your opponent's backhand in the ad court), you or your partner must cover the outside shot possibility with the other player moving to cover the middle lane. The sharp crosscourt angle is not the priority because it is such a difficult shot to make. This outside-outside rule should force the opponents into trying this type of ill-advised, low percentage shot.

The rule for shots to the inside or the middle of the court is that both you and your partner lean to the middle for the main coverage with less attention given to the shot from the middle of the court to the outside. Figures 20-9 and 20-10 show inside-inside/outside-outside coverage at the net.

These same rules apply to any situation when a player and his partner are at the net. Drills should be conducted with two up and two back, or all four players up, to practice good teamwork in tracking and coverage.

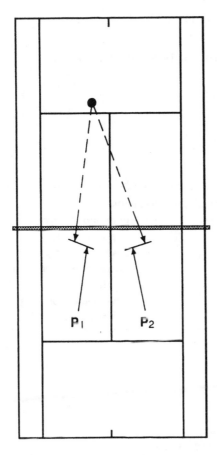

Figure 20-9. Inside-inside coverage on a ball to the middle.

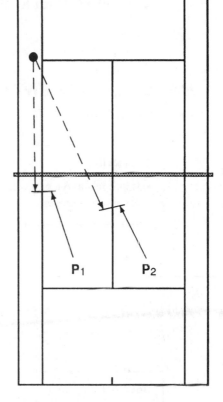

Figure 20-10. Outside-outside coverage on a ball hit wide.

Other Quick Reminders About Effective Doubles Play

1. Control the net and you will control the match. This is almost always true. With two players covering shots, it is hard to put balls away or to be effective without taking the net. Work as a team on closing off the net.

2. Go down the line or down the middle to set up your partner. A crosscourt shot from the baseline against two net men is like a shooting gallery for the team on the net. A down-the-line or down-the-middle shot, if kept low, will usually set up a player's partner.

3. A couple of good rules to remember when poaching:

    a. If my partner is hitting the ball I must look to the weak side opponent to negate his poaching movement first.

    b. If I can't hit a winner, make my shot to my opponent's side of the court.

4. Good positioning, not great shots, wins most often in doubles.

5. Hit to the middle of the court on any ball that cannot be angled off for a winner. Remember that an angled shot opens the court up for your opponent's offensive shot.

6. Hit through your opponents, not around them. This simply means that good doubles teams do not go for great shots but keep angles closed while working to gain better positioning on the net.

7. MOVE, MOVE, MOVE, AND CLOSE, CLOSE, CLOSE for better court positioning.

Figure 20-11. Doubles checklist — fundamentals for competition.

I. BASE FUNDAMENTALS
(100% Efficiency in Execution)

Best Drills:

- Half-court serve and volley
- Emerson matches

1. High percentage of first serves
2. First Volley   • over and in always
3. 2nd returns   • in play always
     • then low, then power
4. Teamwork   • turn in after each point
5. Hitting through   • no checkouts
     • never wide, never net
     • not over or around

II. ADVANCED FUNDAMENTALS
(Talk your time, grow slowly)

Best Drills:

- 2-on-1 tracking, all positions
- 3-on-2 tracking
- negating drills
- singles court sets

1. Tracking and closing
2. Negating and crossing
3. Jobs at each position
4. Shot selection
5. Roles of team members

III. FINISHING TOUCHES
(the last 5 percent to reach the top)

Flow management through the use of momentum guidelines

Tools for	Serving	Receiving
A. Delayed Pressure	1st serve	2 back
	1st volley	1 up / 1 back
B. Quick Pressure	crossing	1 up / 1 back
		offensive play
C. Change-Up Tactics	I Formation (Australian)	2 back

DOUBLES FORMATIONS AND MOMENTUM CONTROL STRATEGIES

Serving Options

A. Delayed pressure fundamentals - First serve and volley to start point. No poaching and no tricks. Use this base fundamental to close out games, when you are ahead or behind by two or three points, or when you are successful at an aggressive play to take a one-point lead.

B. Quick pressure fundamentals - Crossing (poaching) is on! Use this fundamental when you are one point behind, and for the first two points after breaking serve to take the lead. You can cross as often as needed when more offense is needed.

C. Change-up fundamentals - Use I Formation (Australian). This tactic works best when you come from behind to take the lead in a game (the 30-15 point works best), and use often when ahead by more than one break of serve.

Receiving Options

A. Delayed pressure fundamentals - Use two back formation on first serves. One-up and one-back formation on second serve. Use this formation when you are ahead or behind by two or three points, and also when you are ahead by one point in the game after running a successful play in the deuce court. The first point of the game can be played with two back when the better volleyer of the opposing team is on the net.

B. Quick pressure fundamentals - One up and one back on first serves and on second serves. On the first serve, the receiver's partner will be crossing on any low return. On the second serve, a hit (or chip) and charge play should be played when the better volleyer is serving (try to challenge the good volleyer for the net position). Both players should converge on the net in their lanes. On the second serve of the weaker volleyer, the receiver partner poaching play should be set up. Quick pressure on returns should be used always when behind by one point in the game and whenever the score is tied and offense is needed.

C. Change-up fundamentals - Use two back for first serve return and infrequently for second return. Usually run a one-up and one-back play on second serve return. You may also want to hit returns at net person, lob, or other variations. Use these tactics only when way ahead or way behind. Be ready to go to quick pressure fundamental if you lose momentum.

Special Plays

1. Poaching and running an aggressive play for the first two points after you break serve to lead usually works well to lock in leadership role in match. Never be tentative after you break serve. Go with the lead.

2. When up a break and working for the second break, play aggressive on the first point of the game, and then use more delayed pressure tactics to make opponents earn every point. Be ready to return to quick pressure tactics if needed.

3. After your bad shot or great shot take more time if possible between points. After your opponent's bad shot or great shot, take less time. No meetings with partner unless needed.

4. Use signals to direct serves and coordinate poaching.

5. Use quick switch tactic when going from regular to I Formation.

6. When down 0-40, the momentum of the game can be changed if you will play solid fundamentals on the first two points, and then at 30-40 you must poach and play aggressively.

SUMMARY

Figure 20-12. Doubles play — your role at each position.

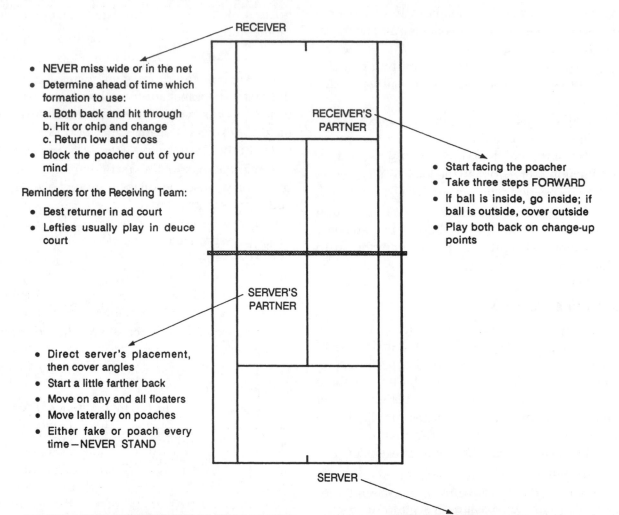

RECEIVER

- NEVER miss wide or in the net
- Determine ahead of time which formation to use:
  a. Both back and hit through
  b. Hit or chip and change
  c. Return low and cross
- Block the poacher out of your mind

Reminders for the Receiving Team:

- Best returner in ad court
- Lefties usually play in deuce court

RECEIVER'S PARTNER

- Start facing the poacher
- Take three steps FORWARD
- If ball is inside, go inside; if ball is outside, cover outside
- Play both back on change-up points

SERVER'S PARTNER

- Direct server's placement, then cover angles
- Start a little farther back
- Move on any and all floaters
- Move laterally on poaches
- Either fake or poach every time — NEVER STAND

SERVER

- Make high percentage of first serves; hit an agressive serve two times per game
- Serve down the middle, and ad court into body
- irst volley deep to middle
- Get one step farther in to volley
- It's the server's responsibility to make all first volleys
- Use the I Formation of change-up

Reminders:

- Control the net and control the match — be one step closer
- Do not go crosscourt from backcourt. Use the middle of the court to set up the point
- Setter in ad court; hitter in deuce court
- Good positioning, not great shots, wins in doubles play
- MOVE, MOVE, MOVE — CLOSE, CLOSE, CLOSE
- Use the middle on any ball that you cannot end the point on
- Hit through your opponents, not around them

Chapter 21

USE EFFECTIVE DRILLS TO SHARPEN YOUR TEAM'S SKILLS

There are six groups of drills in this section:

1. *Feeding drills — important for basic stroke development*
2. *Breakdown or one-on-one rallying drills — for practicing not changing the direction of the ball*
3. *Two-on-one drills — for practicing changing the direction of the ball*
4. *Match simulation drills*
5. *Serving drills*
6. *Simulated set play*

THE CONCEPT OF DRILL WORK

Drills help a player learn new skills and shots that would be difficult to learn by just playing sets. These shots can be developed and grooved until the player is ready to incorporate them into his game and tool box of skills.

In order for a drill to be effective, it must simulate as closely as possible the shots or situations that occur in a match. The most sophisticated drills do not have merit unless they prepare the individual for the situation he will encounter under the pressure of competition. Drills should be simple and specific, and each player should know what he is trying to accomplish.

Strive for excellence, not perfection....

FEEDING DRILLS

Feeding drills have the most benefit when a skill is first being learned. The primary purpose of feeding drills is to allow the player to groove a particular stroke or shot, and this is done by having the coach feed balls to a particular area of the court for the player to make return shots. The coach should try to feed balls with a variety of spins and placement so that the player learns to handle balls of various degrees of difficulty. Although feeding drills do instill confidence, it is quite difficult to simulate the same spins, power and rhythm that occur in a game rally. Each feeding drill should be repeated anywhere from eight to 12 times, depending on the player's fitness and ability.

Figure 21-1. Feeding drill.

1. Wide-Middle Forehand Drill

Objective: To work on wide forehands and forehands from the middle position. The major emphasis is on improving movement and setting up for the forehand from any position on the court.

Description: Standing just behind the service line, the coach (C) feeds a balls deep and wide to the forehand side (1), making the player (P) stretch to return it. The coach then feeds a ball to the middle (2) so the player has to move very quickly in recovery to the middle to hit a forehand. The coach continues hitting balls wide (3) and to the middle (4), mixing up the feeds. He should also feed balls to the backhand corner so that the player can hit inside-out forehands.

2. Wide-Middle Backhand Drill

Objective: To work on wide backhands and backhands from the middle of the court, with the major emphasis on the player's movement and balance in setting up for the shot.

Description: The coach (C) stands behind the service line and feeds a ball to the middle of the court (1) so the player (P) has to stretch to return it. The coach then feeds a ball wide to the backhand side (2), forcing the player to back up into a position to make this backhand shot. The coach continues to hit balls to the middle (3) and wide (4) on the backhand side. As the player becomes more proficient in setting up for each shot, the coach should also feed balls to the forehand side of the court to force the player to develop even better court movement in setting up for balance.

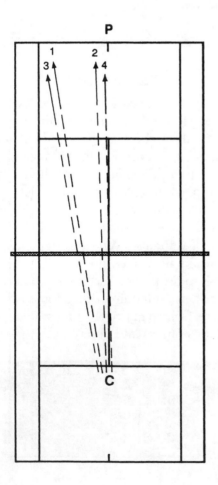

Figure 21-2.

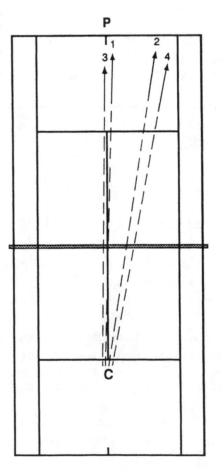

Figure 21-3.

3. Wide-Middle Volley Drill (Forehand and Backhand)

Objective: To work on stretch volleys and volleys from the middle position. The improvement of movement and balance is emphasized.

Description: The coach (C) feeds balls alternately wide and to the middle of the deuce court, forcing the player (P) to stretch for a wide ball (1 and 3) and then recover to the middle for a cramped volley (2 and 4). The drill should also be performed with the player in the ad court so he can work on his backhand volley.

4. Stretch Ground Stroke Drill

Objective: To groove the forehand and backhand while working on footwork and lateral movement.

Description: The coach (C) stands behind the service line and feeds a wide ball to the forehand side of the backcourt (1). The player (P) moves from the center of the backcourt to return the ball, and then recovers to the middle by using good lateral footwork. The coach then feeds the player another wide ball to the forehand side (2) and continues the drill with two consecutive feeds to the backhand side (3 and 4). The player should aim his returns either crosscourt or down the line.

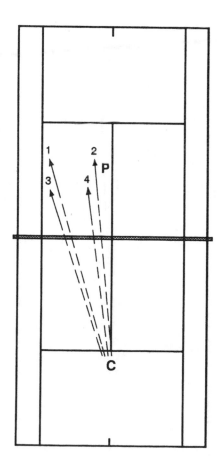

Figure 21-4.

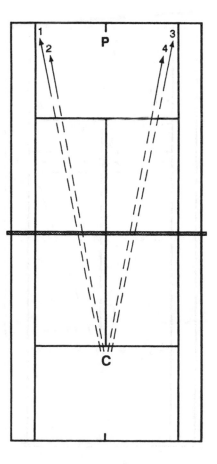

Figure 21-5.

5. Stretch Volley Drill

Objective: To improve movement at the net and learn how to make the volley when fully stretched out.

Description: The coach (C) stands four to five feet behind the service line and feeds balls to the outstretched reach of the player's (P) forehand and backhand volleys. Special emphasis should be placed on the player's recovery back to the middle after each shot before stretching for the next ball. The player should hit the ball deep to the baseline or make a drop volley.

6. Six Ball Drill: All Court Coverage

Objective: To combine the stretch forehand and backhand ground strokes with the stretch forehand and backhand volleys.

Description: The coach (C) stands four to five feet behind the service line. He feeds balls to the player (P) so that the player has to move from one corner to the other and stretch to return the balls (1 and 2). He then brings the player into the net by feeding him a short ball (3). The player hits the approach shot, and then the coach feeds balls to the player's forehand and backhand sides so he has to stretch to volley back (4 and 5). The coach can add an overhead (6) as the last shot.

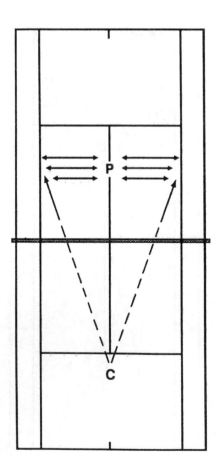

Figure 21-6.

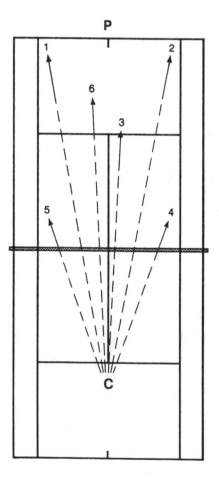

Figure 21-7.

7. *Kill Shot Drill*

Objective: To develop the player's kill shot, or a shot that is virtually impossible to return.

Description: The coach (C) feeds weak balls to different positions on the court (1, 2, 3 and 4), and the player (P) moves to every ball and hits only a forehand or a backhand. This forces the player to develop his footwork and court movement and to learn to hit an aggressive shot off a weak ball. The player should try to hit each shot as aggressively as possible. Shot placement can be made to either corner.

8. *Volley-Close-Smash Drill*

Objective: To develop forward and backward movement.

Description: The coach (C) feeds a low volley to the feet of the player (P), who starts behind the service line (1). The second volley should be a floater that the player closes on to angle away (2), and the third shot should be an overhead that the player moves back for and puts away (3).

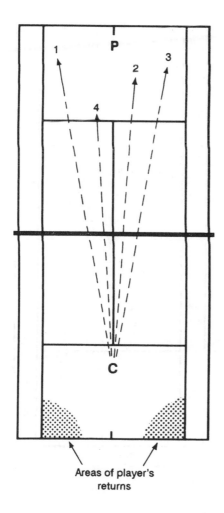

Figure 21-8.

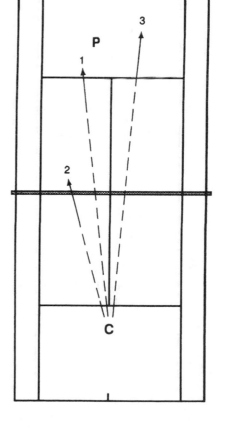

Figure 21-9.

9. Low Ball-High Ball Drill

Objective: To work on forward and backward movement and to improve low volleys and overheads.

Description: The player (P) starts behind the service line and moves up quickly to take a short volley out of the air (1), and then the coach feeds an immediate overhead beyond him (2). The player has to move back quickly for a smash (3) and then close again for a short volley (4).

10. Drop Shot Drill

Objective: To improve forward movement for running down drop shots.

Description: The player (P) starts on the baseline. The coach (C) is at the net and drops a very short ball over the net to the right or the left (1 and 2). The player races from the baseline to make the shot, then backpedals to the start again.

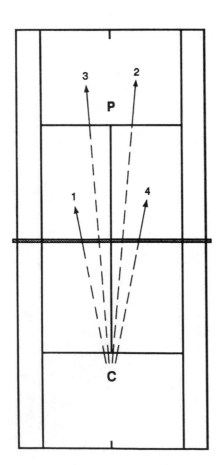

Figure 21-10.

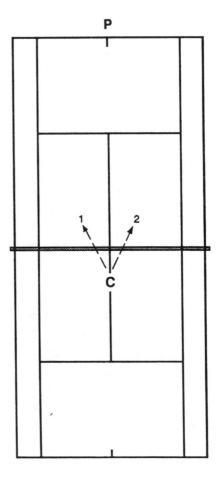

Figure 21-11.

11. Change of Direction Drill (Ground Strokes or Volleys)

Objective: To learn how to change the direction of the ball on ground strokes, and how to improve court movement. The player will also learn his limitations with each shot.

Description: The coach (C) feeds balls from the deep corner of the court to different places all over the court (1-5). The player gets to every ball and hits shots of different speeds and spins to the opposite corner. This can be done with the player at the net, or with the coach up and the player back, or with both the player and the coach at the net.

12. No Change of Direction Drill (Ground Strokes and Volleys)

Objective: To learn how consistency can be developed when the ball is hit right back to where it came from (at a right angle). There is a difference when the player tries to change the direction of the ball. The player will also learn his limitations on each ball.

Description: The coach (C) feeds balls from the deep corner or the side net position. The player (P) has to get to every ball (1-5) and hit it right back to where it came from. This drill can also be done with both the coach and the player up, or with one up and the other back.

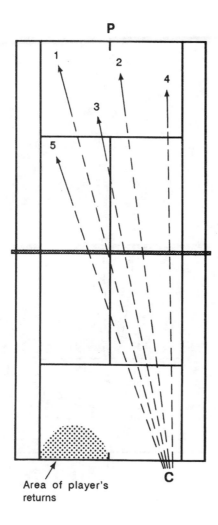

Figure 21-12.

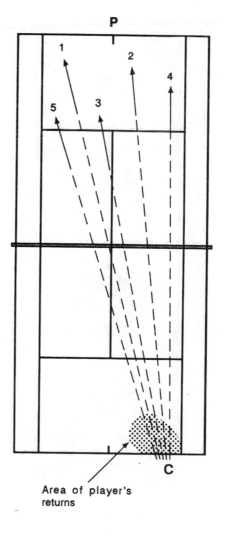

Figure 21-13.

13. The Boykin Bring in Drill

Objective: To learn to use the short angles that are necessary to stretch, and to work on approaching the net and playing from an uncomfortable position.

Description: The coach (C) stands behind the baseline and feeds balls to different areas of the player's court. The player (P1) drives two or three balls deep and then hits a very short angle to the wide part of the service box. If a second player (P2) is used in the drill, he is forced to the net, so the first player hits a passing shot. The drill should be used in preparation for competition against a player who dislikes net play.

14. Approach-Volley-Smash Drill

Objective: To improve upward and backward movement, and to improve the approach shot, volley and overhead smash.

Description: The coach (C) feeds balls from three to five feet behind the service line. The player (P) starts in the middle of the backcourt area. The coach feeds the player an approach shot (1) that he slices, and then he comes into the net. The coach then feeds the player a volley (2) followed by an overhead (3) that makes the player move all the way back to the three-quarter court area again.

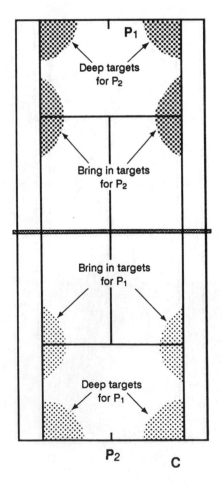

Figure 21-14.

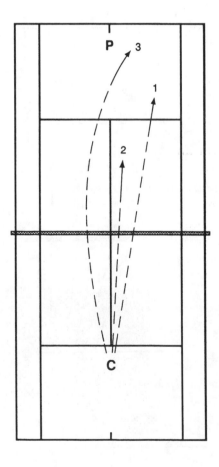

Figure 21-15.

CHANGING THE DIRECTION OF THE BALL VERSUS NOT CHANGING THE DIRECTION OF THE BALL

During a point in tennis, a player may choose to change or to not change the direction of the ball's flight. Not changing the direction of the ball (hitting the ball back to where it came from) allows the player to hit the ball at a right angle. This is very forgiving to slightly mishit shots and also more difficult shots such as the return of serve, first volleys, passing shots, approach shots and balls placed so that a player is stretched and becomes off-balance or out of position for a return. It is a good rule to avoid changing the direction of the ball on any shot that cannot be controlled.

Changing the direction of the ball (hitting the ball to the open court), on the other hand, is a much riskier proposition. Only a slight change in the angle of the racquet face can misdirect a ball out of bounds or into the net. The temptation is to hit the ball to the open court, away from the opponent. However, this is not always a good idea because of the greater chance for error and because a poorly hit ball will sit up, thereby giving the opponent an opportunity for a put-away on his shot.

Of course, put-aways usually have to be hit to the open court or hit with a change of direction. The key is for a player to recognize his limitations with each ball hit in a rally, whether he is in the backcourt or at the net. If the shot cannot be adequately controlled or put away for a winner, the direction of the ball should not be changed. Returning the ball back to where it came from keeps the player in position and sets him up for the next ball, thereby making it difficult for the opponent to hit a winner. If the ball can be controlled or put away, though, the player should hit it to the open court.

Players who compete on extremely fast courts quickly learn that few or no changes of direction can be made. Also, against extremely hard hitters, it is an excellent tactic not to change the direction of the ball, because this will reduce errors and allow the player to use his opponent's pace more effectively for his own shots. It may also tempt the hard hitter to go for the open court too often.

The following rallying drills teach players how and when to use either a change of direction or no change of direction. Following the Wardlaw Directionals will lead to greater proficiency in determining when to change or not to change direction of the ball.

BREAKDOWN (ONE-ON-ONE) RALLYING DRILLS

In these drills the player returns the ball to where it came from and tries to avoid a breakdown in his execution or concentration. The drills show the use of a coach and one player, but can be done with two players or with two players and a coach with the coach acting as a feeder.

Figure 21-16. Breakdown drill.

15. Ground Stroke Breakdown Drill

Objective: To learn how to cover the court and make deep shots with no change of direction.

Description: The coach (C) feeds the ball from the corner of the court (1). The player (P) rallies the ball back to the coach, and the coach hits each successive shot to a different area of the court (2, 3 and 4). The coach stays in the corner, and the player moves for every ball to any place on the court. The rally continues until either the player or the coach misses. Score should be kept. After the game, the coach should go to the opposite corner and repeat the drill. Note: If a ball sets up, the player can finish off the shot by returning it to the open court.

16. Volley Breakdown Drill

Objective: To learn to cover the net well and to return all balls without a change of direction to set up the next ball.

Description: The coach (C) feeds a ball (1) from the corner to the player (P), who stands at the net. The player volleys the ball back to the coach, allowing the coach to hit another shot to make the player stretch in another position (2). The coach should mix in hard and soft balls as well as wide balls and balls to the middle. Score should be kept, and the drill should be done to the opposite corner as well. Note: If a ball sets up, the player can finish off the shot by returning it to the open court.

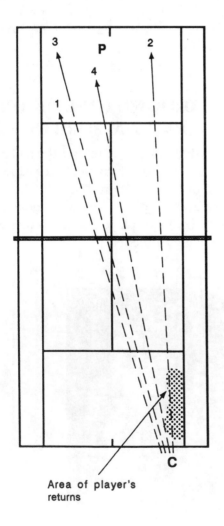

Area of player's returns

Figure 21-17.

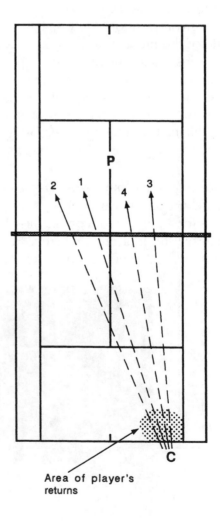

Area of player's returns

Figure 21-18.

17. *Passing Shot Breakdown Drill*

Objective: To learn how to hit first passing shots back to where they came from, and to learn which balls to change the direction of and hit to the open court.

Description: The coach (C) stands in the rear corner position of the service box. He feeds a ball to the player (P), and he and the player rally. The player must hit every shot of the rally back to the coach. The coach runs the player to different areas of the court. Score should be kept, and the drill should be done from the opposite short corner. Note: If an easy ball sets up, the player can finish off the shot by returning it to the open court.

18. *Quick Volley Breakdown Drill*

Objective: To learn not to change the direction of the ball on a stretch-out volley, and to train the hands to be quicker.

Description: The coach (C) stands at the rear corner of the service box, and the player (P) is at the service line. The coach makes shots on both sides low to the player's feet (1-4) to make him stretch and bend to direct them back to the coach. Score should be kept, and the drill should be done from the other side of the court.

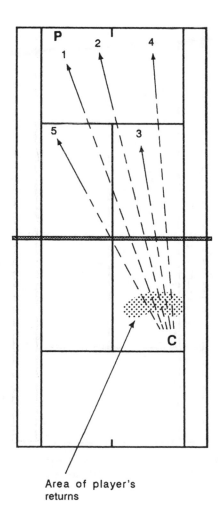

Area of player's returns

Figure 21-19.

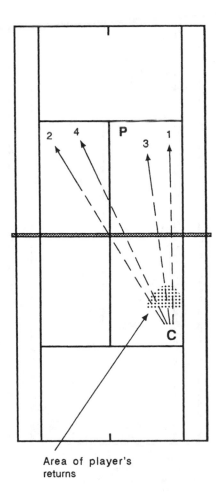

Area of player's returns

Figure 21-20.

19. Overhead Breakdown Drill

Objective: To learn a consistent and reliable overhead smash.

Description: The coach (C) stands to one side behind the baseline and as close to the fence as possible. The player (P) stands close to the net. The player is forced back with a high defensive lob (1). He makes an overhead smash and then tries to close back on the net. The coach then hits another lob up (2) and continues (3 until the player is fatigued. The drill should be repeated with the coach feeding balls to the other side of the court.

20. Offense-Defense (Weapon) Drill

Objective: To turn the player's favorite stroke into a good weapon.

Description: Standing to one side and as far back from the baseline as possible, the coach (C) delivers very easy balls and lofty balls to the player's midcourt area (1, 2, and 3). The player (P) moves around the ball to use his favorite stroke and hits the hardest shot possible that he can still control back to the coach. The coach continues to float balls to the player until the player is fatigued. The drill should also be done with the coach feeding balls to the other side of the midcourt.

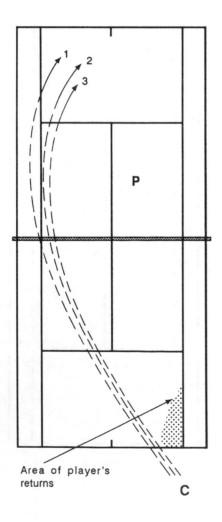

Figure 21-21.

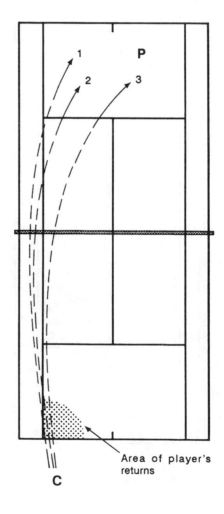

Figure 21-22.

21. Three-Quarters Court Closing Drill

Objective: To learn half-volleys and work on transition with midcourt balls on the way to the net.

Description: The coach (C) stands in the right or left service box to feed the ball. The player (P) starts inside his baseline in the backcourt area. The coach hits the ball to the player's feet (1), and the player makes a pickup and proceeds into the net. The coach, having the better court position, keeps hitting to the player's feet (2-5). As soon as the player misses, he backs up to the baseline and starts again. A drill is successful when the player makes it all the way into the net to put a volley away.

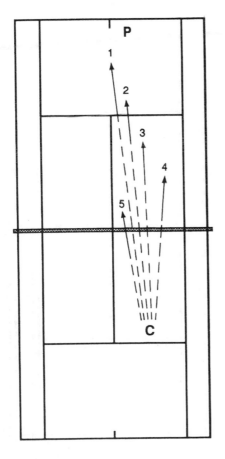

Figure 21-23.

TWO-ON-ONE DRILLS

Two-on-one drills are used routinely to teach players their limitations on every shot, and they are a great way to learn racquet control and good court movement. Players must also learn to hit balls on the run, and in very different positions. Harry Hopman, the famous Australian Davis Cup Coach, made two-on-one training popular worldwide. He trained his Davis Cup teams and many other international champions in this way.

The player who is being drilled should concentrate on hitting through the two players on the other side of the court, never missing wide, and never missing in the net. The player should concentrate on hitting the ball back to where it came from on shots that he cannot control or is off balance on. He can try to change the direction of any ball that pops up to make a penetrating shot. Training in this manner takes on many of the proportions of match play.

As illustrated in the following drills, two-on-one training can be performed in four different formations:

1. *Two players on the baseline versus one on baseline — for ground stroke work.*
2. *Two players at the net versus one on baseline —for passing shots and reflex ground strokes.*
3. *Two players on the baseline versus one at the net — for deep volleys and consistency on volleys.*
4. *Two players at the net versus one at net — for quick volleys and reflexes.*

These drills can be executed with three players; with three players and a coach, who acts as the feeder; or with two players and a coach. Once again, Wardlaw Directionals should be followed.

Figure 21-24. Two-on-one workout.

22. Two-on-One Baseline Rally Drill

Objective: To learn good movement consistency and depth while learning the limitations of each shot and whether or not to change the direction of the ball.

Description: Two players stand at the baseline (P1 and P2), while the third (P3) positions himself at the opposite baseline. P1 and P2 work rallies to P3 as he covers the entire court.

23. Two-on-One Passing Shot Drill

Objective: To work on movement, quick reflexes, the ability to hit on the run, and deciding whether or not to change the direction of the ball.

Description: Two players (P1 and P2) are at the net, while the third player (P3) stands at the baseline. P1 and P2 hit balls to any spot on P3's side of the court. P3 has to move to each shot and hit back through P1 and P2. P3 will quickly learn which balls to change direction and which not to change direction. He should try never to hit shots wide or into the net.

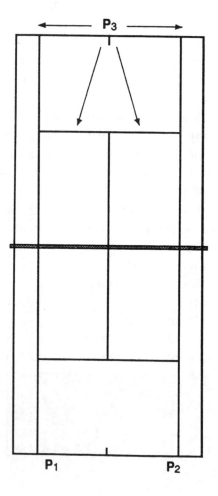

Figure 21-25.

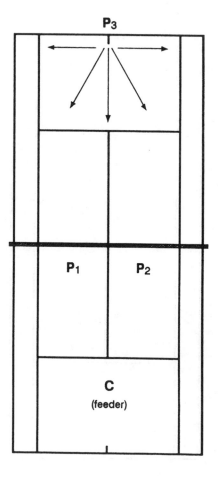

Figure 21-26.

24. Two-on-One Deep Volley Drill

Objective: To develop good movement and consistency of volleys.

Description: Two players (P1 and P2) are on the baseline, and the third player (P3) is at the net. P3 plays each ball hit to him, returning it with a deep volley to either side of the opposite court.

25. Two-on-One Quick Volley Drill

Objective: To improve reflexes and learn limitations in a quick volley situation.

Description: Two players (P1 and P2) are at the service line and face the third player (P3), who stands at the opposite service line. P1 and P2 hit balls at P3 and P3, in turn, reflexes quick, crisp volleys back through his two drill partners.

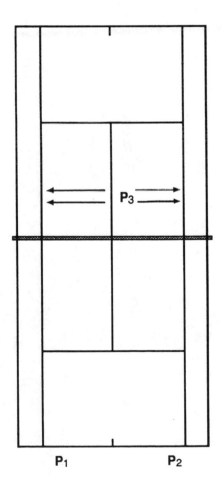

Figure 21-27.

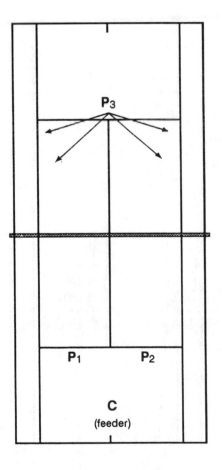

Figure 21-28.

26. Two-on-One Offense/Defense (Weapon) Drill

Objective: To create a good weapon from a player's favorite stroke. This drill is also excellent for learning correct footwork when setting up for floating balls.

Description: Two players (P1 and P2) are far behind the baseline, and the third player (P3) is at midcourt on the opposite side. P1 and P2 alternately deliver very soft floating balls to P3 (1-4). P3 moves around each ball and uses his favorite stroke to hit it, regardless of where it lands. Unlike the one-on-one drill, the player has his choice of hitting to either corner of the opposite side of the court.

27. Two-on-One Three-Quarters Court Closing Drill

Objective: To learn to hit half-volleys and to make reflex shots on the way to the net.

Description: Two players (P1 and P2) stand at the net. The third player (P3) starts at three-quarters court or toward the rear of the backcourt. P1 and P2 take turns hitting balls down and toward P3's feet as he tries to work himself to the net (1-6). If P3 misses a shot, he backs up and begins again. A successful drill finds P3 all the way in the net for a finishing volley.

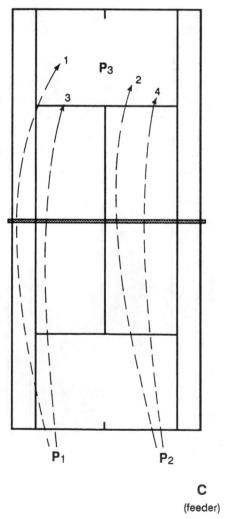

Figure 21-29.

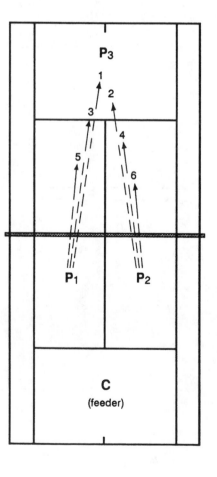

Figure 21-30.

THE KRASS QUICK VOLLEY DRILLS

"Quick hands and quick feet make for volleys that are hard to beat." These three quick volley drills pay big dividends to a player who wants to develop quick reflexes and control of the racquet head. Players should be encouraged to be very aggressive and intense during these high-paced drills.

Figure 21-31. Krass quick volley drill.

28. Shoe Shine Volley Drill

Objective: To develop skills in handling the low volley and half-volley and to develop the skill of placing volleys at the other player's feet.

Description: Both players (P1 and P2) stand behind the service line for the entire drill. Using one-half of the singles court as the boundary, each player tries to hit his volleys to the other player's shoes. Good footwork and use of legs is important. Note: The coach can also feed balls from a side position.

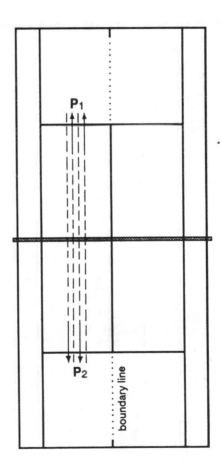

Figure 21-32.

29. One-on-One Closing Volley Drill

Objective: To learn how to close on the net and to develop quick hands, feet, and reflexes.

Description: Both players (P1 and P2) stand in the backcourt. Using one-half of the singles court for the boundary, each player tries to close to the net and win a quick volley point. Score should be kept. Note: The coach may also start the ball out from a side position.

30. Two-on-Two Doubles Tracking Drill (Inside-Inside/Outside-Outside)

Objective: To work on quick volleys and to learn how to track as a doubles team. This drill is excellent practice for doubles movement.

Description: Four players (P1 and P2, P3 and P4) start at their respective service lines. The coach feeds balls to different positions, forcing both pairs to shift or slide together in order to cover the returned shots. Players should also attempt to close together on the net as the drill progresses. This drill can also be done with two players on the net and two on the baseline.

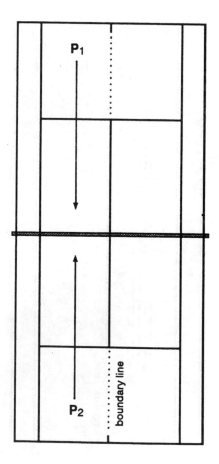

Figure 21-33.

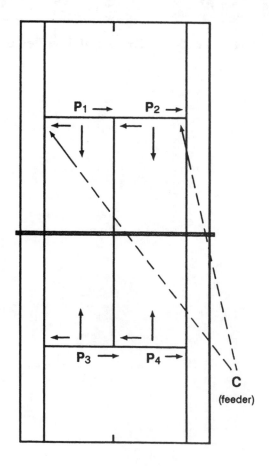

Figure 21-33.

MATCH SIMULATION DRILLS

There are certain patterns that closely simulate situations that occur again and again during match play. The following drills contain some of these patterns that the player can use to develop his skills in playing points in various shot sequences. Although most points cannot be planned from start to finish, the first two or three exchanges usually work well to set up some sequences, and these drills will help the player obtain a good understanding of this concept.

31. The Serve and Volley-Volley Drill

Objective: To work on service placement to the middle of the court, and to work on the first and finishing volleys.

Description: Only one serve is allowed in this drill. The receiver (P2) must return the serve (1) through the middle of the court (2), thereby allowing the server (P1) to make the first volley (3). This first volley should be hit back to where it came from (4), or to the middle of the court. The server then closes off the net and tries to put his second volley away (5). The receiver is allowed to pass on the second ball as well.

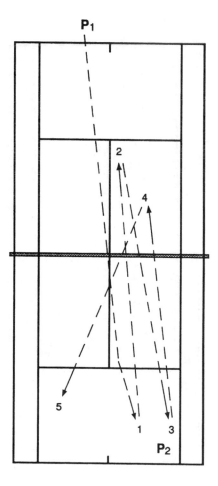

Figure 21-34.

32. The Wide and Glide Drill (Serve Wide and Approach)

Objective: To learn how to pull the receiver out of court and then approach the net.

Description: The server (P1) slices the serve wide into the deuce court or kicks the serve wide into the ad court (1). The receiver (P2) makes his return crosscourt (2). The server makes an approach shot off the first return (3) and comes to the net for the finishing volley (4 and 5).

33. One Serve Receiver Attacks Drill

Objective: To put pressure on the server's second serve, to teach the receiver to come to the net on a return of serve, and to work on the server's passing shot when he is pressed.

Description: The server (P1) is allowed one serve (1). The receiver (P2) must return the serve (2) and come to the net. The server tries to hit a passing shot (3). The receiver now tries to win the point (4) at the net position. Score is kept as in a regular set.

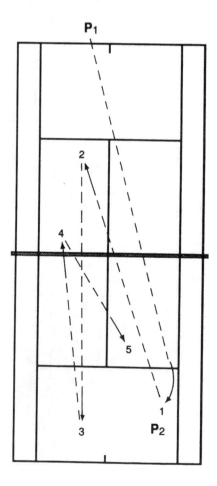

Figure 21-35.

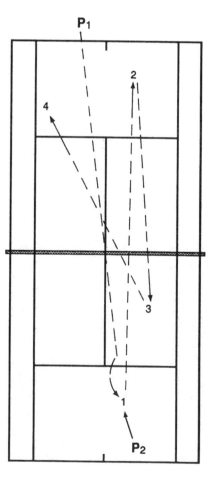

Figure 21-36.

34. Crosscourt Volley with Approach Shot on Short Ball Drill

Objective: To learn the importance of crosscourt rallies, to learn to keep the court closed, and to learn the skills of making consistent crosscourt rallies and down-the-line approach shots.

Description: The two players exchange deep crosscourt forehand or backhand shots (1-3) until a short ball is hit (4). This short ball is the cue for the player to make a down-the-line approach shot (5) and to play the point out. Score should be kept.

35. Crosscourt and Down-the-Line Rallies Drill (Control Drill)

Objective: To become proficient at changing the direction of the ball during the rally.

Description: One player (P2) rallies from the baseline, directing his balls crosscourt, and his partner (P1) returns the balls down the line. This forces the players to run from side to side and change the direction of the ball. Score should be kept, and then the drill should be reversed. Players performing this drill should be concerned with consistency.

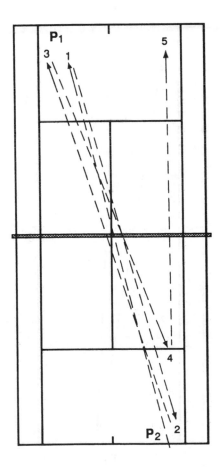

Figure 21-37.

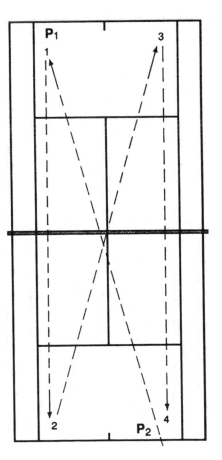

Figure 21-38.

36. Two Volley Passing Shot Drill

Objective: To allow one player to work on the approach volley, and to allow another player to work on the first pass and the second passing shot.

Description: One player (P1) starts behind the service line and feeds a ball as an approach shot (1) to the other player (P2), who is on the baseline. P2 must hit his first pass back to P1 (2). Both P1 and P2 then try to win the point (3 and 4). Score should be kept.

37. Approach-Passing Shot Drill

Objective: To work on approach shots and passing shots.

Description: The coach (C) feeds balls from a position to the side and off the court. Two or more players (P1, P2, and P3) line up at the center of the baseline. One player (P4) is on the coach's side of the court at the baseline. The coach feeds a ball into the midcourt (1); each player takes a turn approaching the net with good under-spin approach shots (2), while the player at the baseline tries to make his passing shot (3). Score should be kept.

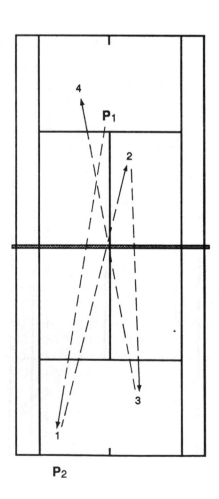

Figure 21-39.

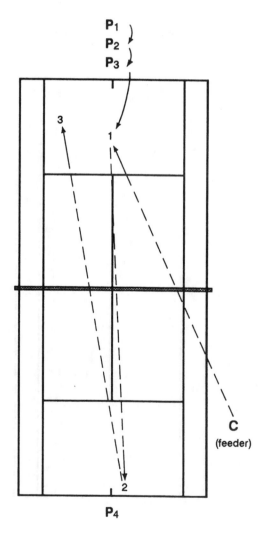

Figure 21-40.

38. One-on-One Stretch Pass and Volley Drill

Objective: To work on stretching to make down-the-line passing shots and stretch crosscourt volleys.

Description: The coach (C) feeds the ball from a position either behind or to the side of the court. He hits a ball to the corner of the passing player's (P1) backcourt, forcing him to stretch for the ball. P1 must make a down-the-line passing shot (2) that the net player (P2) tries to cut off and angle crosscourt (3). The coach then hits a wide ball to the passing player's backhand side (4), and the drill is repeated (5 and 6). The passer may also hit his first shot crosscourt and then move in to finish the point with his second shot.

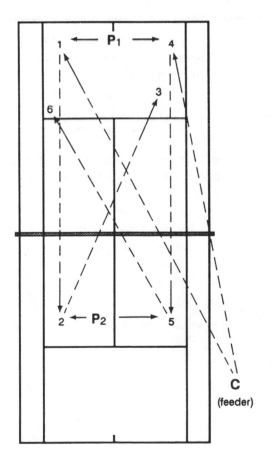

Figure 21-41.

SERVING DRILLS

The following two drills may be used to help players improve their serves.

39. Wrist Serving Drill

Objective: To develop a quicker wrist snap for better racquet head speed on the serve.

Description: The server stands with the side of his body facing the net and both his feet placed firmly on the ground. As the toss is delivered, his whole body is frozen in this sideways position, and the only power used for the stroke comes from the snap of his wrist. It is very important that the feet, legs, hips, upper body, and head all stay sideways so that the wrist action is the predominant power source. The arm, wrist, and racquet head should become one and move like a whip with the racquet head cracking through the ball. The server should serve 50 to 75 balls before regular practice of the serve.

40. The Boykin Placement Cues Drill

Objective: To give the player a very basic concept of placement and accuracy.

Description: (See Figure 21-42 on next page) Just as a bowler looks at the arrows on the lane, and just as a hunter looks through the sight on his gun, so a server can look at an area of the net as a directional target for better service accuracy. A player can improve the placement of middle line serves by standing in the ready position and using the V-shaped area formed by the center strap and the opponent's center service line to direct a serve to Target 1. He can direct a body serve to Target 2 by aligning his opponent's feet with a corresponding spot at the top of the net. A wide corner serve to Target 3 can be directed by lining up part of the net with the target. The diagram illustrates serves to the deuce court, but these targets can also be used when serving to the ad court.

SIMULATED SET PLAY FOR PRACTICE SITUATIONS

A. Play a set, scoring on the service game only, as in volleyball and racquetball. This emphasizes learning how to hold serve.

B. Play a set, scoring on the return game only. This emphasizes learning how to break serve.

C. Play sets in which the server is allowed only one serve, and the receiver must come into the net. This teaches a good second serve as well as coming to the net on a return, and it helps the player develop passing shots.

D. Play a set, in which you must hold serve before you can turn serve over to the opponent. In the first service game, score starts at 0-40; the second service game starts at 0-30, the third game at 0-15, then 0-0, 0-0, as long as it takes to hold serve. This game teaches the server how to come from behind on his service game, and it teaches the receiver to take advantage of early opportunities. This concept works very well in doubles practice sets as well.

E. Play a set serving only to the deuce court, or serving only to the ad court, for the entire set. This allows the server a chance to groove his serve and to learn what his options and plays are to run in each court.

F. Play sets starting at deuce in every game. This system allows multi-sets or competitions to be played in a short time while placing emphasis on the very critical part of each game.

G. Play sets allowing only one serve.

H. Play sets allowing only serve and volley.

I. Play sets allowing no net play.

J. Play sets in which players must stand inside the baseline for all shots. This teaches the player to take balls on the rise and to deal with strange shots and various bounces.

K. Play conversion sets (three points in a row). A game can only be won if three consecutive points are won by a player.

L. Play a set allowing only one serve when you are ahead in the game.

M. Play sets or matches starting every game at deuce.

N. Play groundstroke games to five points where the player has to return to zero for balls in the net, wide, etc.

O. Play games where each player scores two points for winners or loses two points on unforced errors.

P. Play a set using only one half of the doubles court. This requires consistency and focus and makes each player battle to score.

SUMMARY

Nothing can be a substitute for the pressure of actual match play, but drills do work as excellent physical and mental grooving devices. The important emotional training that allows the mental and physical work together can only be trained through the pressure of competition.

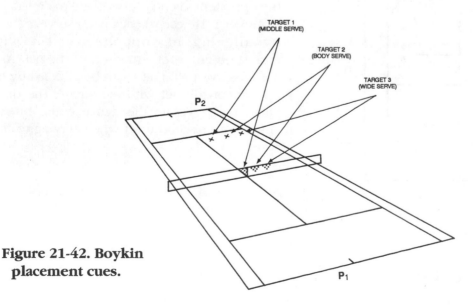

Figure 21-42. Boykin placement cues.

MY FAVORITE INSTRUCTIONAL TOOLS

All teachers of tennis mechanics sometimes run into stumbling blocks in a player's stroking technique. No matter how hard you try, it seems that you can't get it ironed out. Over the years I have learned or developed some effective devices for working out some of those kinks or problem areas that seem to come up. This is a list that has proven quite helpful.

> **T**he greatest waste in the world is the difference between what we are and what we should have become.
> — *Unknown*

THE SERVE

1. Stand in a Box to Serve

For balance and to develop a consistent toss, I use a box or any similar object that will keep the player's feet from moving. This takes care of two things. It demands that the player maintain perfect balance for the ball toss, backswing and contact point and, more importantly, it forces the player to develop a perfect toss. Errant tosses lead the player to lose his or her balance and as a result start to fall over.

Figure 22-1. Standing in a box on serve to practice toss and balance.

2. *Start in Box and Jump Out to Strike the Ball*

A box with shorter sides is necessary in this case. Once the toss and balance are perfected, I will use a box with shorter sides and have the player jump out of it to strike the service toss. This is one of the most effective methods I've ever used to promote extension on the player's serve and to teach the thrust footwork method. I will sometimes use a hat or other object for the player to jump over as well. When using this instuctional technique, make it a point to be mindful of safety and avoid using anything that could cause a sprained ankle or similar injury in the event of player miscue.

3. *Serve (Learning How to Hit Up on the Ball)*

I'll use two different methods for teaching a player how to hit up on the ball when serving. The first is to have the player serve 40 or 50 balls up and over the fence while keeping the feet stationary. At first the player will hit the fence over and over, but as he gets more adept at hitting up on the ball, I will have him do the same thing without the fence and then move him to the tennis court.

Often the second part of this process is to have the player practice serving from a sitting or a kneeling position. This will also force him to develop a feel for hitting up on the ball when serving.

Figure 22-3. Practice hitting up on the serve using the fence.

Figure 22-2. Jumping out of a box on serve to practice extension and thrust footwork.

Figure 22-4. Practice hitting up on the serve from sitting position.

> **I**t is only as we develop others that we permanently succeed.
> — *Harvey S. Firestone*

FOR VOLLEYS

Good volley technique can be relatively easy if a few common problems are avoided. Taking too much backswing is probably the most common mistake teachers run into with students. There are three methods that I consistently use to correct the problem of too much backswing.

1. The Bungi Cord or the Power Groove

I have found the bungi cord invaluable when strapping the arms together in front of the body just above the elbows. This teaches the player to make contact in front of the body with the hands and elbows in front as well.

2. Standing in a Gate

Having the player stand in a gate to practice volleys works equally well for volley technique because the fence prevents the player form taking a backswing. Once this motion is practiced and learned on both the forehand and backhand side, the technique can be easily transferred to the court.

Figures 22-6 thru 22-8. Practice volleys standing in a gate to prevent backswing. Ready position (Fig. 22-6; shown above), forehand volley (Fig. 22-7; below, left) and backhand volley (Fig. 22-8; below, right).

Figure 22-5. Practice making contact in front of the body on volleys by using a bungi cord or the Power Groove.

3. Using a Stretch Cord

I have also found success using a stretch cord to prevent excessive backswing. To use this technique tie one end of the elastic cord around the net strap and the other end around the throat of the racquet. Next have the player step backward until the cord is stretched out. The player should then volley with the aid of this apparatus until he feels comfortable with making contact in front of his body.

4. Using a Wooden Racquet (with racquet cover on)

Use an old-fashioned wooden tennis racquet with the racquet cover on to force the player to make effective contact in front of the body. Proper execution requires crisp movement through the ball; failure to use good technique causes the ball to die or slide off in the wrong direction. This particular drill builds the other volley muscles up as well.

Figure 22-9. Practice volleys using stretch cord to prevent excessive backswing.

Figure 22-10. Practice volleys using a wooden tennis racquet with cover on to encourage effective contact.

5. Kneel-down Position

A common problem in volleying is failure to utilize the legs and bad posture when hitting low balls. An excellent technique to try is to have the player kneel on a towel with the back knee and practice hitting volleys at eye level from this below-the-net position.

Figure 22-11. Practice volleys from a kneel-down position to encourage proper posture on shots.

TEACHING THE UNIT TURN ON GROUNDSTROKES

1. Use a Bungi Cord or the Power Groove

One of the hardest motor skills to develop involves getting the player to use their entire trunk and shoulders for a unit turn when hitting the ball. Beginners generally use only their hands, intermediates only their arms. An old fashioned bungi cord, when strapped above the elbows for hitting ground strokes, works great to practice proper technique. The "Power Groove" (*See Bibliography for more information) is a tool that has been designed specifically for this purpose.

Figure 22-12. Practice proper unit turn using a bungi cord.

Figure 22-13. Practice proper unit turn using the Power Groove—forehand shown.

2. Loading and Unloading

A bench step-up with a medicine ball can also be used to teach the unit turn. An exercise that I have my players do quite often in their physical training is to practice the unit turn with resistance and a bench (an 8-12 inch step works best).

The Forehand — Step up with the right leg and have the trunk and shoulder rotate from the left shoulder under chin to the right shoulder under the chin ("Ike to Mike").

The Two-Handed Backhand — Step up with the left leg and rotate the shoulders from the right shoulder under the chin to the left shoulder under the chin ("Mike to Ike").

Figure 22-15. Practice unit turn using a bench step-up and medicine ball — preparation and loading illustrated.

Figure 22-14. Practice proper unit turn using the Power Groove—backhand shown.

Figure 22-16. Practice unit turn using a bench step-up and medicine ball — step-up and unloading illustrated.

3. Ball Toss from Behind

To teach the player a contact point that is more in front of the body, I'll often toss balls from behind the player so that contact requires a movement forward. I got this idea from the sport of racquetball — specifically from the technique used on shots taken off of the back wall.

BACKHAND POSTURE

In order to hit low backhands properly, the legs must be used properly. Often the player will bend the back instead of the legs and therefore lose leverage due to bad posture. I often use a stool or a chair to help the player get the feel for good posture. The back knee is bent and the back must remain upright.

Figure 22-17. Practice proper contact point in front of the body by hitting balls tossed from behind.

Figure 22-18. Practice hitting low backhands with proper posture by using a stool or chair.

NET CLEARANCE IN GROUNDSTROKE RALLIES

To improve net clearance in groundstroke rallies, use a rope and tie it off 4-5 feet above the height of the net. Instruct your players to hit the ball between the net and the rope for passing shots when the opponent is at the net. Attacking shots should also be hit between the net and rope.

Figure 22-19. Improve net clearance on groundstrokes by practicing with a rope tied above the net.

FURTHER IMPROVEMENTS IN TECHNIQUE

Use a Mirror

A mirror can be used on the court as an aide for technique instruction. This is a big help because the player cannot normally see themselves in action, they only feel themselves. The way a player feels that they are executing a stroke is often inaccurate. The mirror provides a visual impression to refer to. I will also use the player's shadow during instruction to illustrate technique in a similar manner.

Use a Small Racquet

I will often use a small wooden racquet to teach my players better shot technique. Using this as a tool actually frustrates the player into making a good stroke because a small racquet is very unforgiving and will not reward the use of poor technique. I have best results with work on midcourt volleys and transition shots, areas where simple technique is a must.

Figure 22-21. Use a small wooden racquet to teach a player better technique.

SUMMARY

I try to always remain mindful that the player cannot see himself on the court, he can only feel himself. Therefore in the attempt to condition correct muscle memory on shots, I will use anything and everything to help my players develop a better "feel" for technical skills that they are trying to perfect. Once the "feel" is developed, the player has to overlearn it and make it into habit. The payoff is great if the player's strokes can then hold up under the pressure of competition.

Figure 22-20. Use a mirror to provide a visual reference of stroke technique.

Chapter 23

SPORTSMANSHIP:
NOT A JOB FOR THE WEAK

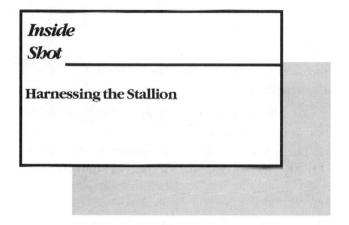

Inside Shot

Harnessing the Stallion

When we talk about sportsmanship, the stereotype that we tend to see is the athlete who never has any sort of problems with teammates, coaches or opponents, someone who is just a nice person in general. Someone once told me that if someone said you were just a "nice guy" it was about the worst thing that could be said about you because it really means that you are probably someone who doesn't really do anything that is noteworthy. I really believe that this is a true statement. Come to think about it, it has always

bothered me to see the sportsmanship awards in competitive events go to those individuals whose temperaments and demeanors are essentially laid back and non-confrontational by nature. It always seemed to me that those are the individuals who really didn't have to struggle much in doing the right thing in pressure situations. What about those individuals who have to struggle daily to do the right thing under the stress of their competition? What about those who completely lose their competitive instincts and become timid sheep when trying to hold back their naturally aggressive nature.

Everyone's Different

It is true that the more passive and peaceful demeanor can be one to be admired, but it is a fact of life that all people are not emotionally wired the same. Competitive sports usually attract competitive people, and under competitive situations, all people do not react the same to pressure, disappointment, humiliation, pain and embarrassment or the setbacks that this extremely tough sport brings; nor likewise the elation, happiness, relief, joy and confidence that success brings as well. Thank goodness that we are all different and those differences are to be praised and nurtured as the gifts from God that they are. Each person's temperament and demeanor are qualities that should never be changed but rather should be directed and groomed into effective assets that choose the right course of action in

It all starts with sportsmanship which in a sense is sort of the golden rule of life. You call the balls fair. You don't try to intimidate. You don't use gamesmanship...the best players that I ever encountered in the world of tennis, the great players were also great sportsmen.

— *Tut Bartzen*

competitive situations. Above all, I believe that the most important thing to remember under the pressure of competition is to be yourself. This is why I repeat over and over to my players the statement "you are number one in the world at being you, and if you copy someone else's demeanor or characteristics or way of doing things, the best that you can ever hope for is to be a good imitation of someone else." The personality types are explained in detail in Chapter 8.

All of us need guidance in what true sportsmanship entails. Although some may automatically have the personality that seems to be perfect under a competitive situation, most have to work on their attitude and actions for competition throughout their careers and lives. That is okay just as long as they are continually trying to get it right. The following chapter discusses some of the specifics regarding what sportsmanship is and includes some guidelines to follow.

HARNESSING THE STALLION

No one enjoys losing, whether it's in a social game or the Wimbledon finals. There's a loser for every winner in most forms of competition, however, and many times the outcome is determined by a competitor's mental approach. That's why it's important to determine just how seriously you want to take the game before you can achieve maximum enjoyment from it.

"Social competitors" play only occasionally, and usually with friends. Although everyone usually gives their best effort, winning and losing are taken in stride and everyone in the group understands that the main objective is to release energy and have fun. This outlook should differ for serious competitors.

The "weekend warrior" emerges when middle age strikes the body of the competitive athlete, but the mind and spirit won't let go of youth. Many of these players take tennis as seriously as ever, and believe they are close to taking their game to another level. They are constantly looking for ways to improve, but job, family and other commitments take up a large part of their time. This can result in frustration if unrealistic expectations are not met. There's nothing worse than seeing this person taking himself too seriously.

Many other players, however, compete as hard as they can every time on the court, but keep winning and losing in perspective. A realistic approach should be considered in terms of player expectations, keeping in mind that the proper attitude is a necessity.

Players should give their best physical, mental and emotional efforts toward winning but understand the balance base on their level of committment.

Understanding The Emotions Of Competition

Competition makes something in all of us surface that we have trouble understanding or controlling.

"I'm just not a competitive person," the young girl said to her parents as she cried and walked away from the tennis court after losing her first match. "When the score got close, I got a big lump in my throat, and I felt like I might be sick to my stomach. My legs got weak and I just felt like not trying any more."

Meanwhile, the girl's friend on the other side of the net was talking with her parents. "It was nice to win, but I felt bad for Jane. She seemed so afraid and nervous; I hope it doesn't hurt our friendship. But WOW! It was so exciting to compete today. I had so much positive energy, I felt I could run all day!"

Regardless of what our standards may be as to how a person should feel and behave during competition, the fact remains that each individual reacts to a competitive situation differently. Some are drawn to it, even inspired by it, while others fear it. Psychologists call it the fight-or-flight syndrome. However, this is something that can be developed until the right perspective is achieved.

Set Goals, Train Hard, Play Fair

Being competitive while playing fair and having fun should be the goal of all of us.

Tennis is an individual sport, and therefore exposes more of our inner feelings and emotions than a team sport would. Winning and losing are basically ours to achieve, and neither the credit nor the blame can be passed to teammates.

One of the great benefits of playing individual sports is that they help you to learn about yourself and what happens to your personality under pressure. I have a framed quote on my office wall that says, "Tennis undresses you like no other sport, sometimes even down to the soul. It is so important to train our fundamentals well so that even in the nakedness of adversity, our substance will endure and prevail."

Through competition, we sometimes like what we find out about ourselves and sometimes we don't. The important thing is that we learn so that we can then grow in a way that enables us to express ourselves competitively in an acceptable fashion.

Athletics is one of the most pure and basic forms of expression. Much like art to the artist and music to the musician, the competitive arena allows the athlete one of the few forums where the inner self can be unleashed for a short period of freedom. Finding the balance between unleashed competitiveness and emotional restraint is the primary goal in becoming a fair but tough competitor.

Corralling The Stallion

Coaching Greg, my senior captain and leader, was one of the most interesting and challenging experiences I've ever had. His disposition and nature away from the tennis court was one of feeling, gentleness, and a very touching warmth that showed a true depth of character.

During competitive situations, however, his moods and actions sometimes shifted dramatically from out-of-control anger to a near total withdrawal of energy. He occasionally had moments of brilliance, when everything came together for him. This "zone" was what we sought for him throughout his career. Because of his sensitive nature, the fierce, competitive image seemed unnatural for him, but it often came out when under attack by his opponent.

The breakthrough that led to finding a proper balance and perspective for him was an observation given by an assistant coach.

"Greg," he said, "with all of his sensitive and calm-hearted tendencies, has a stallion inside of him that is fighting to come out. Greg's calm nature is afraid of the stallion that might run wild all over what he wants to accomplish.

"The key for him is to ride that stallion and use his wonderful inner nature to control its reins so that its strength and energy can be channeled properly into his competitive situations."

This perspective gave Greg an excellent understanding of how to tap his competitiveness and do so in a useful manner, giving him greater inner peace when competing. When the athlete finds this balance, maximum potential can be achieved.

The Fight-or-Flight Syndrome

Robert, a sophomore, was one of my most talented athletes, but also one of the most undisciplined. The player had never made a commitment to being his best, because in high school he was able to succeed without really trying. College was a different matter, however, for soon he found that everyone around him was just as talented as he was. Robert began losing frequently, and it was a painful experience.

I kept telling him that he was going to be successful only if he made a complete commitment to improving his game, and made it quickly. The losses were painful enough that Robert made the commitment, and for six seeks his workouts were exceptional. He gave 100 percent effort in all that he did.

My anticipation was high as our next major tournament arrived. But when the match started, I couldn't believe my eyes. This same player who had worked and trained hard for the six weeks leading up to this moment was "tanking" (giving up) in his first match.

"Why, why, why?" I asked him, "after so much hard work would you just give up?" He replied that he didn't really know why, except that at the moment of battle he became terribly afraid and withdrew energy.

Some refer to it as the "fight-or-flight" syndrome. Under the stress of a competitive situation, some people rise to the occasion, while others retreat. This is especially true when a great commitment has been made to the activity and the person cares a great deal.

After the tournament, I drew up the Black Door diagram (See Chapter 15, Figure 15-1) to help explain that his reaction was quite normal, but that it was important for him to go to the next step.

If you don't care you are taking no risks, and therefore have no fear. The biggest job initially is to bring yourself to the point of commitment and then work through the fear.

> **The measure of a man's character are the choices he makes under pressure.**
> — *Lee Sessions*

Finding "the Zone"

One of the best clutch competitors I've ever coached was Kent Kinnear. Kent seemed to pull out close match after close match during his career. It truly was never over until it was over when you played him. He always seemed to have that sense of calm under pressure that is so hard to teach athletes. As explained earlier, opposing coaches often remarked, "You can sometimes beat Kent's game, but you can never beat Kent."

Kent had a way of finding that elusive balance — taking what he did seriously, but never taking himself too seriously. His maturity in competitive situations seemed to stem from a very solid inner peace, and was a tremendous example to all around him.

One of the best recipes I have seen for tennis players trying to find that balance is by sports psychologist Jim Loehr in his book and video, Mental Toughness. His theory, shown in Figure 23-1, is a very simple formula that helps find that perfect emotional playing "zone" for competition. This tool is one of the most practical I have found to use with competitive players.

Loehr describes four emotional responses that occur under the pressure of competitive situations by the rings on a target.

The outer ring, furthest from the bull's eye, shows giving up, or "tanking." This is the first response many people make under pressure. They tell themselves it's just not worth it to give a 100 percent effort. This response seems to protect the ego, but it never leads to good results in the long run.

The next ring of the target is the anger zone. Many people wind up here during competitive situations. This is a little better than tanking, because you don't completely give up, but it is still quite non-productive. Although it feels good for a moment to lose your temper, good performance rarely results from anger, and your reputation as a sportsman may be damaged as well.

The third ring shows "choking." This is one of the most feared responses for an athlete. To be a choker carries a stigma that is difficult to overcome. However, becoming nervous and unsure of oneself under pressure is not only better than tanking and anger, it is usually the journey the athlete must endure en route to being a good competitor. It means the athletes cares a lot, but hasn't yet learned how to transfer that caring into motor skills. That process takes time for the best of athletes, and is neither an overnight nor an effortless process.

Choking is much better than tanking or anger, and should be recognized as such. An athlete who chokes is only one step away from the very best response in a competitive situation: the challenge response.

Here, all of the athlete's energy is focused. The body, mind and emotions all work as one unit, striving for the same objective. The athlete feels alert, energized and confident, and is able to perform at the peak level. Athletes who experience this "challenge zone" understand the ultimate feeling of competition — a total-release performance without the conflict of emotions that are common under fire.

This target can help athletes bring their best performance from the depths of their souls to the playing field. It is a great guideline for finding that perfect balance of corralling and riding the stallion within.

Figure 23-1. Jim Loehr's mental toughness chart.

In finding your competitive demeanor, it is important to realize that you have a unique disposition that cannot and should not be changed. As a coach, I believe that attitude can be changed, but our innate disposition is the framework we have to work from.

Beginning players, when they are struggling for confidence, should remember that they are the #1 player in the world at their style of play. Then they should believe in it. When the pain is just too tough in handling a loss, the story below is a good one to refer to.

Healing a Wounded Ego

Getting the lead in the senior class play meant everything to me. I was so sure the part was mine that I memorized all the lines even before the audition. To my astonishment, the title role went to another girl and I ended up with a walk-on part.

I was heartsick. I was angry. I was jealous. That evening, at home, I couldn't stop crying. My father, who was a doctor, tried to console me, but I told him, "I'll never get over this."

"Yes, you will," he said, "if you're willing to do something about it."

"Like what," I asked.

He put his arm around me. "The only way to cure a wounded ego is to wash someone else's feet. It heals," Dad said, "Just as surely as a plaster cast mends a broken leg."

I wasn't certain what he meant. "Wash someone else's feet?"

He asked, "What about the girl who got the part? Do you like her?"

"Vivian is all right," I conceded.

"Then congratulate her," Dad said. "Send her a letter."

The letter was the most difficult one I ever wrote in my life, but by the time I finished it, my own pain had disappeared and I really wanted Vivian to succeed. Since then, there have been other times when my ego has gone out of control. But I have always found that the humble act of washing someone else's feet — in one way or another — not only heals but also prevents lingering scars.

— excerpt from Guidepost Magazine

> Sportsmanship is not a job for the weak but it is definitely a job for the meek, for those who possess strength under control.

Five Rules of Sportsmanship to Remember

1. Always give 100% of your entire being when competing. To do so, shows respect for your opponent, honor for your sport, and glorifies God for the talent that He has given you. (The athlete should respect and honor what he does with the same passion that an artist respects his art, or a musician respects his Music.)

2. Confidence (belief in self; respect for your opponent) is admired by all. Cockiness (belief in self; lack of respect for opponent) and self-centeredness is not. Strive for outward and inward confidence.

3. If you win, let it be by the code with your honor held high and have compassion for the opponent that you have beaten. If you should lose, let it also be by the code while giving completely of yourself in that losing cause, and then to honor that opponent who has beaten you. (Someone else's success does not diminish your stature nor your standing. Be genuinely gracious and happy for their good fortune.)

4. Take what you do very seriously, but never take yourself very seriously. Those who try to validate themselves and who they are by how they do in this sport will always be very unhappy and will develop very slowly.

5. Love Winning, and Hate Losing; but never fear the losing. Remember that if you are a true competitor, losing will always hurt. That is just part of the deal about competing. Remember that Pain is not the enemy. Although you should hate losing, you should never fear it. It is a chance for growth and learning if dealt with properly. No matter how hard it is, go back to that court and work on the things that you have learned and a positive result will take place.

Chapter 24

INTERVIEWS ON TENNIS-COACHING EXCELLENCE: WRITTEN BY PAUL GLUCH

I met Paul Gluch in the summer of 1996 as he did research throughout the tennis tournament circuits. After he interviewed me, I was overcome with a curiousity — what were the many fellow tennis coaches were relating to him about their beliefs and philosophies?

It has always been my opinion that too little is shared in the world of tennis. Unlike many other sports, some of the greatest coaching wisdom goes to the grave with its owner because 1) coaches never get the proper vehicle to communicate their ideas to others on a large scale or 2) coaches simply keep their game-related thoughts under lock and key out of fear that sharing ideas will give someone else a competitive edge on the court. This type of situation is a shame and something we should work to change and improve upon. There is a universal law of sharing that works to repay the provider ten fold for his contributions — this should be recognized in the game of tennis.

Paul Gluch's interviews lend some fantastic insight into the ideas, philosophies and beliefs of some of the top coaches in the game.

— Chuck Kriese

THE GLUCH INTERVIEWS

The task of helping others perform better is the message of the book *Everyone's a Coach* co-written by Don Shula and Ken Blanchard. In it Shula talks about his philosophy of coaching excellence:

> People come to you with skills and talents; your job is to instruct, discipline, and inspire them to do things better than they thought they could do them on their own....the real difference in coaching is not about talent. Or personality. Or pride. Or ambition. It's about you believing in someone. And then doing whatever it takes to help that person be his or her very best.

This chapter is based on interviews with almost 70 tennis coaches over a two-year period. Paul Gluch asked them to tell him what tennis-coaching excellence is. He has graciously agreed to the use of these materials in my book and summarized the results — including quotes organized around the themes that emerged from their discussions. The primary focus is on the emotional and mental keys that coaches believe are critical in mentoring tennis players and tennis teams.

Communication with Your Players

Few people would argue that a high level of effective communication is critical to tennis-coaching excellence. In fact, it was the most frequently mentioned topic among coaches of all disciplines. The transmission of information and ideas between coach and athlete (verbally and nonverbally) is the foundation of a good relationship. Without this foundation there is little chance of building a bridge of mutual trust and respect necessary for this relationship to grow and flourish. In order to excel as a communicator, the coach must be able to understand and empathize. Here a coach/father describes how interacting with his young son relates to communicating with his players:

> All players are different. You think you're communicating and you find out you're not even getting to first base. I have a son that's a year and a half old now. If you think about it, here he's trying to communicate with me and tell me what's on his mind and he can't. Once in a while you might hit on the right thing that he really wants. Well, it sometimes feels like the same thing when you're talking with eighteen year-olds on your team — they're trying to tell you in their own way that they're unhappy or they're happy or something's wrong, but they can't quite. So you have to pull it out of them and then you find out it might be something very small to you. Yet for them it's very significant. Be it the fact that they're not playing enough or not playing high enough (on the ladder), or something about their game that they're not happy with, (or something at) home, (or with their) girlfriend — you name it. They seem so mixed up. And when I was eighteen, I was really about the same, and it's all normal.

Dave Barron — Florida State University

The communication process will be different depending on the maturity level and the personality of each individual. In addition, communicating physical and mental skills is very different from communicating sympathetically with the athlete following a setback or injury. Communicating with your "superstar athlete" will be different from communicating with your number 8 or 9 player on the ladder (if you're a college coach). The coach must become sensitive to how he or she adjusts communication skills to meet these roles.

Research suggests there is no other skill that would make you as well-informed, knowledgeable and appealing to others as mastering the skill of really listening to your athletes. This allows a coach to learn from the athletes' perspectives what excites them about their sport and what causes them to lose interest. The coach's ability to listen, to understand and appreciate what the athlete is going through is illustrated in the following quote:

> (The coach) has to understand the pressures that the player experiences out on the court and has to flow with it. I mean there has to be dialogue that is pertinent : how does the player feel? what is he going through? is he tired? Is he emotionally tired? is he physically tired? There has to be a give-and-take somewhere. He has to listen to what the player is really saying.
>
> I think that you have to bend a little bit with the players. I don't think that an authoritative coach is really gonna be effective. I think there has to be guidelines and expectations that the player has to meet for the relationship to be good. There's times when the player really needs you to lay down the law —this is what's expected of you and you're gonna do it, but at times, the coach also has to bend a little bit with the idiosyncrasies of the player. You listen to them to see what they're saying and you flow with it...so you work out their training program, their match strategy, their match play that are unique for them with them. You really gotta have to feel for it — you do with every player. I mean there's times I bend with them and there's times I'm pretty rigid.

Greg Patton — Boise State University

The Art of Tennis Coaching

Providing feedback to the athletes is a process of reflecting on your athletes' performances and giving constructive information on what they might change or refine in order to improve. Since athletes have distorted pictures of their own behaviors, feedback can help them see the reality of the situation. Feedback should be specific and clear, constructive rather than destructive and stress the positive over the negative; it should be timely, simple and most importantly should be directed at the behavior, not the person.

These guidelines do not work all the time, however. This is where the "art" of coaching comes in — saying the right thing at the right time based on the situation and the player's unique personality. Some of the most interesting quotes involved college coaches attempting to change a player's emotional state during a match:

> Once in a while you have to do something drastic. One time I went on-court and said something that got the player angry at me. What had happened was that I redirected his fear and made him angry, and he used that anger to raise his level of play. So being able to change someone's emotion in a pressure situation — knowing what to say to someone and when to say it, based on that person's personality — can make all the difference.

Dick Leach — University of Southern California

After an amusing anecdote of using humor to help his player relax, I remarked to one coach "So you use humor." He replied:

> Yeah. Humor, anger, annoyance... I mean any emotion that I think will trigger a response that I'm looking for in a player. So you have to know your players pretty well. And it's also different based on the opponent and the situation. I have one player on my team who doesn't like to be yelled at or talked harshly to. I have another player that wants me to yell at him — get mad at him. That fires him up. You sort of have to weigh all that. And then a lot of times what they tell you they like still may not be the thing that's best for them. And some of it's trial-and-error and the longer you coach the better you get at it.

Bobby Bayliss —University of Notre Dame

This coach also said that he has also "messed up during matches" at times when he attempted to use humor but failed to get the response he was hoping for. Fortunately, the ability to effectively change a player's emotion usually increases as the coach becomes more experienced.

One final word about communication — the non-verbal type. Several coaches described the importance of displaying the same demeanor and presence they want their players to exhibit:

> I always really try to stay positive and I always try to stay fairly relaxed and poised even when I'm inside really churning up because the last thing I want them to see is me looking like I'm frazzled out there. So you've gotta always be encouraging, always be positive.

Tom Gullickson — United States Davis Cup Coach and USTA National Coach

The coach must project confidence – a sense of calm and composure – especially when the pressure is on. The difficulty here is that, like the players, the coach is often unaware of his or her body language. There might be subtle changes in facial expression that suggest disappointment or anxiety. In this case, the coach may solicit input from assistants or even from the players regarding how they are perceived by others.

Develop the People First

In describing the relationship with his athletes, basketball coach John Wooden said "I often told my players that, next to my own flesh and blood, they were the closest to me. They were my children. I got wrapped up in them, their lives, and their problems."

The coach-athlete relationship is another fundamental aspect of excellence in tennis coaching. However, not all coaches agree on how close this relationship should become. Some believe it is a mistake to be friends with the players they are responsible for. Others believe it is because of a friendly relationship with their players that they are successful. Each of the three coaching levels (juniors, college, and professional) will be distinct in the amount of authority necessary to facilitate moving people towards their own excellence. However, what is clear from the coaches' responses is that common to all successful relationships is a sense of compassion and caring for the person, not just the athlete. A juniors level coach had this to say:

> I think the biggest thing is caring about the person, and not just what the player is accomplishing, caring for them and not just for yourself as the coach. Of course you take pride in your work. But sometimes it can become more important to you that your player wins so that you can look good versus what's best for him. And there can be a lot of that in coaching...the result is putting undue pressure on the kids. The players sense that, and it doesn't produce positive results. The key is bringing something from within (them) and getting the person to perform because of what's inside. It can start because of responding to you because they know you care. You don't want it to be "Well, he's going to be angry or upset if I don't produce." So instead of pushing it from outside onto them, it's bringing it out from within them. That's much more important because they learn what they can accomplish, whereas the other (way) all they're doing is knuckling under pressure.

Bob Pass — USPTA Professional

A number of college coaches expressed similar thoughts:

I have an open door; people can come in and talk about their life. This environment is not only for tennis, it's also an area that encompasses their studies, their personal life, if they have problems. The tennis player...I feel is a circle and it's just not his tennis playing and his competing and his training and his physical conditioning, it also deals with his intellect...with him going to school, his social life, his friends, his dealings with girlfriends, his dealings with his family — all of these things. He brings everything to the court with him so we as coaches can't just throw that baggage out and say "Well, I'm not going to deal with that." We deal with that as much as we do anything about their tennis game.

Greg Patton — Boise State University

I think caring for the person is the key to success anywhere in anything that you're doing. The people that you have working for you or playing for you...I think you have to let them know that you really care about them...just like you do your own children. You care about your children and you love them. You care about your players and love them also. It is as basic and simple as that.

George Acker — former coaching great at Kalamazoo College

Ultimately you have to be committed to them as people...as a person first and what's best for them; and if you're not, your credibility will suffer. They may respect you as a coach but they won't respect you as a person. And when they don't respect you as a person they tend to not respect you in the area that you probably deserve respect: your coaching expertise. But if they don't like you or certainly if they don't respect you they're not going to be as receptive to anything you have to say.

Bobby Bayliss — University of Notre Dame

The importance of this dynamic cannot be underestimated. The amount of caring, concern and respect displayed toward the athlete is often reflected back upon the coach. A former player of basketball coach Jerry Tarkanian once said about him: "We want to win — for ourselves and for the coach. I love Tark. I'd run through a brick wall for him."

Commitment + Passion = Success

To excel at anything one must have a high level of commitment. This was one of the most frequently mentioned values that coaches try to instill in their players, not only to help them improve in tennis but as a "life skill" which will benefit them down the road. Commitment on the coach's part is often expressed through a passion or love for the profession:

Another thing that I'm very, very big on is passion. I refer to my former coach a lot. He told me "Whatever you do in life, do what you like to do the most and what you do best at and you'll never be unhappy." And I really have found that so true in everything that I've done. Whatever it was — if I did it for selfish pride, if I did it for status, if I did it for money, if I did it because it may make me look good — it never turned out right unless I did it because I wanted to do it for the right reason, because I was much more inclined to give of myself completely and do it if it was for the right reasons...one of those is because it's helping somebody else or because I'm going to grow because of it. I think if you live by that and you coach by that and you play by that...you're going to be much happier. I think you'll be much more fulfilled and I think you'll probably stay in coaching a lot longer.

Gene Miller — University of Pennsylvania

One of the most effective methods for instilling a sense of commitment and dedication is for the coach to model this behavior. The dedication with which the coach carries out his or her responsibilities will directly affect how much commitment to excellence is exhibited by the players. The following quote illustrates this:

Being a role model is important. To me it's a big part of the job but in terms of excellence as far as how well your team does, it's just something I think is important to do anyway. When I say commitment, I mean willingness to put in hours and put in quality into the hours; willingness to stay late and hit balls to a player or look at that extra video or take that video you got in the mail home with you and look at it at night instead of some other show on TV. It's about being willing to make that extra phone call in the recruiting area. Write that extra letter. That's kind of what I call commitment, to walk the extra mile for your players, for your school.

Bobby Bayliss — University of Notre Dame

More About Motivation

Motivating people to want to work hard is perhaps the most challenging skill for tennis coaches. Without motivation there is no commitment. Without commitment there is no growth. Since people are usually motivated to fulfill their needs, coaches must be attuned to what these needs are.

Many coaches mentioned the importance of discovering "What makes a player tick?" What is it that excites each person about playing tennis and what causes them to lose interest. This goes back to the communication process, understanding the individual. As one college coach put it:

> You're constantly trying to figure out ways that you can get the most out of the guys on your team. And each individual is different. Certain things that you can do for one player may motivate him and you try to do it to other players and it may make them collapse. So you really have to understand your players on your team, understand their personality and have to know which buttons to push to get those guys going.

Sam Paul — University of North Carolina

Several coaches remarked that the really effective motivators are the people who find what the person does well and then they build on that. There was, however, some disagreement among coaches regarding who is really responsible for the player becoming and remaining motivated:

> A misnomer is that coaches motivate athletes. That's incorrect. They don't motivate athletes. A coach creates an environment which is conducive to an athlete being motivated. Motivation is intrinsic. It comes from within. So if a coach's skill is creating the environment where that player becomes motivated to improve themselves in various areas then you can in turn help someone become an outstanding competitor.

Nick Saviano — USTA National Coach

Another coach who was observing the Boys Championships in Kalamazoo, Michigan intends to have the players be accountable for their own motivation:

> It'd be stupid for me to recruit somebody who I think's going to be motivated by a real hard-nosed kind of approach — typical old-school coaching philosophy — because that's not how (I coach). I'm going to give them more personal responsibility than that. I'm going to be asking them to motivate themselves more. And if they want me to be constantly motivating them and pushing them, they're in the wrong (program). I mean, I'm certainly gonna be there for them all the time and hit with them as much and coach them as much as they want to be coached but I'm not gonna be yelling at them all the time...be on their back all the time to work hard...which might be a shortcoming of mine...which is when you've got to change for different people.

Thomas Johnston — University of Virginia

Believing in the Athlete Has Lasting Impact

In the world of tennis, many players and coaches agree that belief and confidence shown toward the athlete himself can do much in confidence-building for their life. In fact, the success of an athlete is often affected to a great deal by that belief the coach has in the athlete. The coach's beliefs can become self-fulfilling. Some coaches related stories of their playing days when their coach helped them to believe in themselves:

> (My coach) always believed that we could do something and we more or less always rose to those expectations and did it — maybe sometimes we overachieved. But from his standpoint, he believed that we could do it. He instilled that in us. How he did that, I don't know. But again, it was his own way of teaching that personified that confidence.

Gene Orlando — Michigan State University; speaking about his college coach Bill Richards at Ball State University

> I always felt like when (my college coach) watched me play, I just wouldn't lose. He just gave me a lot of confidence. I'm not exactly sure how he did that. I wish I could bottle it. I just felt he had a lot of confidence in me. So part of coaching excellence is trying to instill confidence in your players, feeling confident in them gives them confidence in themselves.

Jay Lapidus — Duke University; speaking about Dave Benjamin at Princeton

The use of confidence-building strategies by coaches is a major factor in helping a young person believe in him or herself. The following quotes from the same coach illustrate methods of achieving this:

> You talk about excellence — I think tennis coaches are in the esteem-building business. I mean, you just don't build esteem. You give them opportunities to succeed and you create opportunities for them to excel so that you can build their esteem. You set goals for them that sometimes they don't believe they can reach...and you really make them believe in what they can achieve and you give them confidence. "Yes, you can do this." 'Cause I think there's a lot of doubt —self-doubt that goes through all athletes. And the coach through the training, through the dialogue, through re-examining match play shows the athlete what he's capable of doing.

Greg Patton — Boise State University

I think there's passion that's involved; you become very passionate about what they do well. And then you set up the practices so that they are successful and you affirm that too. You relive a lot of their successes. It's best that you don't dwell on the negatives or their failures but more (their) achievements.

Greg Patton — Boise State University

Through building self-confidence and self-esteem, the person learns a valuable skill, something that will enhance the quality of life regardless of the endeavor.

About Organization

Nothing can shake a player's confidence faster than a stressed-out, unorganized coach. It is an absolute necessity for the coach to be detail oriented or hire an assistant who is. Making all the arrangements for an out-of-state tournament or an "away" match is a formidable task (plane tickets, hotel reservations, ground transportation, itineraries, court time, meals, phone numbers, practice balls, etc).

The issue of organization was brought up numerous times by coaches. In any competitive situation, a chief duty of leadership is to minimize the impact of unexpected conditions and distractions on the individual and the team. Effective organization skills help reduce stress levels of the coaches and the players and increase the chances for quality performance.

Sport psychologist Dr. Jim Loehr has developed a long checklist of things coaches need to consider to be effective and organized leaders. For example, when training a player/team ask yourself, "What are my goals today? What is it I want to accomplish in today's practice? How can I use our time most efficiently? When traveling with the player/team what am I responsible for? What are players responsible for?" Dr. Loehr emphasizes that the effective tennis coach is someone who is well prepared and totally organized. There are no insignificant details. Taking care of the "little things" is critical in the pursuit of excellence. It begins with managing yourself and your resources:

> Probably the first thing (in tennis-coaching excellence) is more or less the day-to-day attributes that you have to bring to the profession. Excellence to me means being organized with yourself first which means you'll be organized with the team. If you're organized and you think ahead of what you need to do then you'll probably bring more to the

team on the practice court. The big emphasis is the practices and how you conduct your practices: how the player performs in practice is pretty much how he is going to perform in the matches. My job is to make sure that all of our ducks are in a row. I have a role and we try to be organized to teach the players how to be organized as well.

Dave Barron — Florida State University

Keep on Learning

Just as there is no single best way to play tennis, there is no single best way to coach it. Each situation provides a unique opportunity to learn. The excellent coach is literally a student of the game, continually looking for new approaches to enhance the performance of individuals and teams. Information on coaching excellence comes from a variety of sources: the advice of mentors, attending coaching clinics and seminars, reading books, and interaction with colleagues. I asked a juniors coach if he felt it was important for a coach to be open to input from his peers. His response:

> Oh yes, definitely. I feel like a good coach is one that knows that he has got to keep on learning the game of tennis: learning how to communicate. If he already knows what this other coach is saying that's good but if they communicate it in a better way than I can then that coach really has something to offer to me. So I always feel like it's always beneficial for me to listen to somebody else. If nothing more (than to) just say "Yeah, I've listened to that and tried it and it didn't work out." So there's always something I can pick up from somebody. I'm hoping to have as much knowledge as I can.

Curly Davis — The Palmer Tennis Academy, Tampa, Florida

The successful tennis player capitalizes on his strengths, and so does the successful coach. At the same time, he knows where he is not strong and seeks help in those areas. Here's one college coach's definition of tennis-coaching excellence:

> We have a lot of resources at our school. The money generated by football gives us the chance to use a sports psychologist and other experts such as strength coaches, etc. I know something about sports psychology and about strength training, but I would prefer to turn over my players to them for their expertise. A better job can be done and I learn a lot more through that process as well. If we didn't have those resources available to us, it might be quite different.

Bobby Bayliss — University of Notre Dame

It is estimated by some sports scientists that as much as 70% to 80% of what coaches do relates to psychological issues. When it is broken down, factors mentioned as part of tennis-coaching excellence consist of the same three factors discussed by Chuck Kriese in this book: the physical, the mental, and the emotional. What is most certainly clear from these interviews is that the coach wears many hats. Rainer Martens said, "Coaching tennis today incorporates the teaching skills of an educator, the administrative leadership of a business executive, and the counseling wisdom of a psychologist."

At the Boys Championships one coach expressed the numerous responsibilities of the college tennis coach. His response to "What is tennis-coaching excellence?"

A lot of diversity I think. There's so many different parts to coaching in terms of having a good understanding of the fundamentals; being able to recognize talent; being able to develop that talent with a sound understanding of the fundamentals; being able to motivate; being able to help a player analyze match situations; helping a player control emotions and anxiety; maximizing their concentration level. I mean it's just so diverse and then when you throw in the whole team aspect of taking an individual sport and making it a team sport like we do at the collegiate level: having to work with several different personality types, having to blend egos together... There are so many different aspects to it you can almost drive yourself crazy thinking about it, but I think the excellent coaches are outstanding at least a couple of those things and not really poor at any of them.

Bill Richards — Ball State University

The roles of the college coach are even more varied considering he or she has the duties of fund raising and promoting the program within the university and within the community. In fact, one coach indicated he spends up to forty percent of his time raising money to keep the program going.

Regardless of the role he or she is playing, coaches must understand excellence as a process. It takes years of practice. Ideally, coaches would like to have the wisdom gained from experience without the frustration of failure. Unfortunately, it can't be done. The coach must remember that failure is positive feedback. It is part of the process which stimulates growth. The coach who is on the path of excellence persists in the face of challenges or obstacles and keeps a positive outlook.

In addition, excellent coaches maintain a sense of humility and are open to change. Said Louisville basketball coach Denny Crum in describing his mentor John Wooden:

Coach (Wooden) never gave the impression that he knew everything; he was always open to changing and moving forward. It was his greatest strength as a coach, and that's why he had such phenomenal success over the years with his teams and with individual players.

Changing With the Times

A number of coaches spoke about the differences in today's player. The tennis coach of 1997, it seems, has more to deal with than the coach of 1987 or 1977. There are changes in technology. There are changes in strategy based on changes in technology. And there are changes in our society:

I think college tennis players...if there's one thing that they probably don't do as effectively is that they tend to go for short-term fixes. This match is important versus what are the skills that you want to develop over four years. Just in the same way that Americans are not very patient developing things. That's our mentality; we want it faster and quicker and with less effort. That's a value. It's opposed to what your student needs. So first you have to be effective enough in communicating and have them buy into another model, because they're not going to get anywhere if they keep after that model (of short-term fixes).

Dave Fish — Harvard University

Another coach talked about how he has adjusted his coaching philosophy to adjust for today's players:

I think I've always been more on the side of...if anything, practicing too much than too little. I think my coach was always that way, but in some ways I've had to change my thinking a little bit. The younger generation nowadays does not have as hard-work ethic as maybe the older generation that I grew up with. Actually what I'm trying to say is that everybody is a little bit more of an individual these days. Some guys need that. I could have a guy that just needs to be pushed three (hours) and an hour and a half is good (for another guy). Each can still can compete and perform to his maximum potential. But...especially with the college teams now you have to be a little bit more specialized with each individual in the preparation which they like to do. I don't know if it's really possible to go out and have a team workout that is going to be really great for everybody. I don't know if that can be done in this day and age. I was brought up in a much different way, but I've had to change my philosophy a little bit. And tennis is enough of an individual sport where you can do that.

Billy Martin — UCLA

The nature of coaching is dynamic. Adapting becomes a difficult job indeed considering the changes in our society are evolving at an more rapid pace than ever before. The coach of tomorrow must be able to adjust and compensate with the athletes of tomorrow.

Helping Young People Grow into Adulthood

Another aspect unique to coaching tennis at the collegiate level, is that many of the players are experiencing a sense of independence and freedom for the first time. This critical time in their development provides coaches with the added duty of teaching young people how to behave in a mature and responsible manner. Many discussed how tennis is used as a vehicle for imparting values and "life-skills" that will carry them through adulthood:

Well, it all starts I guess with sportsmanship which in the sense is sort of the golden rule of life. You call the balls fair. You don't try to intimidate. You don't use gamesmanship. All of that is just something that's so self-evident to people like me that have been around for a long time...that the best players that I ever encountered in the world of tennis, the great players were also great sportsmen as well. They never took a point if they didn't feel like they'd earned it. And I think this is something that you keep stressing all the time. Winning is important but not to the extent that you have to violate the rules or sort of tippy-toe through the rules to win. And I think while you're doing this—I have a lot of opportunities in pre-practice talks or after-practice talks to mention things that I've seen or read that showed character, not just in athletics but in a lot of other fields. And I think the guys, whether they admit it or not, I think they like to hear some of those stories from other walks of life.

I try to keep my eyes open in all sorts of magazines and articles, anything that I read that I think has any remote implication to them playing better as an athlete, or acting better or living better as a person. I think it all ties in. I think tennis is a great game for learning how to operate within the rules under a lot of pressure — center stage, thrills, disappointments and all of those things and still keep a balance in your life. So I use any and all stuff that I run across. I can't even tell you where or when. Sometime it might even be scripture — a lot of good stories in there too. But they can always kind of read between

the lines and relate it or correlate it to what they're doing.

Tut Bartzen — Texas Christian University

And another coach:

The bottom line is you try to get these kids set for life. You're trying to give them some skills that when they leave college, when they graduate with a degree, that they've got skills that whatever they get into, whether its sports or business or medicine or law that they have got the confidence developed from a tennis program. Here's how I correct a weakness; here's how I improve myself; here's how I get better; here's how I know that there are no limits.

Brent Abel — Junior Coach, Northern California Tennis Association

****

The following are excerpts from interviews on various other topics from top college, junior and professional coaches.

On Recruiting:

In recruiting I usually look for players who have not gotten their growth spurt yet but are playing at a pretty good level already...when they're not yet strong and not fast yet and they're physically weaker than the other people, you can bet that they have to use their head and they have to play the game with their whole being to have had the success that they have had. When they do get the growth spurt they really take off with their game. The kids who get the growth spurt early in the 12's or 14's usually win because of their physical strength and size but aren't forced to develope the critical process in their patterns that they need to play the game at the higher levels. They can hit the ball but they can't play the game.

Chuck Kriese — Clemson University

If you're smart, you'll recruit people that are going to work well with you. You don't want to just recruit anybody. If you have a choice on recruiting two people of relatively equal ability the person that you're going to communicate better with is the person you should recruit. And how do you know that? Well, its just a feel you get from talking with (a player), talking to the parents...and that's part of the recruiting game.

Thomas Johnston — University of Virginia

I think if you go about it with a philosophy where you show the kids what you have to offer and your first thought is what's best for the kid...try to find them the best situation where they're going to excel. When a kid finds a place where he's really gonna be happy, then that's where he's going to play his best. So if I feel like a kid's really gonna be happy at the University of Tennessee then I'm eager to get him there 'cause I really feel like they'll fulfill their potential. If I feel like I'm coercing a kid to come that is not going to be happy there, it's not going to be good for him or me either.

When a kid's looking at schools, it's difficult 'cause you get one official visit. I'm not sure how true a picture you get coming in for one weekend and trying to hang out a few hours or a couple of days with the players on the team. That's the tough part about the process. We're limited how much we can contact the kids and get to know them. The less time we get to spend with the kids in the recruiting process the more difficult it is to really get a feel for them and for them to get a feel for the schools they're looking at. But you have to take the situation as it is and make the best of it. I think you can do it but the kids, have to be diligent. The parents have to be diligent at it and the coaches have to work hard at it. If everybody does that, then you can usually get a good fit.

John Kreis — The University of Tennessee

On Moving out of Your Comfort Zone:

I think in order to improve, you've got to get out of your comfort zone. And I think what happens a lot of times is... you know, whether it's you or I and whether it's tennis or any other game, we enjoy doing the things that are comfortable. And then all of a sudden somebody asks us to do something different. For instance, for me I'm trying to learn how to play golf. Well, I'm just trying to hit the ball straight right now. If somebody talks to me about a slice or a fade or change this grip or try this, that's all very much out of my comfort zone right now. But I know the only way I'll get to be a better player is if I experiment and try and then practice those types of things.

Scott Perelman — coach for Chris Woodruff

I think a (coach) has got to really be able to make his players want to improve and feel like there's a purpose for trying to improve and trying to stretch their limits...trying to get them out of their comfort zone as often as possible to expand the comfort-zone limits. I think most of us are sort of creatures of comfort in terms of...we have a limit and I think the good coaches can get these guys to believe that they can do a little bit more. And every day's a little more, a little more and then you look back a month later and go "We've just taken the ceiling from here and now the ceiling's up here." And I think the good ones are able to do that (not only) with their individual players but also with their team as a whole.

— Brent Abel

It's a mistake to try to make things easy in pursuit of anything involved in excellence because in order to achieve excellence, by the nature of it you have to stretch yourself. You have to get out of your comfort zone. You have to reach beyond where you have in the past to keep improving. And in order to do that, you're gonna have ups and downs and it will not be easy. And if it's easy all the time, then you're really not achieving excellence. Relative to what you're capable of, you're achieving mediocrity and that's how I gauge excellence. Excellence is based on an individual's own skill level and talents and are they pushing what they have to the maximum. Unlike the public often perceives just winning as achieving excellence. That is not necessarily a good barometer of excellence.

—Nick Saviano

On Risk Management:

I read a management book once and it said they took a poll of 153 of the nation's top managers and said "If you had to do it over again, what would you do differently?" And to a man they all said "I would take more risk." And when you take risks there's a greater chance of failure but there's also a greater chance of success. I used to think that failure was bad, the last thing I wanted to do was fail. But if by taking a risk to try to win you end up making a mistake and failing you're gonna learn and you're gonna have a knowledge that you didn't the time before and it's gonna cause you to be a success down the road. I'm not talking about way-out risks where it's just wild and you're not being smart about it. I'm talking about legitimate risk. Anyone who competes knows the difference. The key thing though is to act and not to just wait on good things to happen.

— Gene Miller

I think you have to look and understand human differences in the same way that you have to understand that there may be three or four different ways to coach a player — based on that person's personality — how they respond to risk. That's going to tell you can this person stand to become a net rusher. Can they stand points (snaps his fingers twice) winning and losing fast based on making a gamble or is this guy more temperamentally suited, the longer the point goes on the better the chances.

— Dave Fish

On Enjoying the Process:

Another frequently mentioned topic was enjoying the process of pursuing excellence. Several coaches remarked how this perspective stimulated their players' technical development and motivation level.

Some of the things that I really focus on...that the person is enjoying it and they're improving. If they're enjoying the experience then they'll usually improve and if they improve that makes it more enjoyable. If you can make that kind of an experience for them then I believe that you're approaching excellence.

Bill Reynolds — Cal State Fullerton

...if they're really motivated and happy and loving it and enthusiastic about it — and passionate and crazy — they're gonna be pretty good right there. You can be a great technical coach or a great mental skills coach or a great physical trainer and if the player's not having any fun, you may as well hang it up. It doesn't do any good. So it starts with that player lovin' the game. The greatest players I've ever known were the people that loved it the most. They want to go out and tinker with their game by the hour and play it and do it and hit it whether it's hot or cold or whether they've lost a big match — they want to get out there and do it again.

Wayne Bryan — Tennis 'n Music in Camarillo, CA

Besides making the experience enjoyable for the athletes, successful coaches are most often enjoying the experience themselves. Not even long commutes on California freeways can dampen the enthusiasm of Dick Leach:

(My job is) not work for me. It's fun and enjoyable. (I'm the) luckiest guy in the world. People say "How can you drive 50 miles to work every day?" I say "It's real easy 'cause I don't have to do it." I'm doing it 'cause I want to do it. When I get (to the university) I'm happy and when I'm finished for the day — when I get home, I get home. It's not that pressure of having to be at a job at eight o'clock that you don't like and leaving at five. I've got the greatest job in the world and I get paid for it. Not very much, but I get paid for it.

On "The Big Picture":

Whether you win or lose, you do it with class. It's really important to portray that to your players. A tennis match is certainly not the most important thing in this world. And it certainly cannot in any way be brought up as such. Each match,

individually or collectively as a team, is simply another step...a learning experience. The idea is that winning or losing is taken in context. You avoid the real highs or real lows —that you try to keep it as everyday life, just another day in which there are some disappointments and some great things...frustrating things and some outstanding things. That happens to all of us every day.

I hope that what I do off-the-court also carries over. I do a lot of things off the court. This is a 10 million dollar building program we're completing. We raised every penny ourselves. I hope the team takes pride in the result...realize that they have been a part in creating this themselves. I think instilling a pride in the program...that's very, very important. I do a lot of work with "inner city kids" so to speak in East Palo Alto. In fact I have a luncheon meeting today talking about buying property to put in courts and a study center — things like that — in addition to the court complex we built on a school site. I'm just one of the people in this. But I think that this idea of giving back to the community is very, very important. And hopefully they learn from me off-the-court in this regard. I hope they learn the importance of being well organized from me. I hope they learn to accept individual responsibility for their actions on-the-court and off...from me. I would be very disappointed if the kids ever came to practice and knew that I had little sleep the night before or that something went wrong in my personal life...or that I had a big setback with my department or I just got called on the carpet by my boss, or something like that. I'd be very disappointed if those emotions came out to them on the court. I would be very disappointed if they ever heard me use an alibi...And I hope that these "tennants" become a part of their personal life and a part of their personal experience as well — there are many things beyond the on-court things that are very philosophically important to convey to a 20-year-old kid.

Dick Gould — Stanford University

On Preparation for Big Matches:

Several of the coaches I spoke with were interested in what Coach Gould did differently or how he prepared his team to play UCLA after losing to the Bruins three times during the season. (Stanford defeated UCLA for the National Championship in the last match of the 1996 collegiate year.)

I can't tell you anything special. I'm not aware of anything we did differently than what we'd been doing all year. Maybe that's why the year was successful, because we didn't really emphasize or do anything different. If you ask the kids they might pick out something that they thought was different. I don't think we did anything differently. You don't tell the kids it's a big match because it is a big match. You don't tell them "You only have to beat them once and this is it" because they know that. You don't go out and add to their anxiety level in what's a very anxious situation by making something big out of that. I think our thrust was "Let's get out there and get after our doubles and play solid doubles." And obviously in each match there are little things we ask them to do against certain opponents or certain styles of play.

I also asked Coach Gould "What stands out as something you feel is a critical aspect that you really want to focus on day in and day out?"

I think being positive. Looking ahead, not looking back. You're looking ahead. That point's over. You learn by it. Go on. You accept it and go on. Hopefully you don't accept it blindly. You accept it by learning by it. But go on. Don't dwell on it. That's done. Let's go to the next thing. What's up? Well we lost today. Let's go on. We lost that set. Let's go on. What are you going to do about it? I think that's probably the — if there's any one thing — I mean that's a very important part of my coaching philosophy: being positive, looking ahead. You always have a chance. You can always get better. It doesn't mean you're going to win. I think stressing improvement is very important, rather than the end result. We might talk about the backswing on the forehand as one area that can be improved for example. I think that stressing improvement is critical — being positive and accepting responsibility and moving on.

On Controlling Things You Have Control Over:

I talk with all the players that I've worked with about controlling the things that you can control. You can always control your effort. You can always control your attitude. You can always control your behavior on the court. Those kind of things are things that are absolutely and completely within your control. And it's a decision-making process. You can decide to get crazy on the court. You can decide not to put in a great effort. But hopefully you don't let yourself do that. And there's that temptation all the time — if things aren't going well — to let yourself go crazy on the court, to let yourself start to just kind of fade

into "Ah, I don't care. It doesn't really make any difference. There's another match next week." And that's the thing that hopefully...like I said over that long term you've created an atmosphere where a guy may have that thought for a second but he just says "I'm not gonna allow that to creep into my mind." I'm gonna say "C'mon, keep fighting, keep fighting, keep fighting" and see what happens.

Brad Stine — coach for Jonathan Stark

(My players) always knew that if they lost and they gave it a hundred percent, I never had a negative word to say...never was down on a guy for losing, ever. If they played a good match I'd often congratulate them even if we lost. Tell 'em I was proud of 'em. I was looking for a guy to show courage. That's what I wanted. I wanted him to show courage. By courage I don't mean that you make the shot on the big point. I mean that if you miss the shot on the big point you don't whine about it. And you come back without ducking your head for the next point. That's courage. That you can control and the other, you can't. Anything that they could control and that they did, I was happy with. If they couldn't control it, it didn't bother me that they lost.

Dr. Allen Fox — Psychologist and former Pepperdine University Coach

On "Building the Player":

What I think is really essential in terms of excellence is to have the ability to figure out what is the base of that person. Just like if you're going to build a building you've got to take a look at the soil that's going to be underneath that building before you construct it. You can't put in on a wet land and not put in some sort of decent foundation. In tennis, I always look for the person's core foundation — whether it's their head, whether it's their speed, whether it's their heart, whether it's their hands — whatever it may be and always build from that.

Peter Burwash — Peter Burwash International, Tennis Specialists

On Working with a Top Professional Player:

At this level in tennis—and I'm talking now professional level in tennis — it has to be a partnership. To begin with, it has to be a dictatorship from the coach's point of view, 'cause he has to get in there disciplines that he believes are the right way that that player's got to go. But then once you've got the disciplines in, then it's a partnership. And if both partners contribute the same amount but in different ways the end product will always, I believe, be far better than what either of you ever dreamed of.

One thing you have to remember is from an excellence point of view, a coach can never wake up miserable. A coach has always got to be happy. A coach has always got to see the good things in the day...must never see the bad things in the day. The only time he can see the bad things in the day is when he shuts the hotel door room and he's on his own. Then he can think of that. But everyday you have to wake up happy. You can't have a depression. You have got to be the one that's putting the life into everything that you're trying to do.

Tony Pickard — former coach for Stefan Edberg

A final note from Coach Kriese....On Being Selfless

It is quite appropriate to me that the final thoughts on coaching excellence should come from someone whom I feel is one of the greatest coaches in the world today. I say this because long before Tom Gullickson became our top national coach and Captain of the Davis Cup Team, I once worked with him at a very small clinic at a club in Michigan. Knowing of he and his brother's playing greatness, I was very eager to learn more about this man by seeing him work as a teacher. To my great satisfaction, it was not new and exciting tennis techniques or gimmicks that I learned from him, but a true sense of what a teacher and a coach is as he worked unselfishly for hours with little kids, older folks, young folks, good players, and bad players; treating everyone the same and giving everyone the same thing: HIS WHOLE HEART!! No ego involved whatsover.

And one more...

I think being an athlete is kind of a selfish profession because what's good for me...the focus is all on me, especially in the individual sports. I think being a coach in an individual sport or any sport really...coaching is pretty selfless. You really can't let your own ego get attached too much. It's like "What can I do that can help the players play their best tennis." And my ego can't be involved. I've got to subjugate any of my wants or desires for what's best for this particular player. How can I help him the most and how can we create that good team feeling within an individual sport like tennis.

— Tom Gullickson

****

Again my sincere thanks to Paul Gluch for conducting all of these fantastic interviews and for letting his work be relayed to the many who will benefit from its reading.

**Coach and player — a winning combination.
Coach Chuck Kriese (left) pictured here with Kent Kinnear.**

COACHING NOTES

COACHING NOTES

COACHING NOTES

BIBLIOGRAPHY

Bass, Ruth U. "An Analysis of the Components of Tests of Semi-circular Canal Function and of Static Dynamic Balance." *Research Quarterly* May 1939:33.

Benjamin, David. *The ITCA Guide to Coaching Winning Tennis.* New York: Prentice Hall, 1988.

Chui, Edward. "Effect of Systematic Weight Training on Athletic Power." *Research Quarterly* October 1950:188-194.

Endres, John P. "The Effect of Weight Training Exercise Upon Speed of Muscular Movements." Masters Thesis University of Wisconsin, 1953.

Fox, Edward L. and Donald K. Matthews. *Interval Training.* Philadelphia: W. B. Saunders Co., 1974.

Gluch, Paul. "Interviews on Tennis-Coaching Excellence." 1996.

Grawunder, Ralph and Marion Steinmann. *Life and Health.* 3rd. ed. New York: Random House Inc., 1980.

Hoffman, Marshal and Gabe Mirkin, M.D. *The Sports Medicine Book.* Boston: Little, Brown and Co., 1978.

Hoyt, Creig, et. al. *Food for Fitness.* 6th ed. Mountain View, CA: World Publications and Bike World Magazine, 1978.

Loehr, Jim. "The Sixteen Second Cure."

Leone, Ray. "Ray Leone's Sales Funnel." 1997.

Johnson, Barry I. and Jack K. Nelson. *Practical Measurements for Evaluation in Physical Education.* Minneapolis: Burgess Publishing Co., 1969.

Kraft, Steve and Connie Haynes. *The Tennis Player's Diet.* New York: Doubleday and Co., Inc., 1975.

Kriese, Chuck. *Total Tennis Training.* Indianapolis: Masters Press, 1989.

Kriesc, Chuck. *Winning Tennis.* Indianapolis: Masters Press, 1993.

Kriese, Chuck. *Youth Tennis.* Indianapolis: Masters Press, 1994.

Lisciandro, Frank. *The Sugar Film.* Santa Barbara, CA: Image Associates, 1980.

Littauer, Fred and Florence. Whole Again Conference. Bryan, Texas.

Masley, John W., Ara Hairabedian, and Donald N. Donaldson. "Weight Training in Relation to Strength, Speed, and Coordination." *Research Quarterly* October 1953:308-315.

O'Xendine, Joseph B. "Emotional Arousal and Motor Performance," *Quest* 13:23-31, 1970.

Promise Keepers. *Seven Promises of a Promise Keeper.* Focus on the Family Publishing, 1994.

Sprague, Ken. *The Athlete's Body.* Los Angeles: Jeremy P. Tarcher, Inc., 1981.

Wardlaw, Paul. "Wardlaw Directionals: Tactical Guidelines for Tennis." 1994.

Wilkin, Bruce M. "The Effect of Weight Training on Speed of Movement." *Research Quarterly* October 1952:361-369.

Zorbas, William S. and Peter Karpovich. "The Effect of Weight Lifting Upon the Speed of Muscular Contraction." *Research Quarterly* May 1951:145-148.

For more information on "The Power Groove"
write: c\o The Institute   132 Powell Road   Anderson, SC 29625
or call: toll free (800) 868-5465   local (864) 224-0066   fax (864) 885-9080

ABOUT THE AUTHORS

Since taking over as men's head tennis coach at Clemson University in 1975, Chuck Kriese has developed a program that consistently ranks among the best in the nation. His teams have posted eight national top ten finishes, produced thirty All-Americans, and won eleven Atlantic Coast Conference titles including the 1997 championship. He was named the National Coach of the Year by the ITCA in 1981 and the USPTA in 1981 & '86. Add to this six ACC Coach of the Year awards and the distinction of being the all-time winningest coach in ACC history.

But his influence on the game of tennis reaches far beyond his accomplishments. Kriese is widely recognized as one of the top educators and motivators in his profession. His winning formula can be described as a recipe for total player development that focuses on the physical, mental, and emotional challenges of the game. It is a motivational program proven by champions and beginners alike.

Among his former players and assistants you will find twelve who are currently coaching programs at the collegiate level, carrying on a legacy of competitive tennis. Having coached the U.S. Junior Davis Cup team, the U.S. Sunshine Cup team, and twenty-three former collegiate players who have gone on to play at the professional level, Kriese is truly deserving of the respect he has earned — a respect perhaps equal but never greater than that which he gives the game.

Chuck Kriese received his BA and MA from Tennessee Tech and completed his coaching apprenticeship under Harry Hopman. He has written three other books on the sport — *Total Tennis Training*, *Winning Tennis*, and *Youth Tennis* — and speaks internationally on the topic of tennis.

At Kenyon College, hard work and dedication have become constants in the highly successful women's tennis program under the guidance of eight-year head coach Paul Wardlaw.

Wardlaw's comprehensive coaching skills have helped the Kenyon Ladies evolve into a perennial national NCAA Division III power with a combined record of 171-37 over the last eight years. They have entered four of the last five Division III national tournaments as the top seeded team, claiming national championships in 1993, 1995 and 1997. The Ladies have also finished as national runners-up three times and captured eleven North Coast Athletic Conference championships in thirteen years of league competition.

Wardlaw's accomplishments have not gone unrewarded. He was named the Wilson/ Intercollegiate Tennis Association National Coach of the Year in 1993; the ITA/Midwest Region Coach of the Year in 1993 & '97; and the NCAC Coach of the Year in 1990, '95, & '96. His program has produced thirteen All-American tennis honors for Kenyon College.

Wardlaw received both his bachelor's degree (College of Wooster) and master's degree (University of Illinois) in philosophy.

Paul Gluch, Ph.D., has a doctorate degree in exercise and sport science. As a certified sport psychologist his primary focus is helping athletes enhance their mental skills. He is currently developing a center for performance education in Orange County, California.

TENNIS IS OUR RACKET

Spalding Winning Tennis

Chuck Kriese

Written for beginning through advanced players, *Winning Tennis* includes instruction on fundamental technical skills and physical training, the use of basic strategies, and excellent motivational programs that address the emotional side of the game for the student. *Winning Tennis* also gives the student a solid understanding of rules and etiquette while incorporating the rich heritage of the sport.

$14.95 • paper • 192 pages • 7 x 10 • illus.
ISBN: 0-940279-61-4

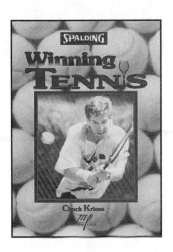

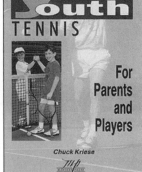

Spalding Youth Tennis

Chuck Kriese

Youth Tennis provides participants, as well as their parents and coaches, with a complete look at a game that can be enjoyed for a lifetime. Not only does it cover all of the game's fundamentals — with drills for improving performance — it discusses the all-important mental and emotional aspects of play. An overview of the game's history, its most notable figures, and a glossary make this book an invaluable resource for anyone involved with young tennis players.

$12.95 • paper • 192 pages • 5¼ x 8¼ • illus.
ISBN: 0-940279-88-6

*All Masters Press books are available at better bookstores or by calling
Masters Press at 1-800-9-SPORTS. Catalogs available by request.*

Become a Champion with Masters Press!

Masters Press has a complete line of books to cover favorite sports and help coaches and participants alike "master their game."

All of our books are available at better bookstores or by calling Masters Press at 1-800-9-SPORTS. Catalogs available by request.

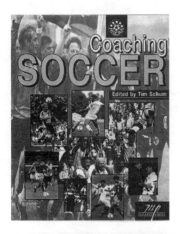

Coaching Soccer

National Soccer Coaches Association of America
Edited by Tim Schum

Fundamental skills, offensive and defensive strategy, team offense and defense, conditioning and motivational techniques — every conceivable aspect of the world's most popular sport is discussed in this official coaching handbook. Never before has so much information by so many renowned soccer authorities been collected in one volume.

$22.95 • paper • 448 pages • 8½ x 11 • illus.
ISBN: 1-57028-094-0

Coaching Volleyball

The American Volleyball Coaches Association

The most complete and indispensable collection of volleyball writings available. Includes articles from Terry Liskevych, Head Coach, USA Women's Team; Doug Beal, Head Coach, 1984 USA Men's Olympic Gold Medal Team; and Jim Coleman, Technical Advisor, USA National Men's Team.

$19.95 • paper • 352 pages • 8½ x 11 • illus.
ISBN: 1-57028-124-6

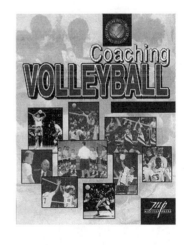

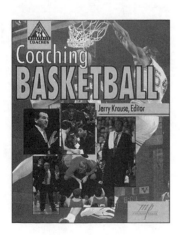

Coaching Basketball

Edited by Jerry Krause

Sponsored by the National Association of Basketball Coaches, this book is a collection of more than 130 articles and essays by the games leading coaches, covering every aspect of the game.

$22.95 • paper • 320 pages • 8½ x 11 • diagrams throughout
ISBN: 0-940279-86-X